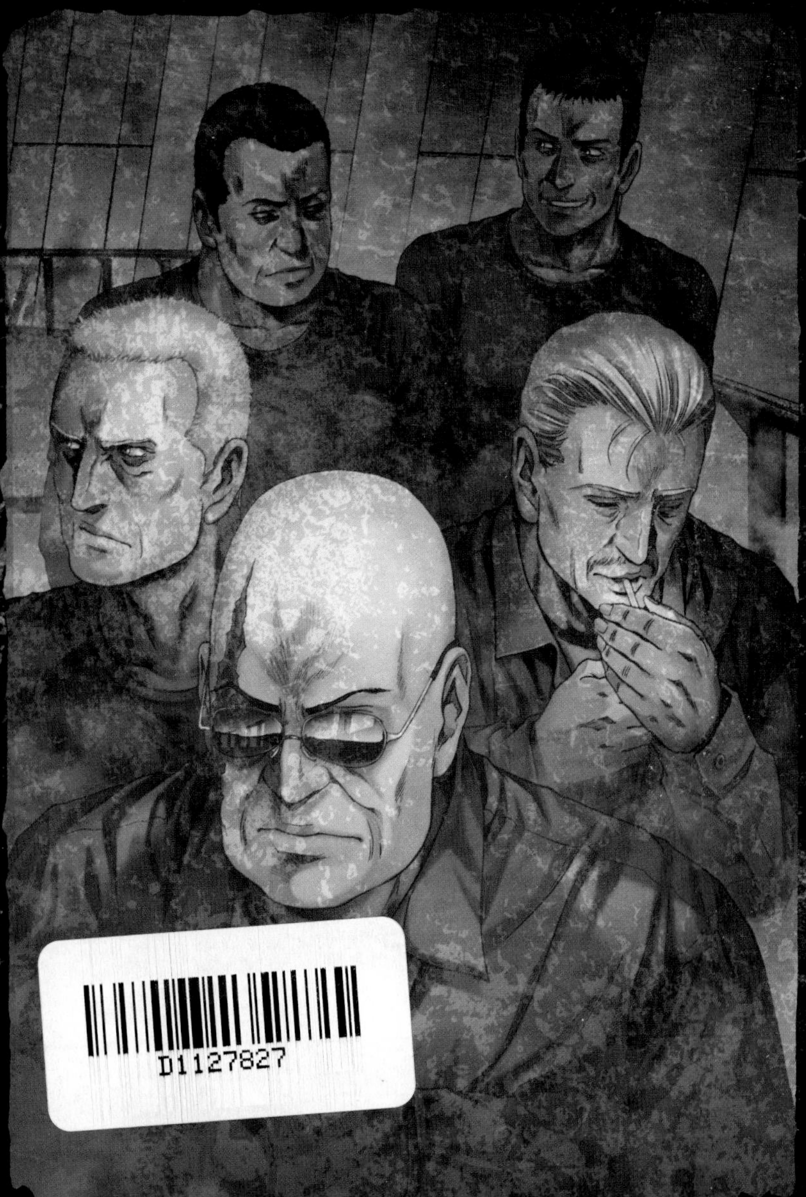

BTOOOM!

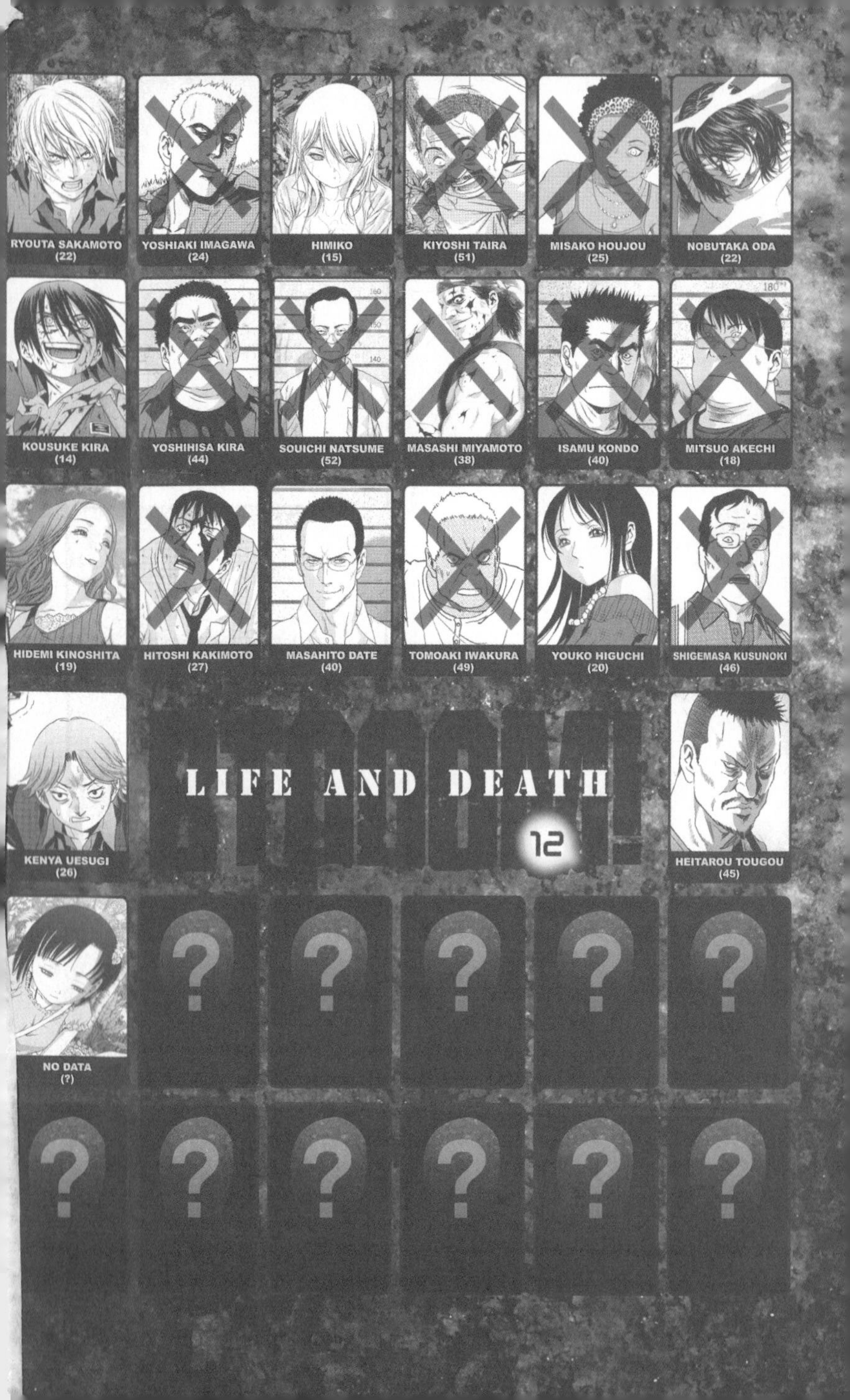
RYOUTA SAKAMOTO (22)
YOSHIAKI IMAGAWA (24)
HIMIKO (15)
KIYOSHI TAIRA (51)
MISAKO HOUJOU (25)
NOBUTAKA ODA (22)
KOUSUKE KIRA (14)
YOSHIHISA KIRA (44)
SOUICHI NATSUME (52)
MASASHI MIYAMOTO (38)
ISAMU KONDO (40)
MITSUO AKECHI (18)
HIDEMI KINOSHITA (19)
HITOSHI KAKIMOTO (27)
MASAHITO DATE (40)
TOMOAKI IWAKURA (49)
YOUKO HIGUCHI (20)
SHIGEMASA KUSUNOKI (46)
KENYA UESUGI (26)
LIFE AND DEATH
12
HEITAROU TOUGOU (45)
NO DATA (?)
?
?
?
?
?
?
?
?
?
?
?

BTOOOM!

JUNYA INOUE

CHARACTER

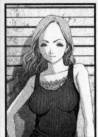

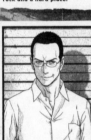

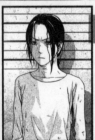

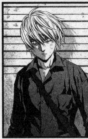

RYOUTA SAKAMOTO

GENDER: Male
AGE: 22
BLOOD TYPE: B
JOB: Unemployed
HOME: Tokyo
BIM TYPE: Cracker, timer, homing

After spending every day cooped up in his home gaming online, he suddenly finds himself forced to participate in "BTOOOM! GAMERS," a killing game taking place on a mysterious uninhabited island. As a world ranker in the online third-person shooter "BTOOOM!", he uses his experience and natural instincts to survive and concoct a plan to get off the island along with his comrades.

HIDEMI KINOSHITA

GENDER: Female
AGE: 19
BLOOD TYPE: A
JOB: Part-timer
HOME: Gunma
BIM TYPE: Timer

As Oda's partner, this female player tackled Himiko with her skillful wrestling moves. She's essentially an egomaniac and wants to be admired by everyone around her. It eventually led to her getting nominated for the island. Now her partner Oda has mercilessly abandoned her, forcing her between a rock and a hard place.

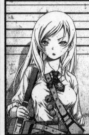

HIMIKO

GENDER: Female
AGE: 15
BLOOD TYPE: B
JOB: High school student
HOME: Tokyo
BIM TYPE: Cracker, timer, gas, homing

A half-Japanese high school girl who has teamed up with Sakamoto. She harbors a deep resentment against men after a sordid experience in her past, but after surviving some battles thanks to Sakamoto, she begins to trust him. Her character in the online version of "BTOOOM!" is actually married to Sakamoto's character, but she's starting to fall in love with the real Sakamoto too.

MASAHITO DATE

GENDER: Male
AGE: 40
BLOOD TYPE: AB
JOB: Doctor
HOME: Chiba
BIM TYPE: Remote control

A former elite doctor. He took advantage of his status to commit malpractice and placed all the blame on Murasaki. The man has a sinister nature. Having survived a previous run of "BTOOOM! GAMERS," he was eventually sent right back to the island. That experience and the information he possesses as a result makes him a key man in Sakamoto's escape plan.

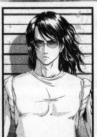

NOBUTAKA ODA

GENDER: Male
AGE: 22
BLOOD TYPE: AB
JOB: Restaurant manager
HOME: Tokyo
BIM TYPE: Cracker, gas, flame

Sakamoto's biggest rival and an old classmate of his from high school. His elaborate plans and surprisingly daring athleticism have helped him procure weapons and chips at a rapid pace as he plans for his own departure from the island. Engaging in life-or-death battles with his former best friend Sakamoto, he has demonstrated himself to be an unequaled master at combat.

SHIKI MURASAKI

GENDER: Female
AGE: 39
BLOOD TYPE: O
JOB: Nurse
HOME: Chiba
BIM TYPE: NO DATA

A former nurse. She was wrongly blamed for Date's wrongdoings and sent to the island where she fought in the previous version of "BTOOOM! GAMERS." She and Date had teamed up, but she was betrayed by him once more and left to scrape by on the island. She has survived on her own for a long time but sides with Sakamoto and his team to provide information.

BTOOOM! 12

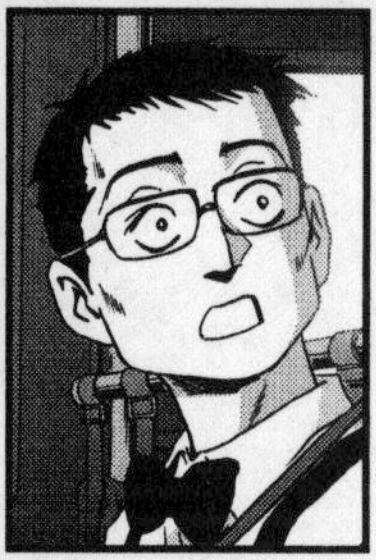

TETSUO WAKAMOTO

GENDER: Male
AGE: 30
BLOOD TYPE: B
JOB: System engineer
HOME: Tokyo

A system programmer for "BTOOOM! GAMERS," he is involved in the development of both versions of the game. He's amiable enough but tends to speak without thinking.

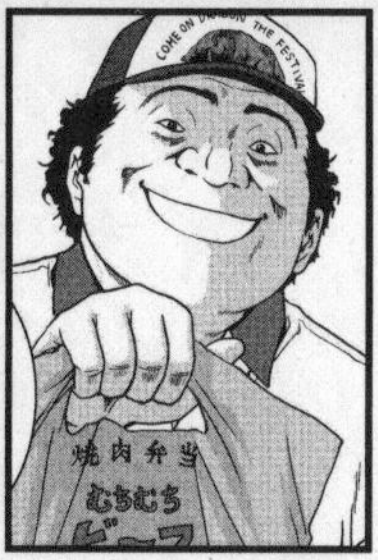

TAKANO-HASHI

GENDER: Male
AGE: 45
BLOOD TYPE: AB
JOB: Game planner
HOME: Hokkaido

An executive staff member at Tyrannos Japan, he is the leader behind all the development of the online game, as well as the live-action version, "BTOOOM! GAMERS." He considers Sakamoto a valuable player and debugger who will serve as a key player in the completion of "BTOOOM! GAMERS."

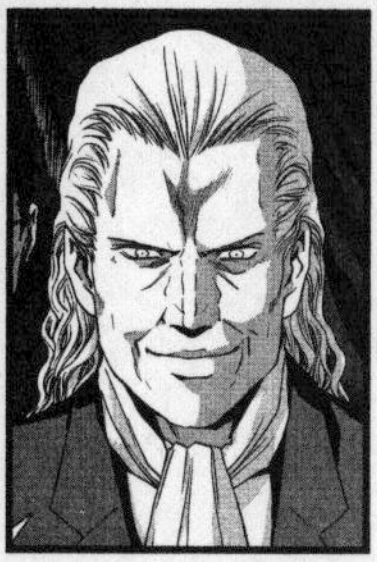

LONGER SCHWARITZ

GENDER: Male
AGE: 77
BLOOD TYPE: O
JOB: Capitalist
HOME: New York

A descendant of European aristocracy, he is a powerful man who runs the world behind the scenes with his considerable capital. In order to more thoroughly control the online world, he founds the THEMIS project and has high hopes for "BTOOOM! GAMERS."

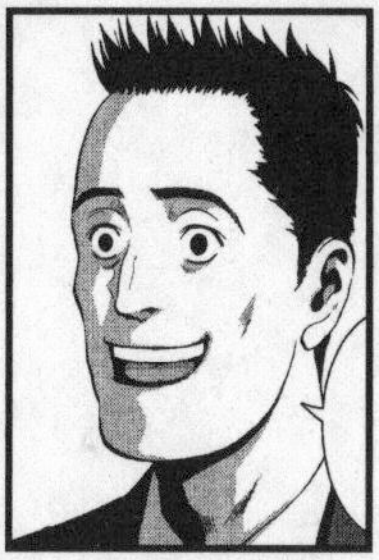

TSUNEAKI IIDA

GENDER: Male
AGE: 24
BLOOD TYPE: A
JOB: Game programmer
HOME: Tokyo

An employee at Tyrannos Japan and Sakamoto's senpai from college. He's an excellent programmer and works under Takanohashi on the development of "BTOOOM! GAMERS." But he doesn't agree with the inhuman nature of the game and approaches Sakamoto with the proposal and strategy to put a stop to the game's development.

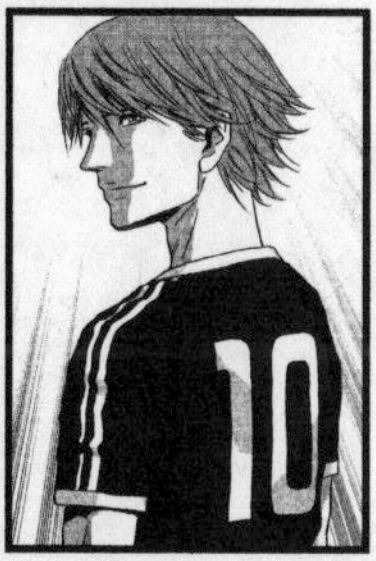
10

SEIYA

GENDER: Male
AGE: 22
BLOOD TYPE: A
JOB: College student
HOME: Gunma

Hidemi Kinoshita's ex-boyfriend. Due to an injury, he had to give up his dreams of being a soccer player. While mired in despair, he was driven to take his own life by Hidemi's cheerful blog posts detailing her life without him.

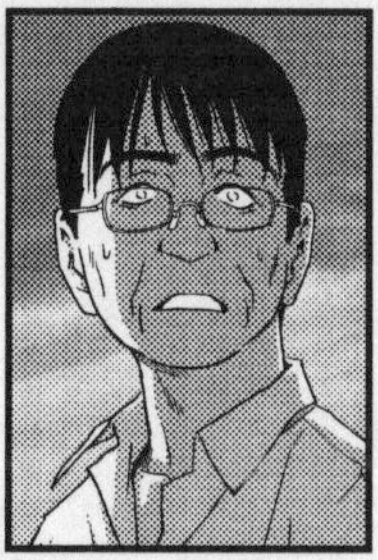

HISANOBU

GENDER: Male
AGE: 55
BLOOD TYPE: A
JOB: Unemployed
HOME: Tokyo

Yukie's new husband and Sakamoto's stepfather. He's worried about how much time his stepson spends up in his room and scolds him only to be attacked. Having just been laid off, he racks up debt because of his praiseworthy efforts to preserve his family's lifestyle. However, Yukie is frail in body and mind and attempts to kill herself. Fate has dealt him an unfair card in life.

CONTENTS

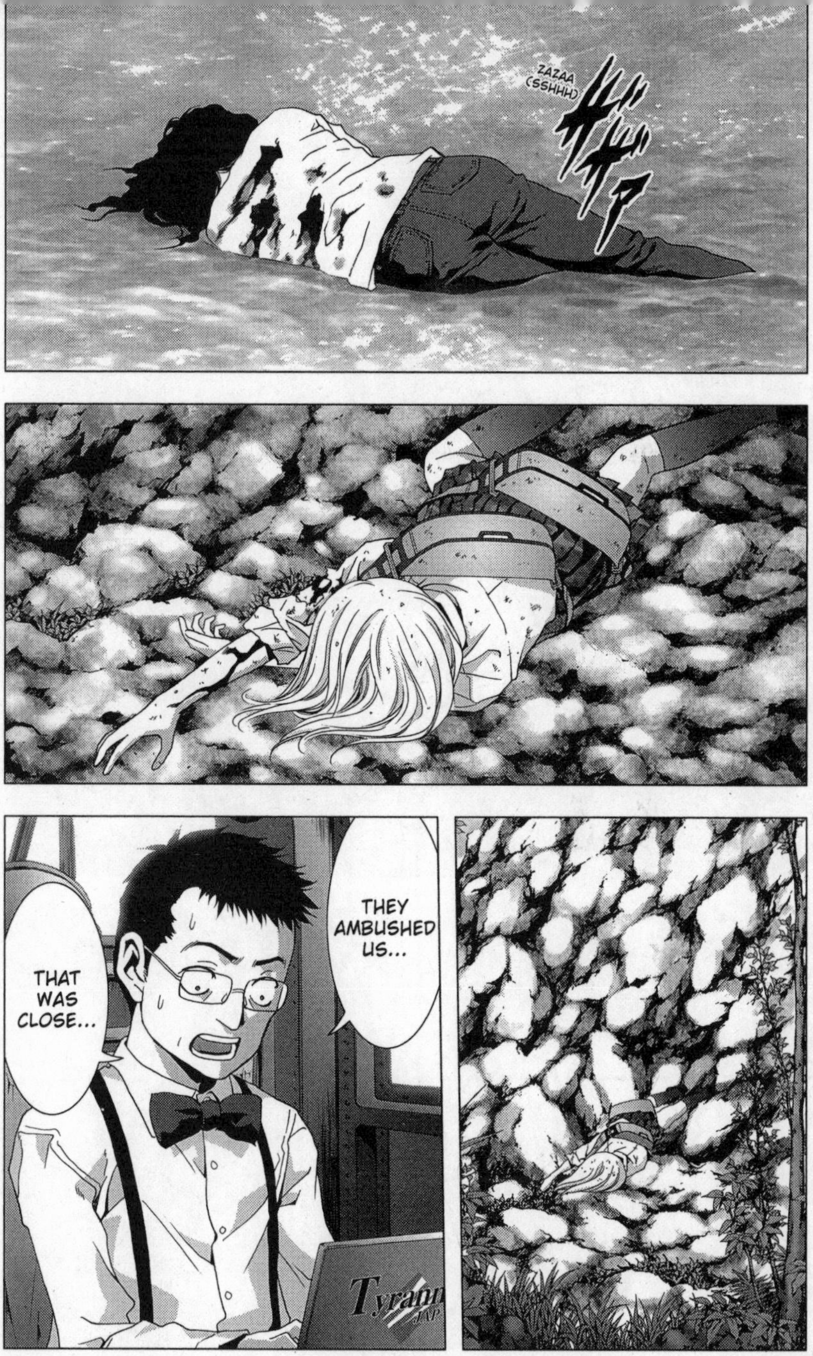
ZAZAA (SSHHH)
ザザァ
THEY AMBUSHED US...
THAT WAS CLOSE...

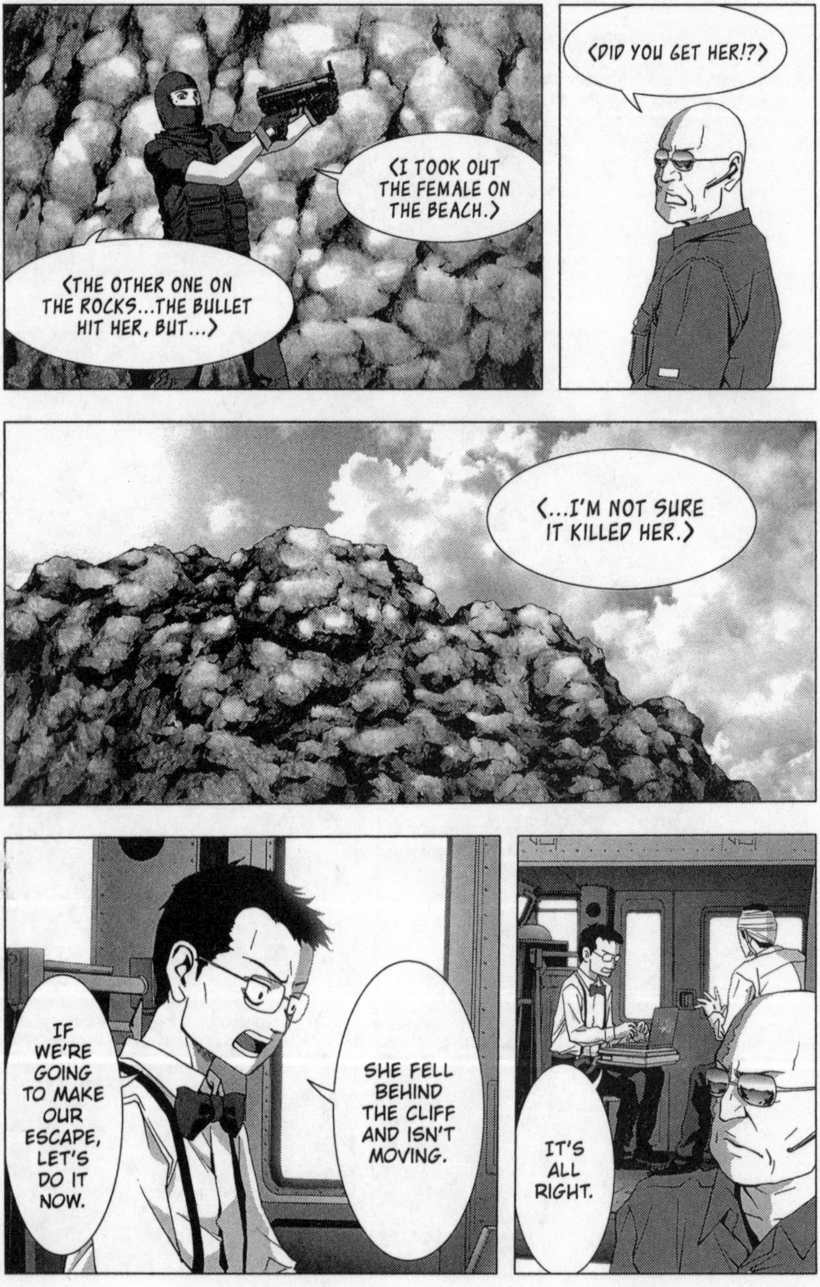
<DID YOU GET HER!?>
<I TOOK OUT THE FEMALE ON THE BEACH.>
<THE OTHER ONE ON THE ROCKS...THE BULLET HIT HER, BUT...>
<...I'M NOT SURE IT KILLED HER.>
IT'S ALL RIGHT.
SHE FELL BEHIND THE CLIFF AND ISN'T MOVING.
IF WE'RE GOING TO MAKE OUR ESCAPE, LET'S DO IT NOW.

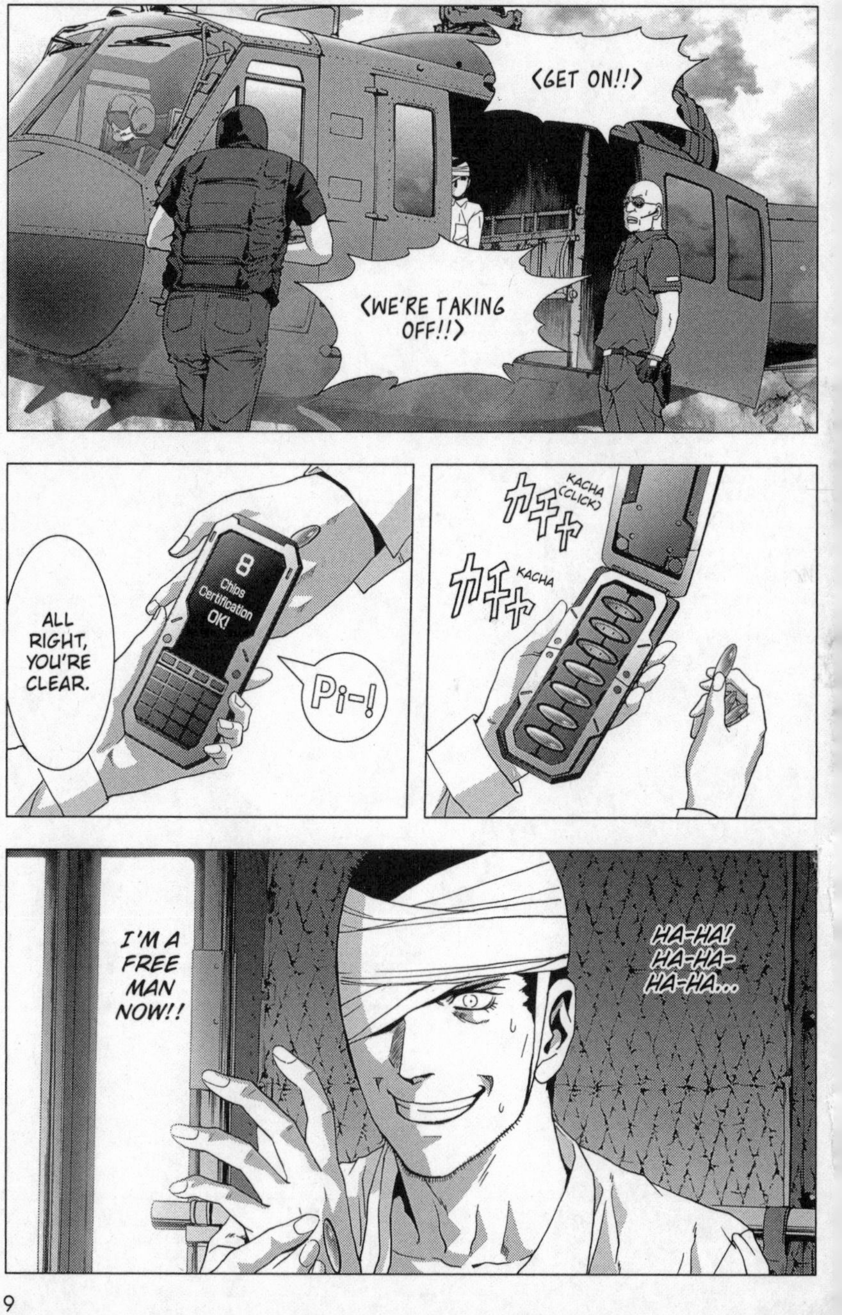
<GET ON!!>
<WE'RE TAKING OFF!!>
カチャ
KACHA (CLICK)
カチャ
KACHA
8 Chips Certification OK!
Pi-!
ALL RIGHT, YOU'RE CLEAR.
HA-HA! HA-HA-HA-HA...
I'M A FREE MAN NOW!!

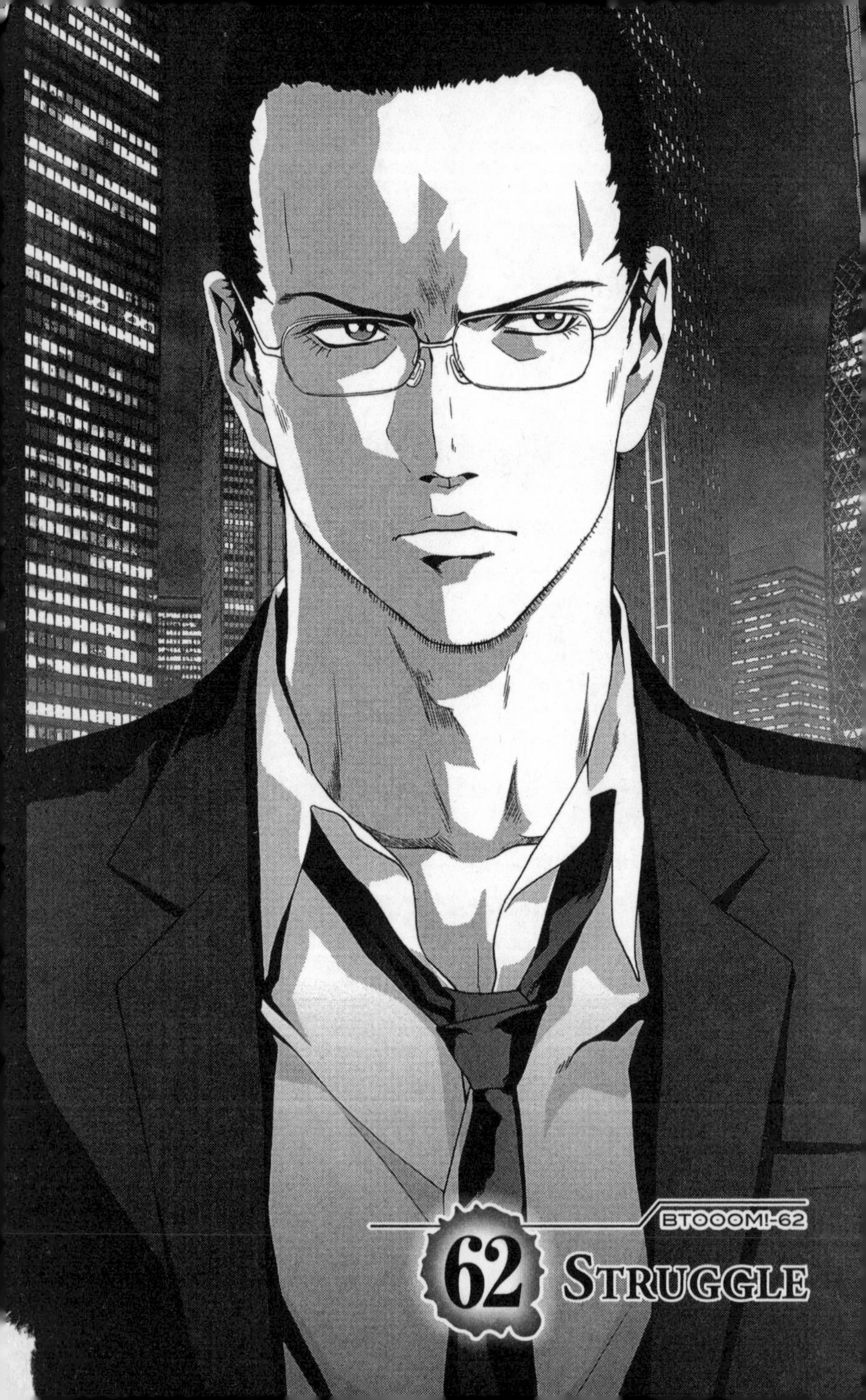
BTOOOM!-62
62
STRUGGLE

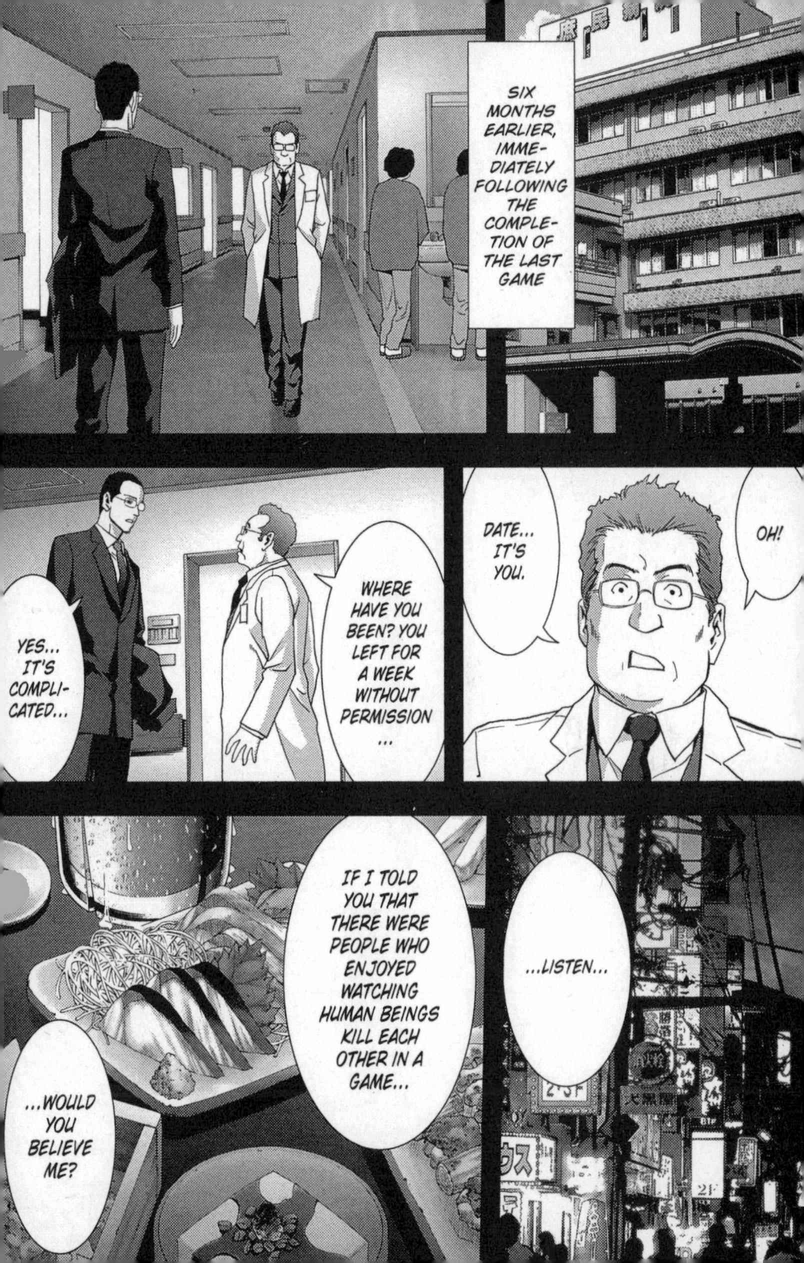
SIX MONTHS EARLIER, IMMEDIATELY FOLLOWING THE COMPLETION OF THE LAST GAME
OH!
DATE... IT'S YOU.
WHERE HAVE YOU BEEN? YOU LEFT FOR A WEEK WITHOUT PERMISSION ...
YES... IT'S COMPLICATED...
...LISTEN...
IF I TOLD YOU THAT THERE WERE PEOPLE WHO ENJOYED WATCHING HUMAN BEINGS KILL EACH OTHER IN A GAME...
...WOULD YOU BELIEVE ME?

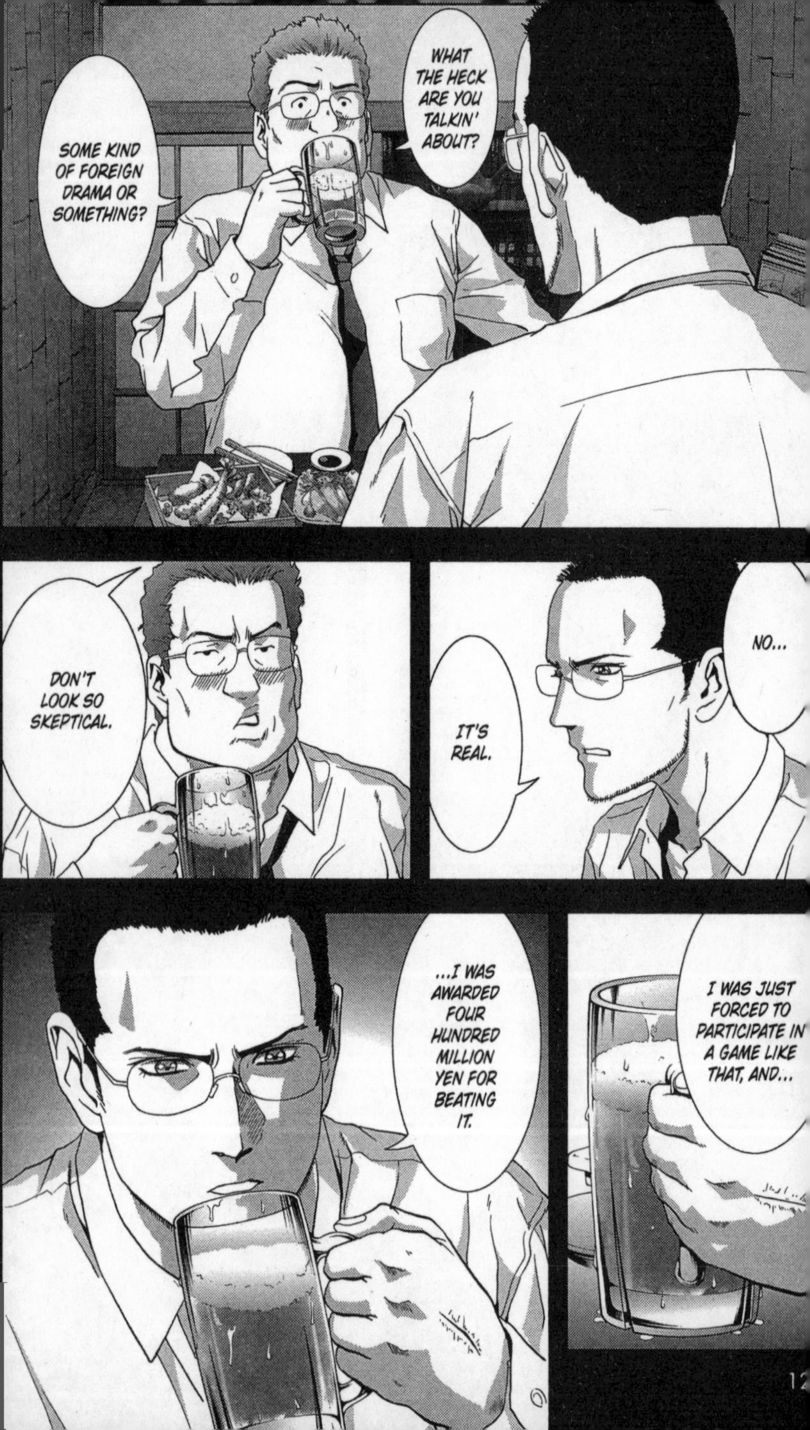
WHAT THE HECK ARE YOU TALKIN' ABOUT?
SOME KIND OF FOREIGN DRAMA OR SOMETHING?
NO...
IT'S REAL.
DON'T LOOK SO SKEPTICAL.
I WAS JUST FORCED TO PARTICIPATE IN A GAME LIKE THAT, AND...
...I WAS AWARDED FOUR HUNDRED MILLION YEN FOR BEATING IT.

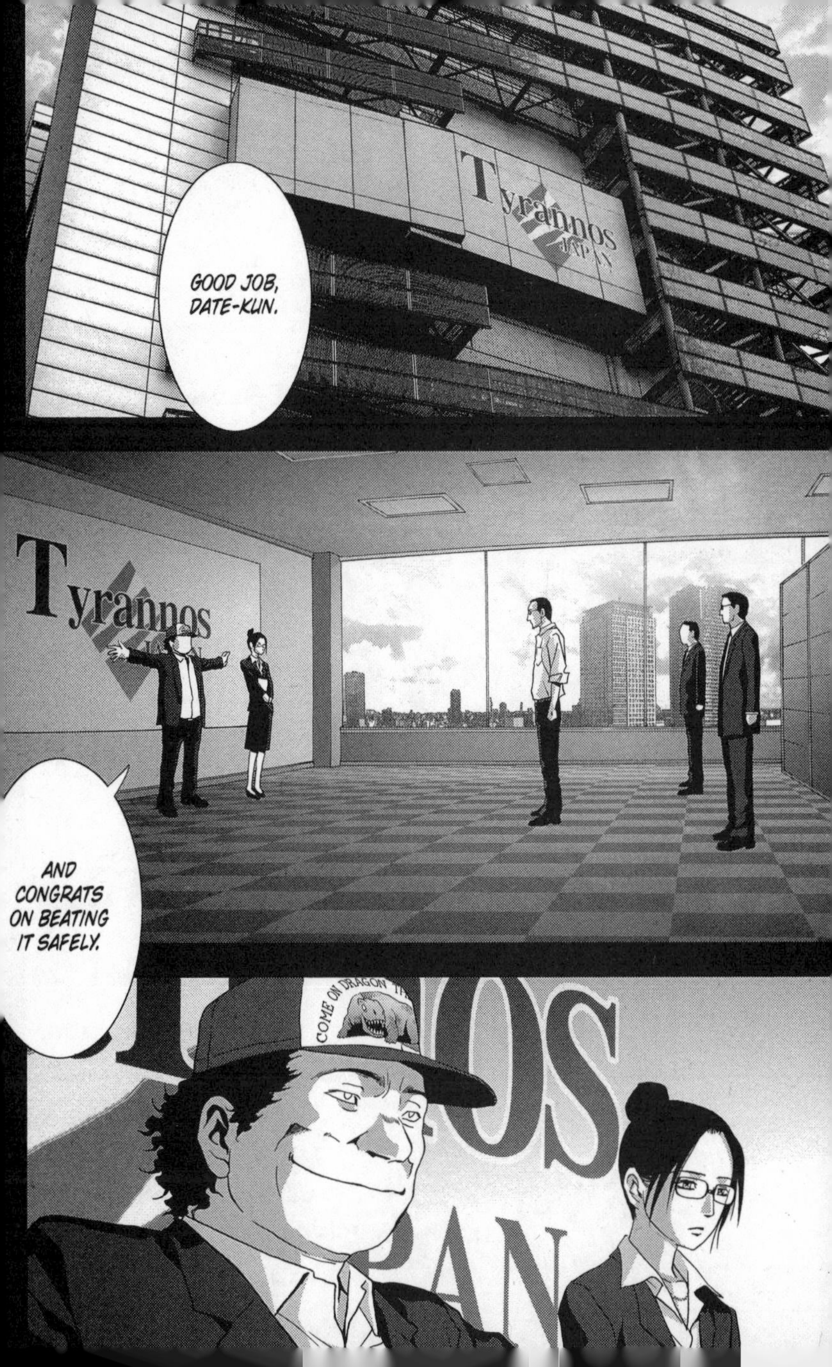
Tyrannos
GOOD JOB, DATE-KUN.
Tyrannos
AND CONGRATS ON BEATING IT SAFELY.
COME ON DRAGON

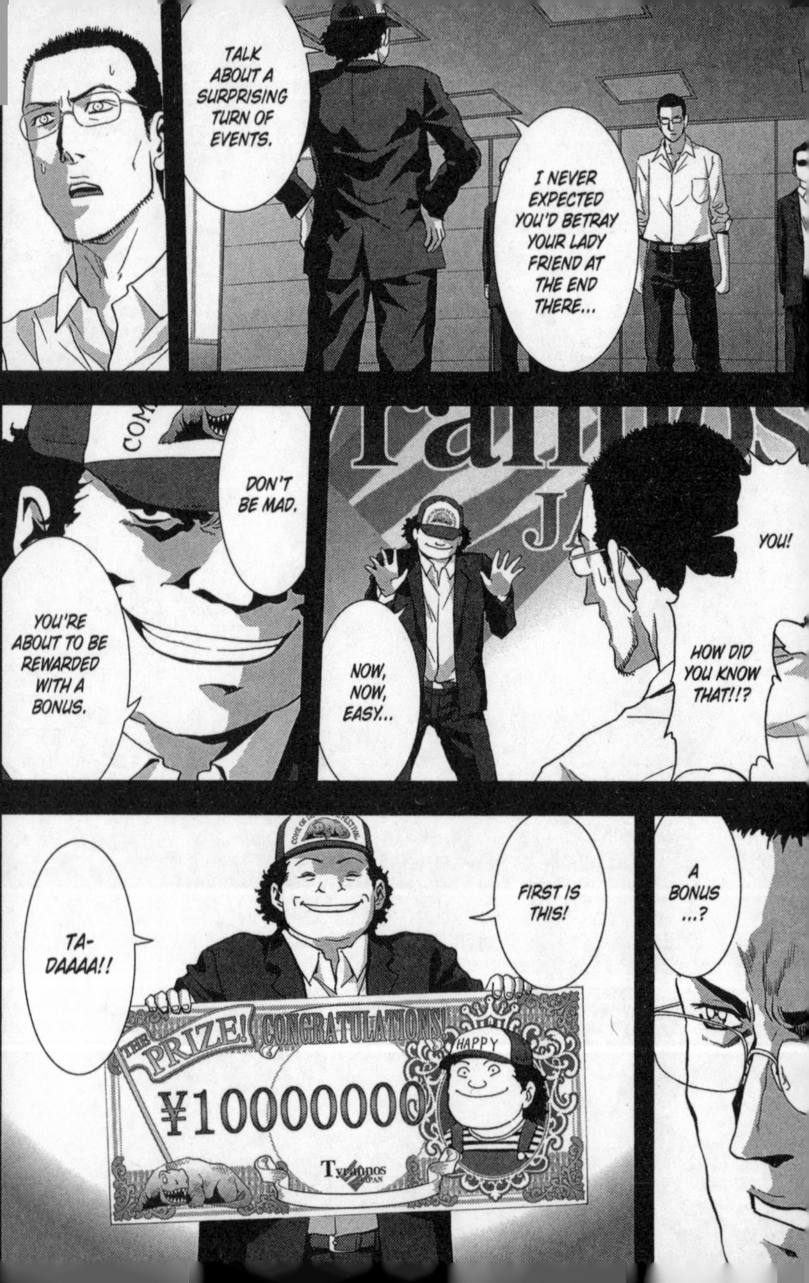
TALK ABOUT A SURPRISING TURN OF EVENTS.
I NEVER EXPECTED YOU'D BETRAY YOUR LADY FRIEND AT THE END THERE...
YOU!
HOW DID YOU KNOW THAT!!?
NOW, NOW, EASY...
DON'T BE MAD.
YOU'RE ABOUT TO BE REWARDED WITH A BONUS.
A BONUS ...?
FIRST IS THIS!
TA-DAAAA!!
THE PRIZE!
CONGRATULATIONS!
HAPPY
¥10000000
Tyrannos
JAPAN

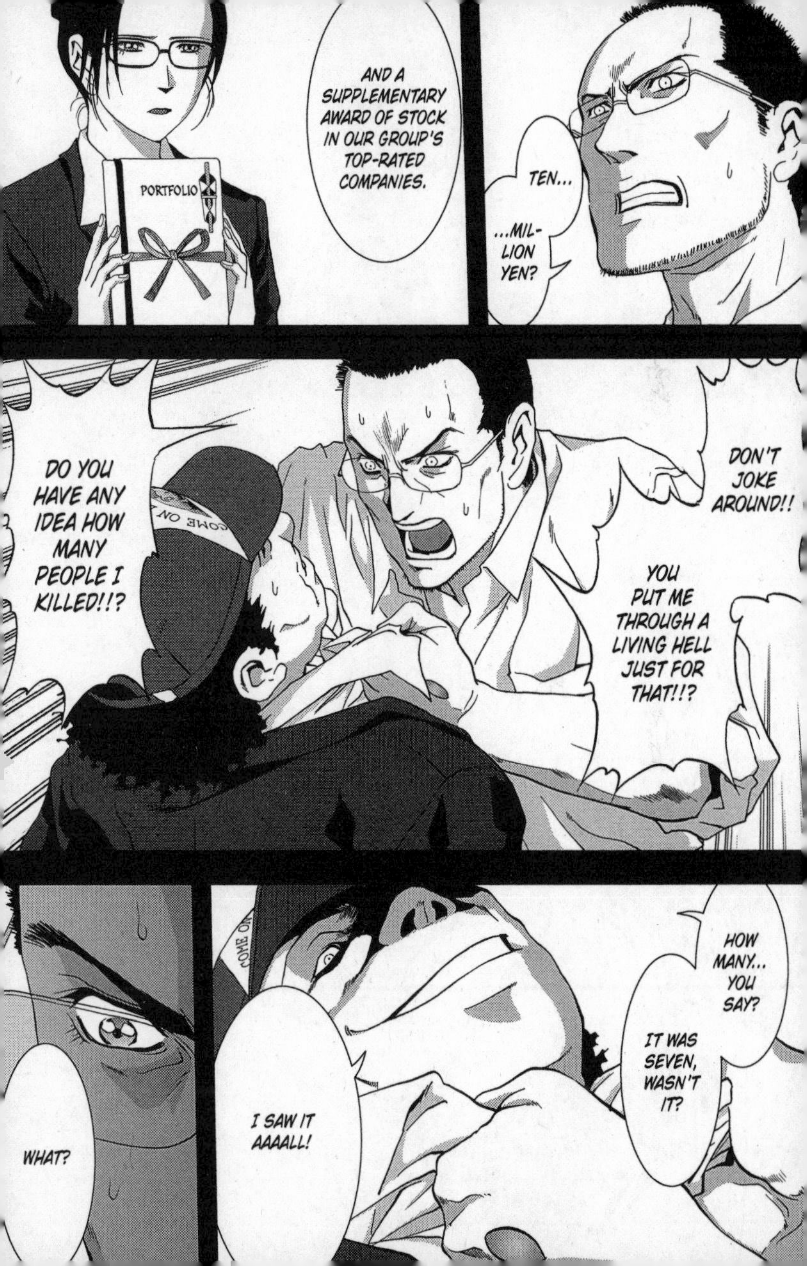
TEN...
...MIL-LION YEN?
AND A SUPPLEMENTARY AWARD OF STOCK IN OUR GROUP'S TOP-RATED COMPANIES.
PORTFOLIO
DON'T JOKE AROUND!!
YOU PUT ME THROUGH A LIVING HELL JUST FOR THAT!!?
DO YOU HAVE ANY IDEA HOW MANY PEOPLE I KILLED!!?
HOW MANY... YOU SAY?
IT WAS SEVEN, WASN'T IT?
I SAW IT AAAALL!
WHAT?

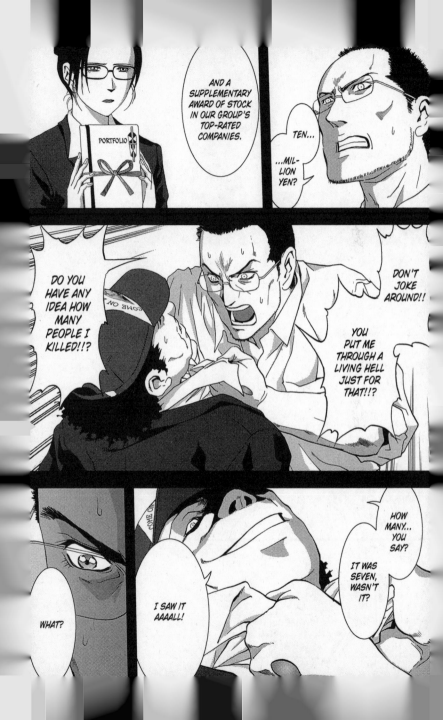

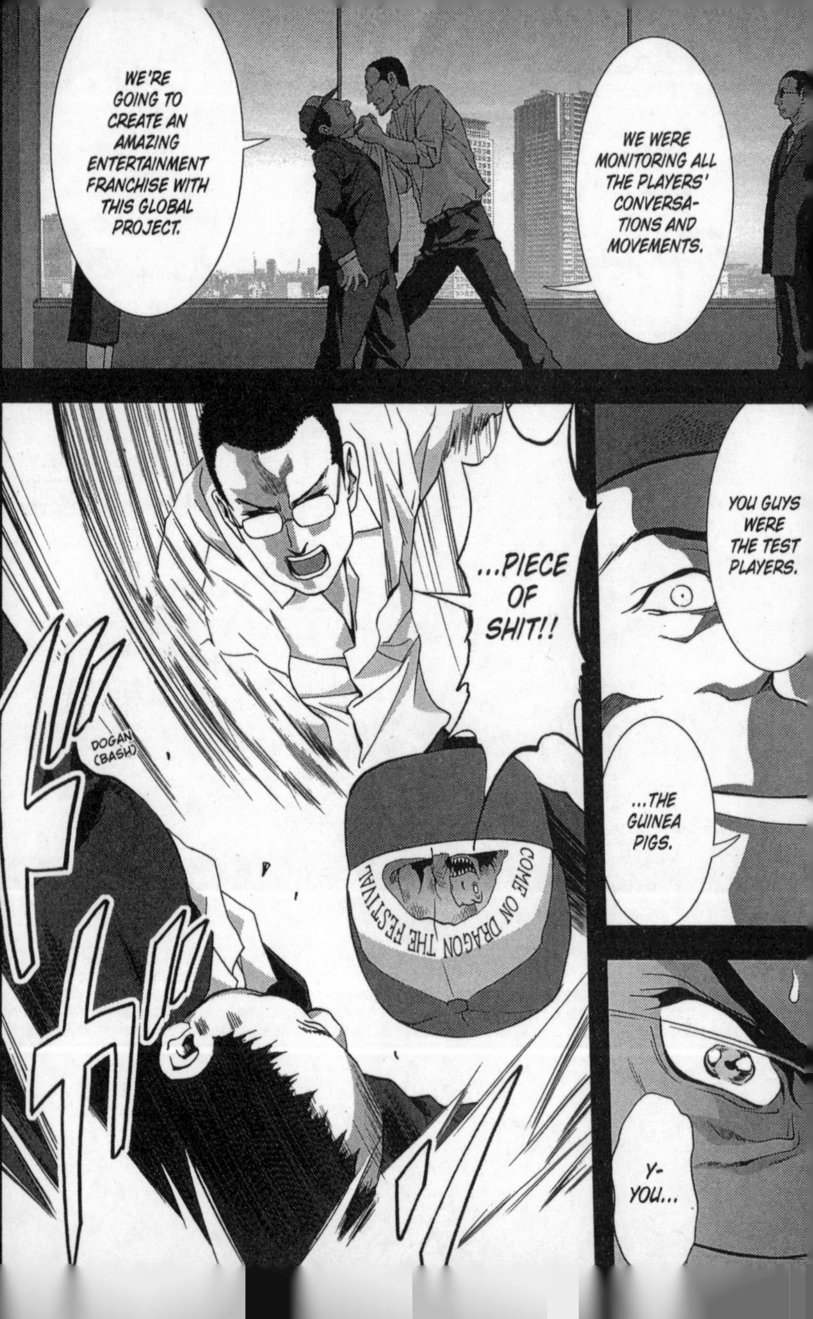
WE WERE MONITORING ALL THE PLAYERS' CONVERSA- TIONS AND MOVEMENTS.
WE'RE GOING TO CREATE AN AMAZING ENTERTAINMENT FRANCHISE WITH THIS GLOBAL PROJECT.
YOU GUYS WERE THE TEST PLAYERS.
...THE GUINEA PIGS.
Y- YOU...
...PIECE OF SHIT!!
DOGAN (BASH)
COME ON DRAGON THE FESTIVAL

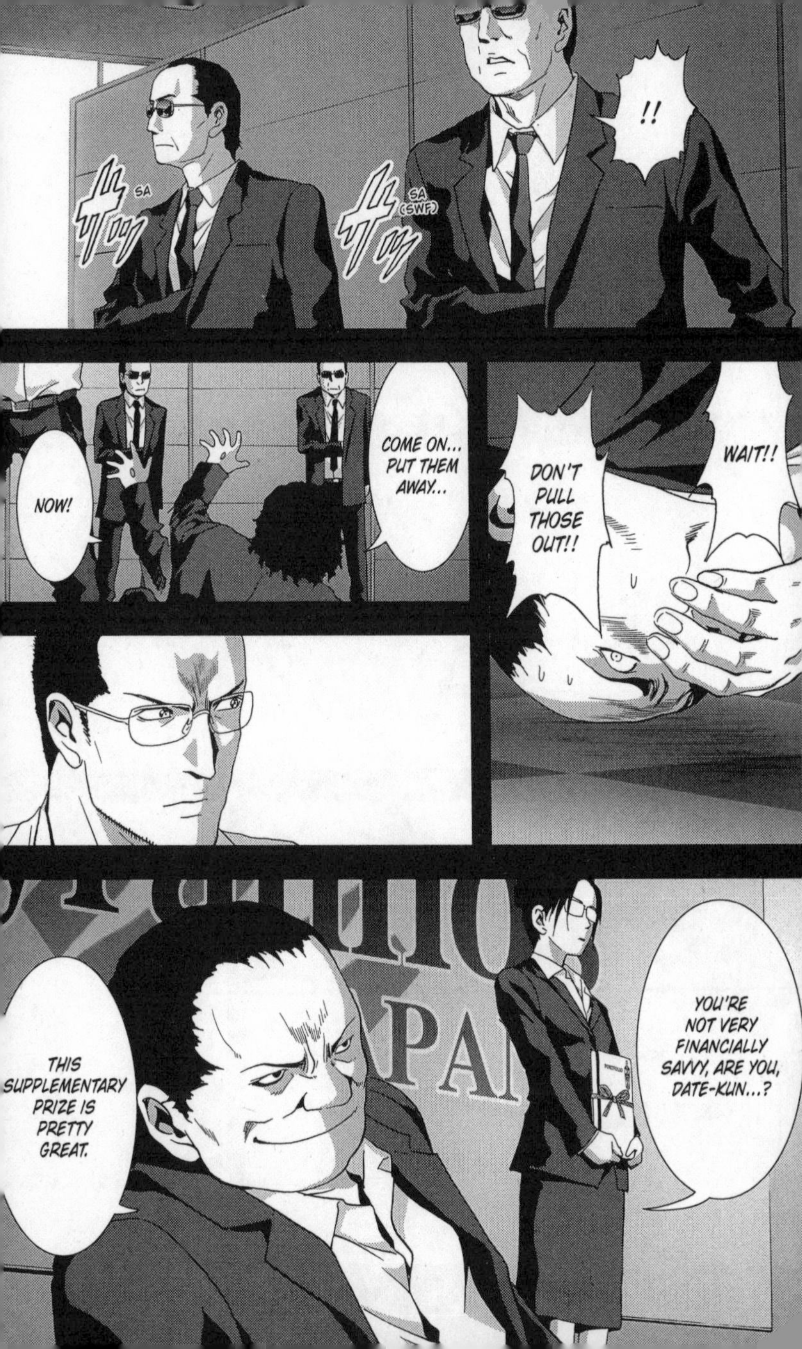
!!
SA (SWF)
SA
WAIT!!
DON'T PULL THOSE OUT!!
COME ON... PUT THEM AWAY...
NOW!
YOU'RE NOT VERY FINANCIALLY SAVVY, ARE YOU, DATE-KUN...?
THIS SUPPLEMENTARY PRIZE IS PRETTY GREAT.

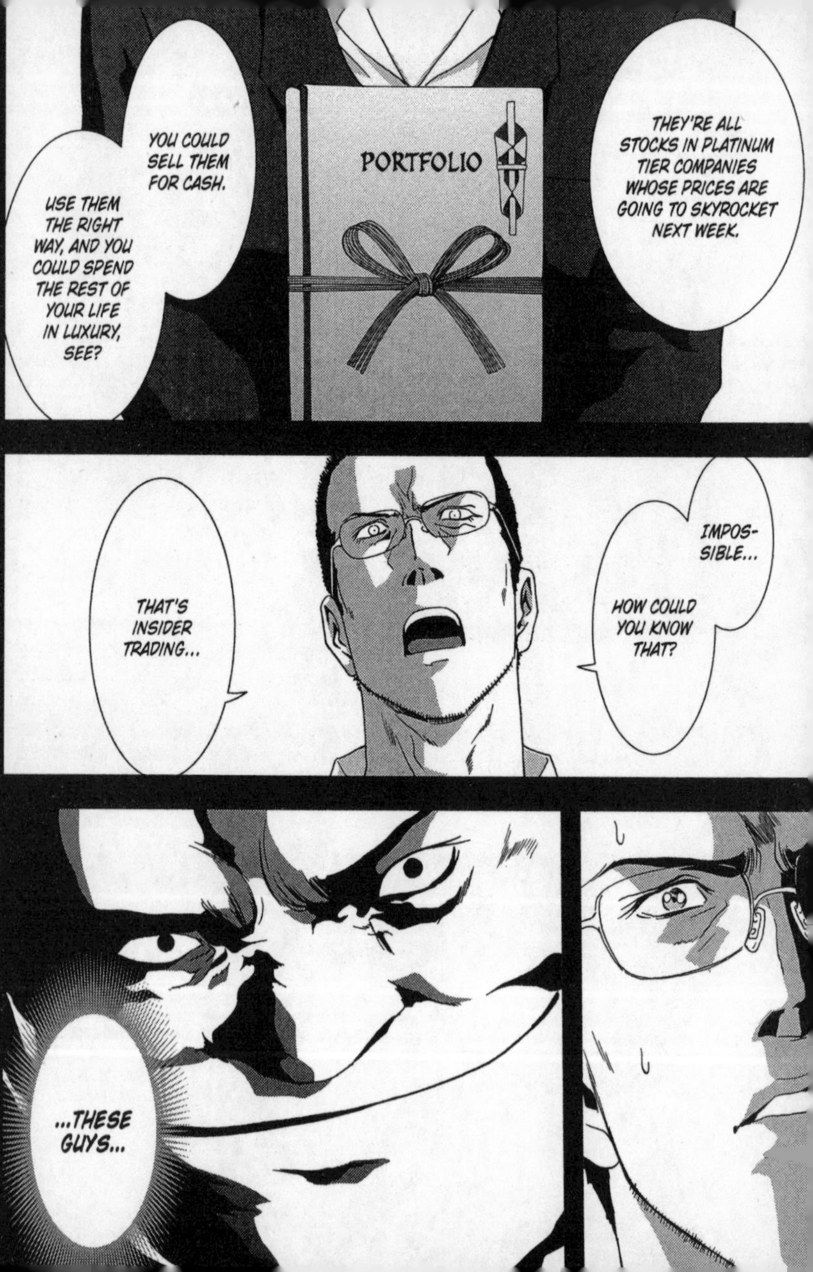
THEY'RE ALL STOCKS IN PLATINUM TIER COMPANIES WHOSE PRICES ARE GOING TO SKYROCKET NEXT WEEK.
PORTFOLIO
YOU COULD SELL THEM FOR CASH.
USE THEM THE RIGHT WAY, AND YOU COULD SPEND THE REST OF YOUR LIFE IN LUXURY, SEE?
IMPOS-SIBLE...
HOW COULD YOU KNOW THAT?
THAT'S INSIDER TRADING...
...THESE GUYS...

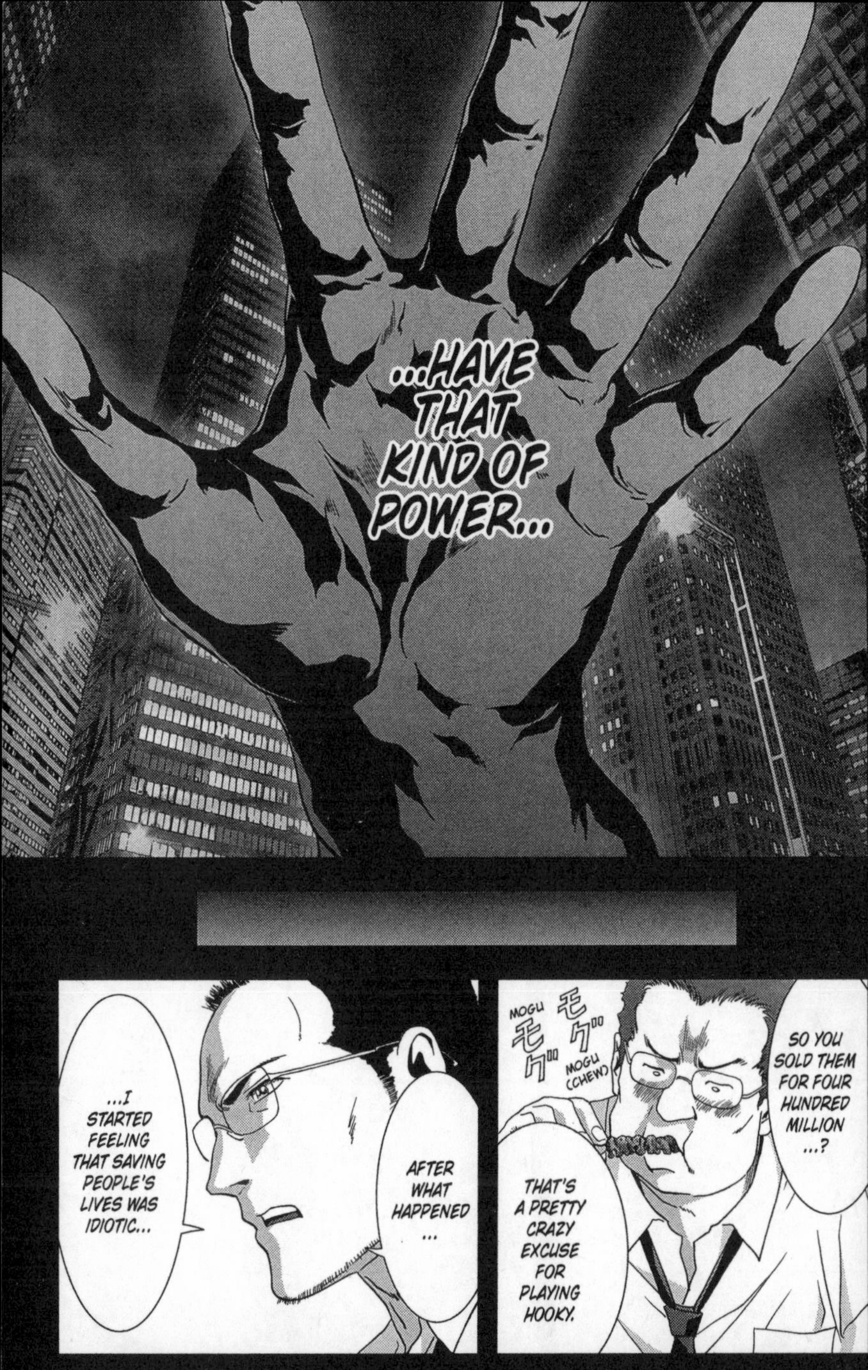
...HAVE THAT KIND OF POWER...
SO YOU SOLD THEM FOR FOUR HUNDRED MILLION ...?
MOGU MOGU (CHEW)
THAT'S A PRETTY CRAZY EXCUSE FOR PLAYING HOOKY.
AFTER WHAT HAPPENED ...
...I STARTED FEELING THAT SAVING PEOPLE'S LIVES WAS IDIOTIC...

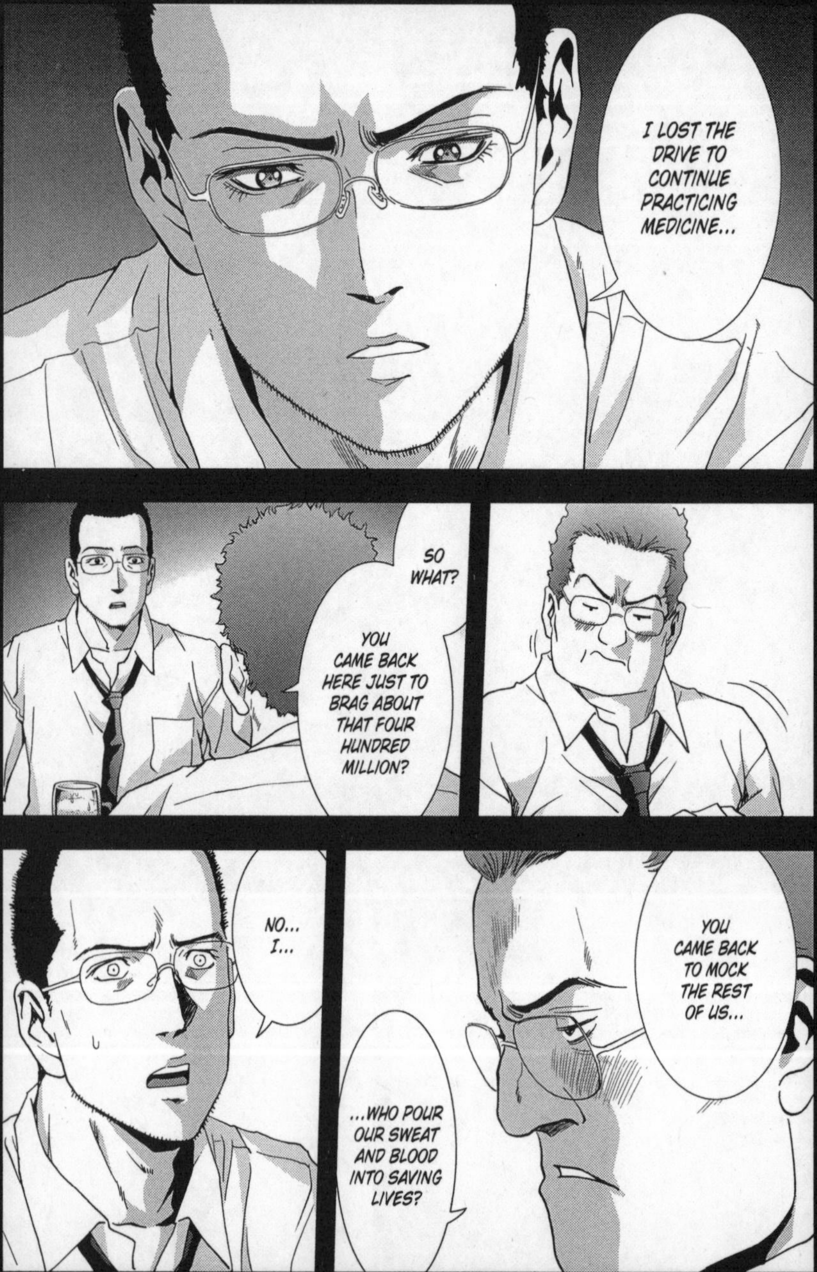
I LOST THE DRIVE TO CONTINUE PRACTICING MEDICINE...
SO WHAT?
YOU CAME BACK HERE JUST TO BRAG ABOUT THAT FOUR HUNDRED MILLION?
YOU CAME BACK TO MOCK THE REST OF US...
...WHO POUR OUR SWEAT AND BLOOD INTO SAVING LIVES?
NO... I...

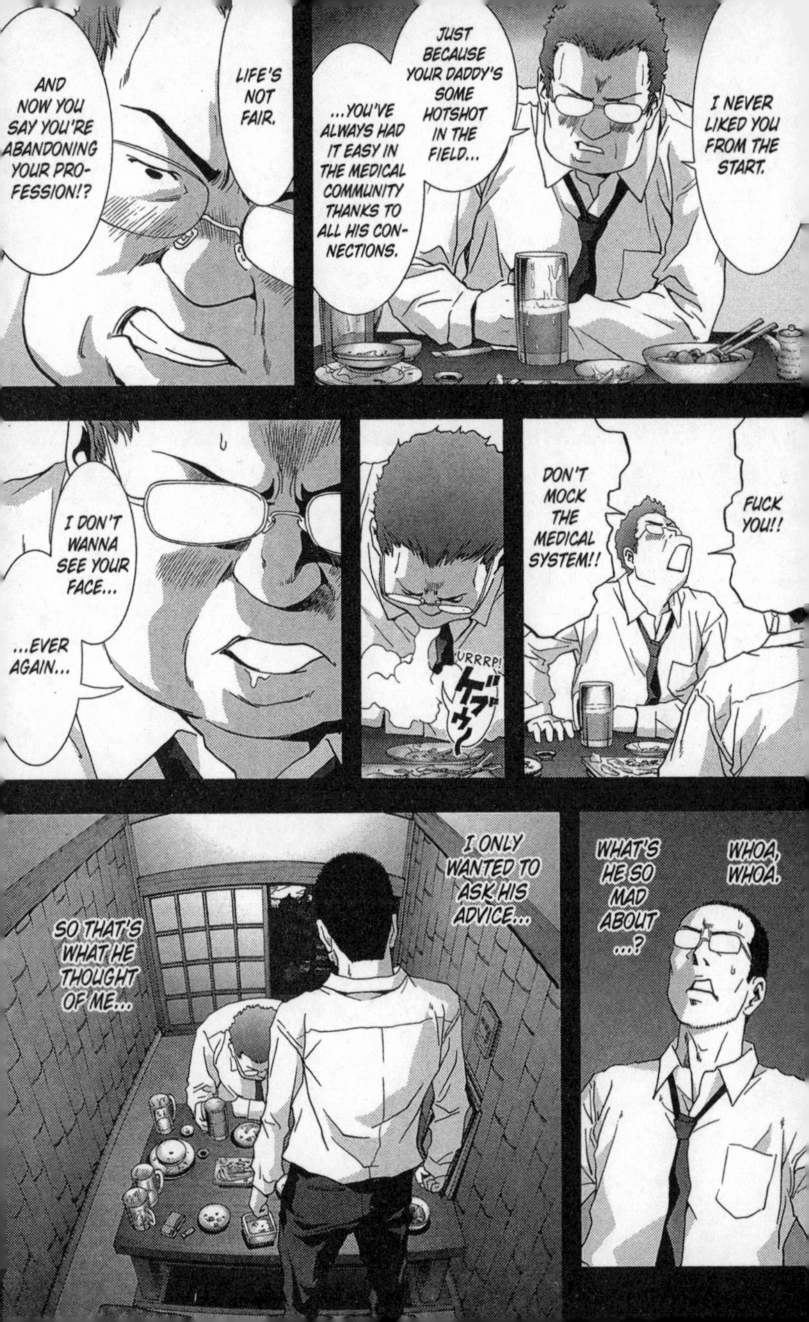
I NEVER LIKED YOU FROM THE START.
JUST BECAUSE YOUR DADDY'S SOME HOTSHOT IN THE FIELD...
...YOU'VE ALWAYS HAD IT EASY IN THE MEDICAL COMMUNITY THANKS TO ALL HIS CON- NECTIONS.
LIFE'S NOT FAIR.
AND NOW YOU SAY YOU'RE ABANDONING YOUR PRO- FESSION!?
FUCK YOU!!
DON'T MOCK THE MEDICAL SYSTEM!!
URRRP!
I DON'T WANNA SEE YOUR FACE...
...EVER AGAIN...
WHOA, WHOA.
WHAT'S HE SO MAD ABOUT ...?
I ONLY WANTED TO ASK HIS ADVICE...
SO THAT'S WHAT HE THOUGHT OF ME...

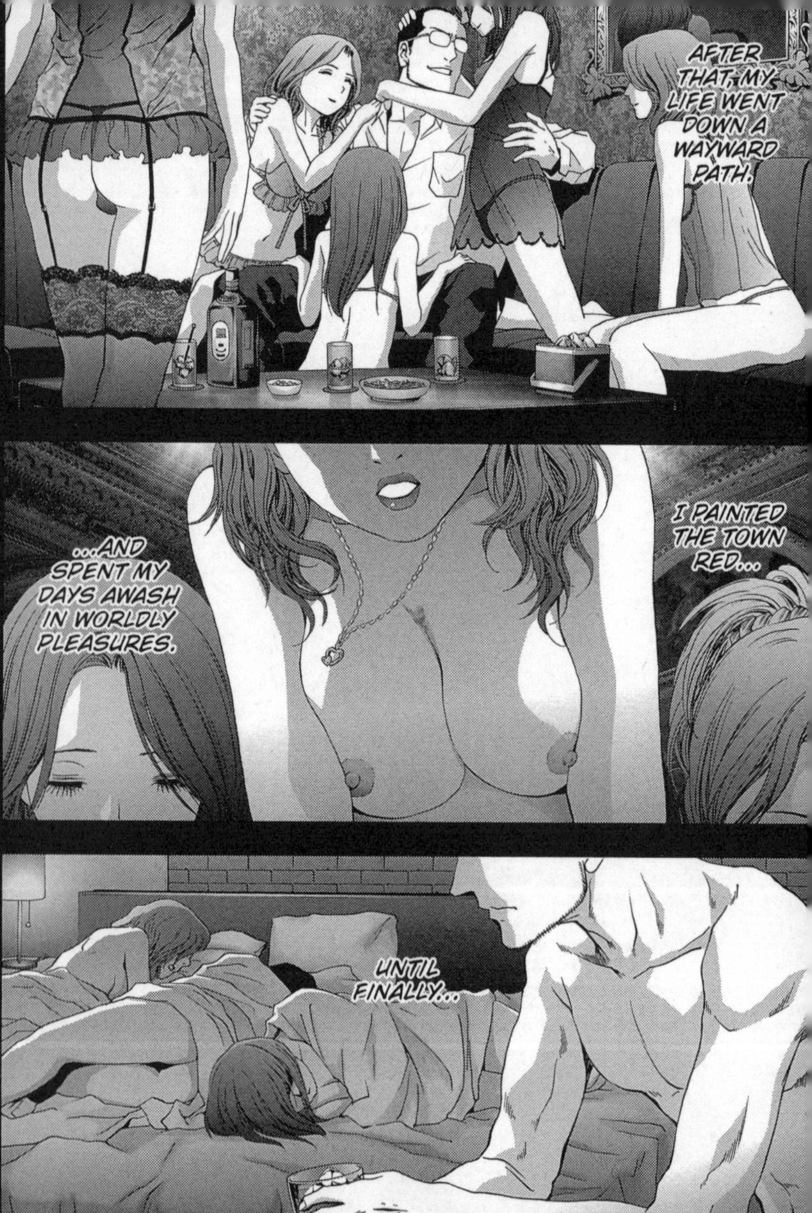
AFTER THAT, MY LIFE WENT DOWN A WAYWARD PATH.
I PAINTED THE TOWN RED...
...AND SPENT MY DAYS AWASH IN WORLDLY PLEASURES.
UNTIL FINALLY...

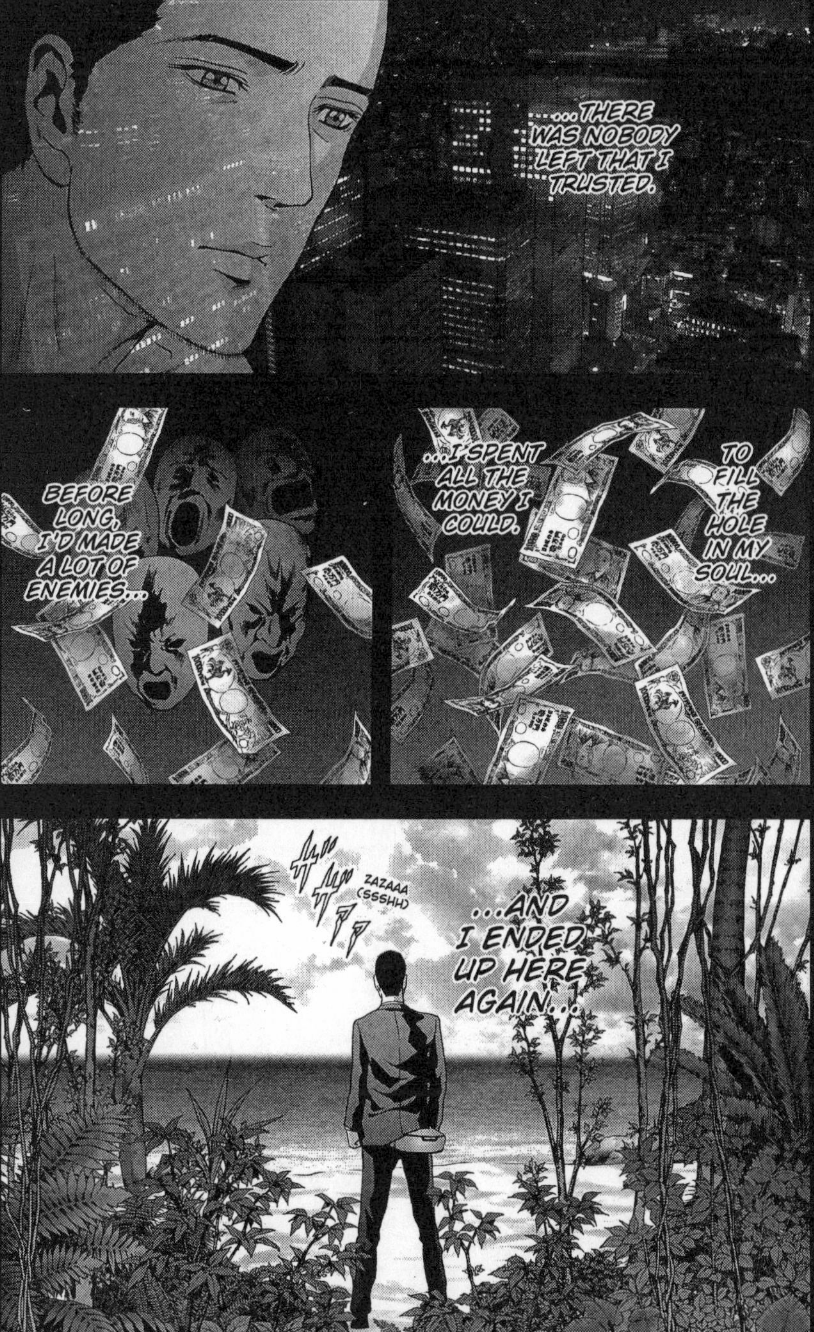
...THERE WAS NOBODY LEFT THAT I TRUSTED.
...I SPENT ALL THE MONEY I COULD.
TO FILL THE HOLE IN MY SOUL...
BEFORE LONG, I'D MADE A LOT OF ENEMIES...
ZAZAAA (SSSHH)
...AND I ENDED UP HERE AGAIN...

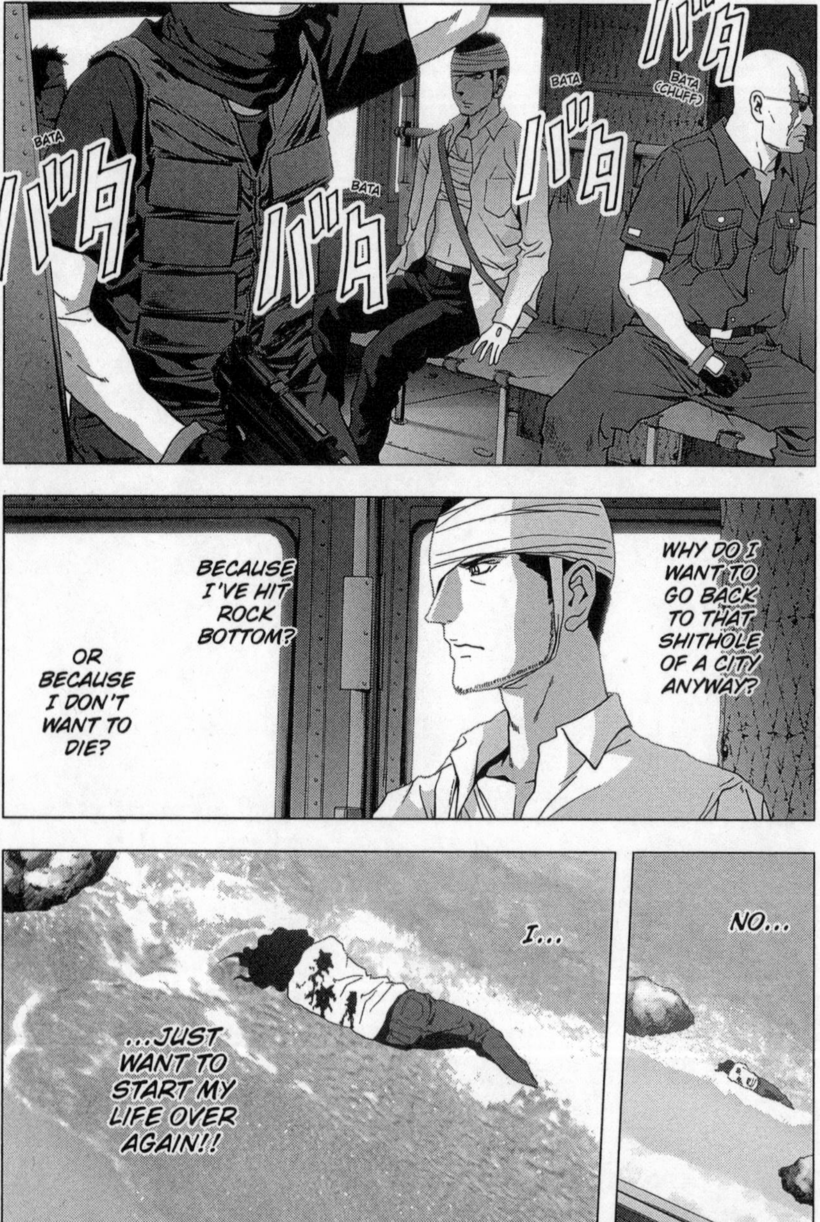
バタ
BATA (CHUFF)
バタ
BATA
バタ
BATA
バタ
BATA
WHY DO I WANT TO GO BACK TO THAT SHITHOLE OF A CITY ANYWAY?
BECAUSE I'VE HIT ROCK BOTTOM?
OR BECAUSE I DON'T WANT TO DIE?
NO...
I...
...JUST WANT TO START MY LIFE OVER AGAIN!!

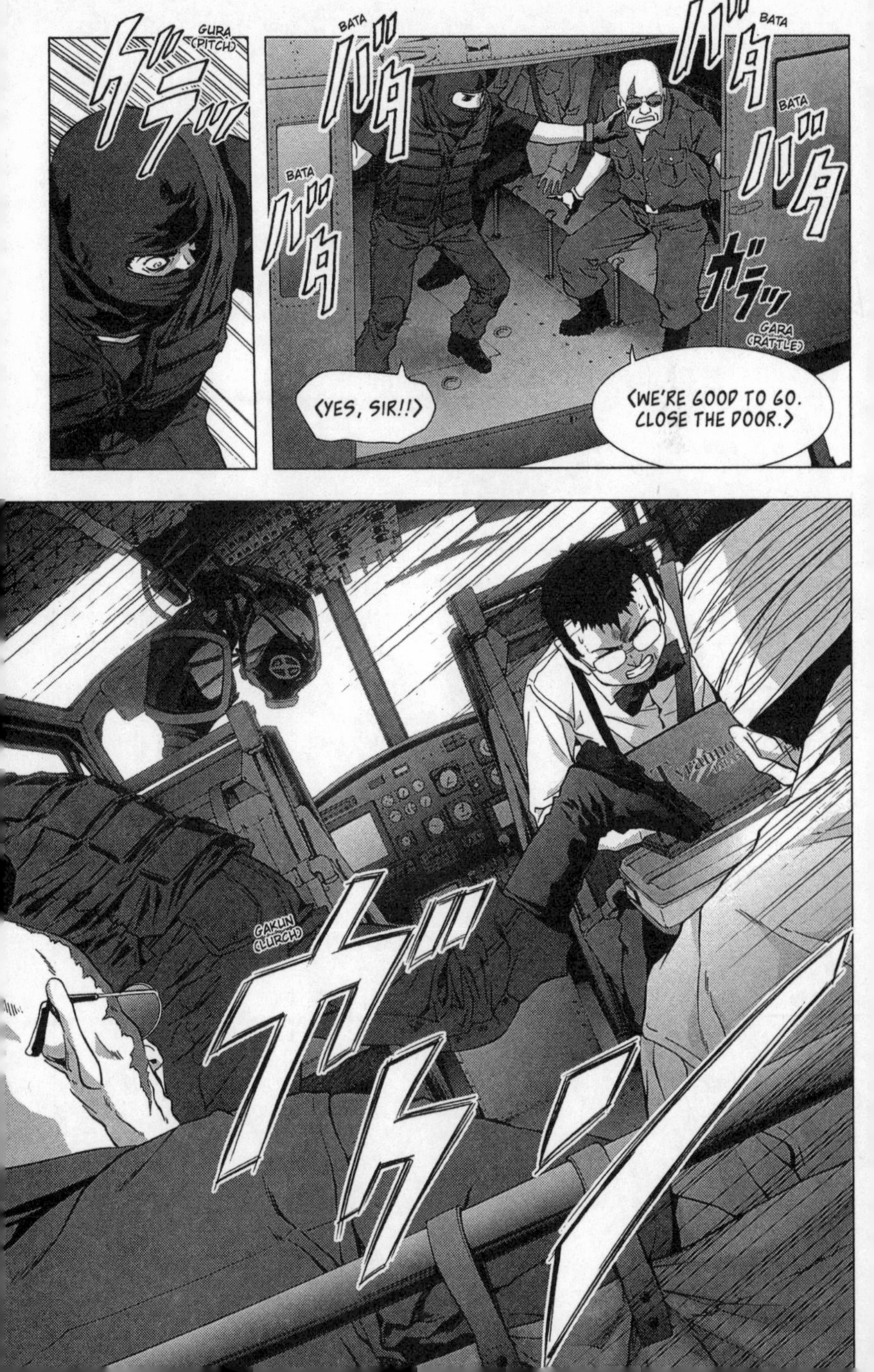
BATA
BATA
GARA (RATTLE)
<WE'RE GOOD TO GO. CLOSE THE DOOR.>
BATA
BATA
<YES, SIR!!>
GURA (PITCH)
GAKUN (LURCH)

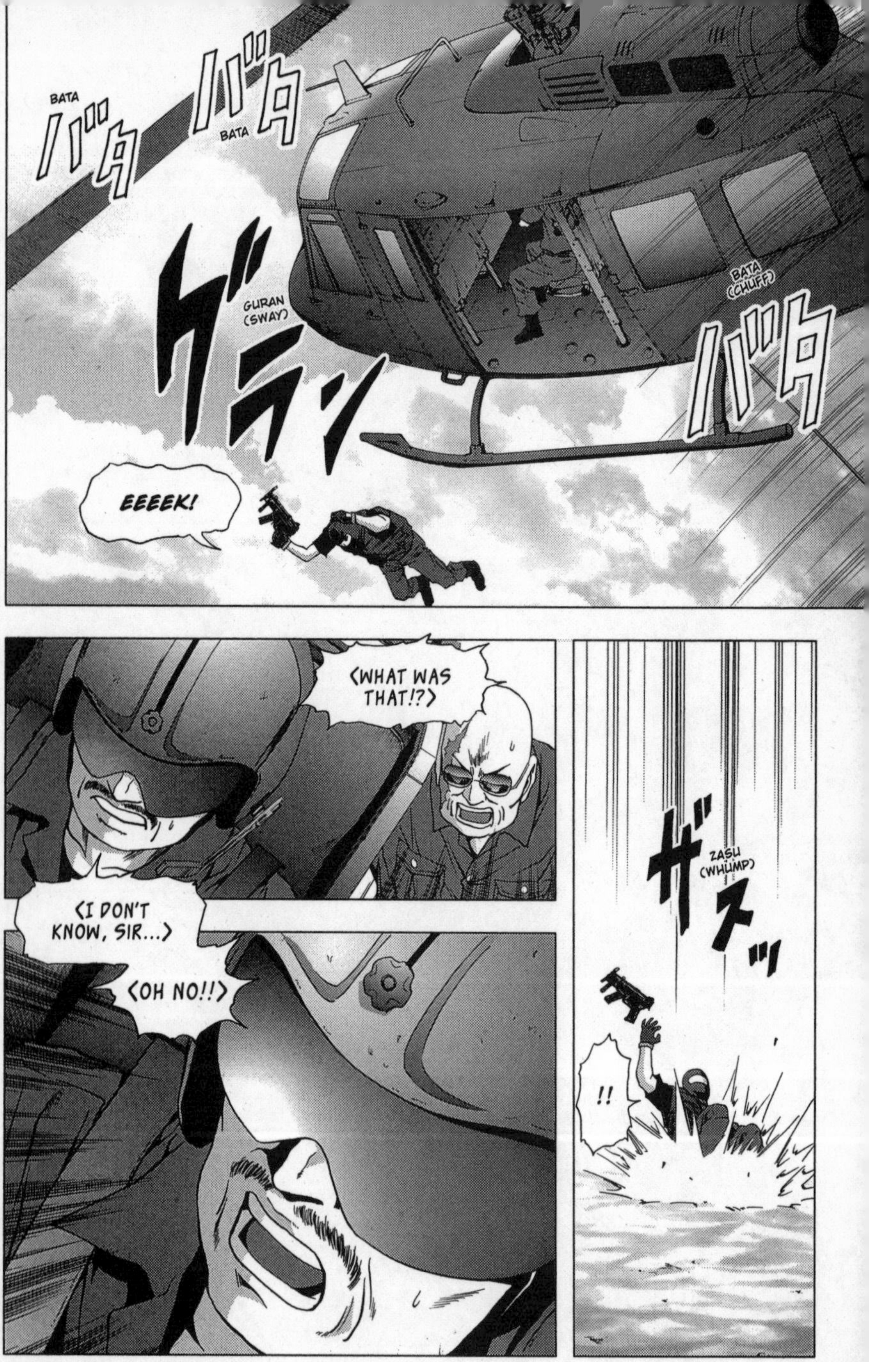
BATA
BATA
BATA (CHUFF)
GURAN (SWAY)
EEEEK!
ZASU (WHUMP)
!!
<WHAT WAS THAT!?>
<I DON'T KNOW, SIR...>
<OH NO!!>

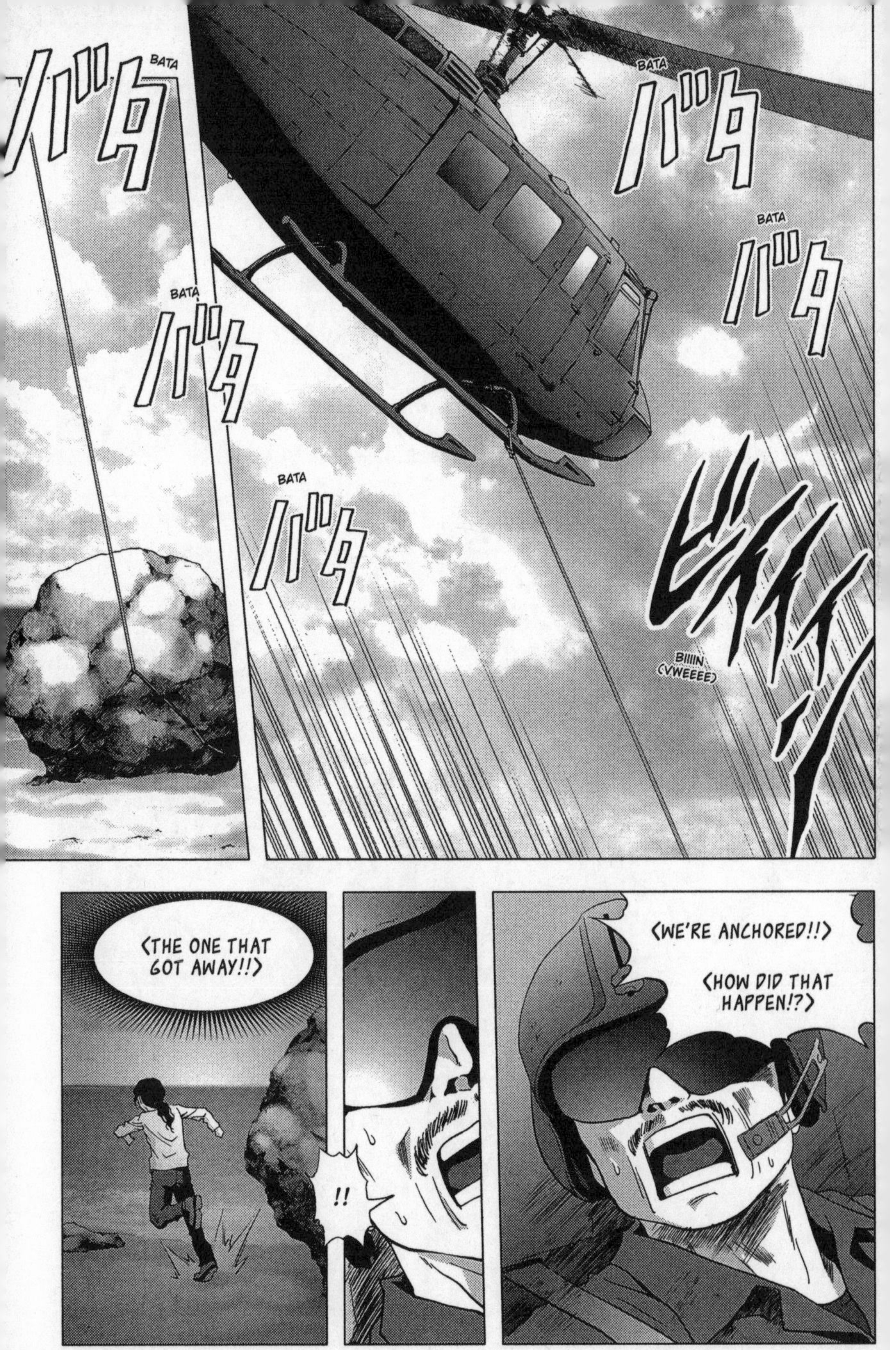
BATA
BATA
BATA
BIIIN (VWEEEE)
BATA
BATA
〈WE'RE ANCHORED!!〉
〈HOW DID THAT HAPPEN!?〉
!!
〈THE ONE THAT GOT AWAY!!〉

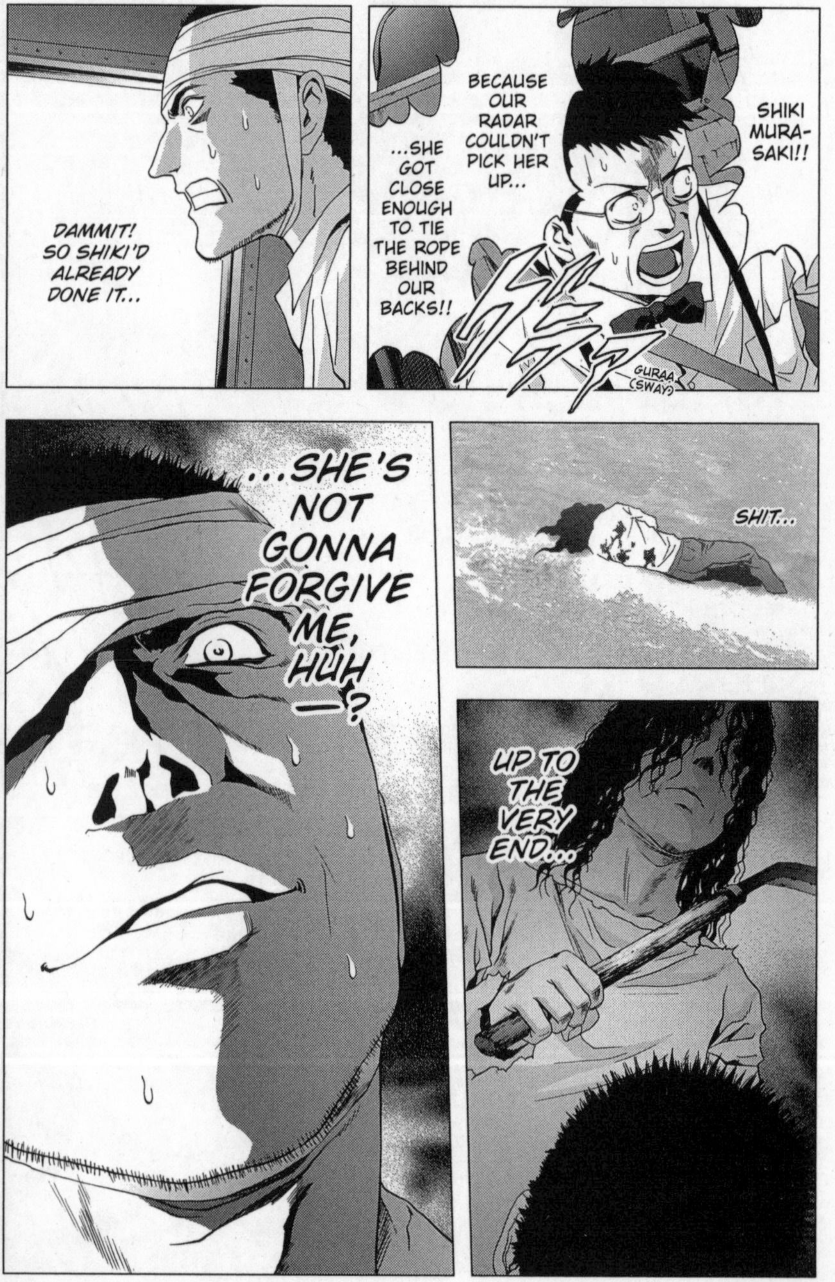
SHIKI MURA-SAKI!!
BECAUSE OUR RADAR COULDN'T PICK HER UP...
...SHE GOT CLOSE ENOUGH TO TIE THE ROPE BEHIND OUR BACKS!!
GURAA (SWAY)
DAMMIT! SO SHIKI'D ALREADY DONE IT...
SHIT...
UP TO THE VERY END...
...SHE'S NOT GONNA FORGIVE ME, HUH—?

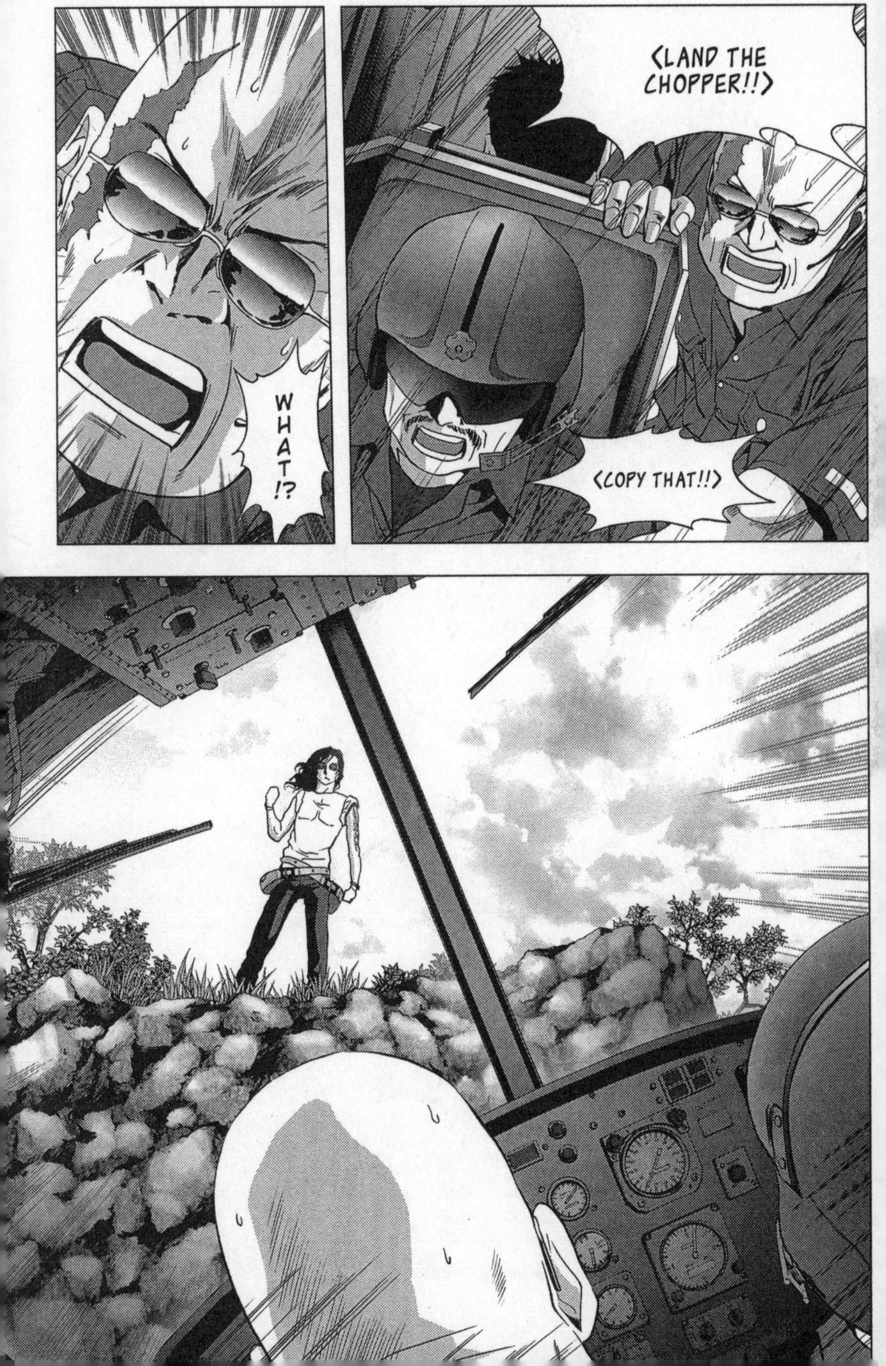
<LAND THE CHOPPER!!>
<COPY THAT!!>
WHAT!?

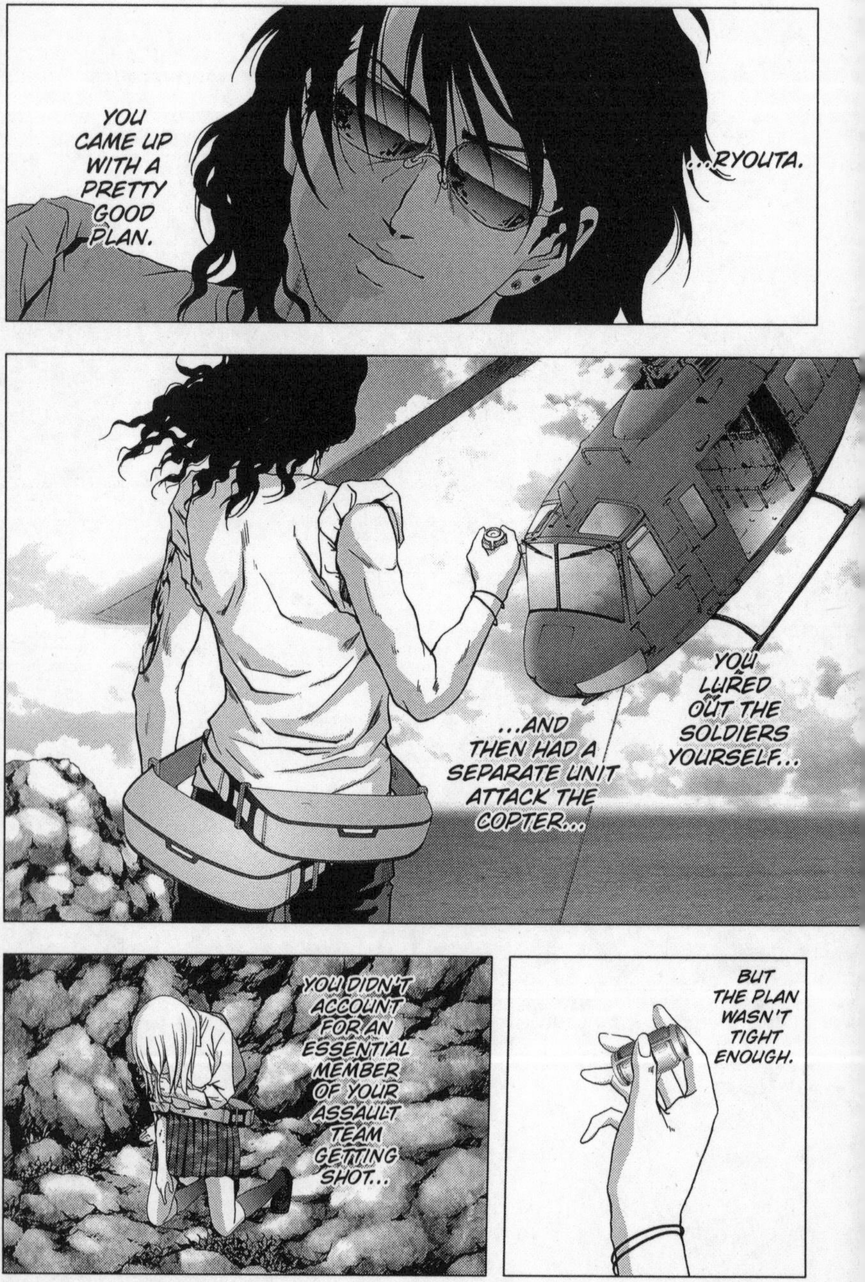
YOU CAME UP WITH A PRETTY GOOD PLAN.
...RYOUTA.
YOU LURED OUT THE SOLDIERS YOURSELF...
...AND THEN HAD A SEPARATE UNIT ATTACK THE COPTER...
BUT THE PLAN WASN'T TIGHT ENOUGH.
YOU DIDN'T ACCOUNT FOR AN ESSENTIAL MEMBER OF YOUR ASSAULT TEAM GETTING SHOT...

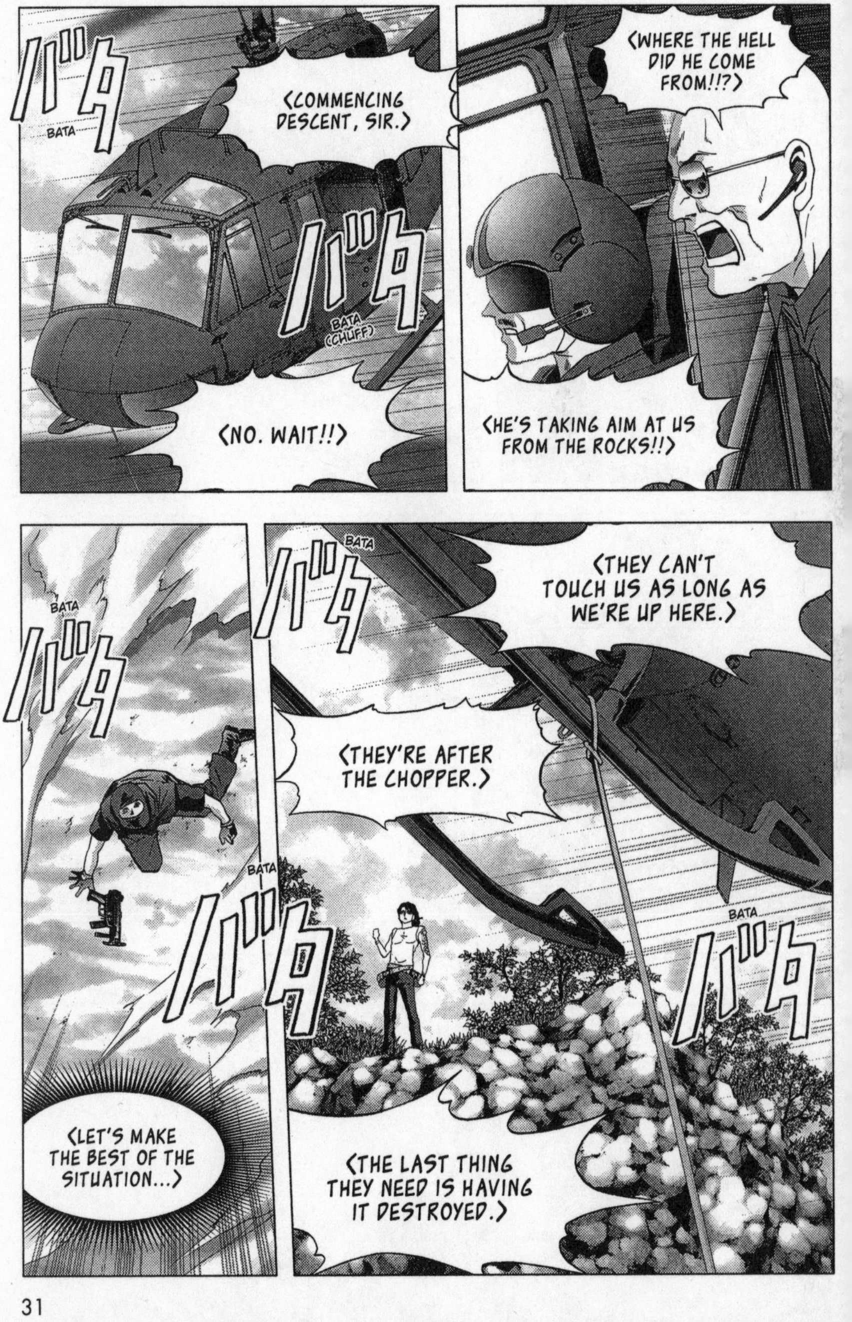
‹WHERE THE HELL DID HE COME FROM!!?›
‹HE'S TAKING AIM AT US FROM THE ROCKS!!›
バタ
BATA
‹COMMENCING DESCENT, SIR.›
バタ
BATA (CHUFF)
‹NO. WAIT!!›
バタ
BATA
‹THEY CAN'T TOUCH US AS LONG AS WE'RE UP HERE.›
‹THEY'RE AFTER THE CHOPPER.›
バタ
BATA
‹THE LAST THING THEY NEED IS HAVING IT DESTROYED.›
バタ
BATA
バタ
BATA
‹LET'S MAKE THE BEST OF THE SITUATION...›

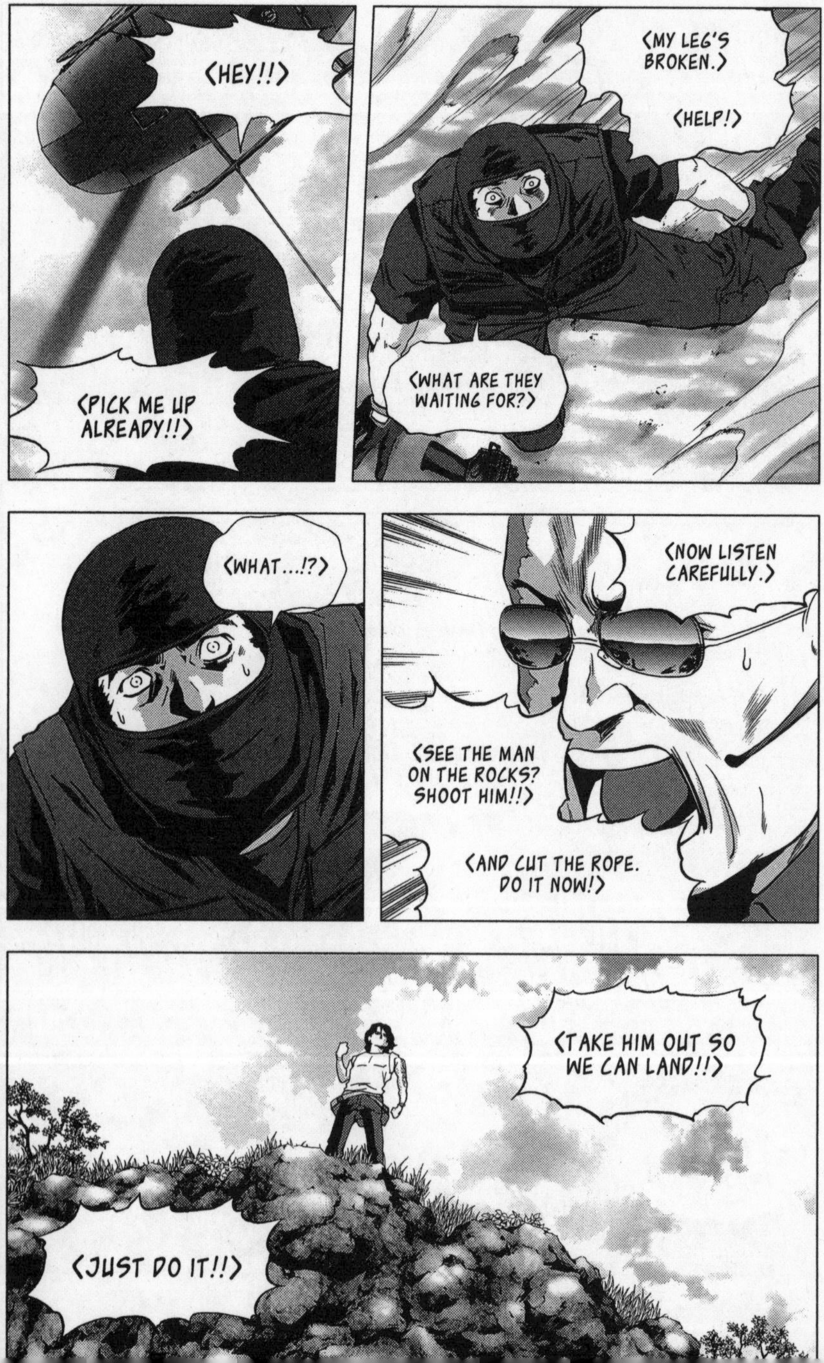
〈MY LEG'S BROKEN.〉
〈HELP!〉
〈WHAT ARE THEY WAITING FOR?〉
〈HEY!!〉
〈PICK ME UP ALREADY!!〉
〈NOW LISTEN CAREFULLY.〉
〈SEE THE MAN ON THE ROCKS? SHOOT HIM!!〉
〈AND CUT THE ROPE. DO IT NOW!〉
〈WHAT...!?〉
〈TAKE HIM OUT SO WE CAN LAND!!〉
〈JUST DO IT!!〉

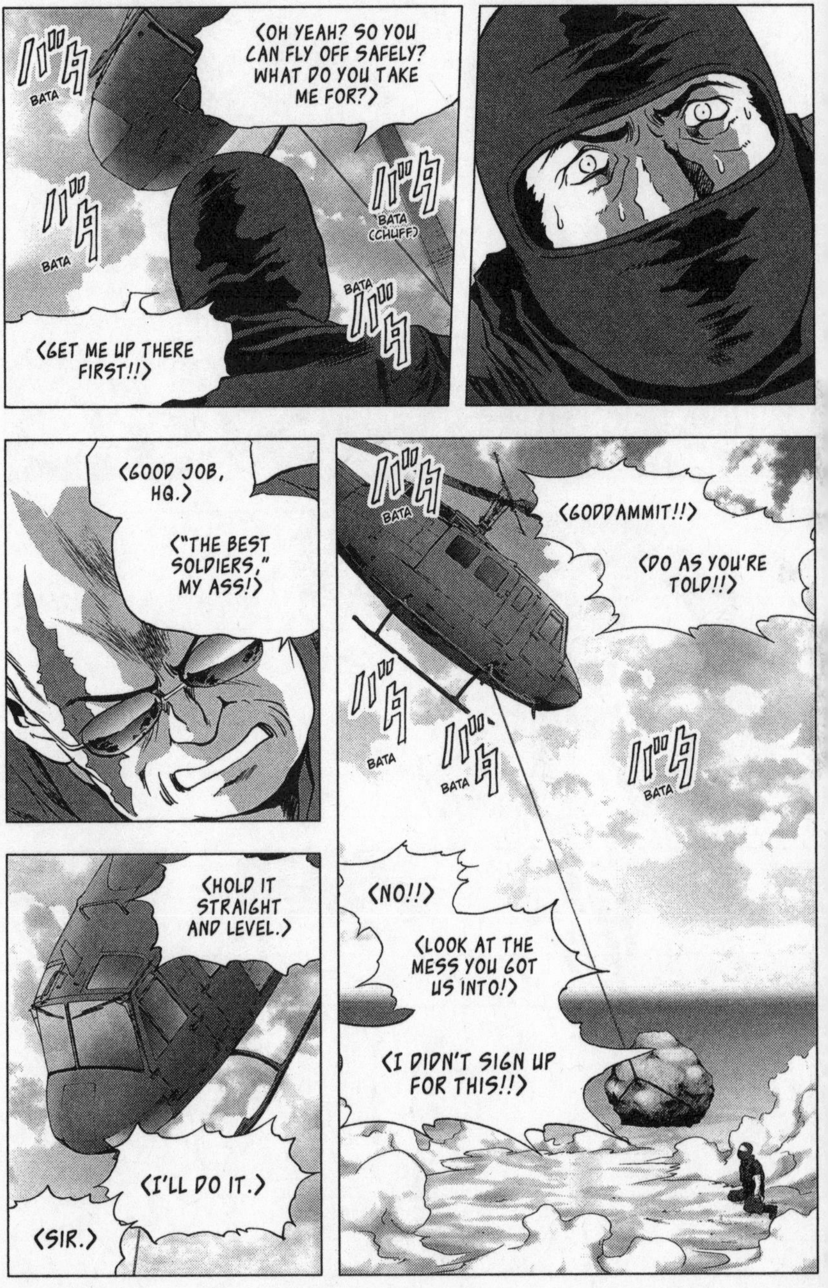
〈OH YEAH? SO YOU CAN FLY OFF SAFELY? WHAT DO YOU TAKE ME FOR?〉
バタ
BATA
バタ
BATA (CHUFF)
バタ
BATA
BATA
バタ
〈GET ME UP THERE FIRST!!〉
〈GODDAMMIT!!〉
〈DO AS YOU'RE TOLD!!〉
バタ
BATA
バタ
BATA
バタ
BATA
バタ
BATA
〈NO!!〉
〈LOOK AT THE MESS YOU GOT US INTO!〉
〈I DIDN'T SIGN UP FOR THIS!!〉
〈GOOD JOB, HQ.〉
〈"THE BEST SOLDIERS," MY ASS!〉
〈HOLD IT STRAIGHT AND LEVEL.〉
〈I'LL DO IT.〉
〈SIR.〉

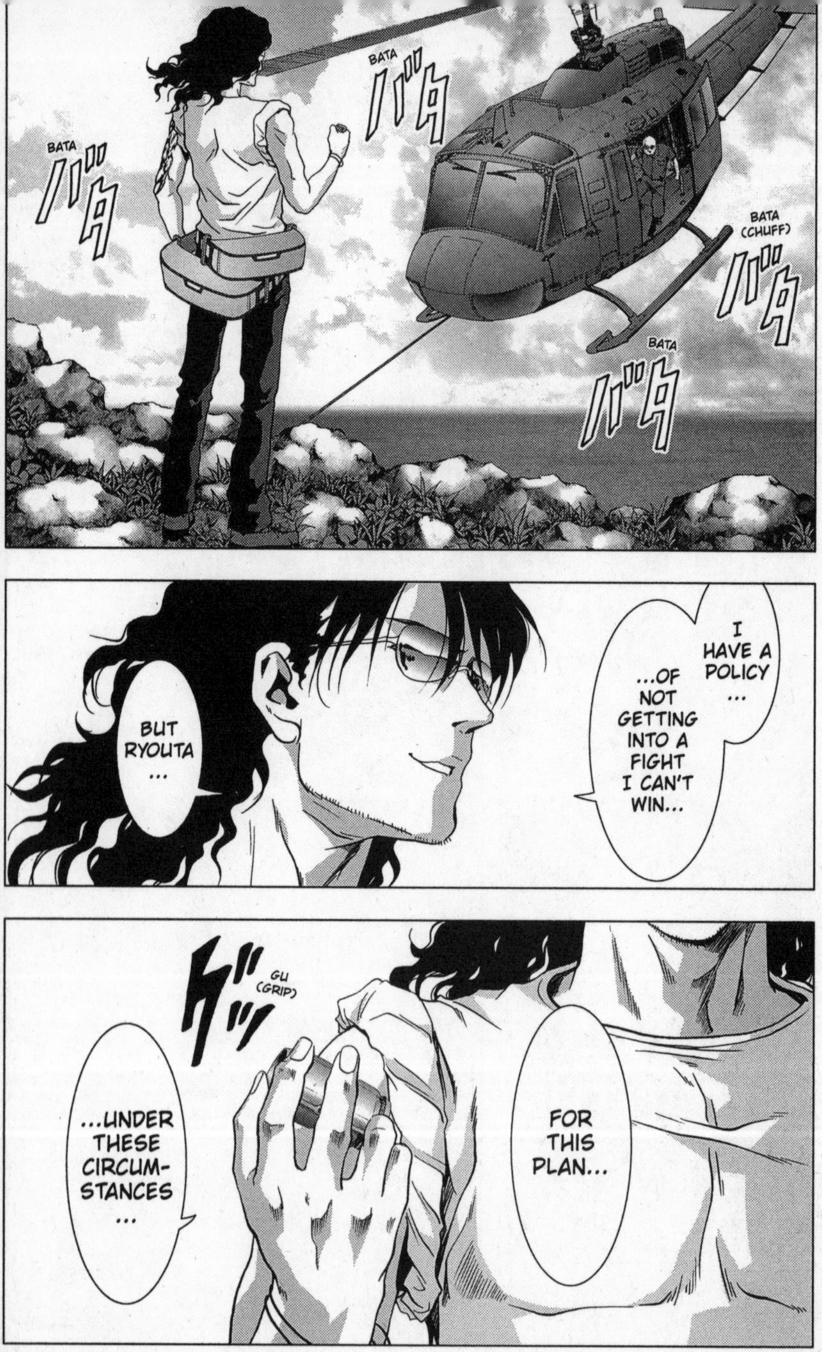
BATA (CHUFF)
バタ
BATA
バタ
BATA
バタ
BATA
バタ
I HAVE A POLICY ...
...OF NOT GETTING INTO A FIGHT I CAN'T WIN...
BUT RYOUTA ...
FOR THIS PLAN...
GU (GRIP)
グッ
...UNDER THESE CIRCUM-STANCES ...

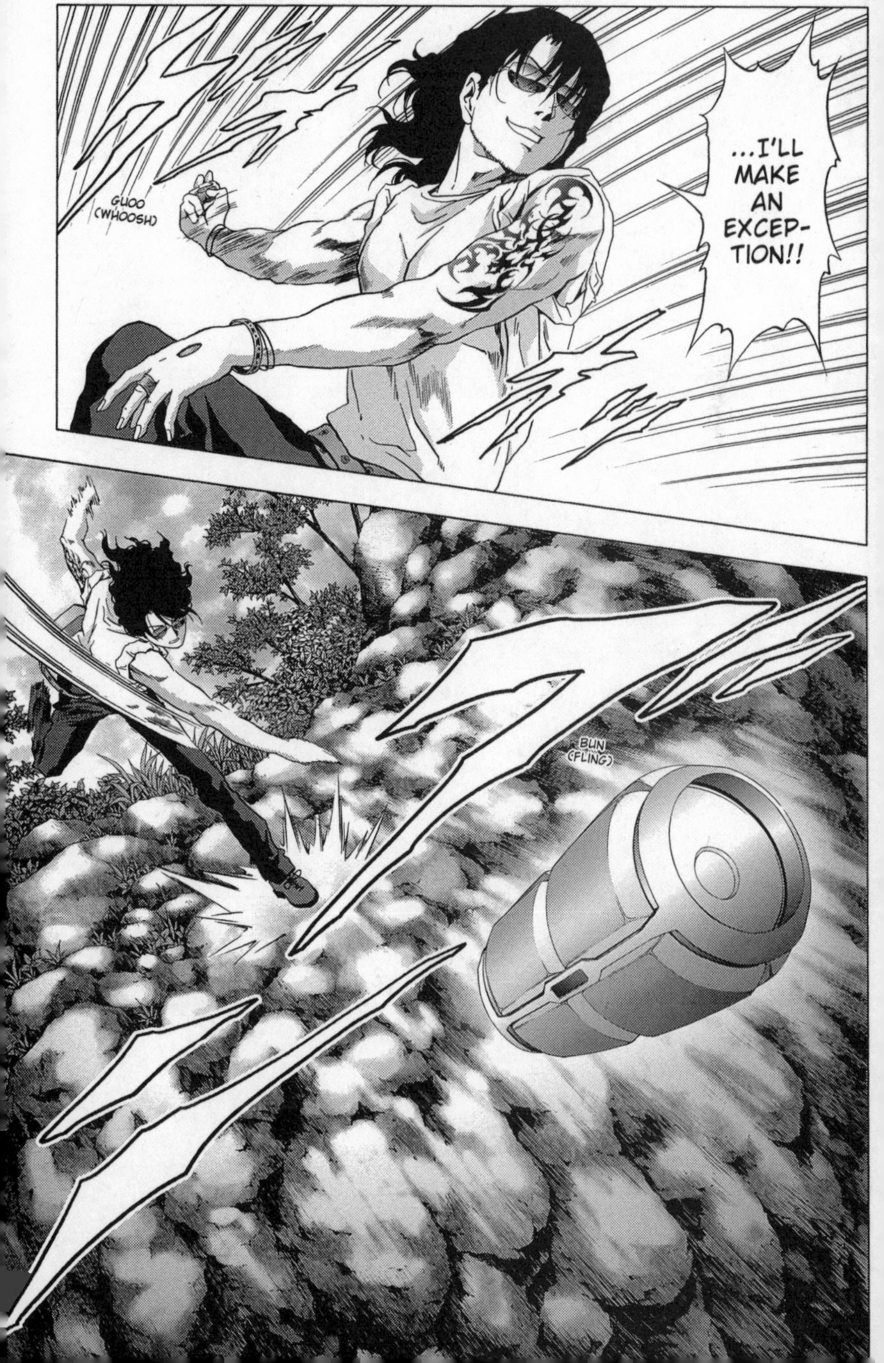
...I'LL MAKE AN EXCEPTION!!
GUOO (WHOOSH)
BUN (FLING)

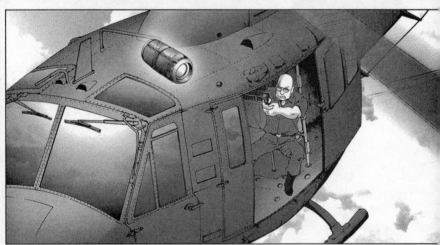

36

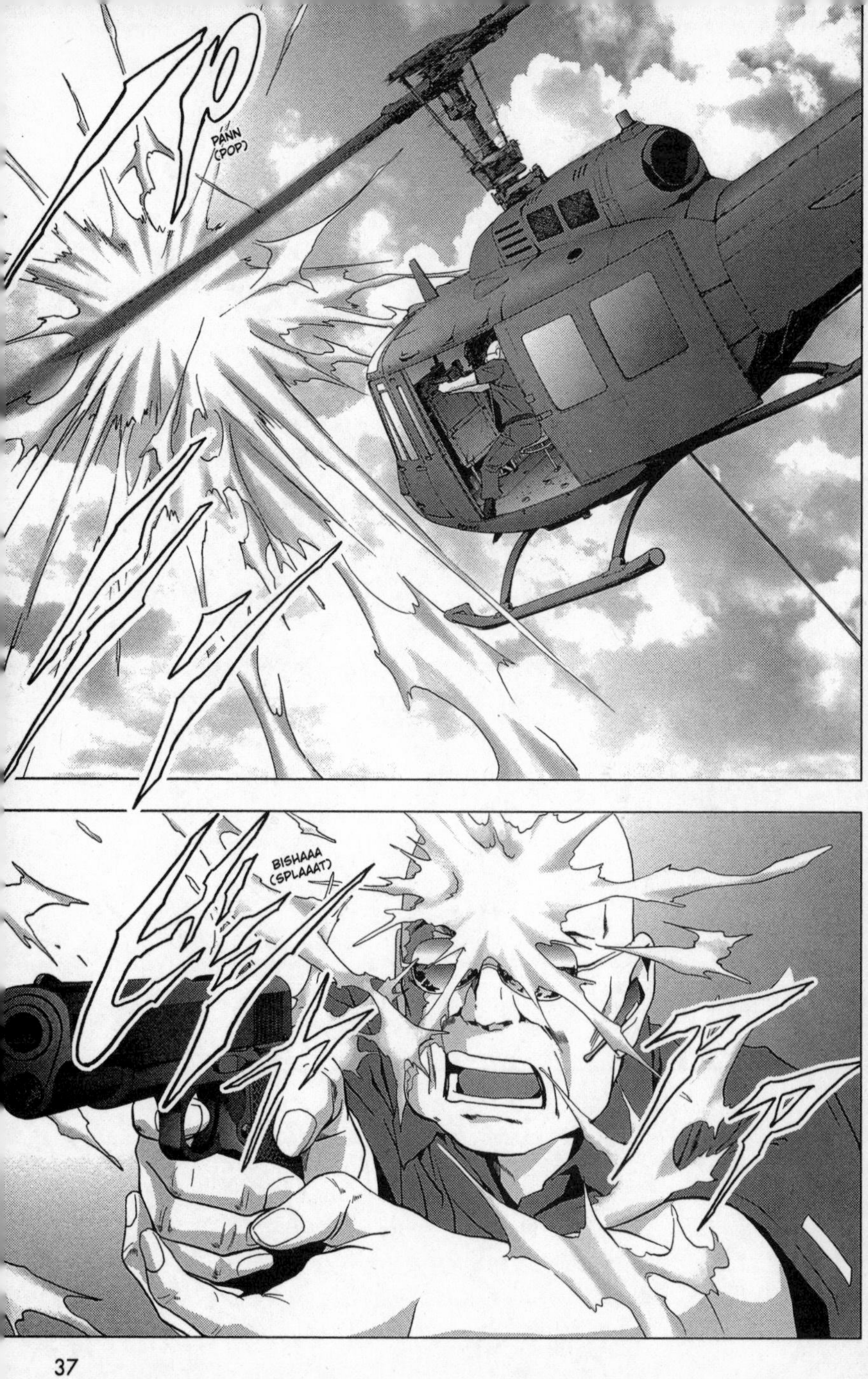
PANN
(POP)
BISHAAA
(SPLAAAT)

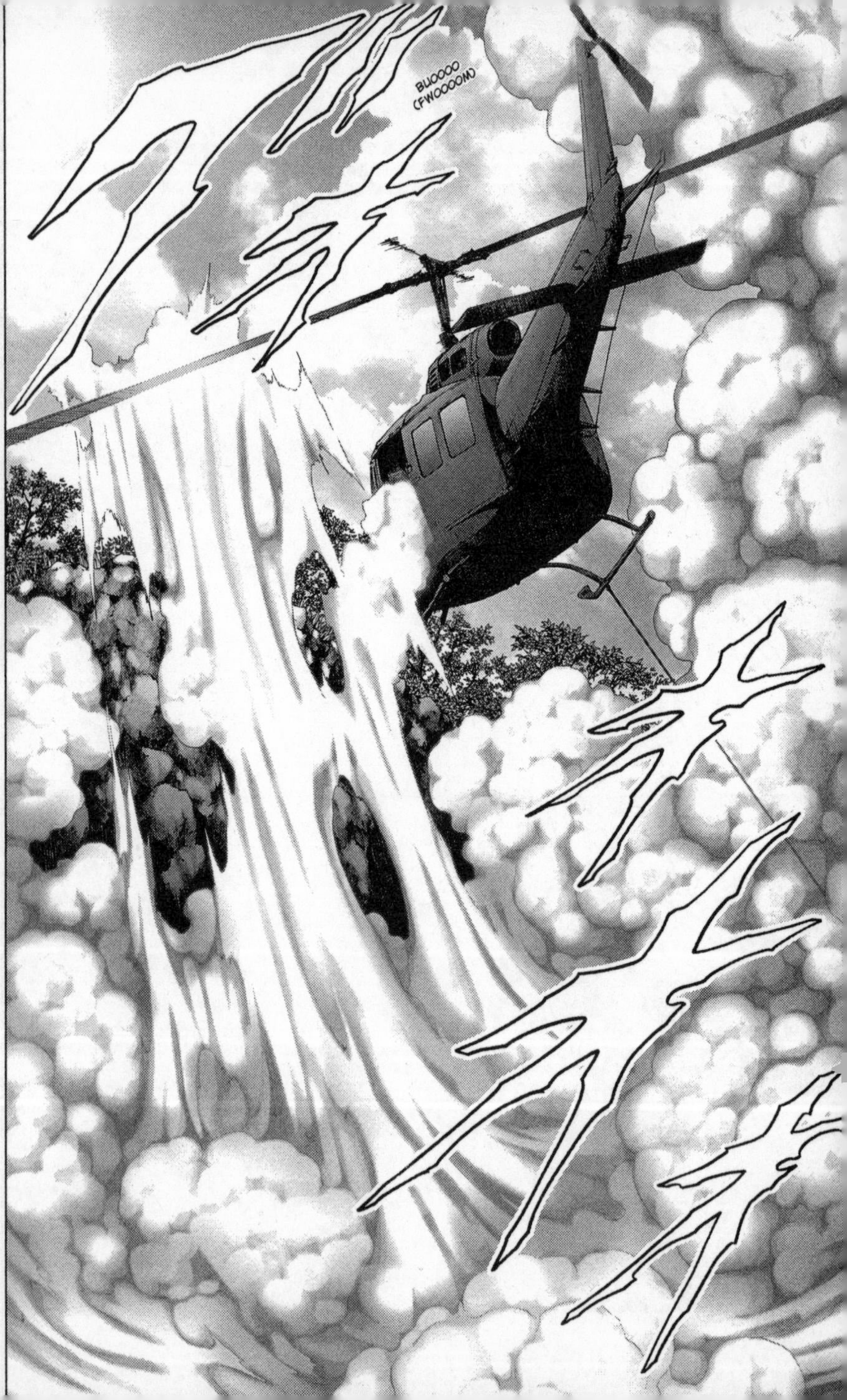
BUOOOO
(FWOOOOM)

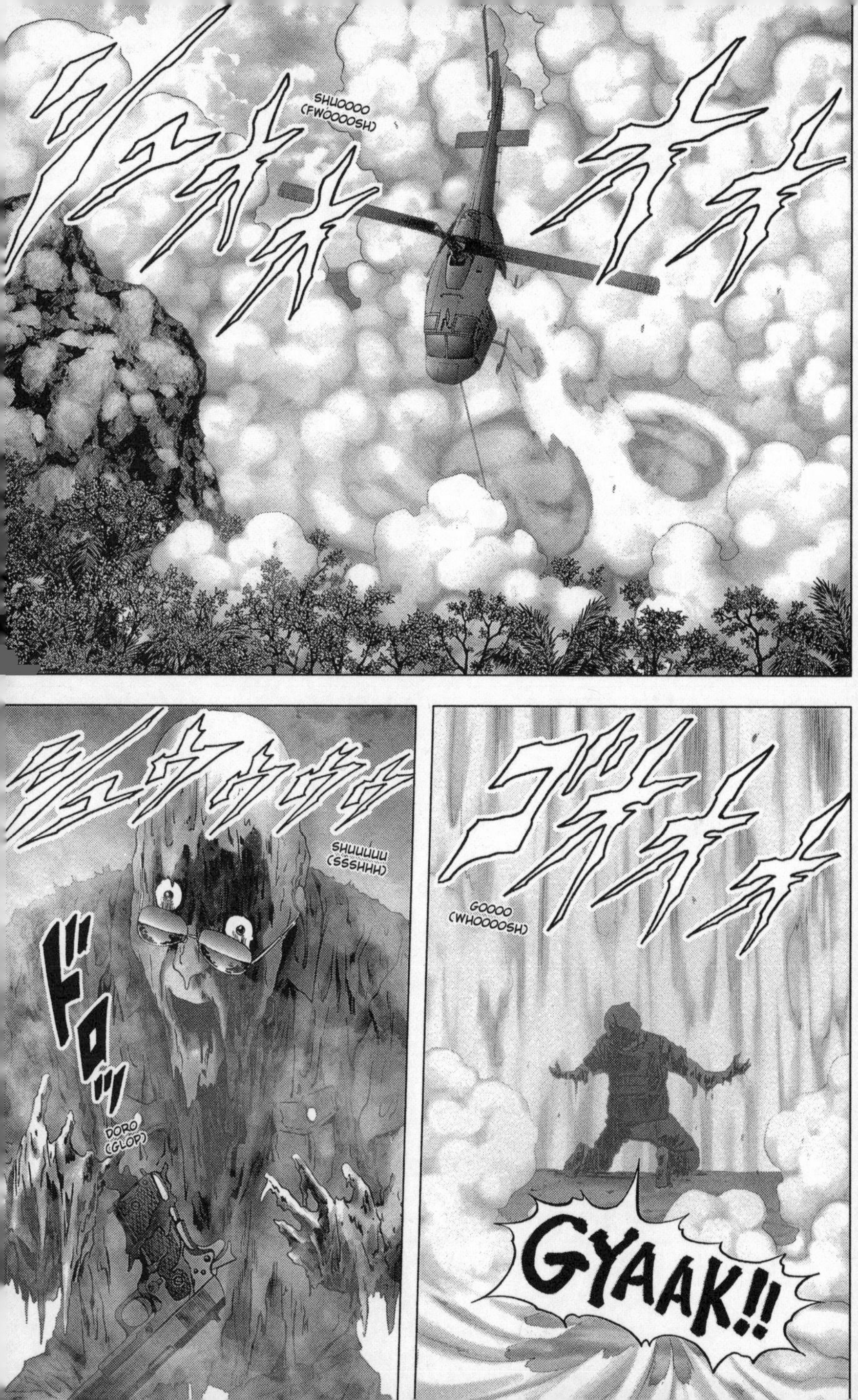
SHUOOOO
(FWOOOOSH)
GOOOO
(WHOOOOSH)
GYAAK!!
SHUUUUU
(SSSHHH)
DORO
(GLOP)

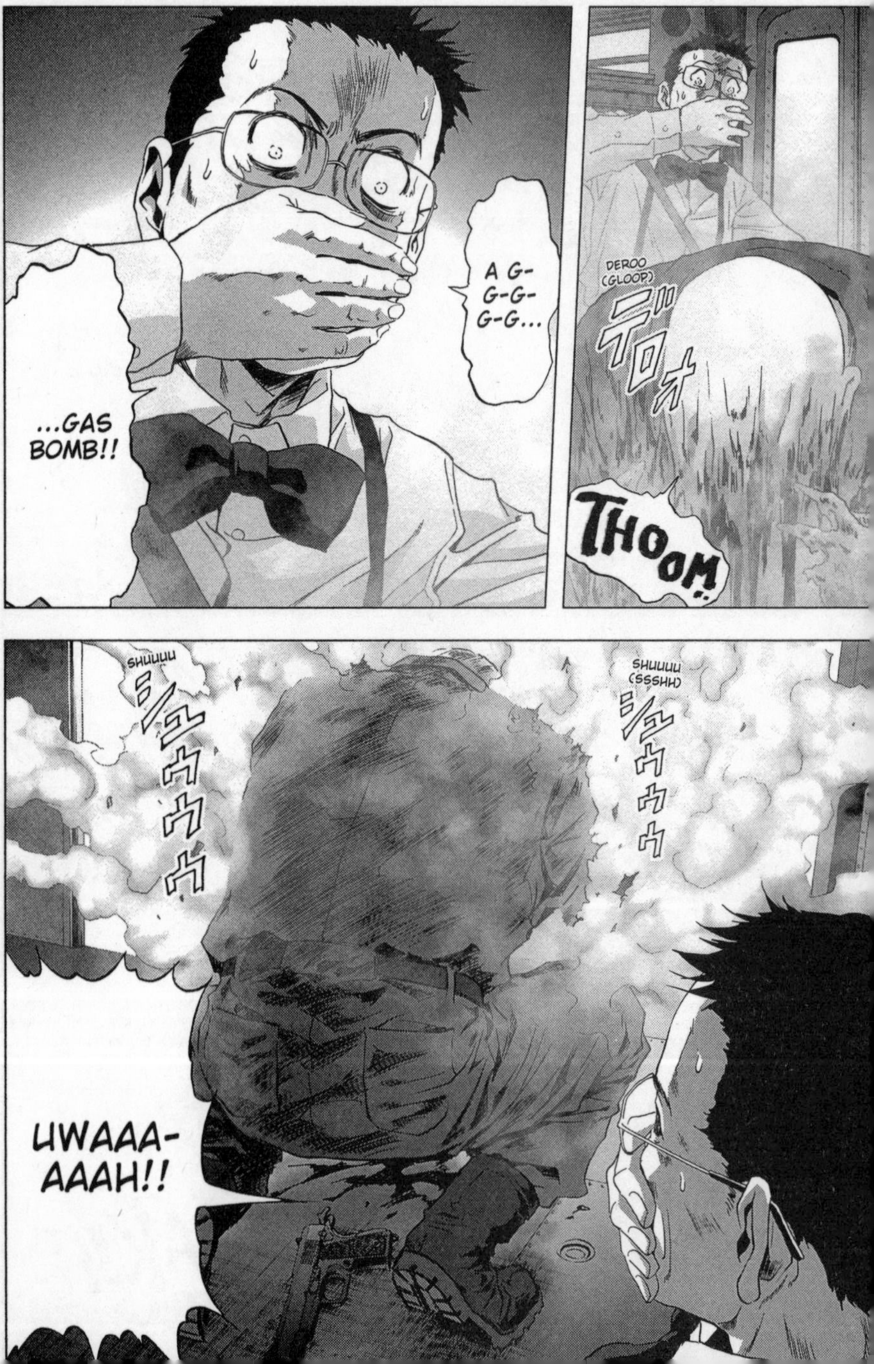
DEROO (GLOOP)
デロォ
THOOM
A G- G-G- G-G...
...GAS BOMB!!
SHUUUU (SSSHH)
シュウウウ
SHUUUU
シュウウウウ
UWAAA-AAAH!!

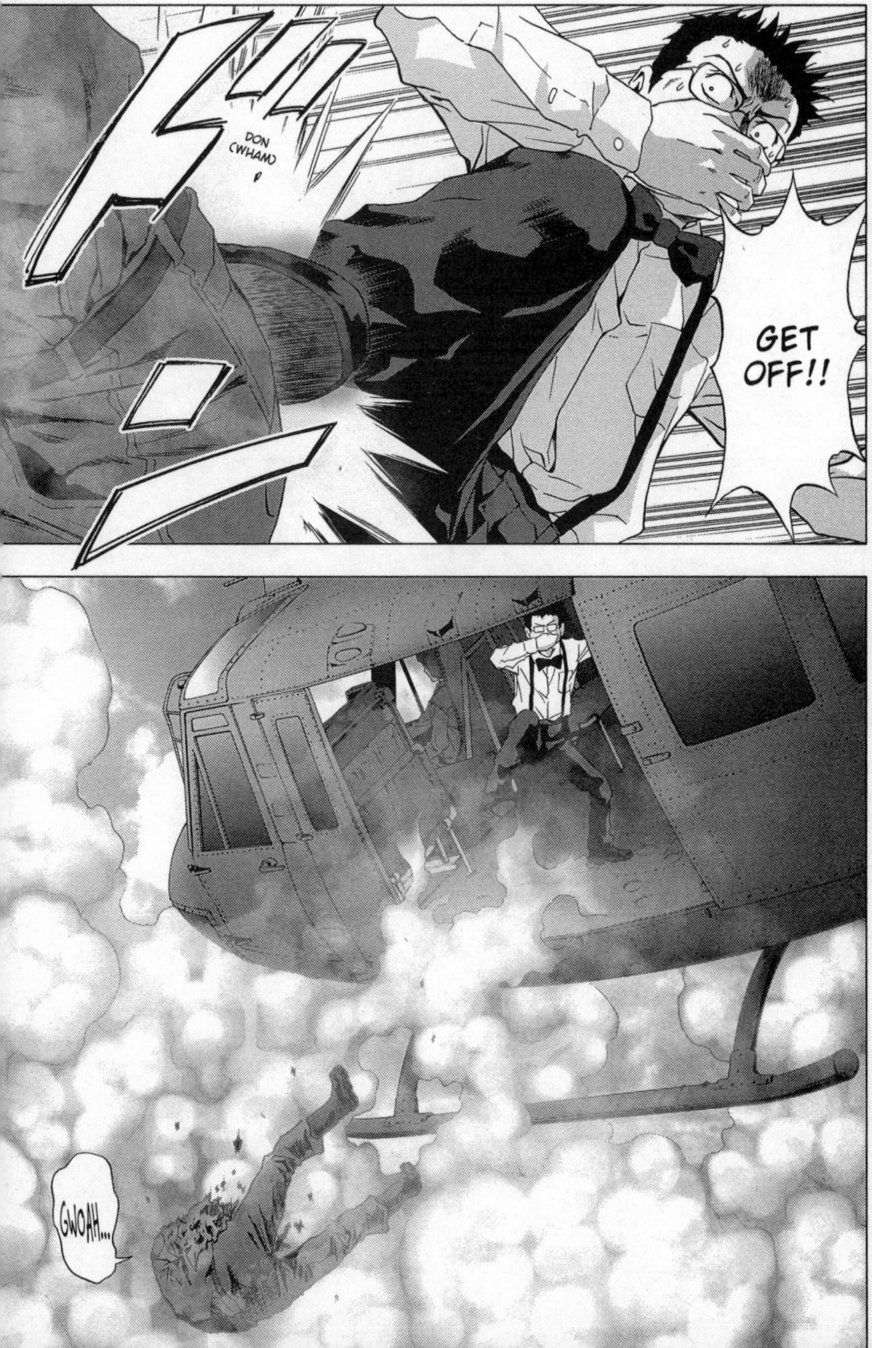
GET OFF!!
DON (WHAM)
GWOAH...

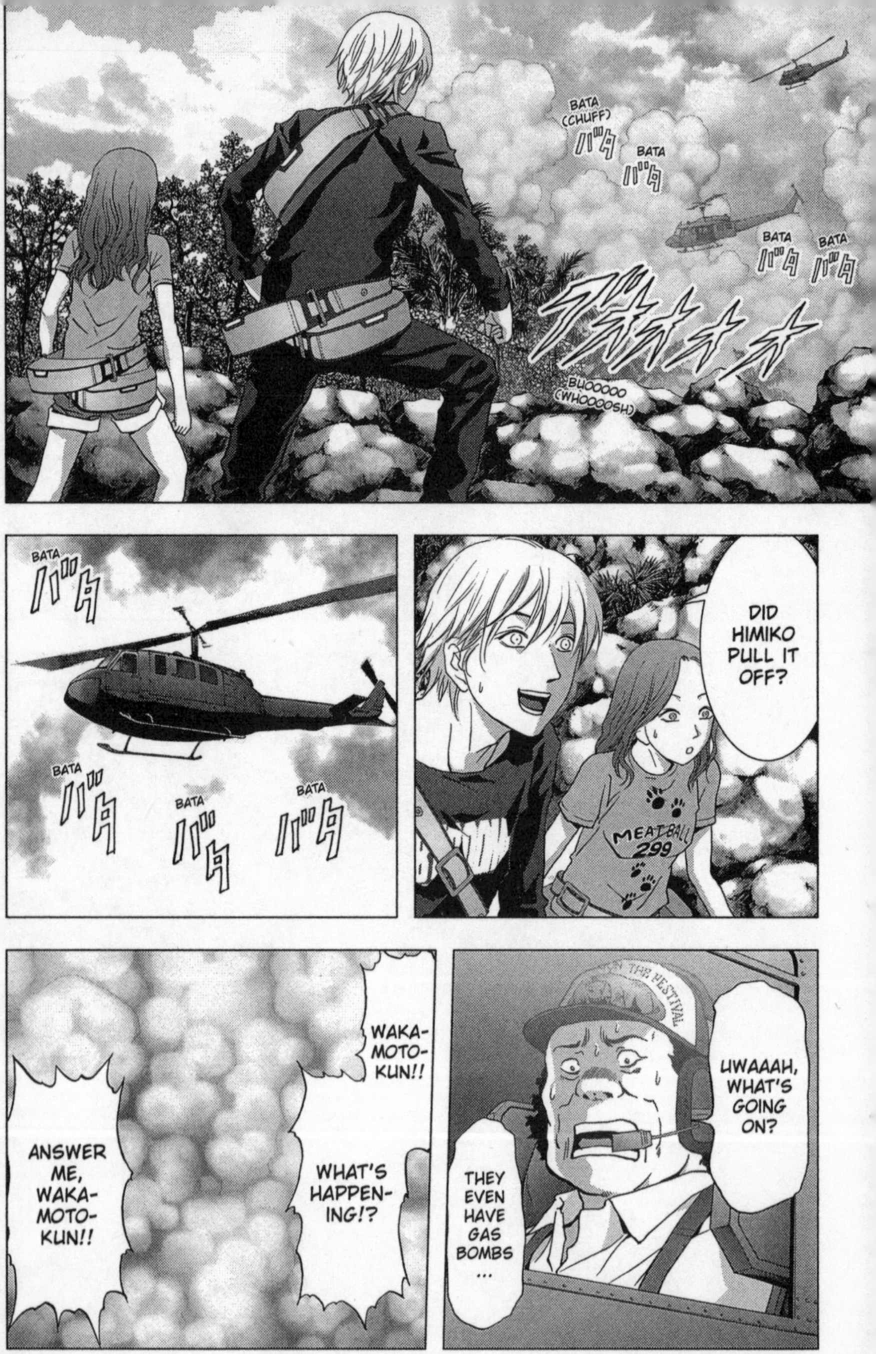
BATA
BATA
BATA
BATA (CHUFF)
BUOOOO (WHOOOOSH)
DID HIMIKO PULL IT OFF?
BATA
BATA
BATA
BATA
UWAAAH, WHAT'S GOING ON?
THEY EVEN HAVE GAS BOMBS ...
WAKA-MOTO-KUN!!
WHAT'S HAPPEN-ING!?
ANSWER ME, WAKA-MOTO-KUN!!

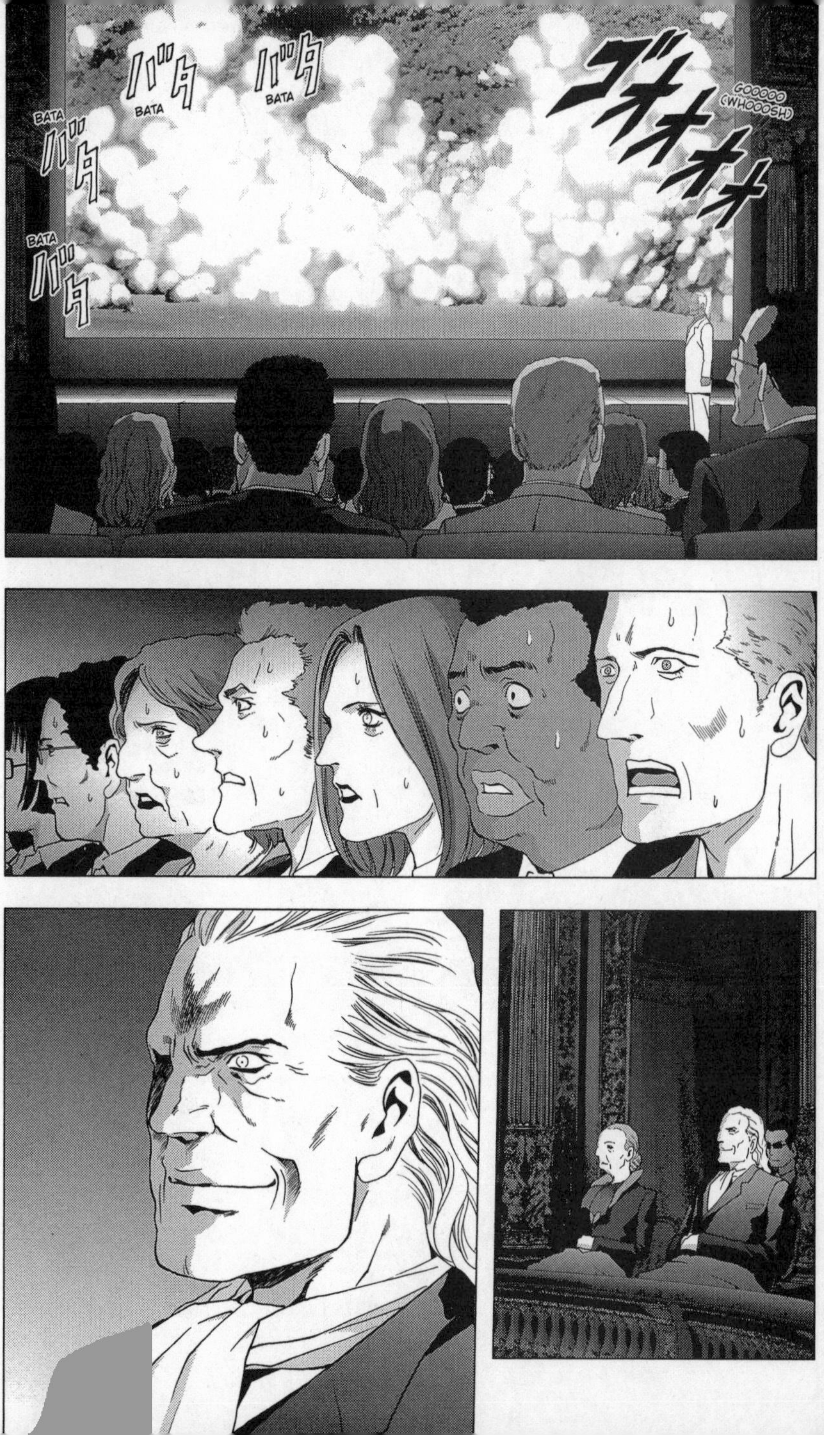
ゴオオオオ
GOOOOO (WHOOOSH)
バタ
BATA
バタ
BATA
BATA
バタ
BATA
バタ

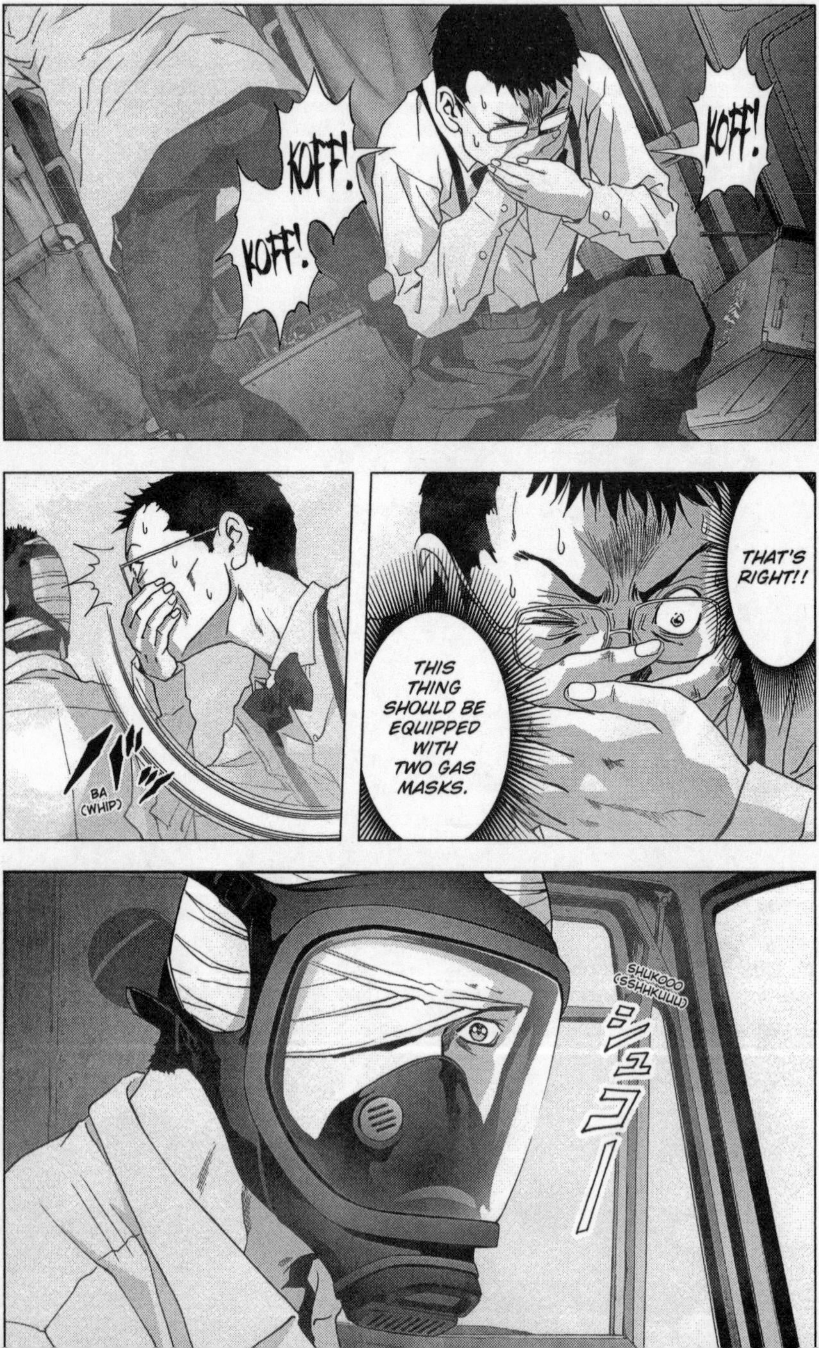
KOFF!
KOFF!
KOFF!
THAT'S RIGHT!!
THIS THING SHOULD BE EQUIPPED WITH TWO GAS MASKS.
BA (WHIP)
SHUKOOO (SSHHKUUU)
シュコー

WHAT ...!?

HUH ...?

SHUKOOO

HUH!?

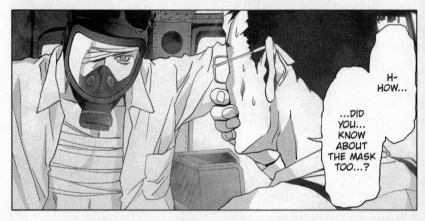

H-HOW...

...DID YOU... KNOW ABOUT THE MASK TOO...?

OH MY GOD...

YOU...

SHUKOOO

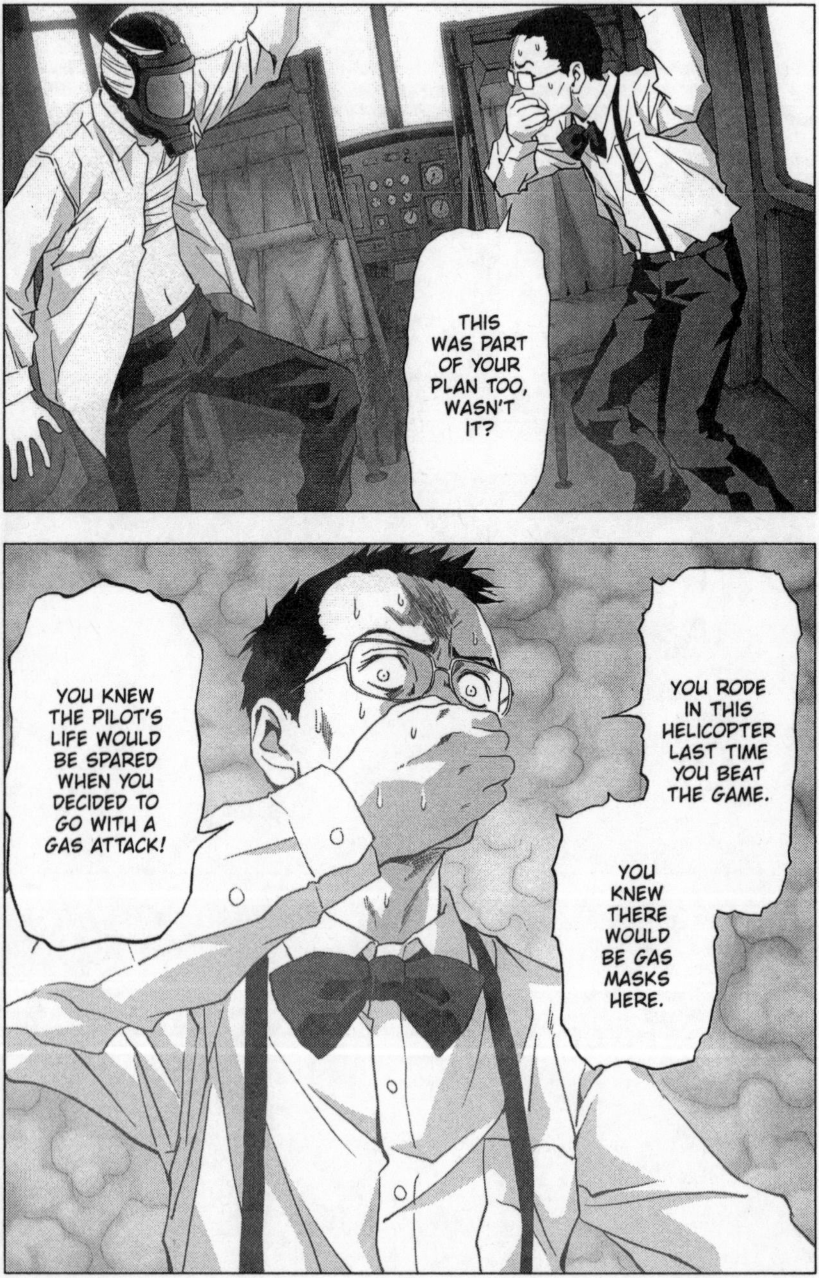
THIS WAS PART OF YOUR PLAN TOO, WASN'T IT?
YOU RODE IN THIS HELICOPTER LAST TIME YOU BEAT THE GAME.
YOU KNEW THERE WOULD BE GAS MASKS HERE.
YOU KNEW THE PILOT'S LIFE WOULD BE SPARED WHEN YOU DECIDED TO GO WITH A GAS ATTACK!

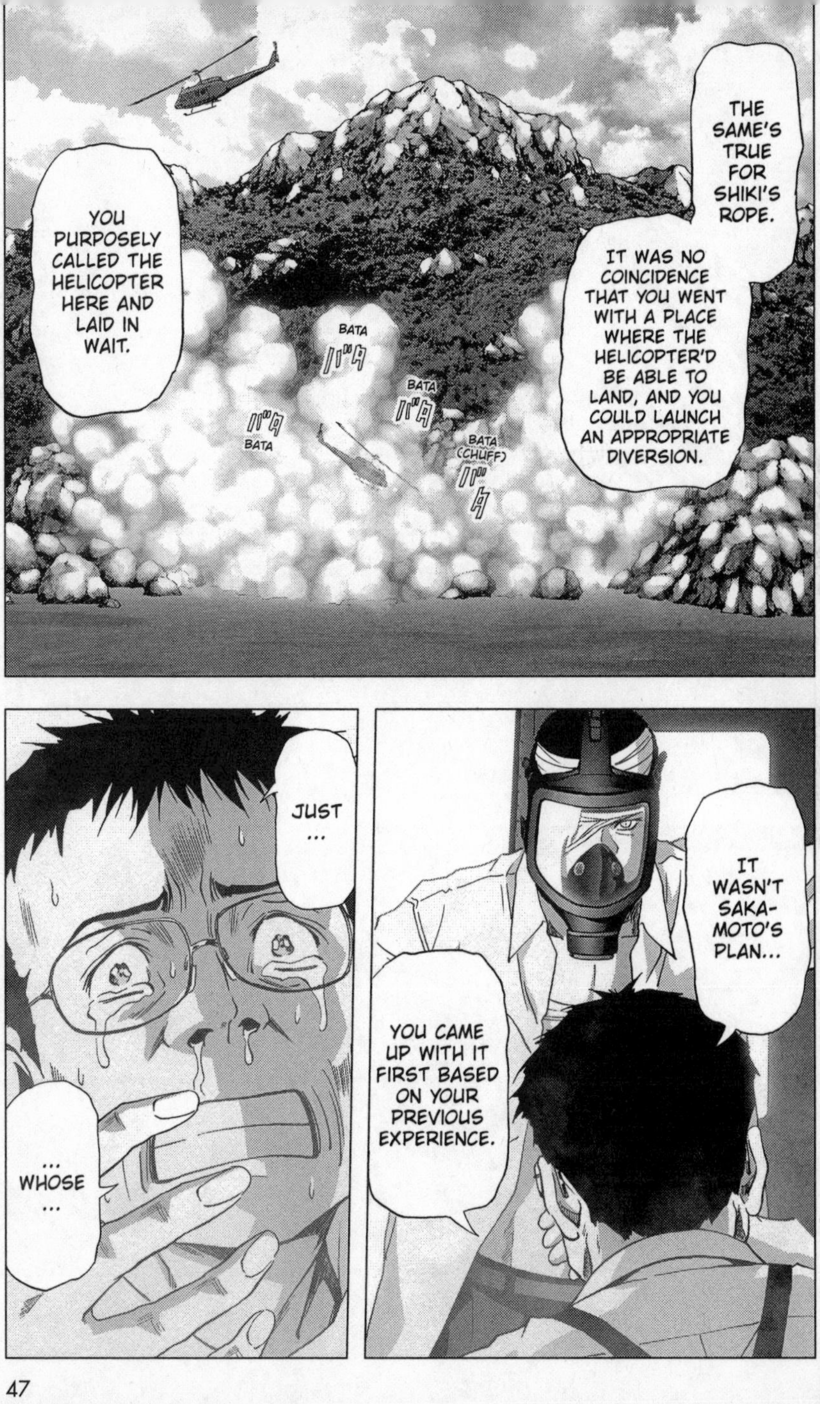

THE SAME'S TRUE FOR SHIKI'S ROPE.
IT WAS NO COINCIDENCE THAT YOU WENT WITH A PLACE WHERE THE HELICOPTER'D BE ABLE TO LAND, AND YOU COULD LAUNCH AN APPROPRIATE DIVERSION.
BATA (CHUFF)
BATA
BATA
BATA
YOU PURPOSELY CALLED THE HELICOPTER HERE AND LAID IN WAIT.
IT WASN'T SAKA-MOTO'S PLAN...
YOU CAME UP WITH IT FIRST BASED ON YOUR PREVIOUS EXPERIENCE.
JUST ...
... WHOSE ...

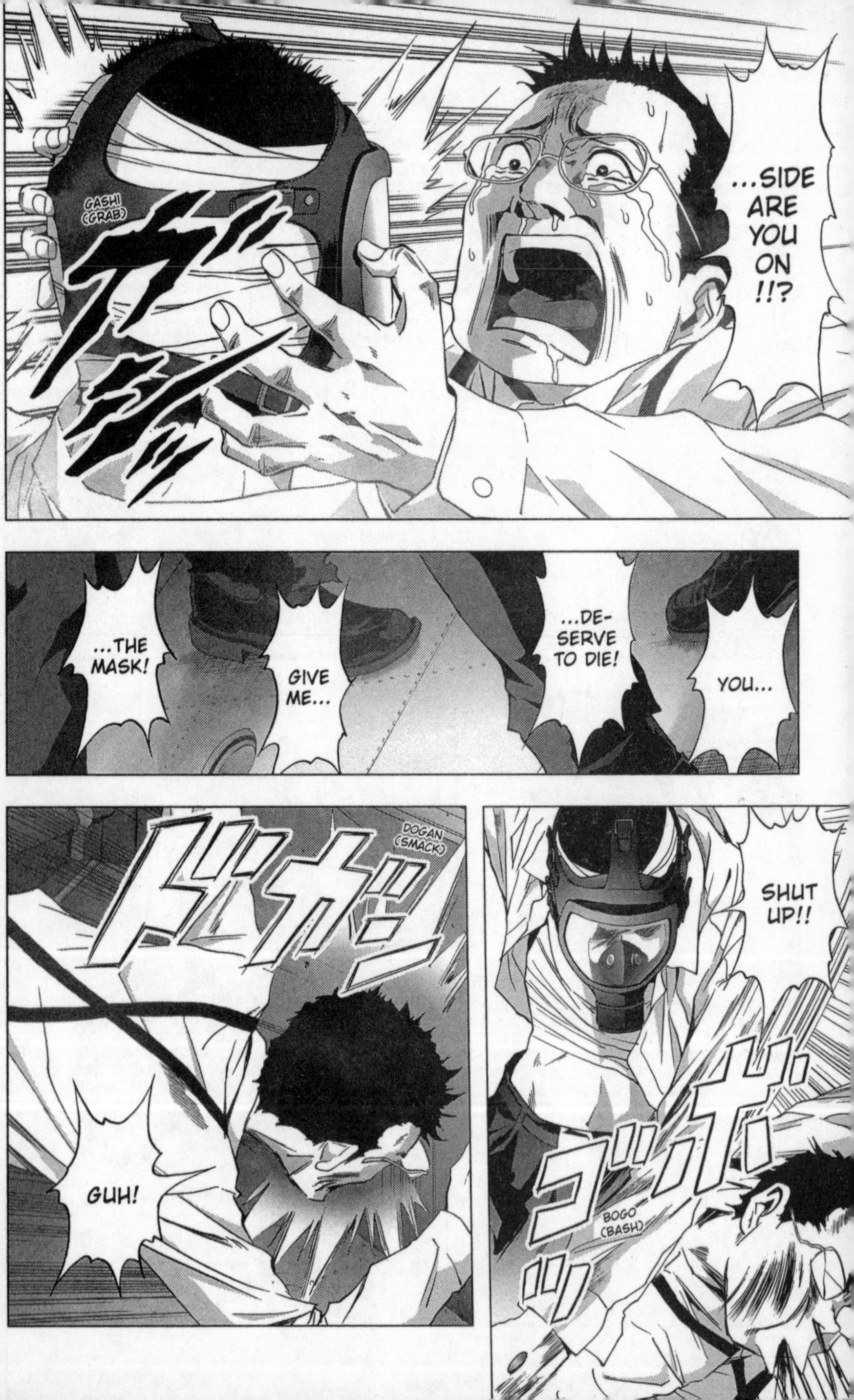
...SIDE ARE YOU ON!!?
GASHI (GRAB)
YOU...
...DE-SERVE TO DIE!
GIVE ME...
...THE MASK!
SHUT UP!!
BOGO (BASH)
DOGAN (SMACK)
GUH!

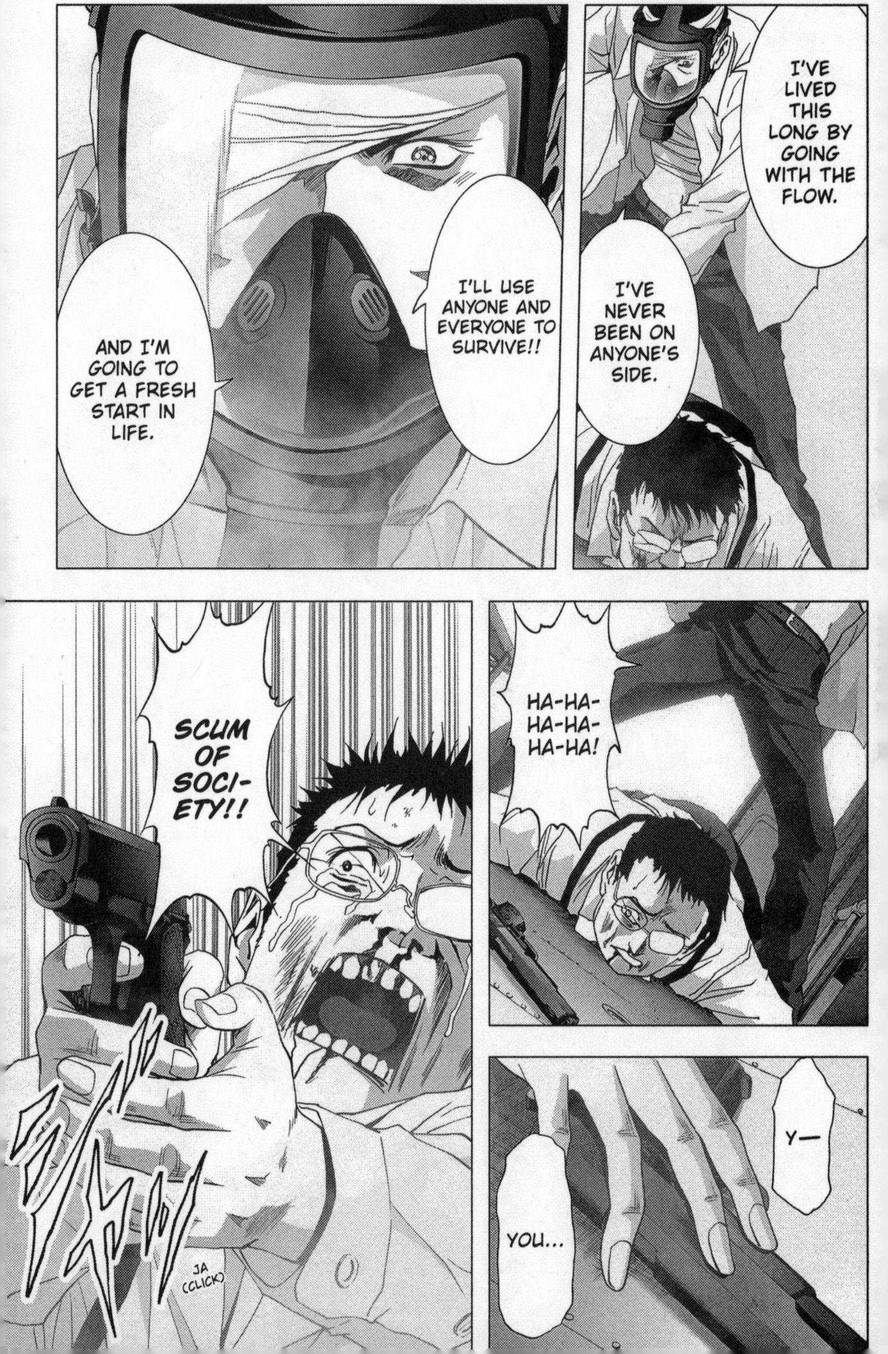
I'VE LIVED THIS LONG BY GOING WITH THE FLOW.
I'VE NEVER BEEN ON ANYONE'S SIDE.
I'LL USE ANYONE AND EVERYONE TO SURVIVE!!
AND I'M GOING TO GET A FRESH START IN LIFE.
HA-HA-HA-HA-HA-HA!
Y—
YOU...
SCUM OF SOCI-ETY!!
JA (CLICK)

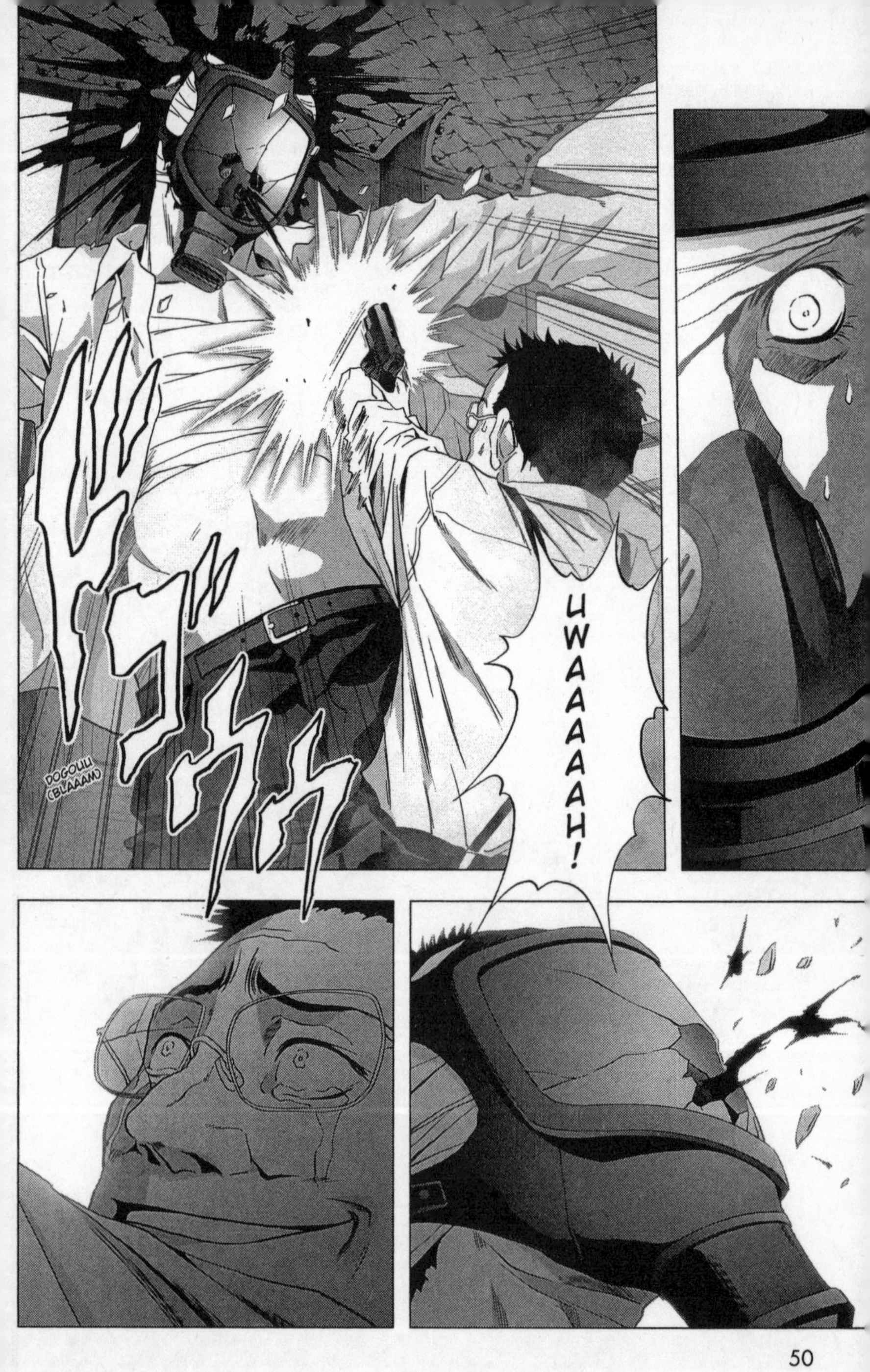
UWAAAAAAAH!
DOGOUU (BLAAAM)

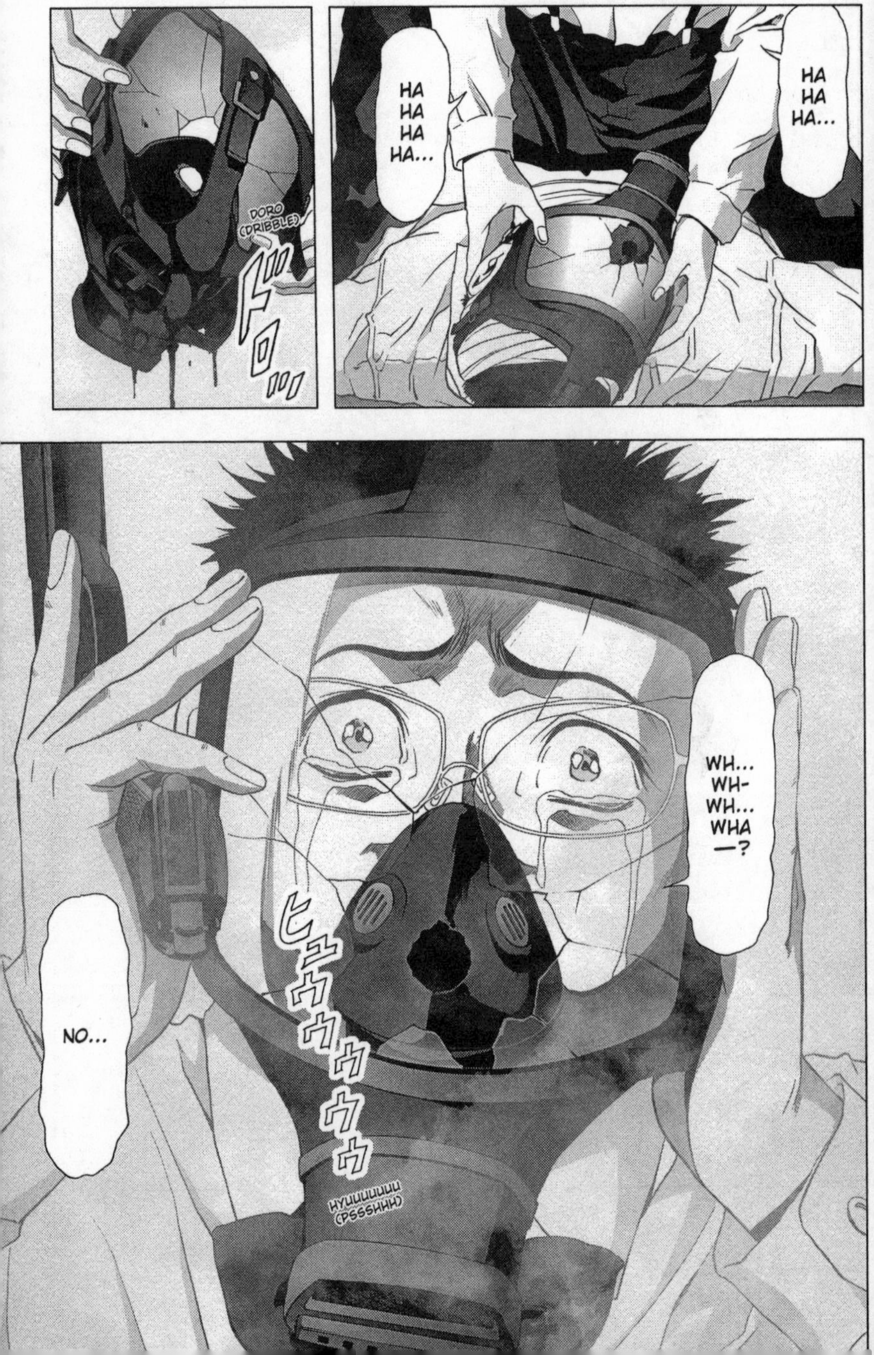
HA HA HA...
HA HA HA HA...
DORO (DRIBBLE)
WH... WH-WH... WHA—?
NO...
HYUUUUUUUU (PSSSHHH)

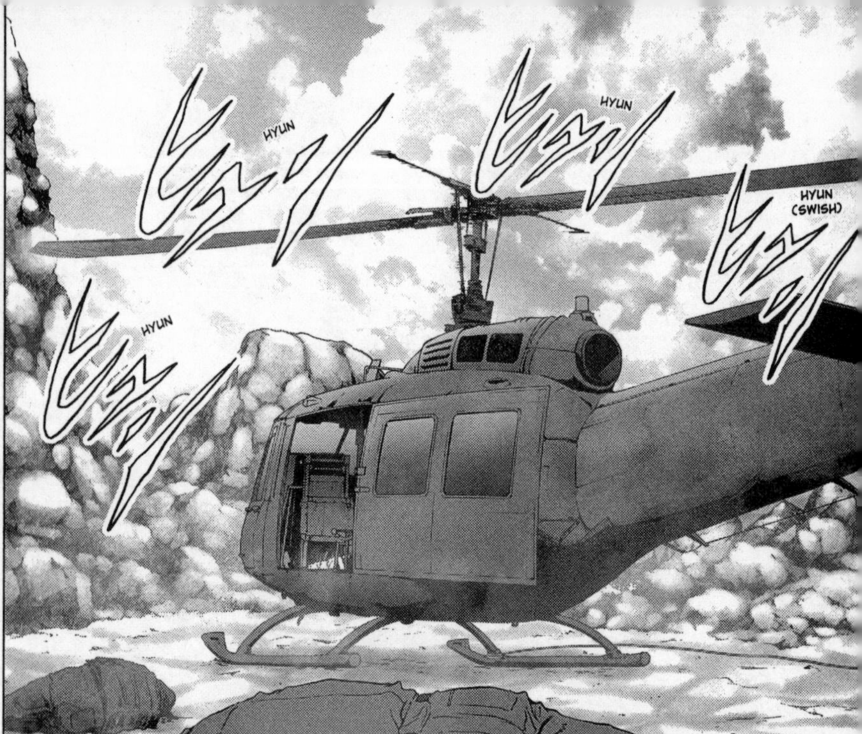
HYUN
(SWISH)
HYUN
HYUN
HYUN

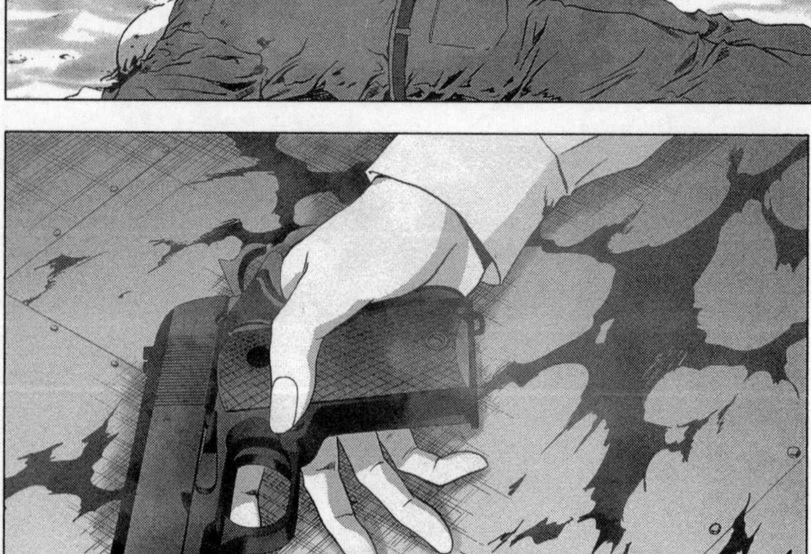

63 HEAVY SACRIFICE

#.#.#.#

ZAZAA
(SSSHH)

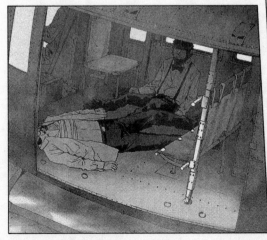

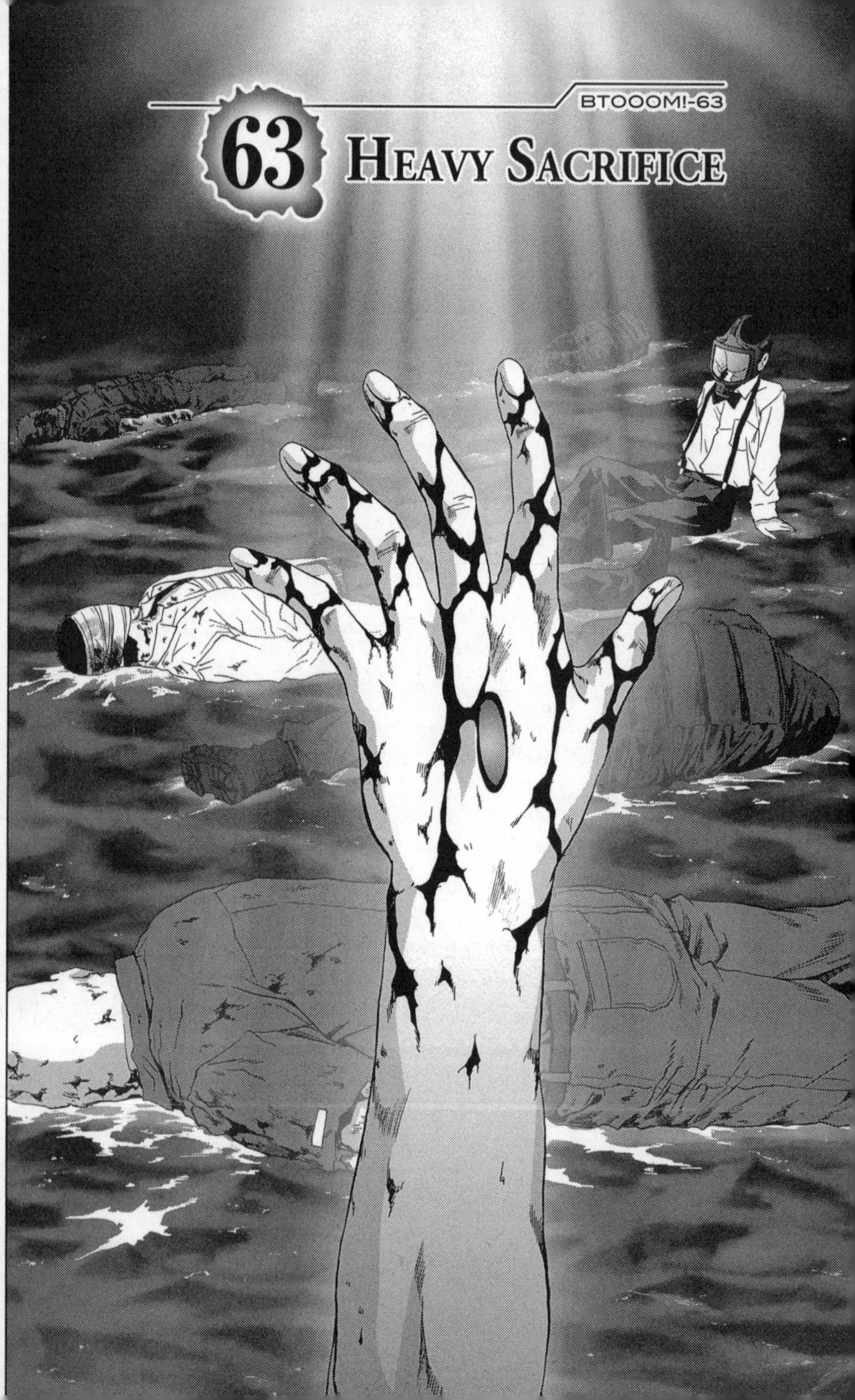
BTOOOM!-63
63 HEAVY SACRIFICE

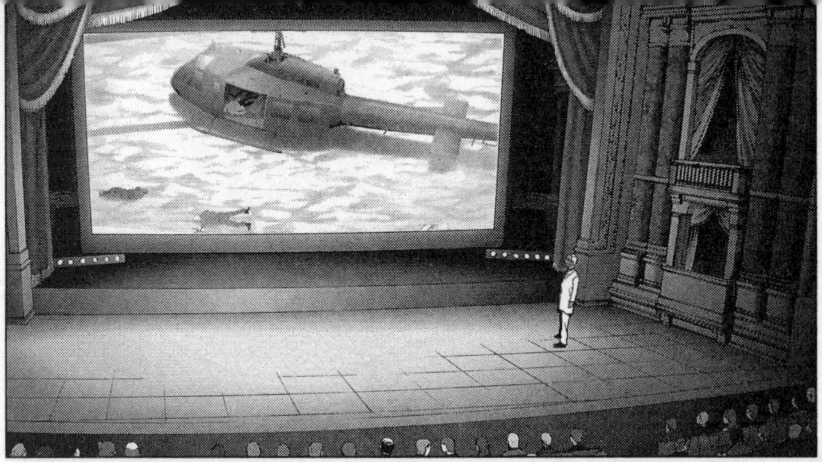

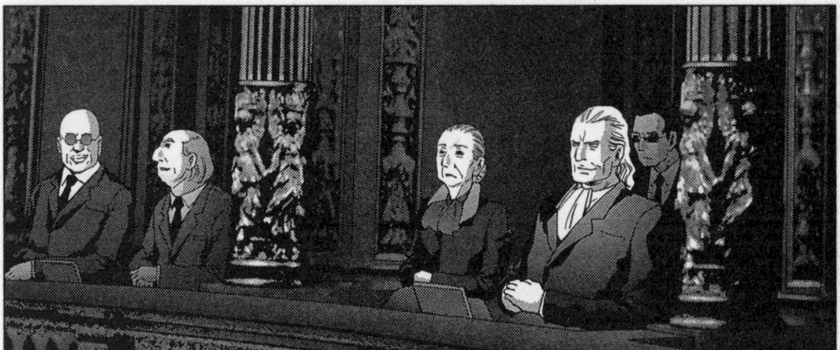

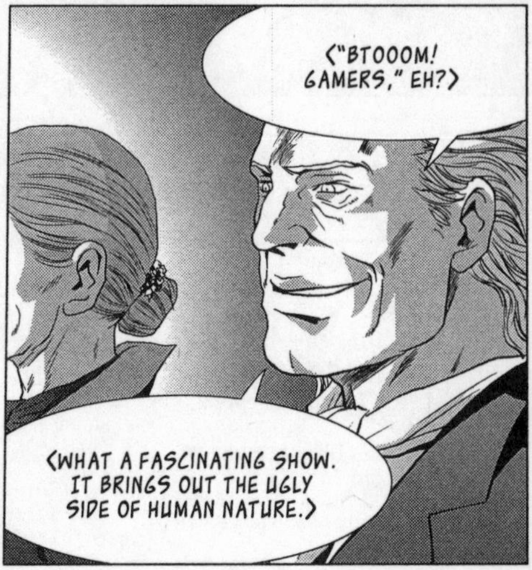
<"BTOOOM! GAMERS," EH?>
<WHAT A FASCINATING SHOW. IT BRINGS OUT THE UGLY SIDE OF HUMAN NATURE.>

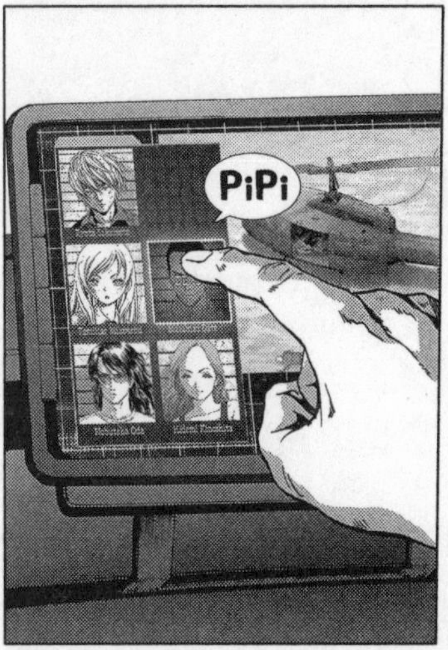
PiPi

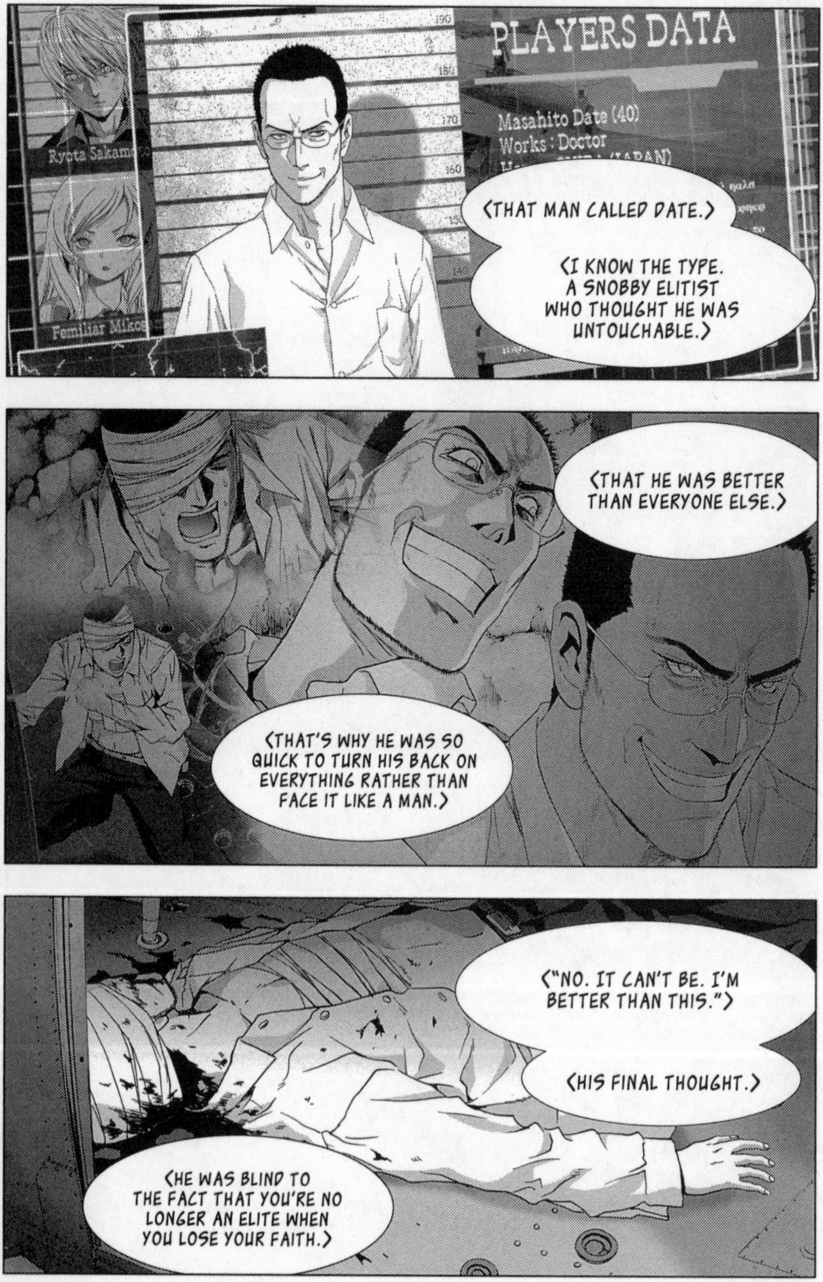
PLAYERS DATA
Masahito Date (40)
Works : Doctor
〈THAT MAN CALLED DATE.〉
〈I KNOW THE TYPE. A SNOBBY ELITIST WHO THOUGHT HE WAS UNTOUCHABLE.〉
〈THAT HE WAS BETTER THAN EVERYONE ELSE.〉
〈THAT'S WHY HE WAS SO QUICK TO TURN HIS BACK ON EVERYTHING RATHER THAN FACE IT LIKE A MAN.〉
〈"NO. IT CAN'T BE. I'M BETTER THAN THIS."〉
〈HIS FINAL THOUGHT.〉
〈HE WAS BLIND TO THE FACT THAT YOU'RE NO LONGER AN ELITE WHEN YOU LOSE YOUR FAITH.〉

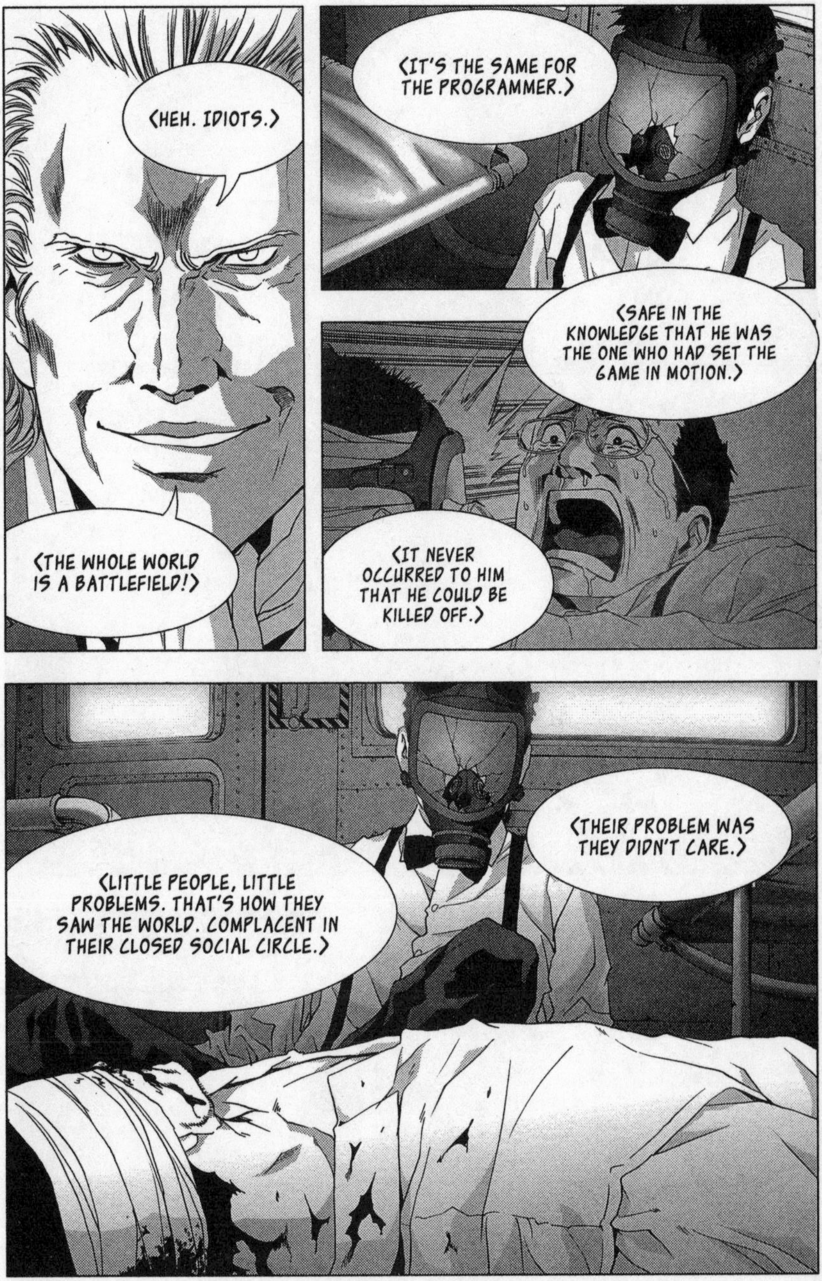
<IT'S THE SAME FOR THE PROGRAMMER.>
<SAFE IN THE KNOWLEDGE THAT HE WAS THE ONE WHO HAD SET THE GAME IN MOTION.>
<IT NEVER OCCURRED TO HIM THAT HE COULD BE KILLED OFF.>
<HEH. IDIOTS.>
<THE WHOLE WORLD IS A BATTLEFIELD!>
<THEIR PROBLEM WAS THEY DIDN'T CARE.>
<LITTLE PEOPLE, LITTLE PROBLEMS. THAT'S HOW THEY SAW THE WORLD. COMPLACENT IN THEIR CLOSED SOCIAL CIRCLE.>

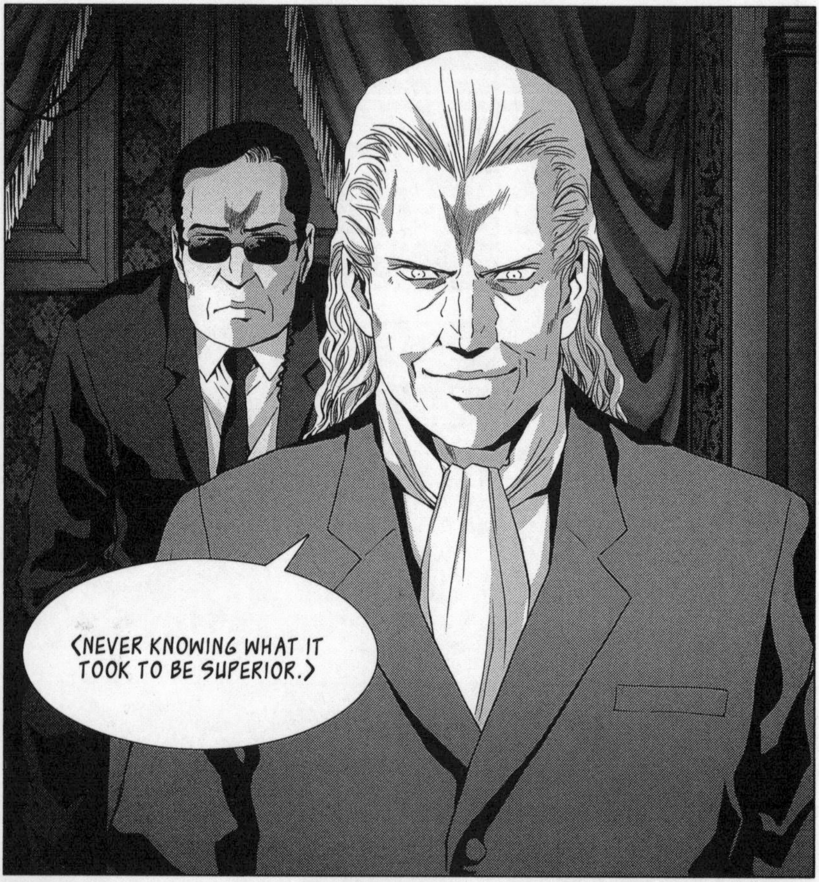
‹NEVER KNOWING WHAT IT TOOK TO BE SUPERIOR.›

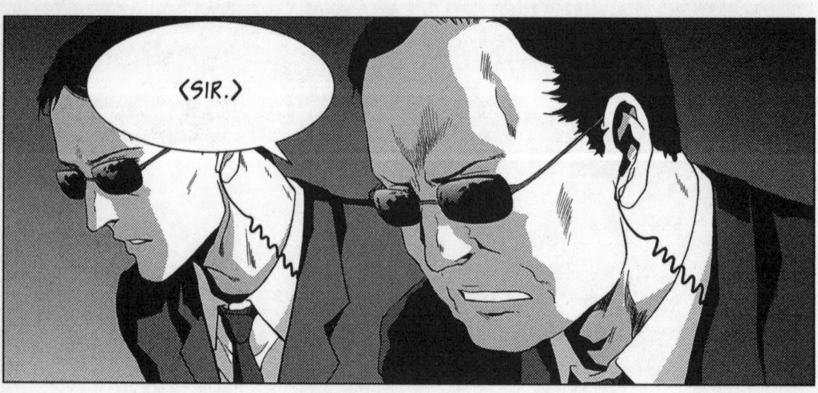
‹SIR.›

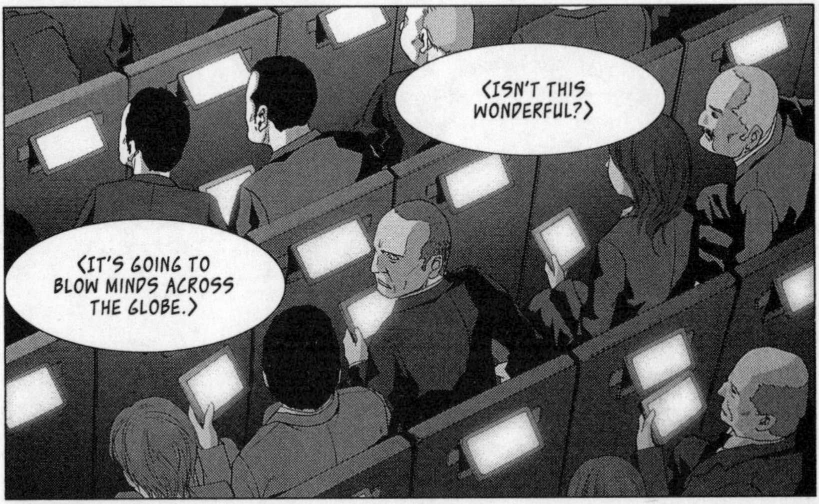
‹ISN'T THIS WONDERFUL?›
‹IT'S GOING TO BLOW MINDS ACROSS THE GLOBE.›

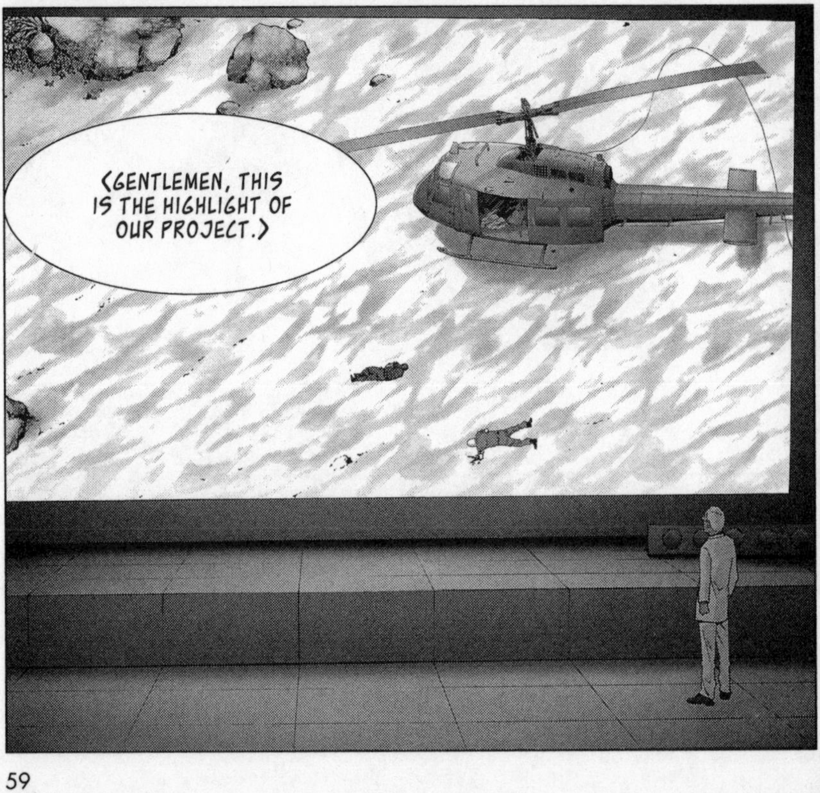
‹GENTLEMEN, THIS IS THE HIGHLIGHT OF OUR PROJECT.›

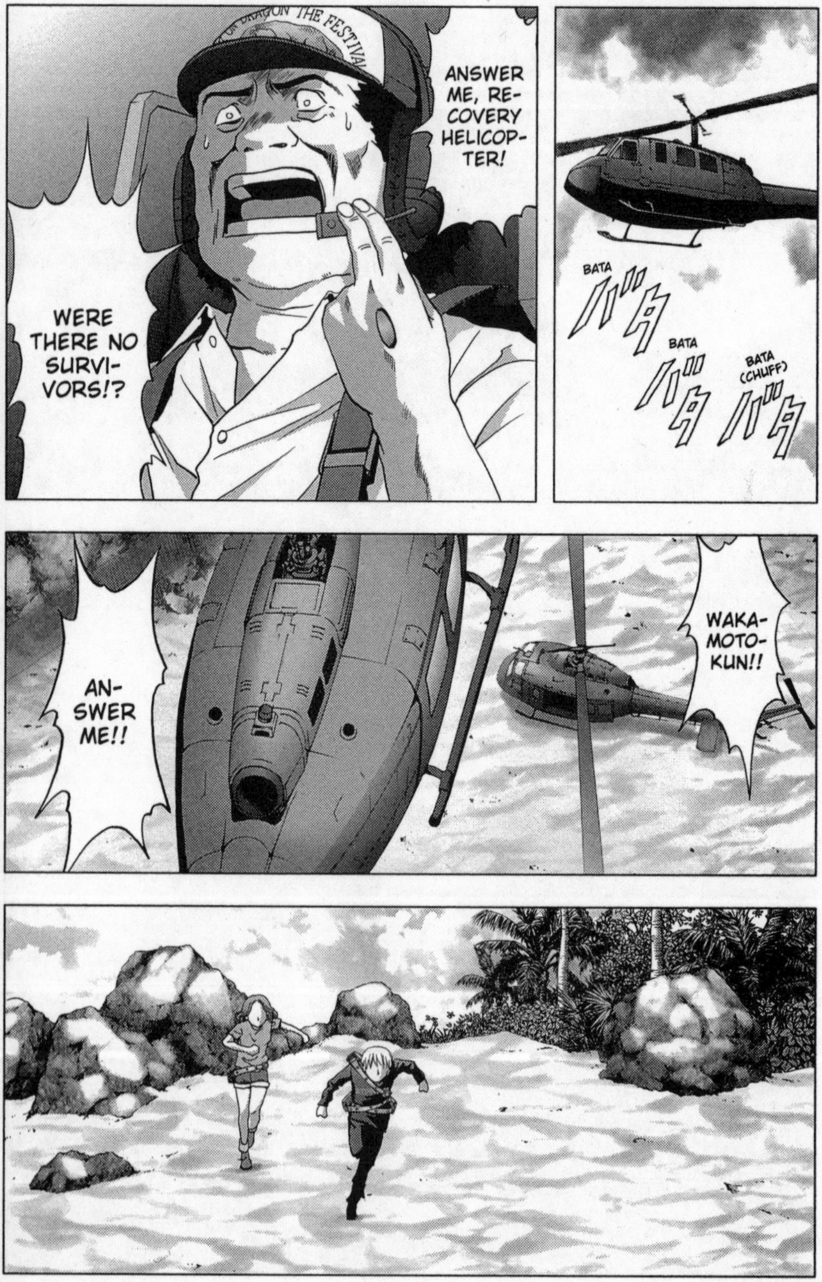

BATA
バタ
BATA
バタ
BATA (CHUFF)
バタ
ANSWER ME, RECOVERY HELICOPTER!
WERE THERE NO SURVIVORS!?
WAKAMOTO-KUN!!
ANSWER ME!!

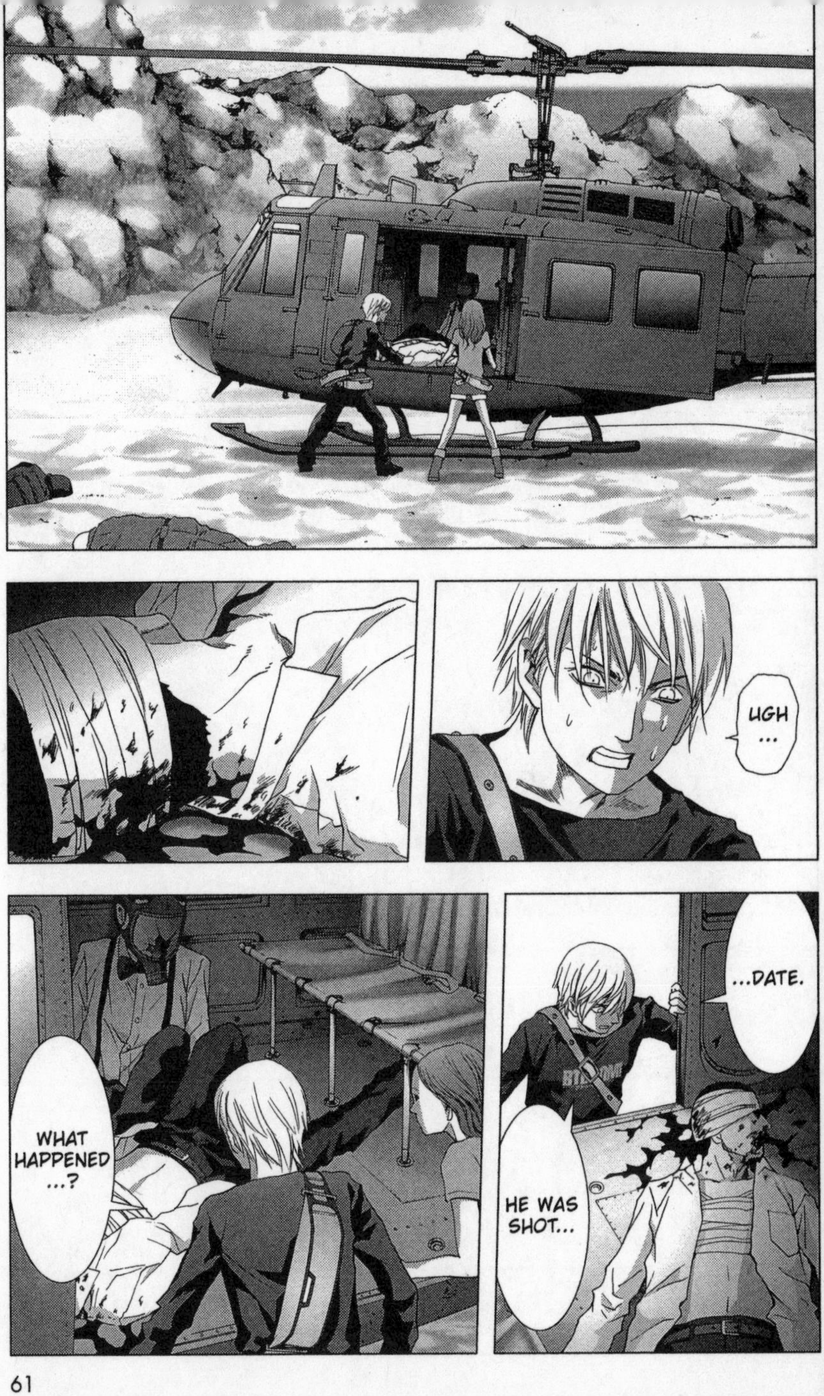
UGH ...
...DATE.
HE WAS SHOT...
WHAT HAPPENED ...?

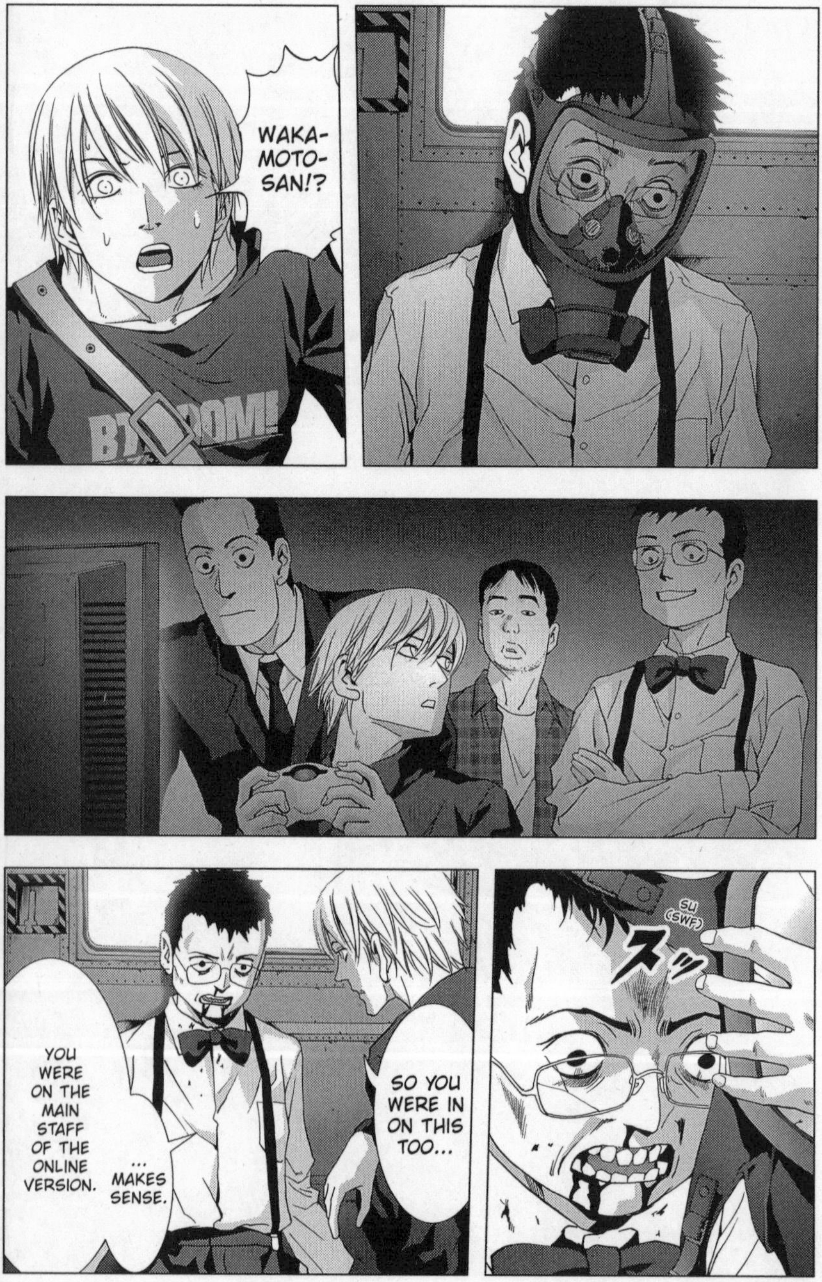
WAKA-MOTO-SAN!?
スッ
SU (SWF)
SO YOU WERE IN ON THIS TOO...
YOU WERE ON THE MAIN STAFF OF THE ONLINE VERSION.
... MAKES SENSE.

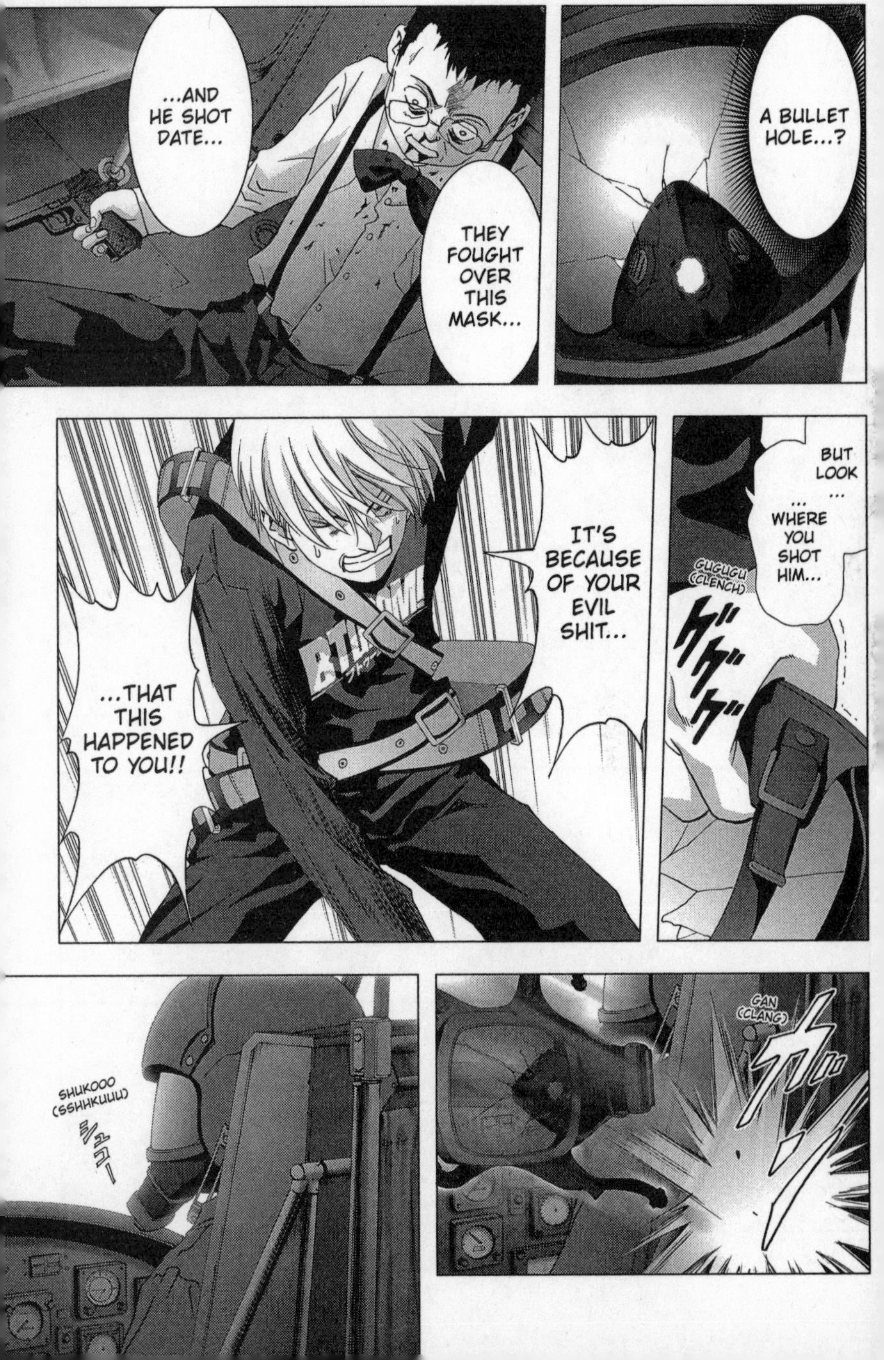
A BULLET HOLE...?
...AND HE SHOT DATE...
THEY FOUGHT OVER THIS MASK...
BUT LOOK... ...WHERE YOU SHOT HIM...
GUGUGU (CLENCH)
IT'S BECAUSE OF YOUR EVIL SHIT...
...THAT THIS HAPPENED TO YOU!!
GAN (CLANG)
SHUKOOO (SSHHKUUU)

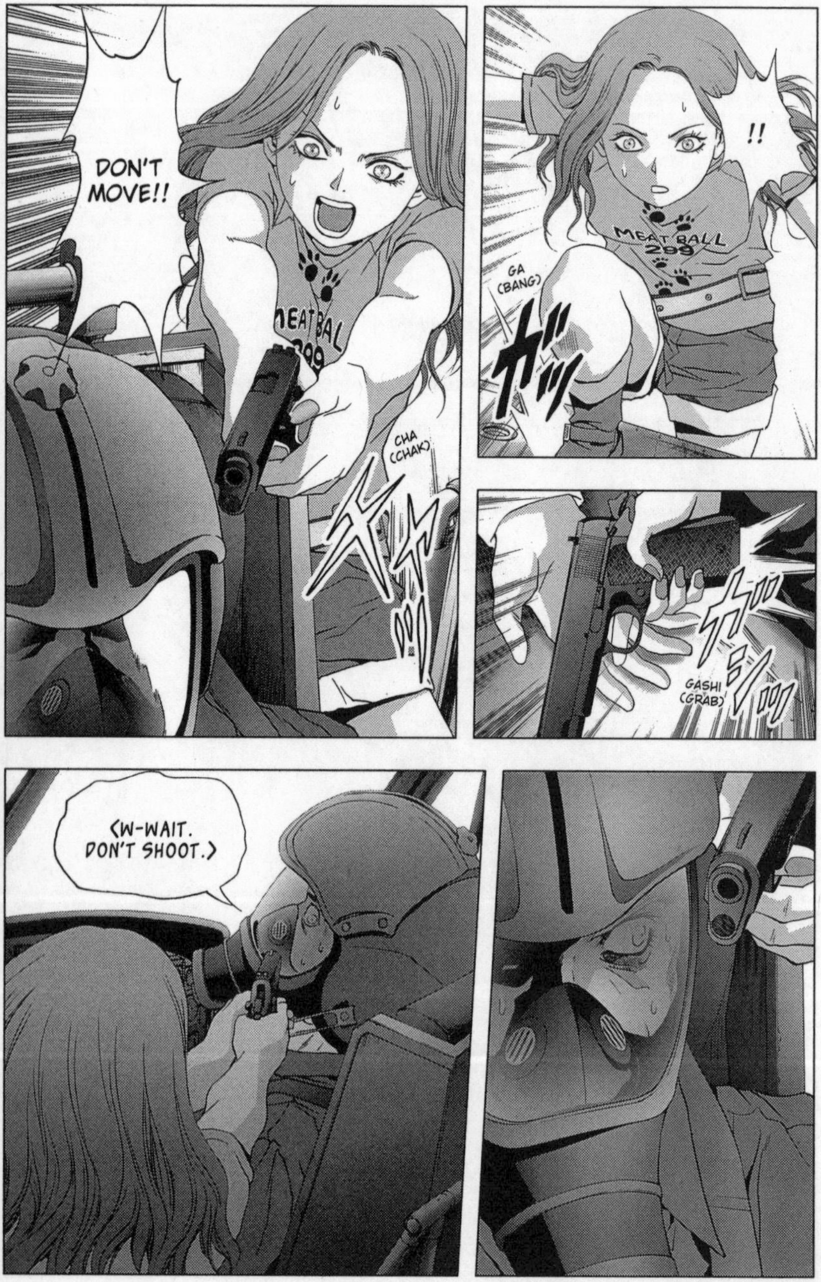
!!
GA (BANG)
GASHI (GRAB)
DON'T MOVE!!
CHA (CHAK)
<W-WAIT. DON'T SHOOT.>

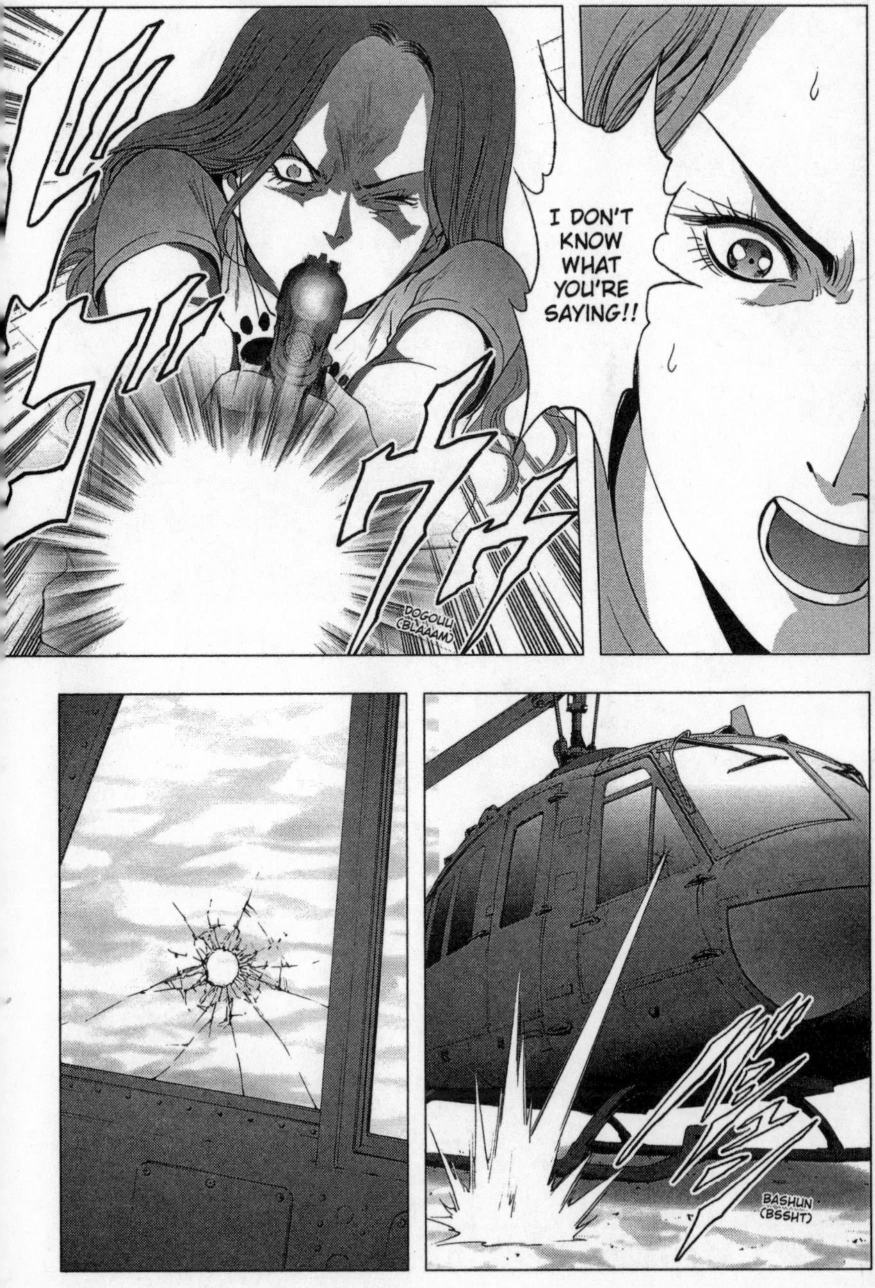
I DON'T KNOW WHAT YOU'RE SAYING!!
DOGOUU (BLAAAM)
BASHUN (BSSHT)

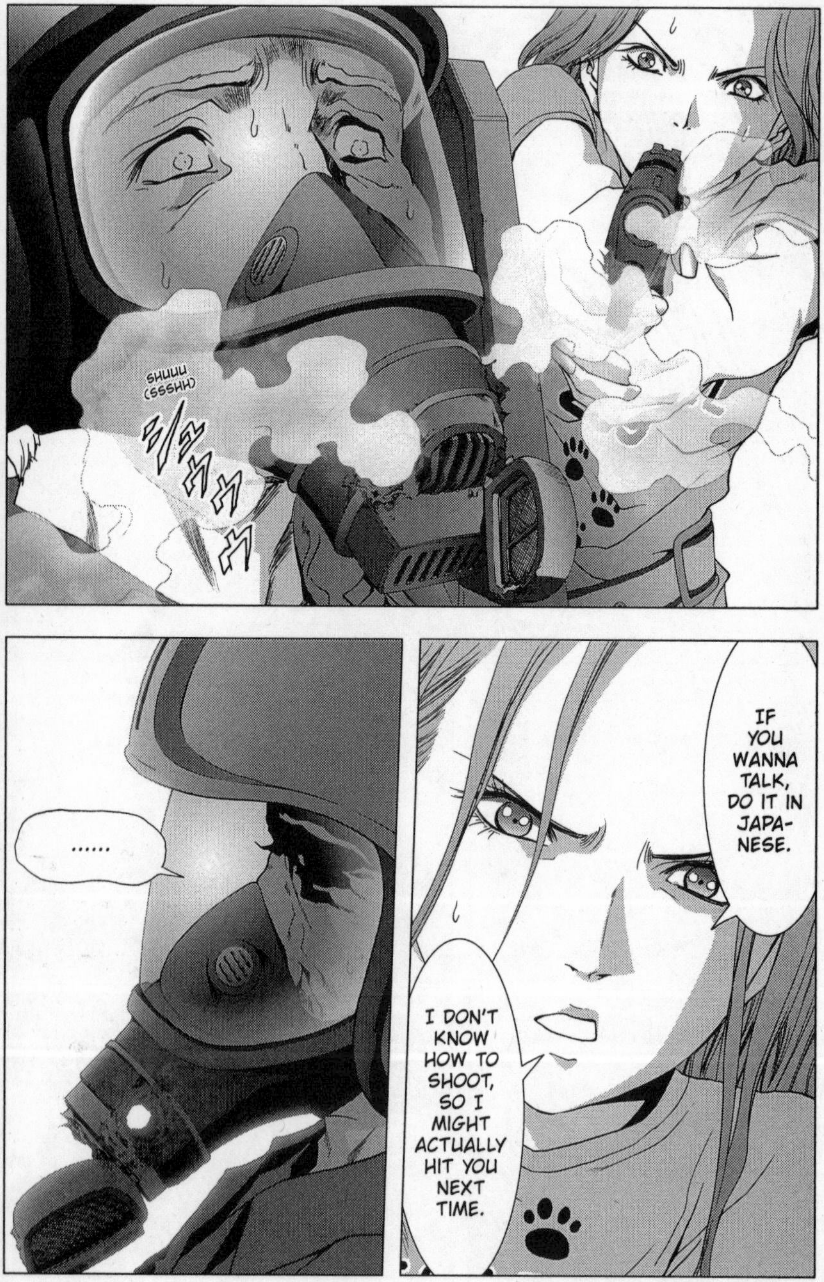
SHUUU (SSSHH)
IF YOU WANNA TALK, DO IT IN JAPA- NESE.
......
I DON'T KNOW HOW TO SHOOT, SO I MIGHT ACTUALLY HIT YOU NEXT TIME.

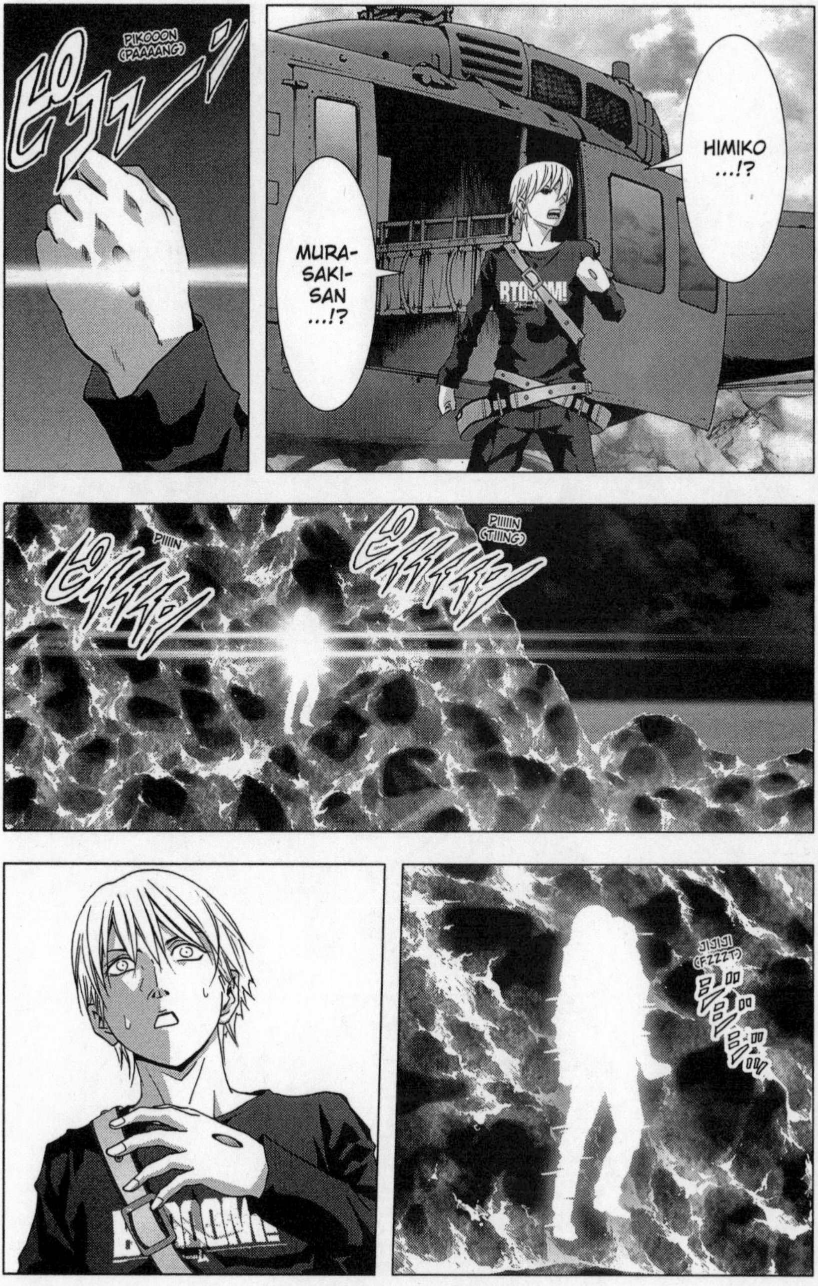
HIMIKO ...!?
MURA-SAKI-SAN ...!?
PIKOOON (PAAAANG)
PIIIIN (TIIING)
PIIIN
JIJIJI (FZZZT)

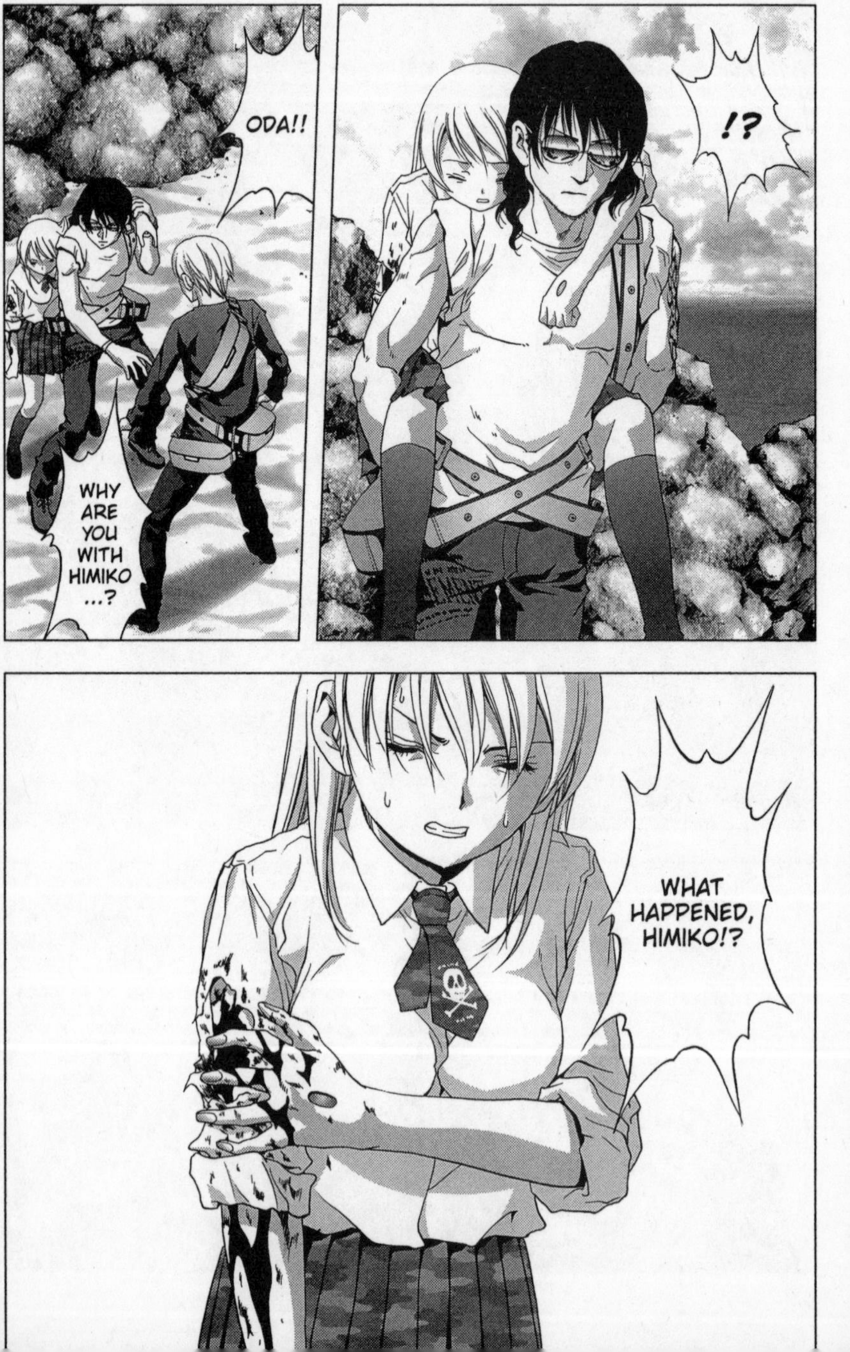
!?
ODA!!
WHY ARE YOU WITH HIMIKO ...?
WHAT HAPPENED, HIMIKO!?

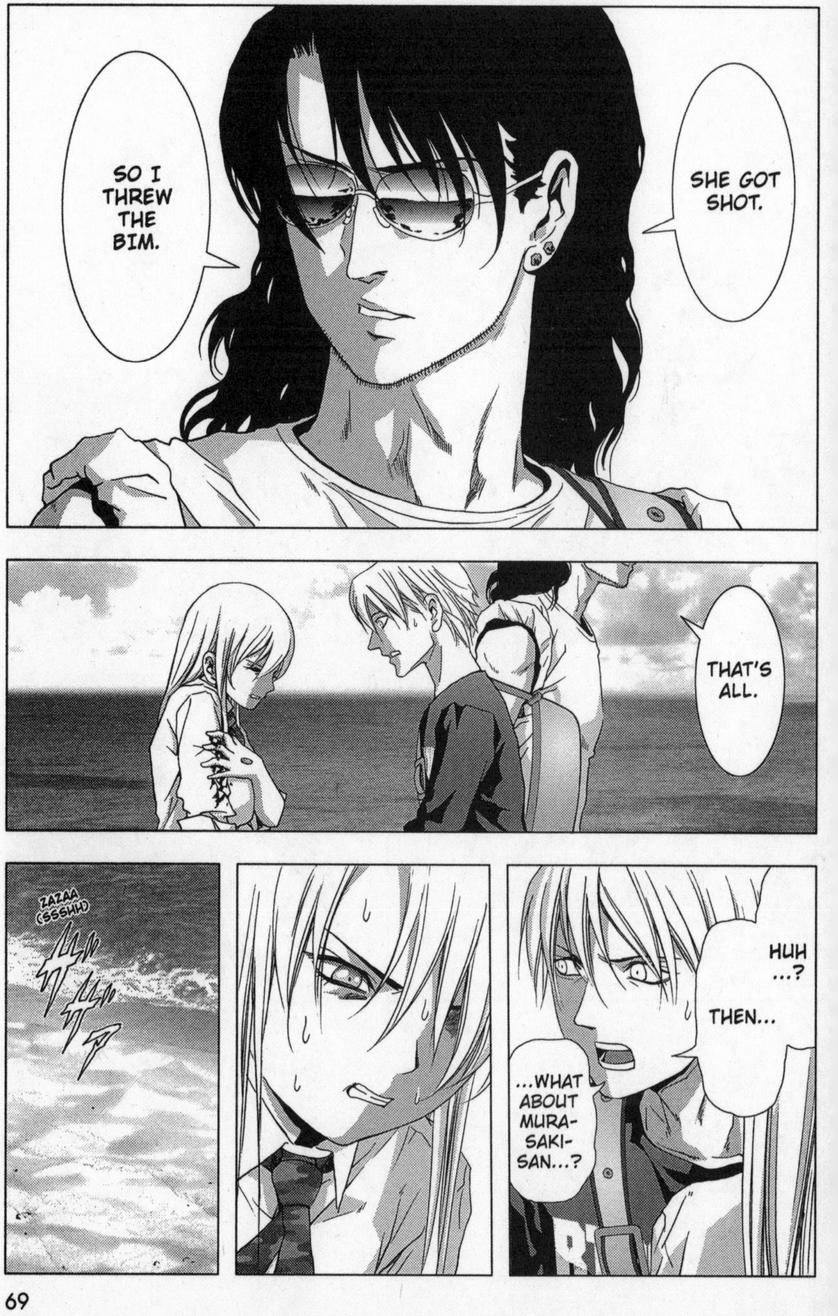
SHE GOT SHOT.
SO I THREW THE BIM.
THAT'S ALL.
HUH ...?
THEN...
...WHAT ABOUT MURA-SAKI-SAN...?
ZAZAA (SSSHH)

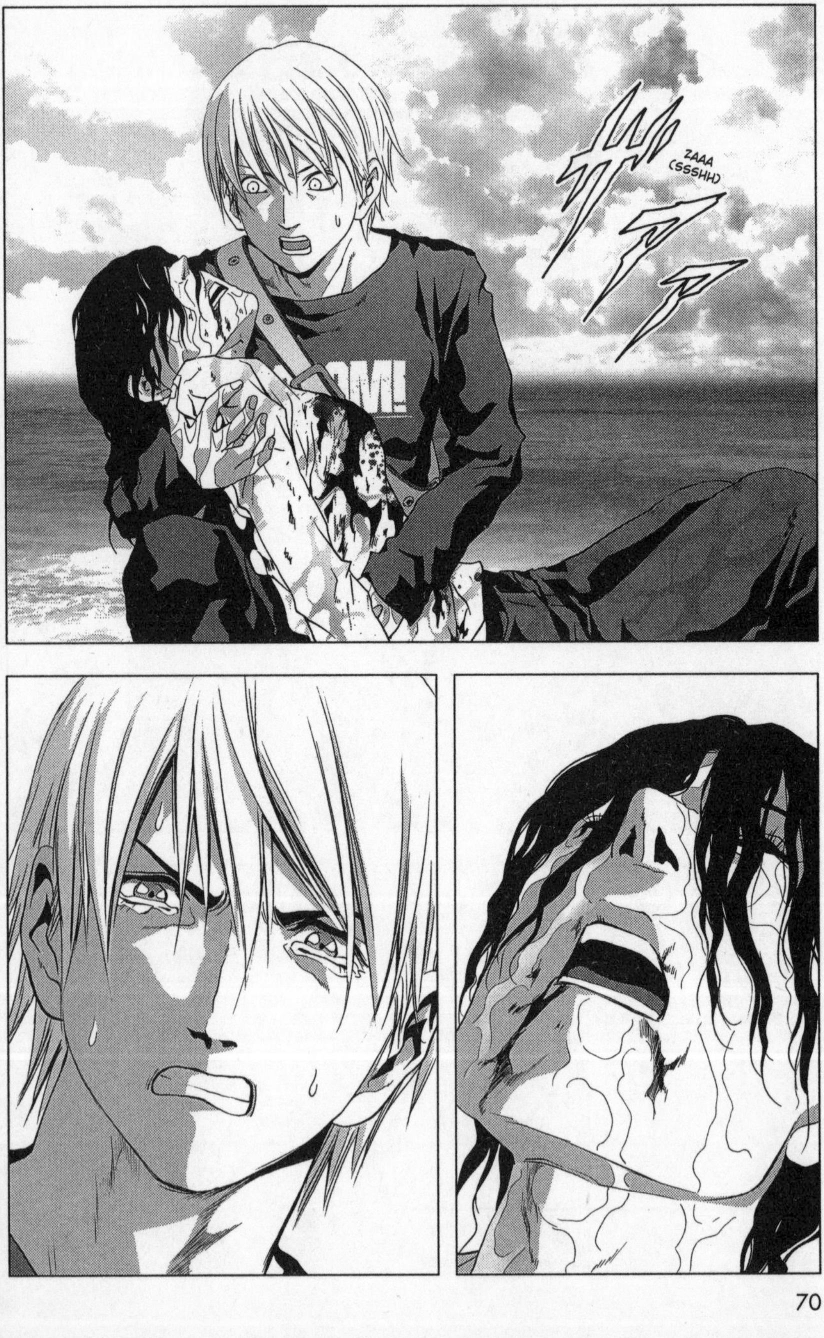
ZAAA
(SSSHH)

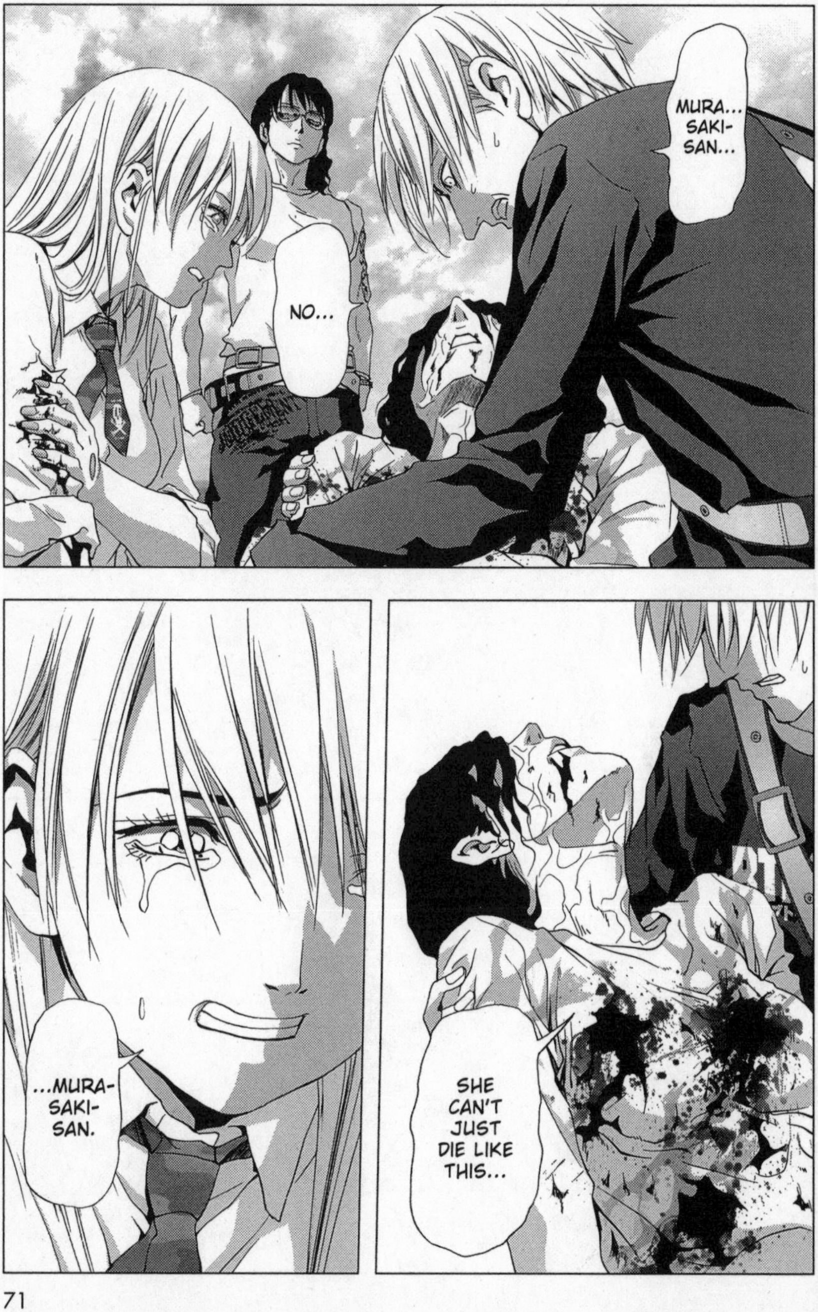
MURA... SAKI-SAN...
NO...
SHE CAN'T JUST DIE LIKE THIS...
...MURA-SAKI-SAN.

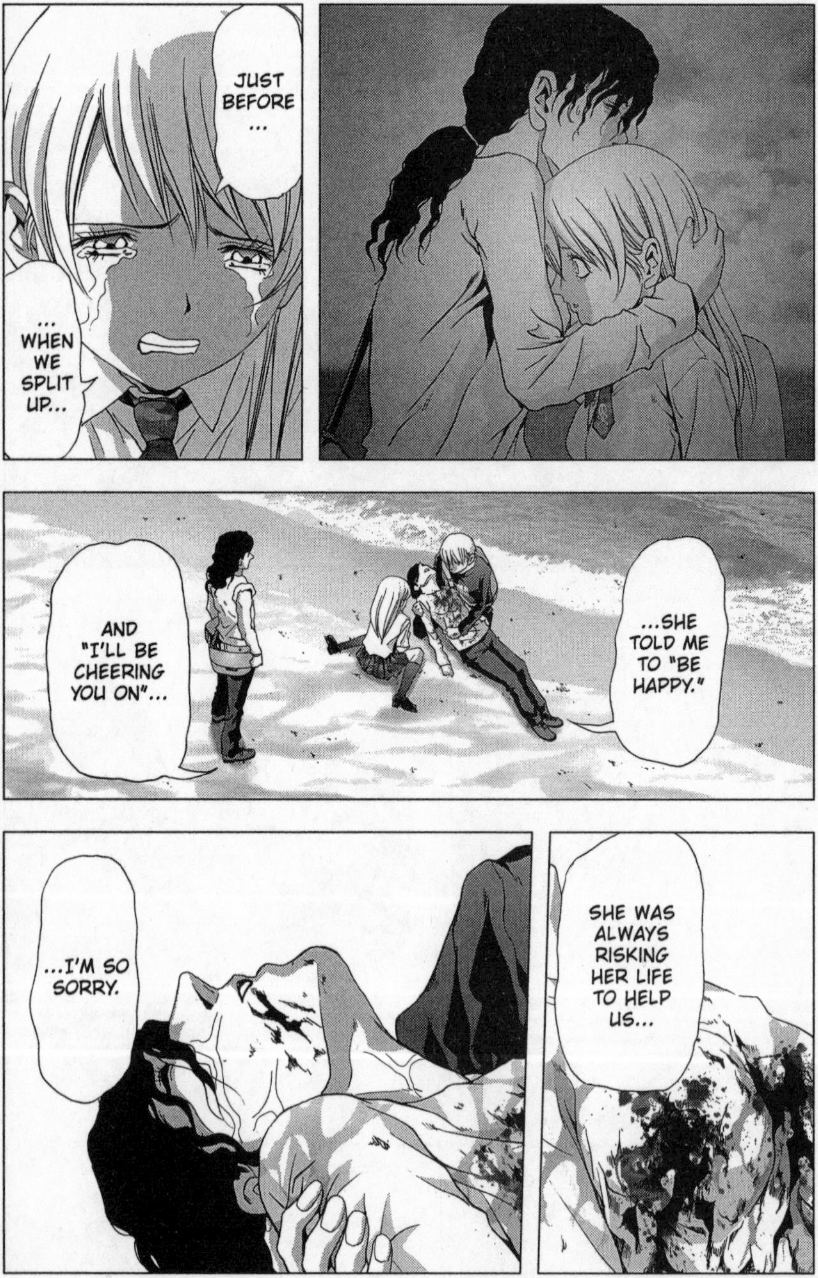
JUST BEFORE ...
... WHEN WE SPLIT UP...
...SHE TOLD ME TO "BE HAPPY."
AND "I'LL BE CHEERING YOU ON"...
SHE WAS ALWAYS RISKING HER LIFE TO HELP US...
...I'M SO SORRY.

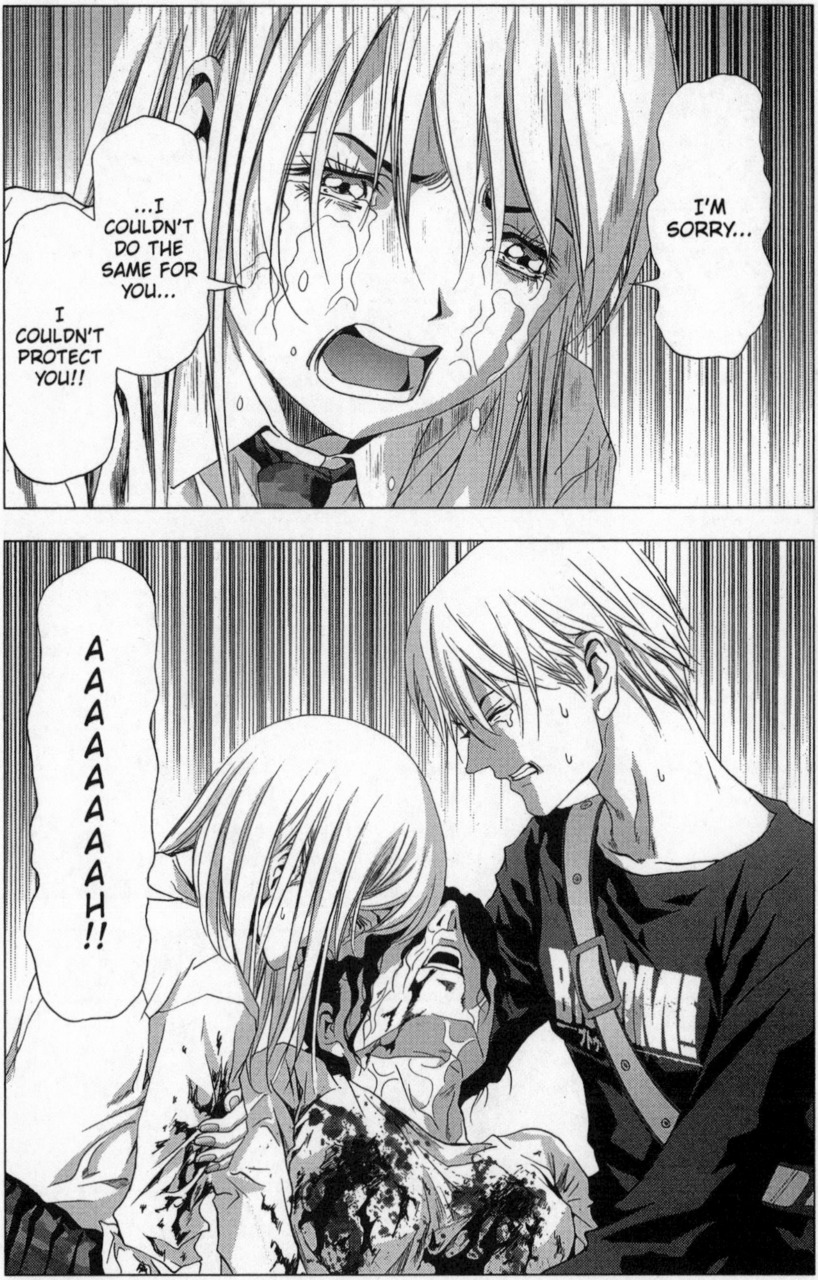
I'M SORRY...
...I COULDN'T DO THE SAME FOR YOU...
I COULDN'T PROTECT YOU!!
AAAAAAAAH!!

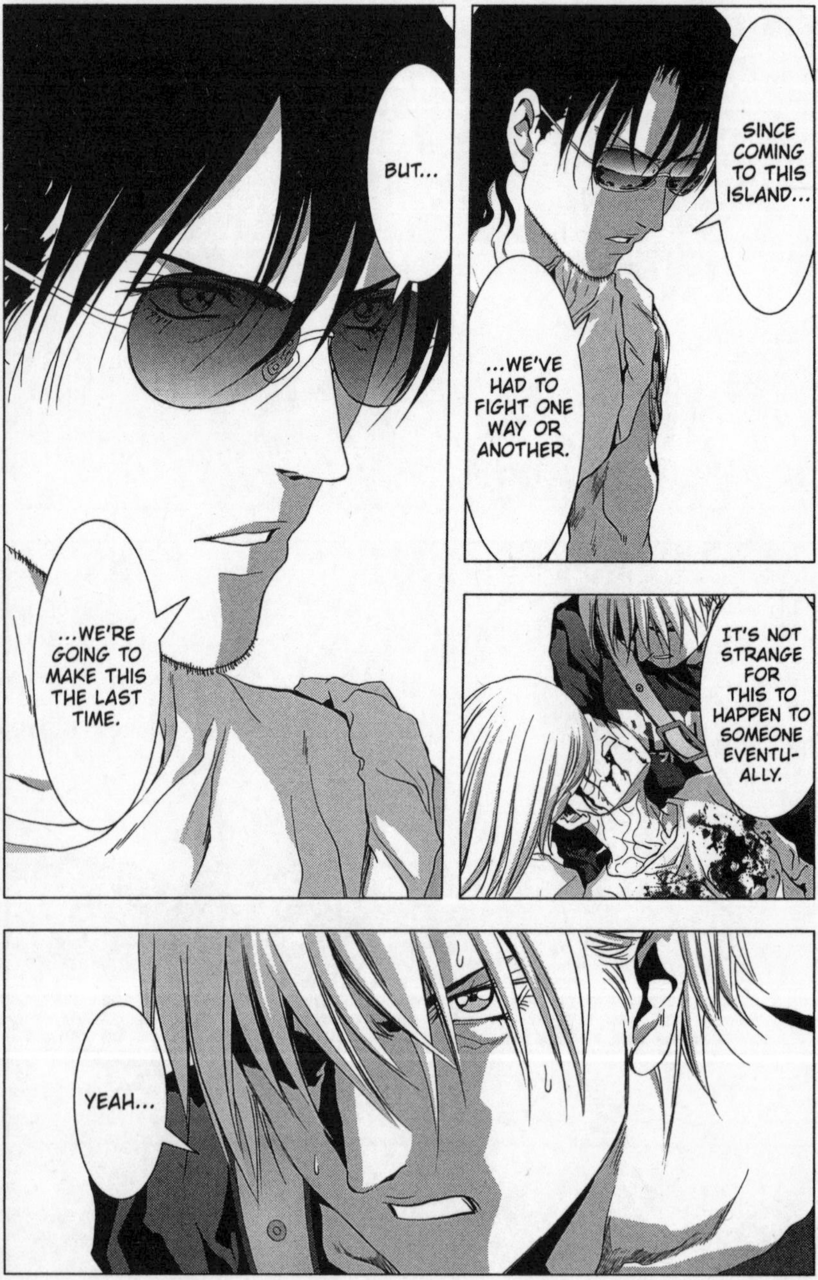
SINCE COMING TO THIS ISLAND...
...WE'VE HAD TO FIGHT ONE WAY OR ANOTHER.
IT'S NOT STRANGE FOR THIS TO HAPPEN TO SOMEONE EVENTU-ALLY.
BUT...
...WE'RE GOING TO MAKE THIS THE LAST TIME.
YEAH...

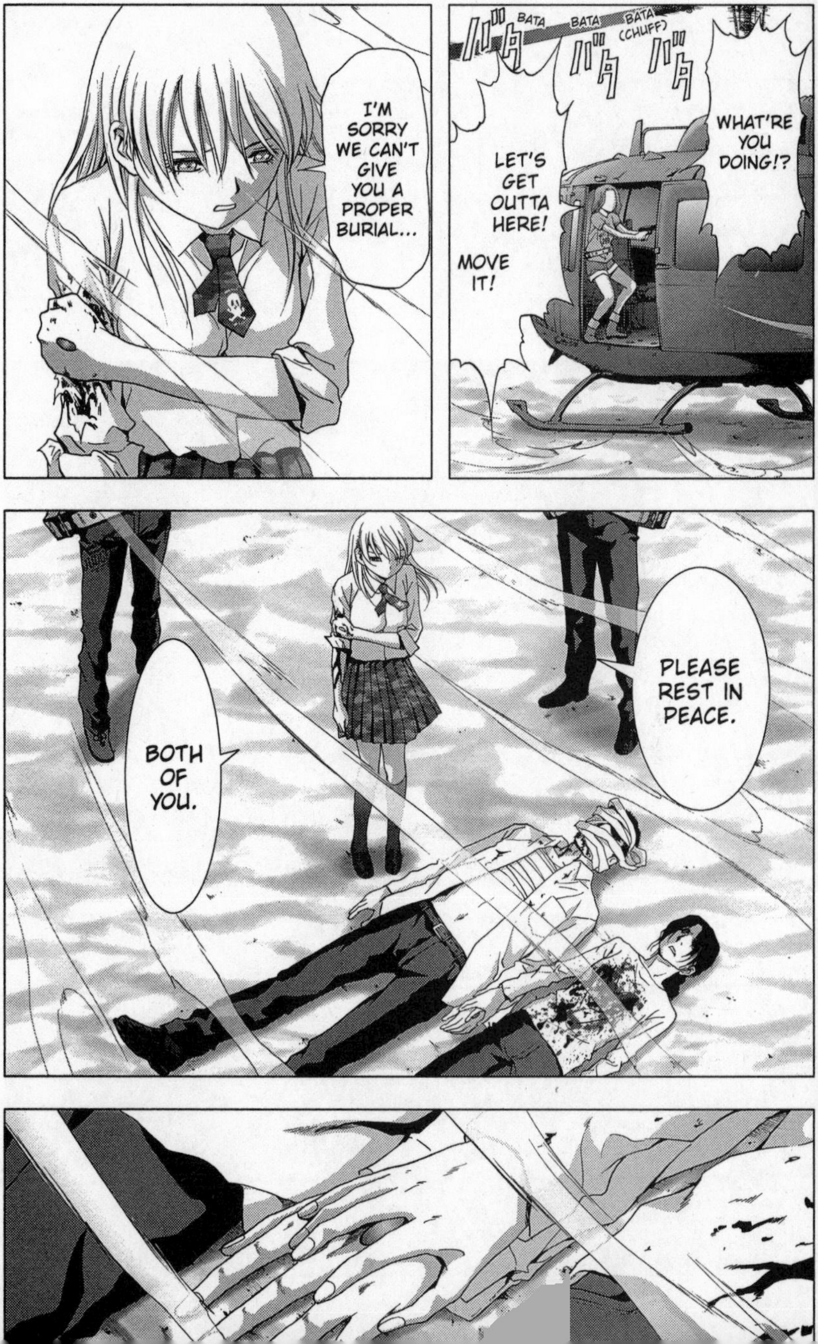
バタ BATA
バタ BATA
バタ BATA (CHUFF)
WHAT'RE YOU DOING!?
LET'S GET OUTTA HERE!
MOVE IT!
I'M SORRY WE CAN'T GIVE YOU A PROPER BURIAL...
PLEASE REST IN PEACE.
BOTH OF YOU.

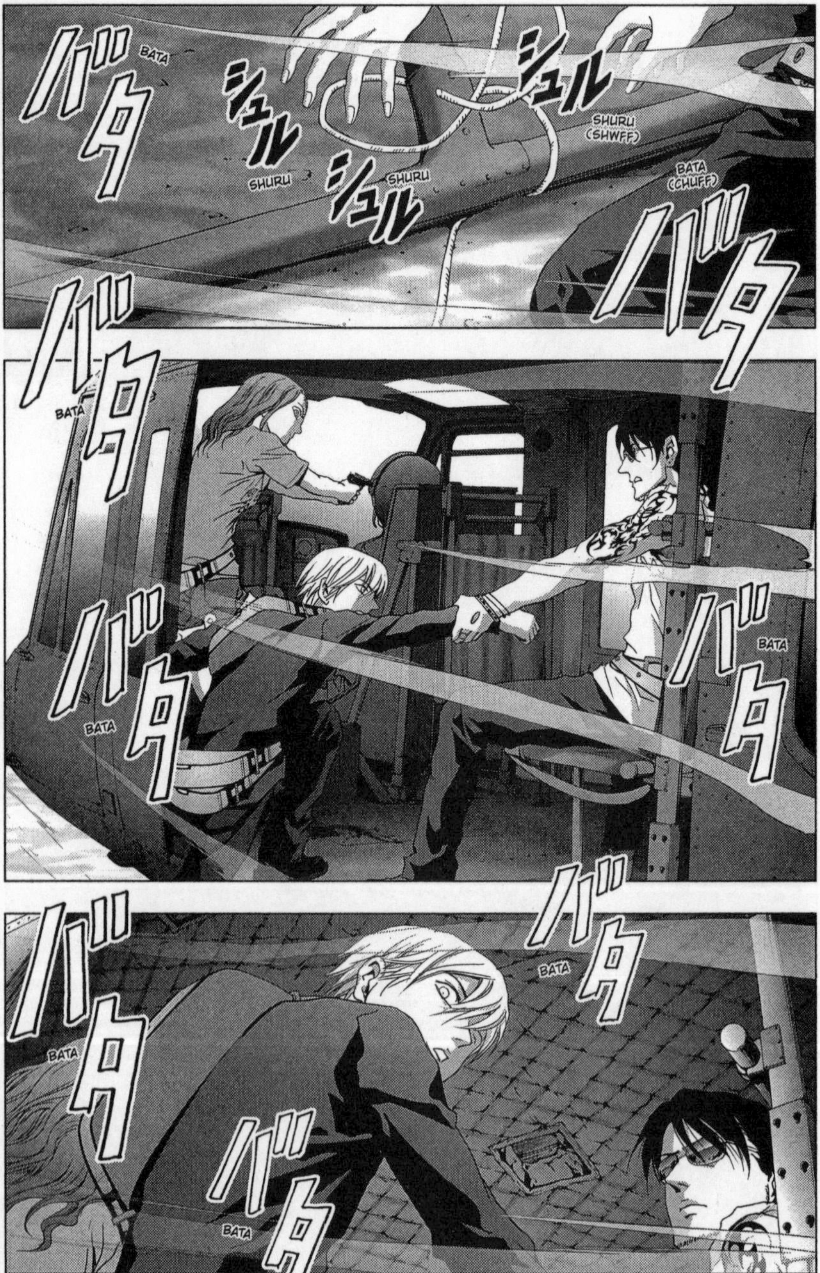

シュル
SHURU
(SHWFF)
バタ
BATA
(CHUFF)
シュル
SHURU
シュル
SHURU
バタ
BATA
バタ
BATA
バタ
BATA
バタ
BATA
バタ
BATA
バタ
BATA
バタ
BATA

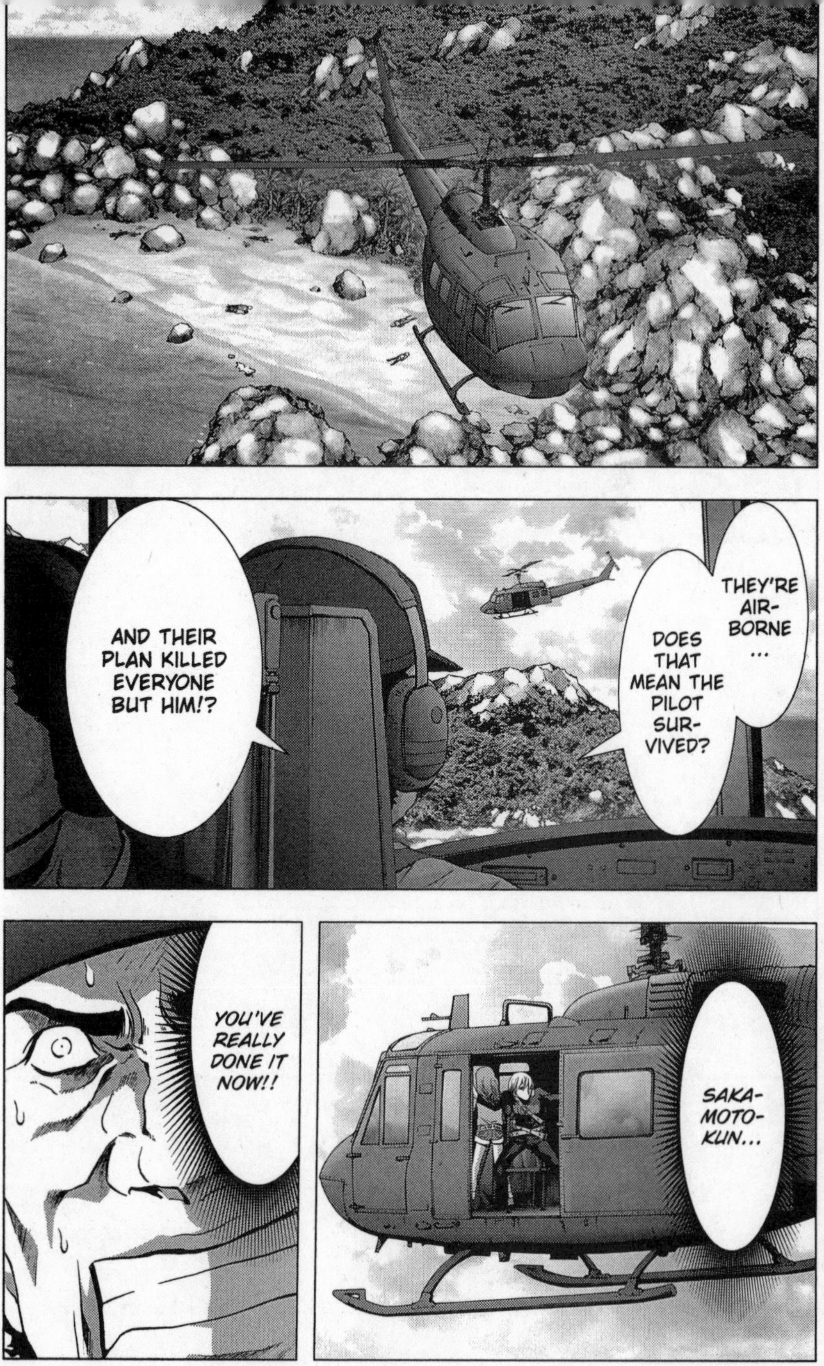
THEY'RE AIR-BORNE ...
DOES THAT MEAN THE PILOT SUR-VIVED?
AND THEIR PLAN KILLED EVERYONE BUT HIM!?
SAKA-MOTO-KUN...
YOU'VE REALLY DONE IT NOW!!

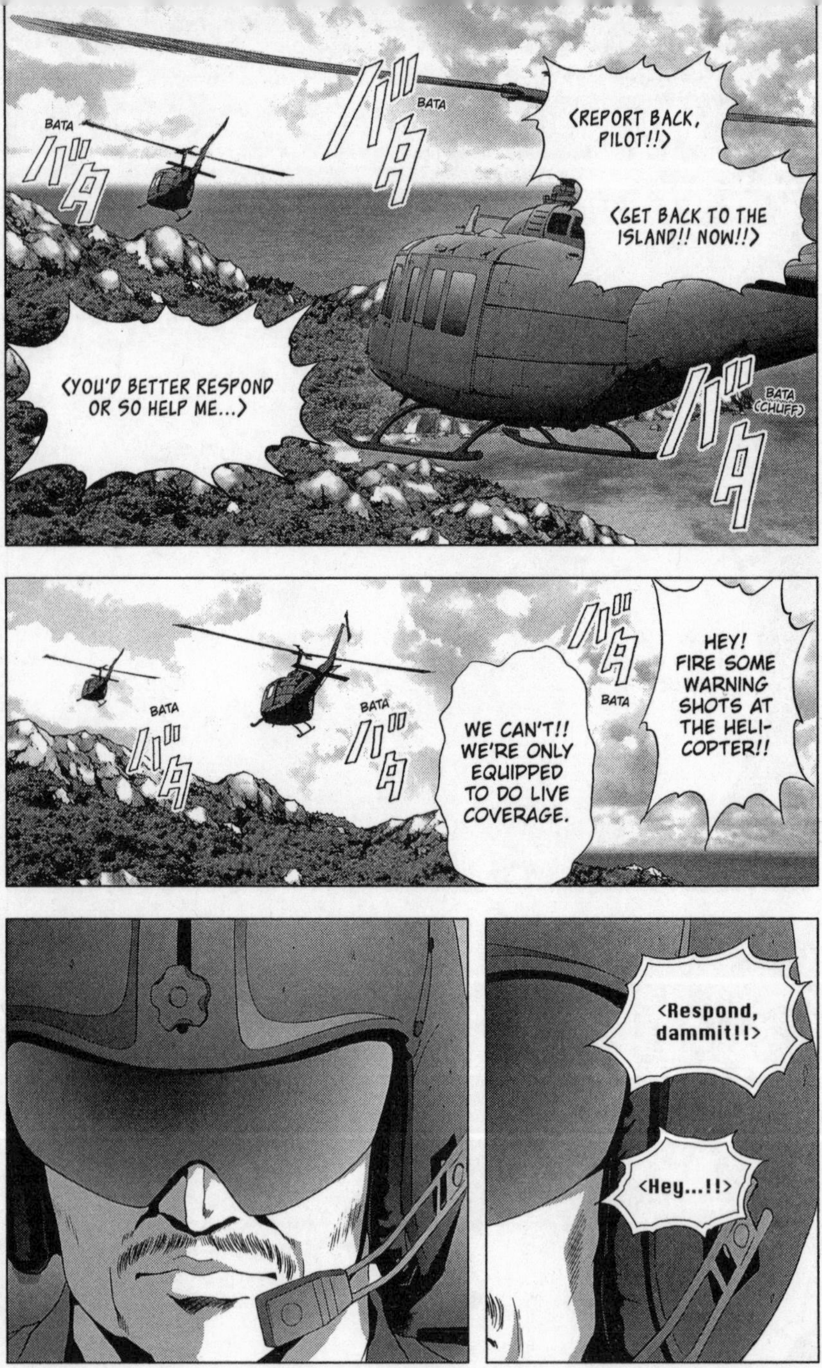
<REPORT BACK, PILOT!!>
<GET BACK TO THE ISLAND!! NOW!!>
BATA (CHUFF)
BATA
BATA
<YOU'D BETTER RESPOND OR SO HELP ME...>
HEY! FIRE SOME WARNING SHOTS AT THE HELI-COPTER!!
BATA
WE CAN'T!! WE'RE ONLY EQUIPPED TO DO LIVE COVERAGE.
BATA
BATA
<Respond, dammit!!>
<Hey...!!>

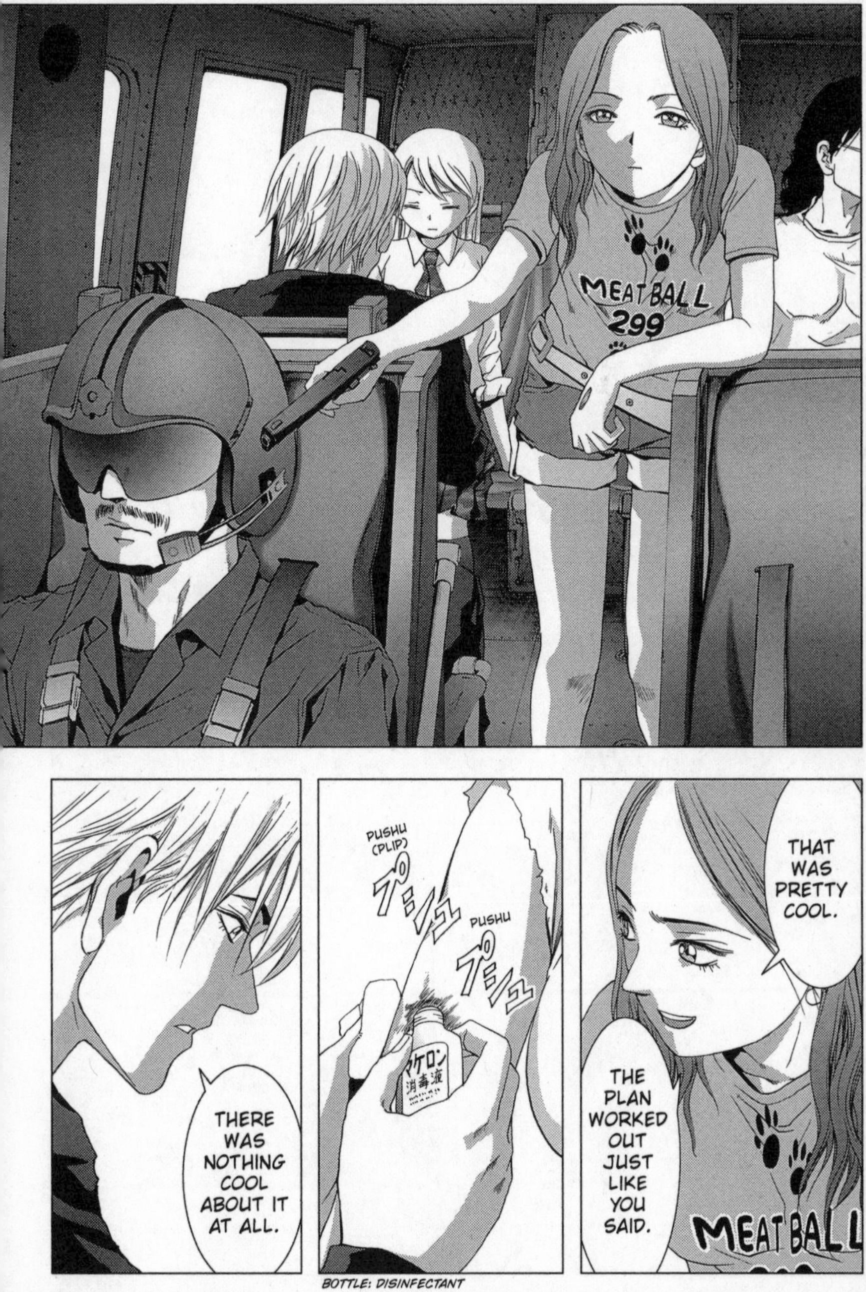
MEAT BALL 299
THAT WAS PRETTY COOL.
THE PLAN WORKED OUT JUST LIKE YOU SAID.
MEAT BALL
PUSHU (PLIP)
プシュ
PUSHU
プシュ
マケロン 消毒液
THERE WAS NOTHING COOL ABOUT IT AT ALL.

BOTTLE: DISINFECTANT

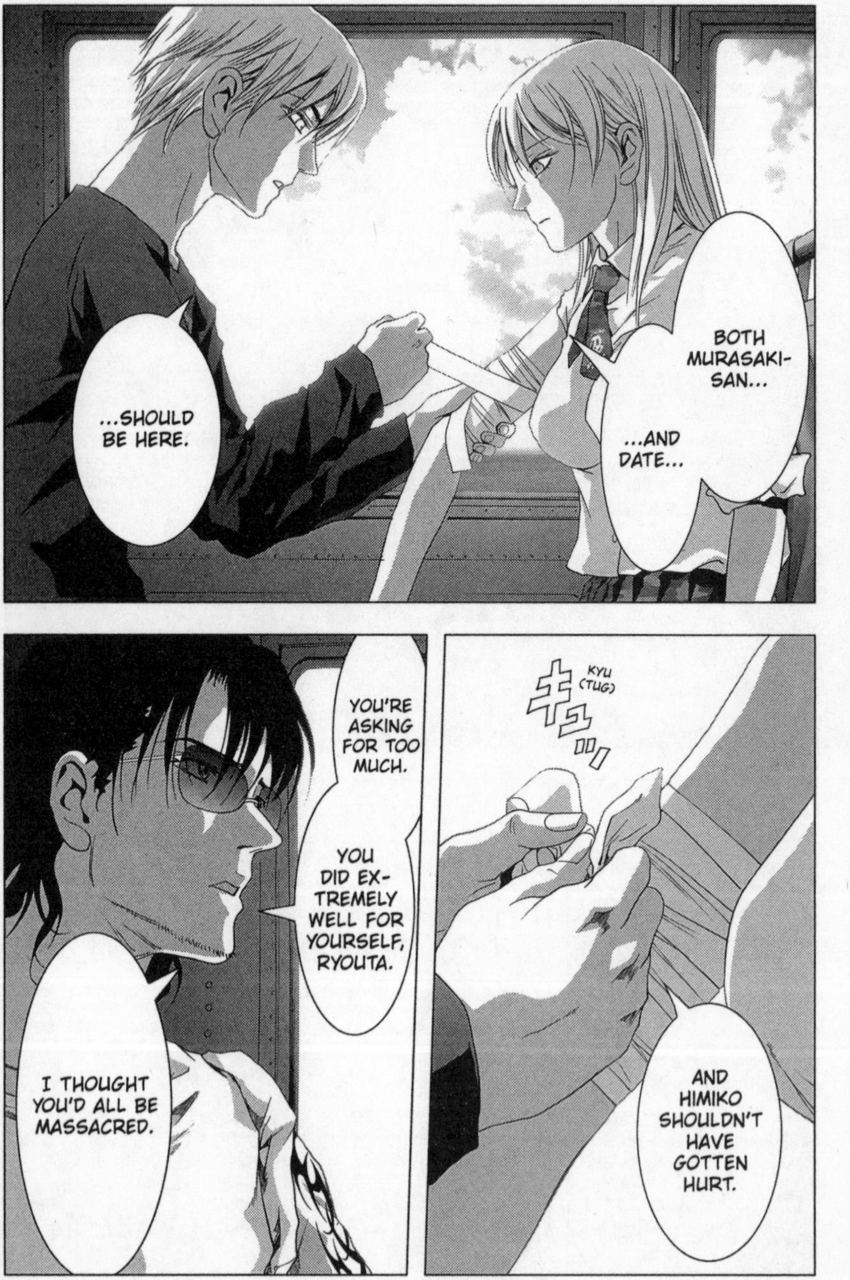
BOTH MURASAKI-SAN...
...AND DATE...
...SHOULD BE HERE.
KYU (TUG)
AND HIMIKO SHOULDN'T HAVE GOTTEN HURT.
YOU'RE ASKING FOR TOO MUCH.
YOU DID EXTREMELY WELL FOR YOURSELF, RYOUTA.
I THOUGHT YOU'D ALL BE MASSACRED.

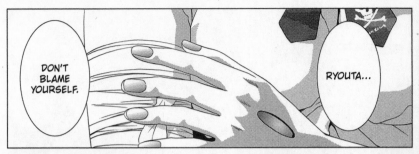

DON'T BLAME YOURSELF.

RYOUTA...

MURASAKI-SAN PUT US BEFORE HER OWN SAFETY...

I THINK...

...SHE WAS TRYING TO TELL US SOMETHING...

IF OUR ESCAPE FROM THE ISLAND...

...WILL LEAD TO THE COLLAPSE OF THE GAME...

...THEN WE HAVE TO MAKE THIS PLAN A SUCCESS.

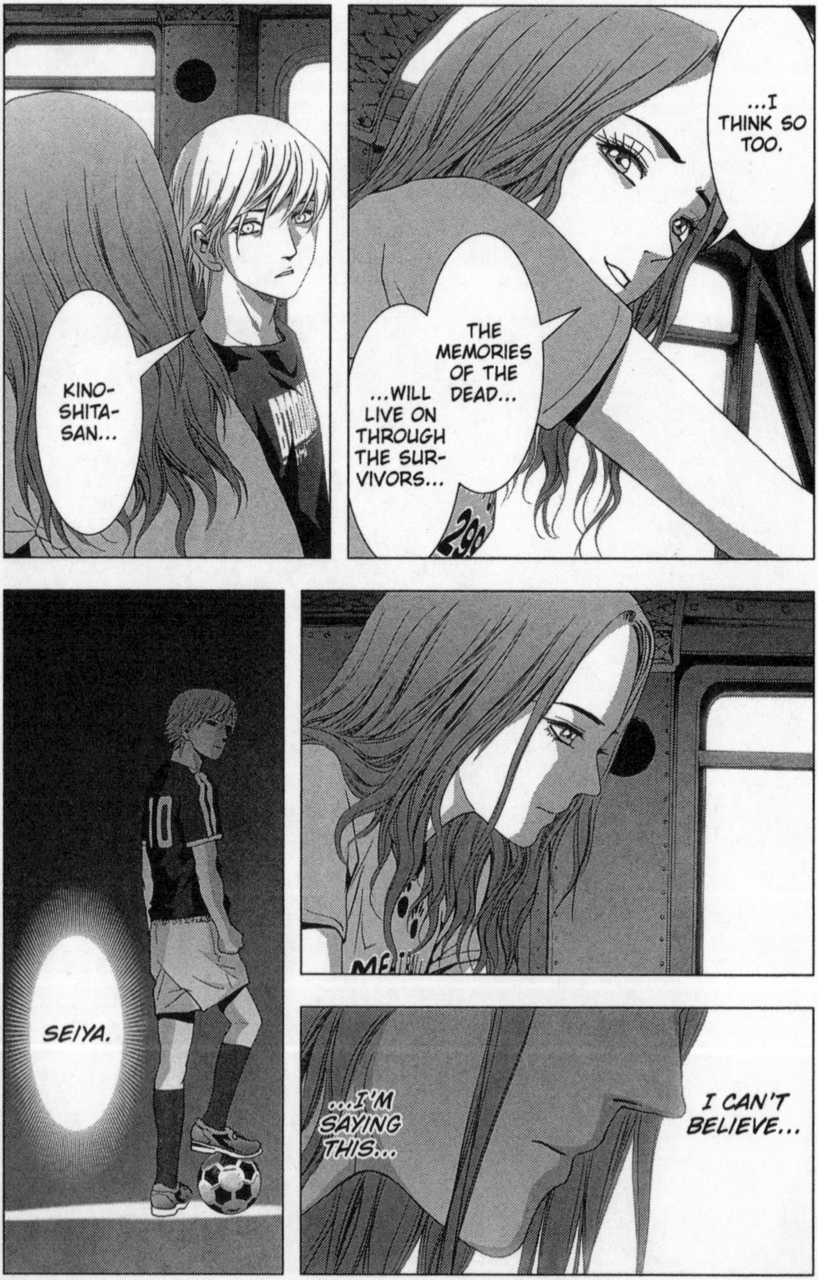
...I THINK SO TOO.
THE MEMORIES OF THE DEAD...
...WILL LIVE ON THROUGH THE SUR-VIVORS...
KINO-SHITA-SAN...
I CAN'T BELIEVE...
...I'M SAYING THIS...
SEIYA.

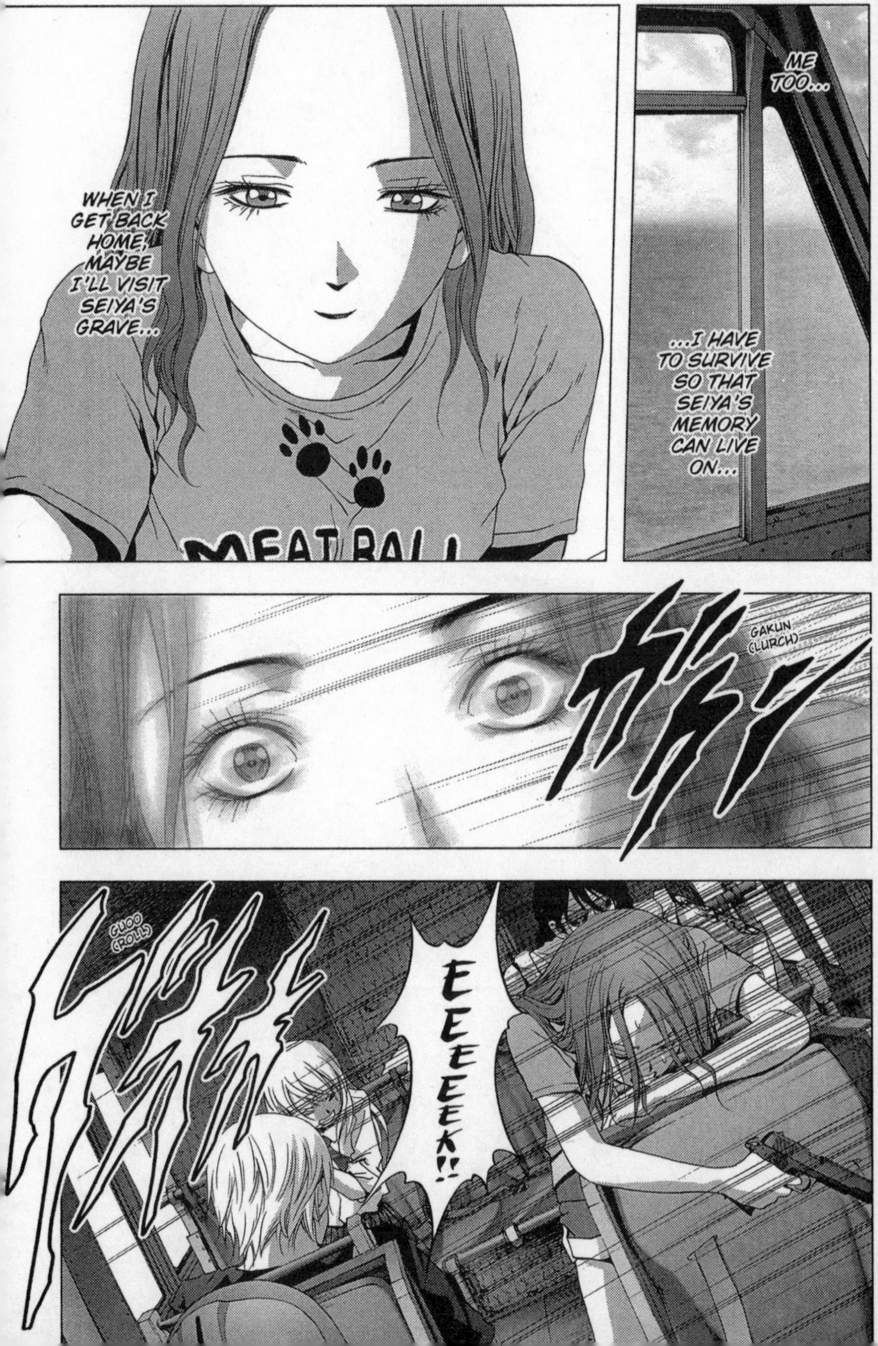
ME TOO...
...I HAVE TO SURVIVE SO THAT SEIYA'S MEMORY CAN LIVE ON...
WHEN I GET BACK HOME, MAYBE I'LL VISIT SEIYA'S GRAVE...
GAKUN (LURCH)
EEEEEEEK!!
GUOO (ROLL)

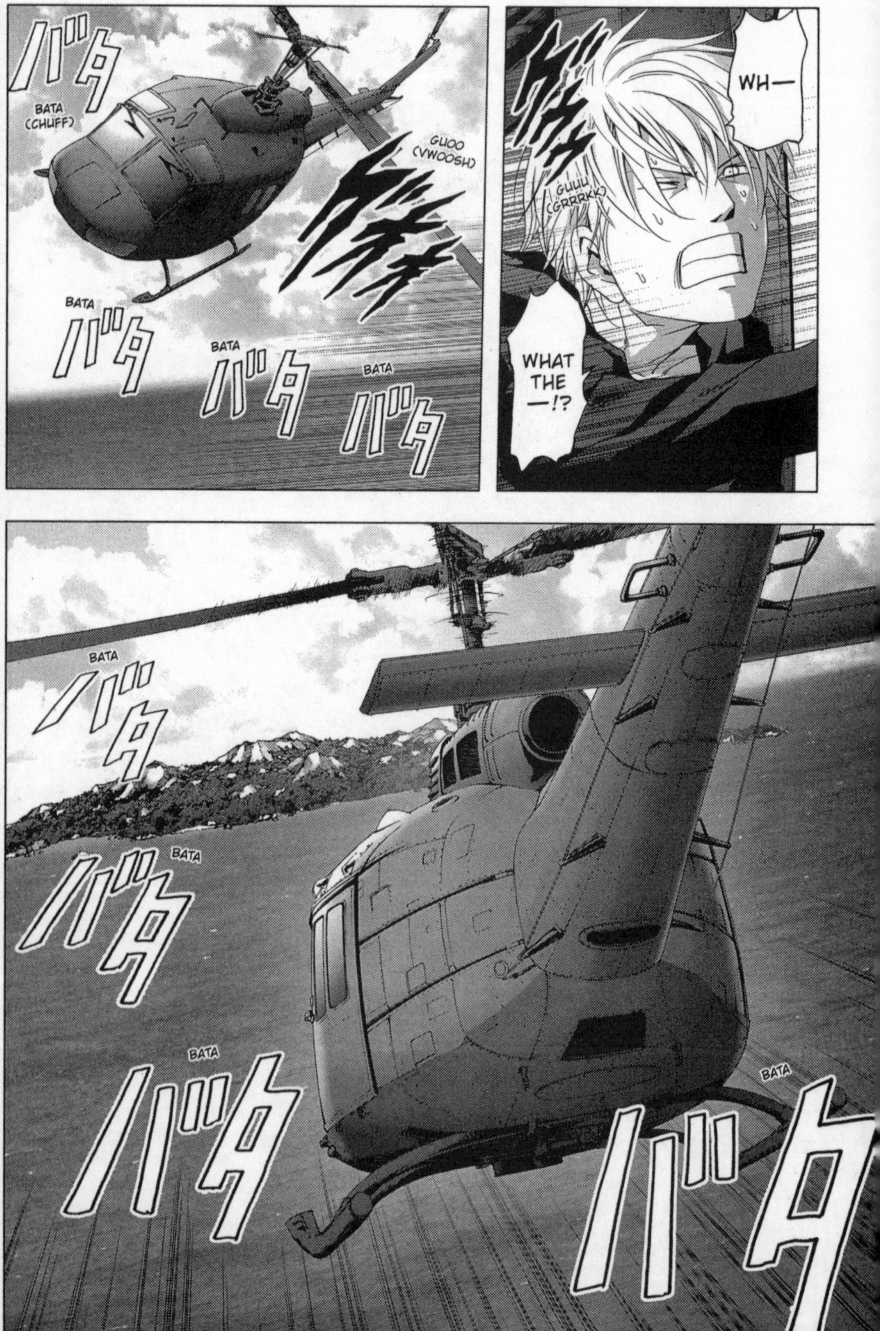
WH—
GUUU (GRRRKK)
WHAT THE —!?
BATA (CHUFF)
GUOO (VWOOSH)
BATA
BATA
BATA
BATA
BATA
BATA
BATA

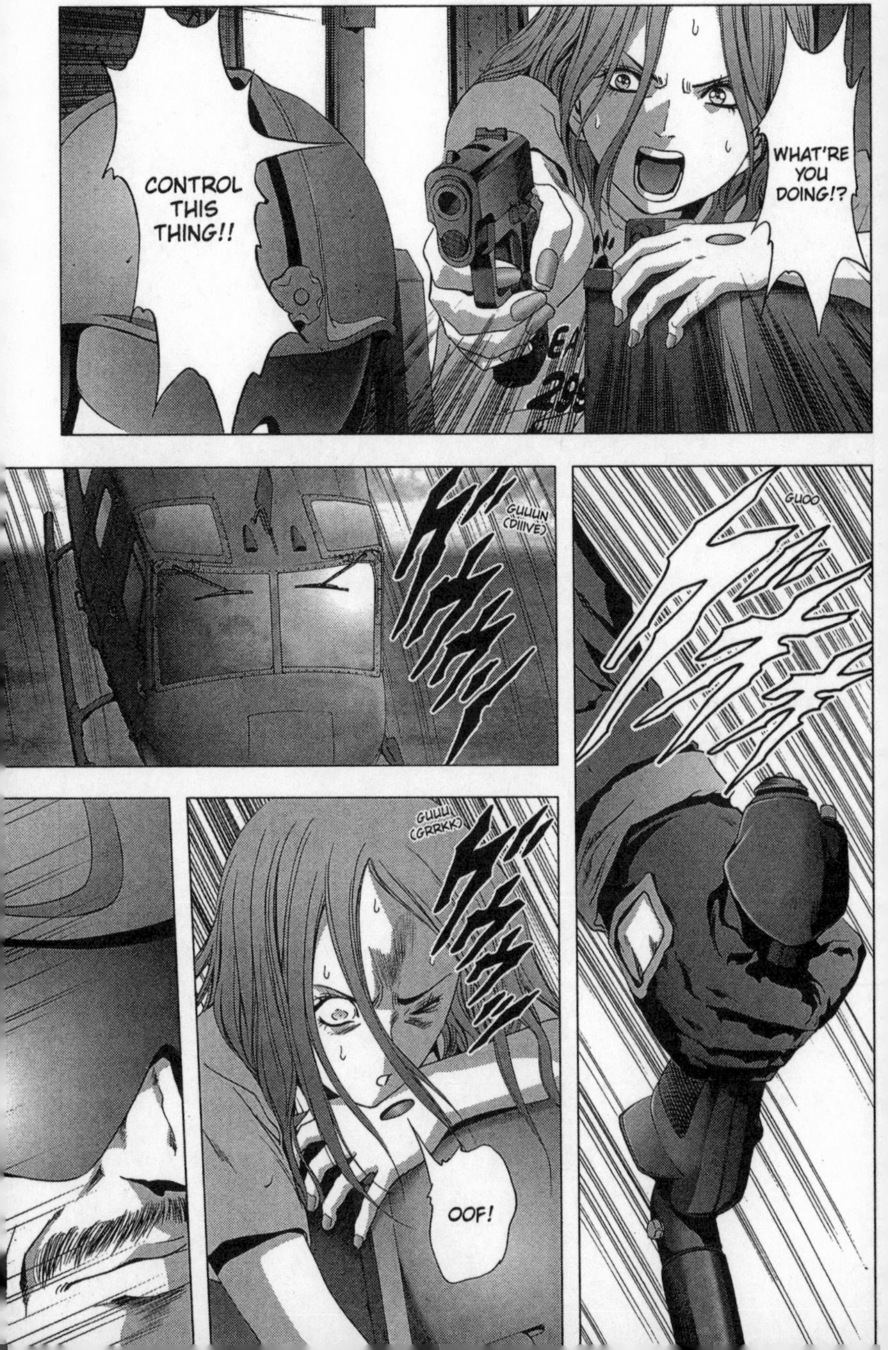
WHAT'RE YOU DOING!?
CONTROL THIS THING!!
GUOO
GUUUN (DIIVE)
GUUU (GRRKK)
OOF!

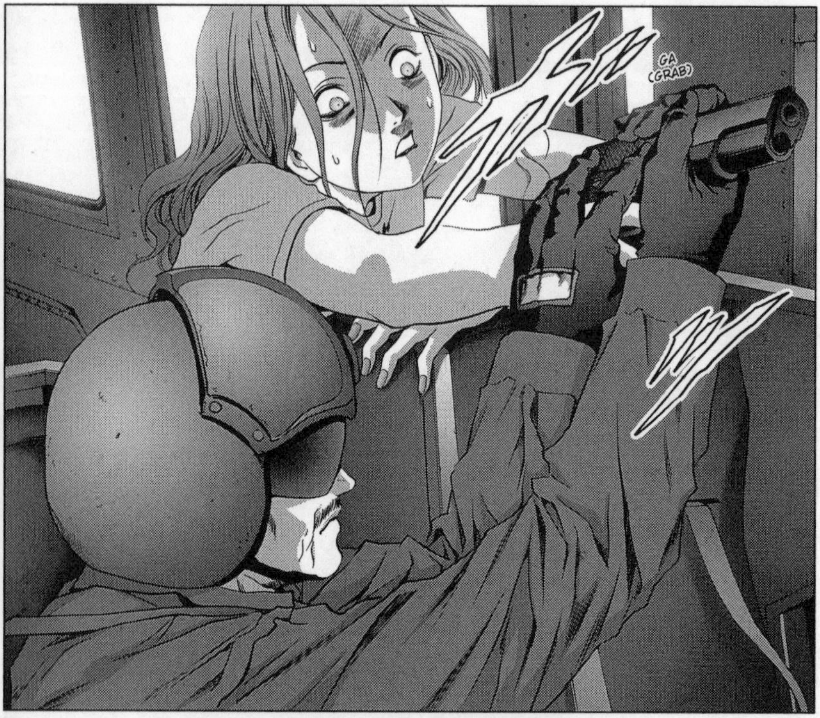
GA
(GRAB)
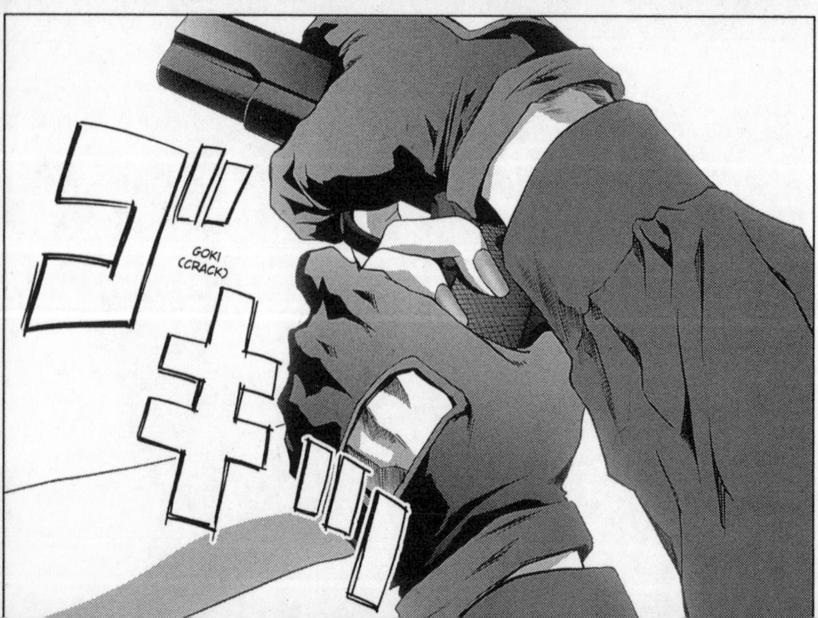
GOKI
(CRACK)

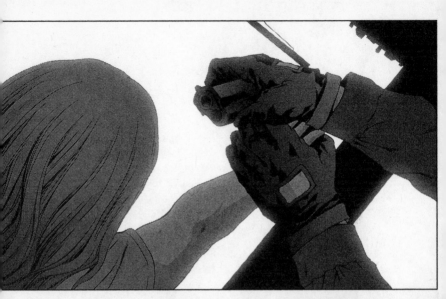

!!

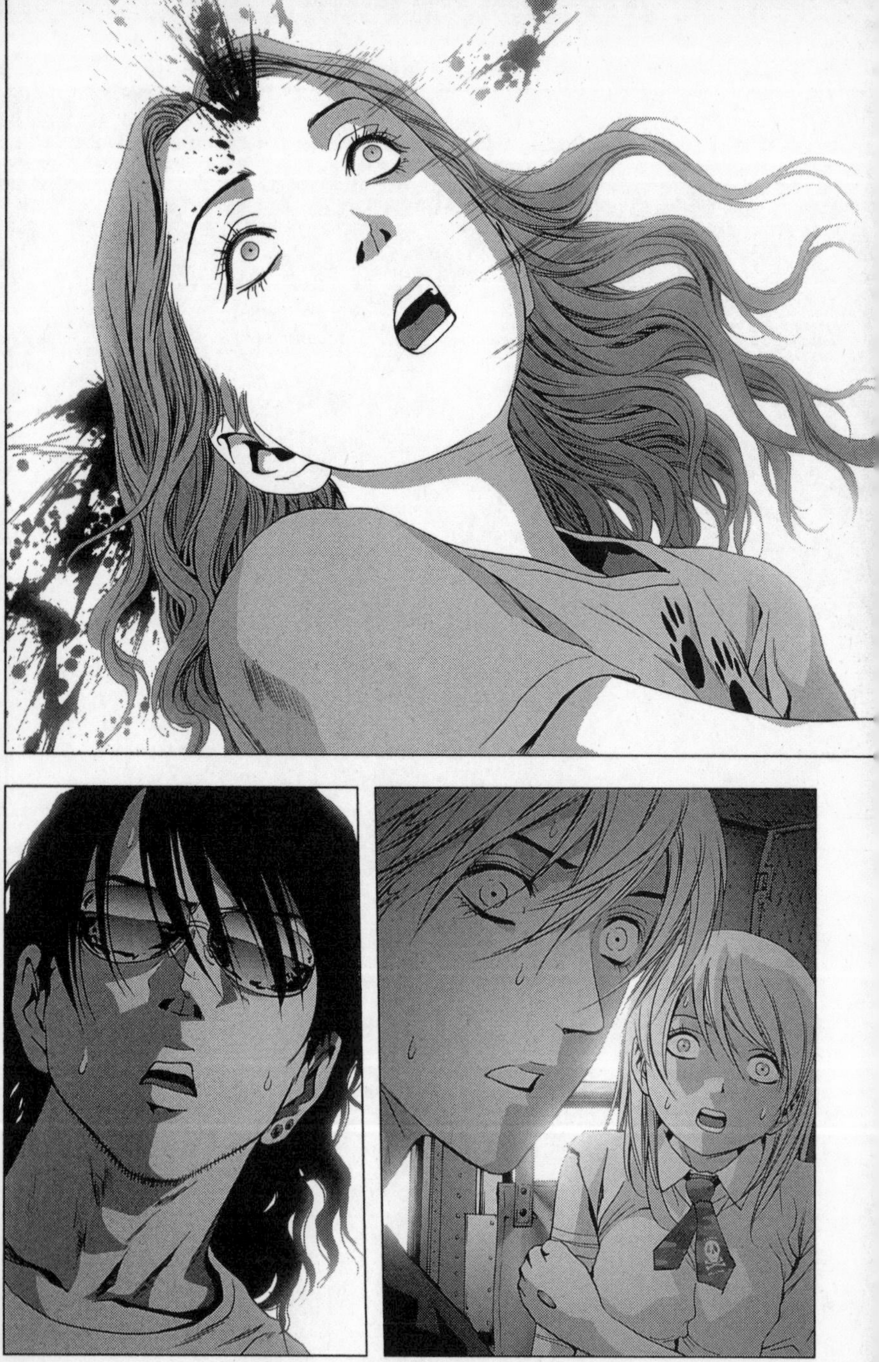

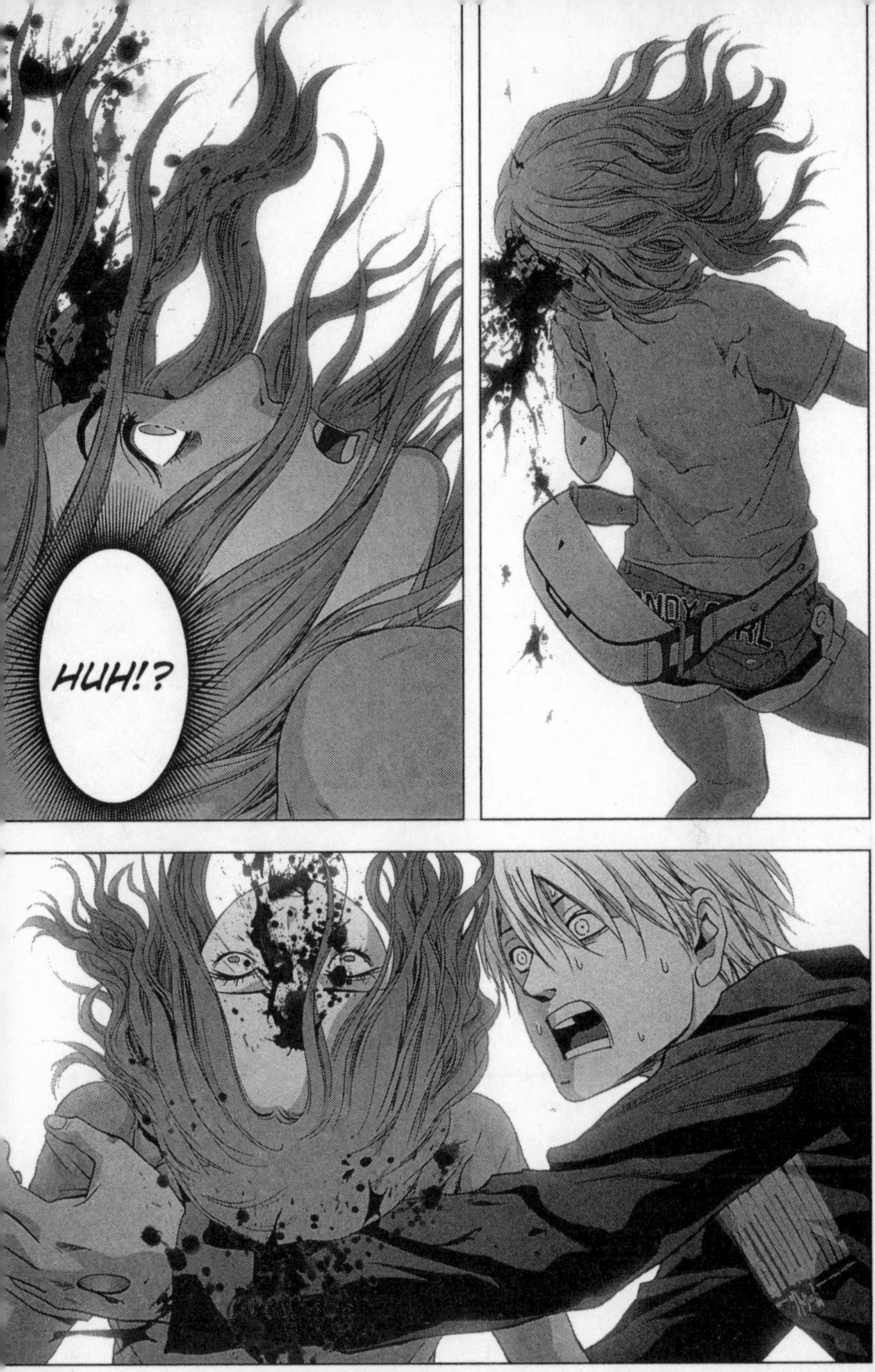
HUH!?

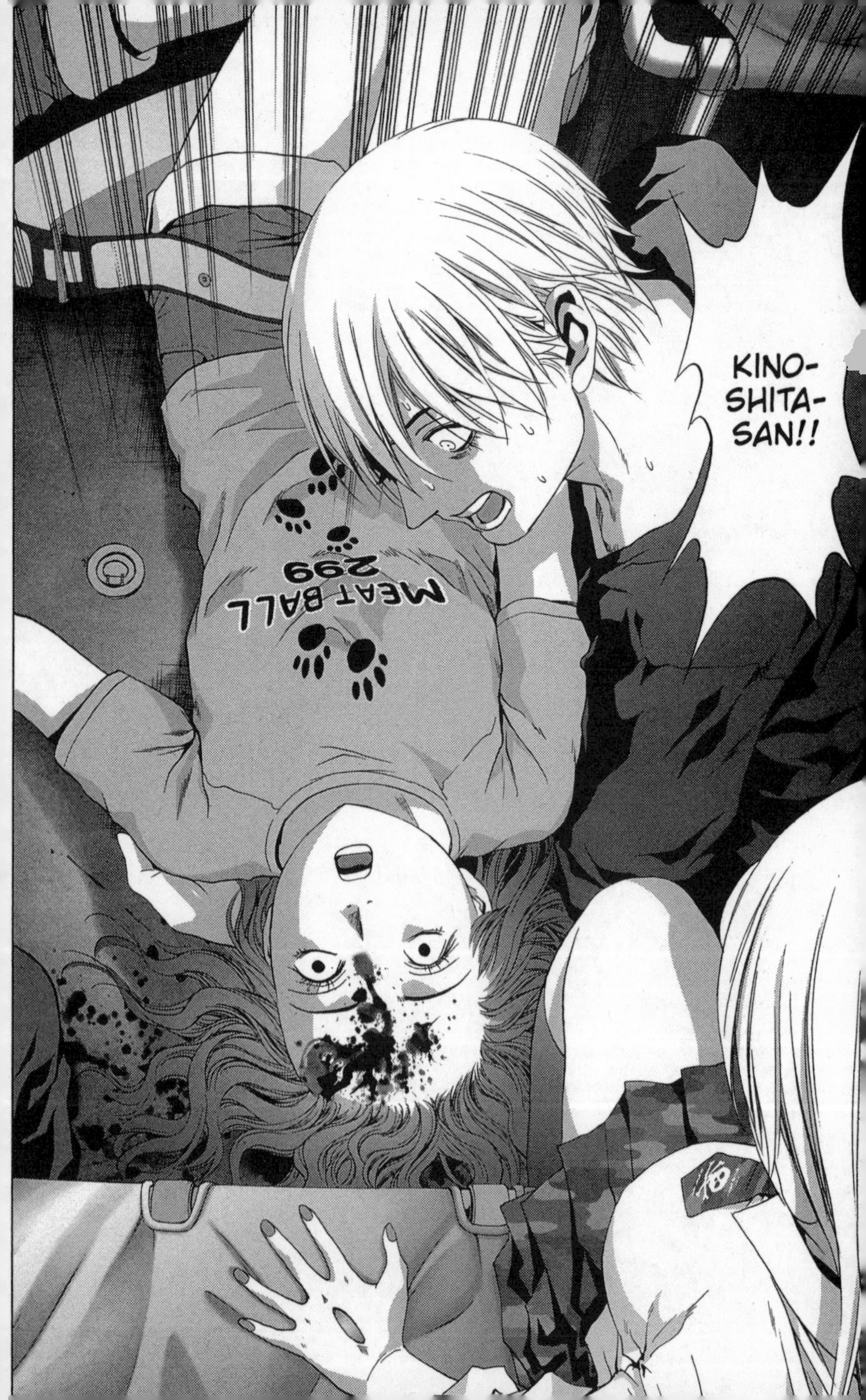
KINO-SHITA-SAN!!
MEAT BALL 299

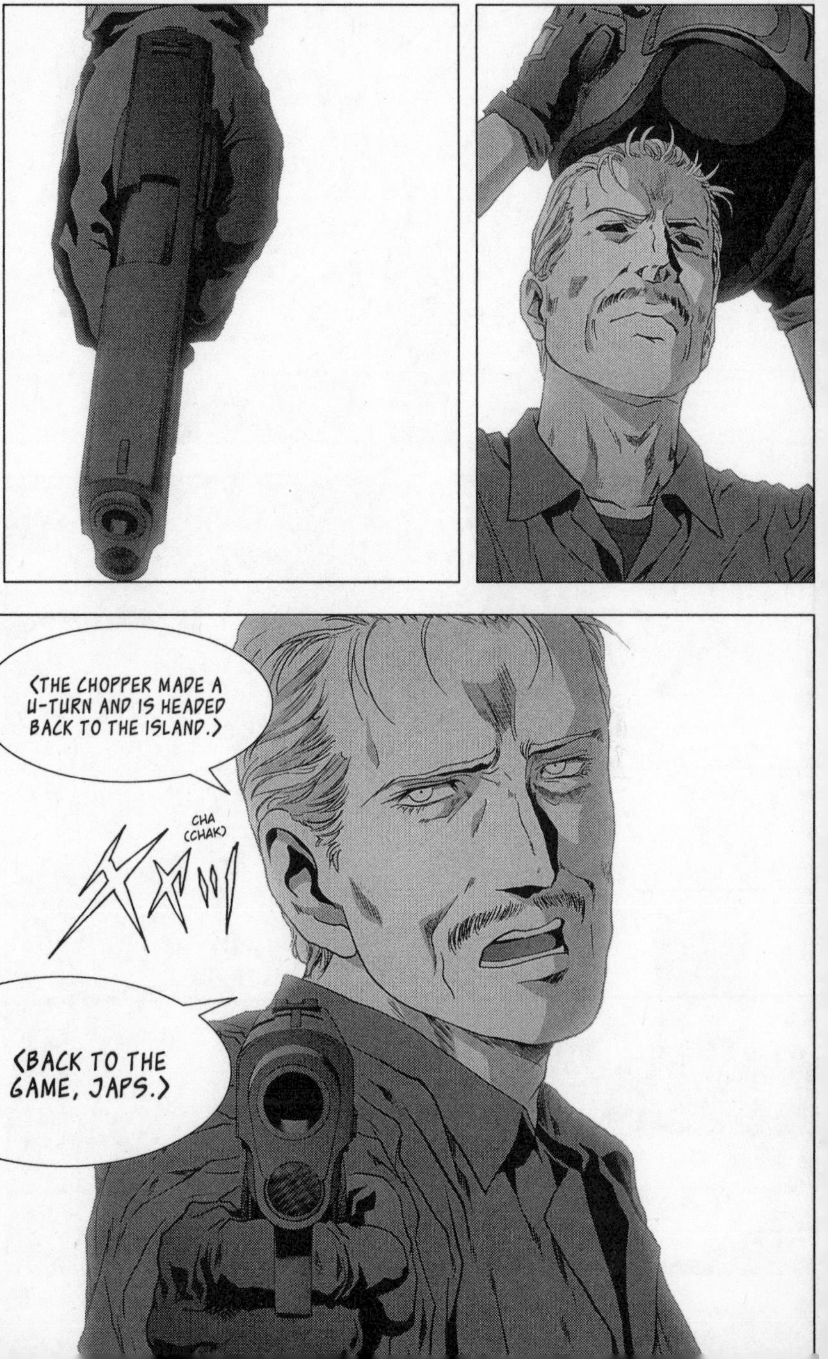
<THE CHOPPER MADE A U-TURN AND IS HEADED BACK TO THE ISLAND.>
CHA (CHAK)
<BACK TO THE GAME, JAPS.>

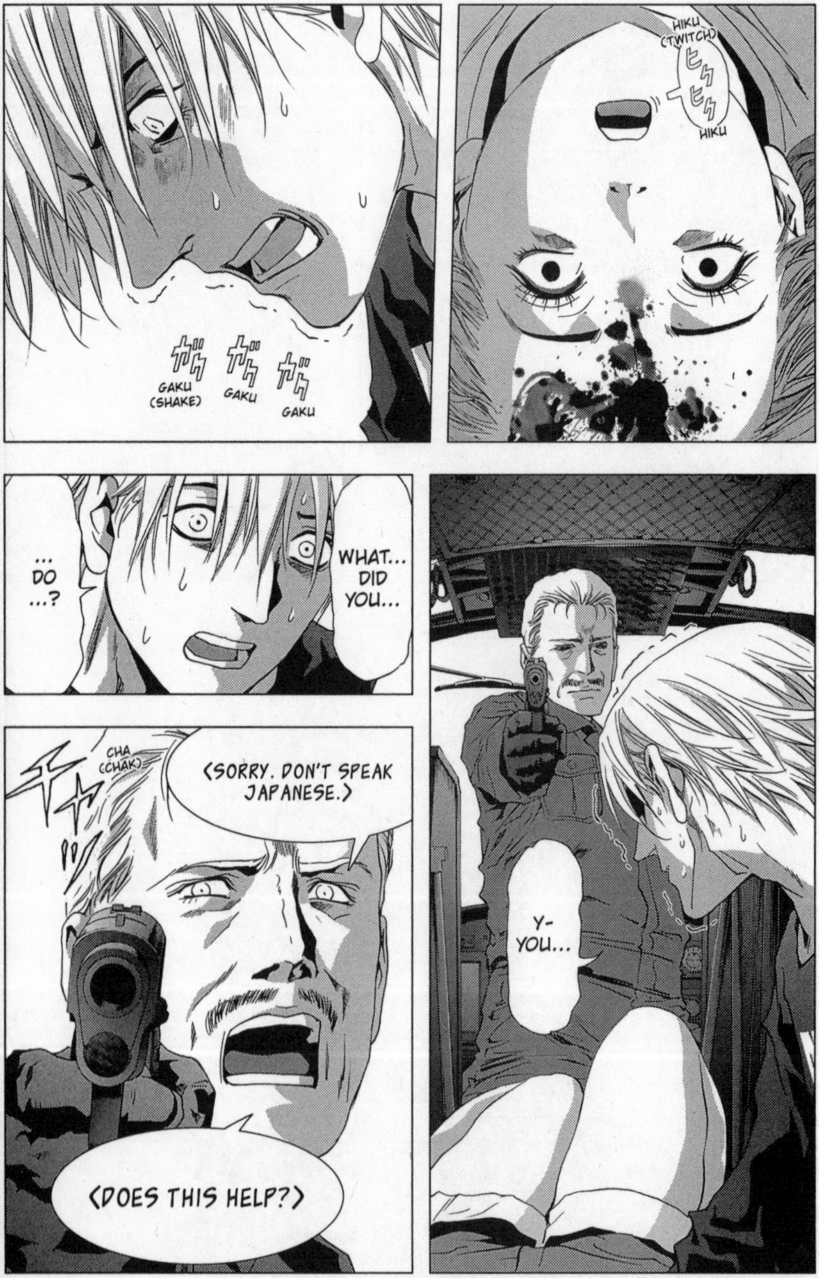
HIKU (TWITCH) ヒク ヒク HIKU
ガク ガク ガク
GAKU (SHAKE) GAKU GAKU
Y- YOU...
WHAT... DID YOU...
... DO ...?
チャ CHA (CHAK)
⟨SORRY. DON'T SPEAK JAPANESE.⟩
⟨DOES THIS HELP?⟩

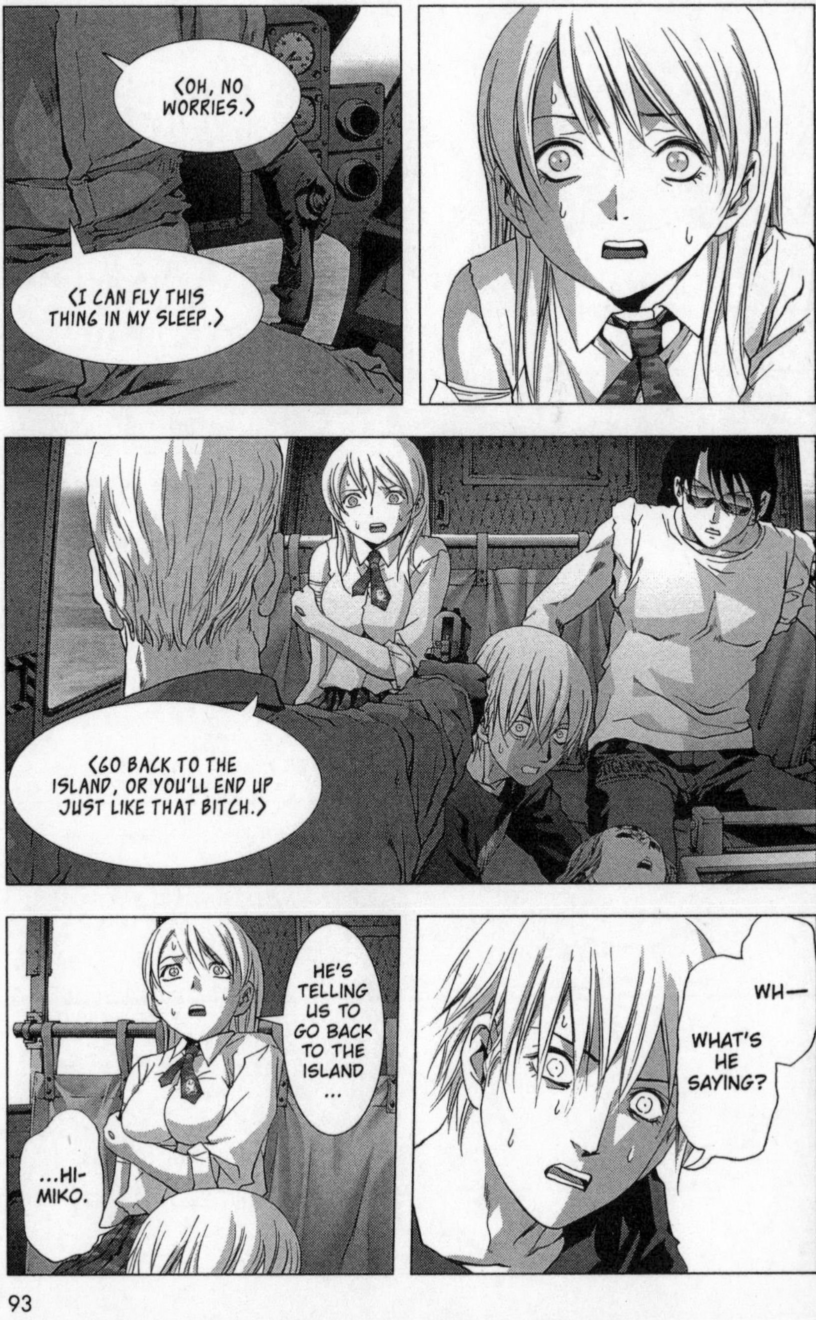
<OH, NO WORRIES.>
<I CAN FLY THIS THING IN MY SLEEP.>
<GO BACK TO THE ISLAND, OR YOU'LL END UP JUST LIKE THAT BITCH.>
WH—
WHAT'S HE SAYING?
HE'S TELLING US TO GO BACK TO THE ISLAND ...
...HI-MIKO.

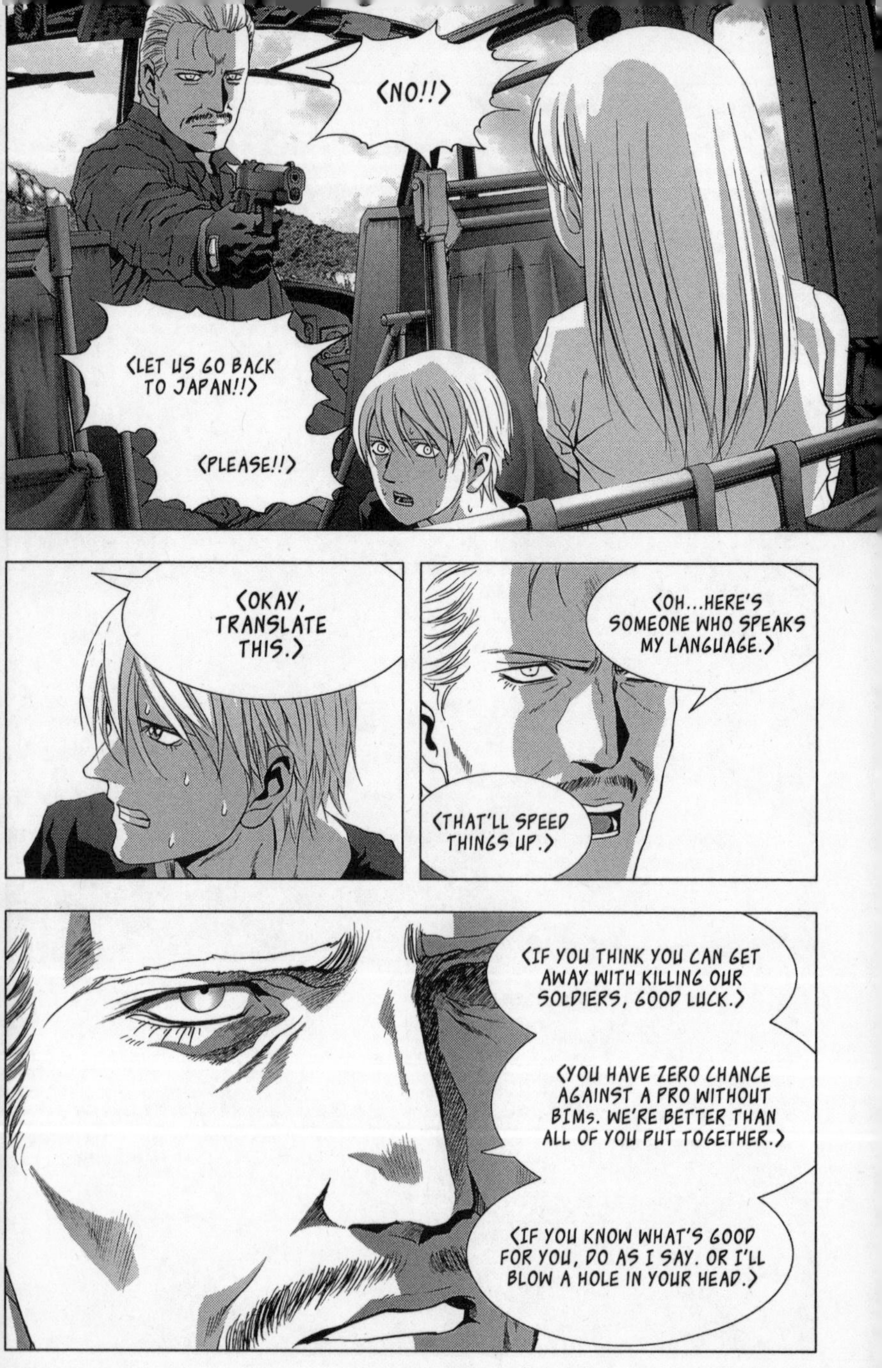
<NO!!>
<LET US GO BACK TO JAPAN!!>
<PLEASE!!>
<OH...HERE'S SOMEONE WHO SPEAKS MY LANGUAGE.>
<THAT'LL SPEED THINGS UP.>
<OKAY, TRANSLATE THIS.>
<IF YOU THINK YOU CAN GET AWAY WITH KILLING OUR SOLDIERS, GOOD LUCK.>
<YOU HAVE ZERO CHANCE AGAINST A PRO WITHOUT BIMs. WE'RE BETTER THAN ALL OF YOU PUT TOGETHER.>
<IF YOU KNOW WHAT'S GOOD FOR YOU, DO AS I SAY. OR I'LL BLOW A HOLE IN YOUR HEAD.>

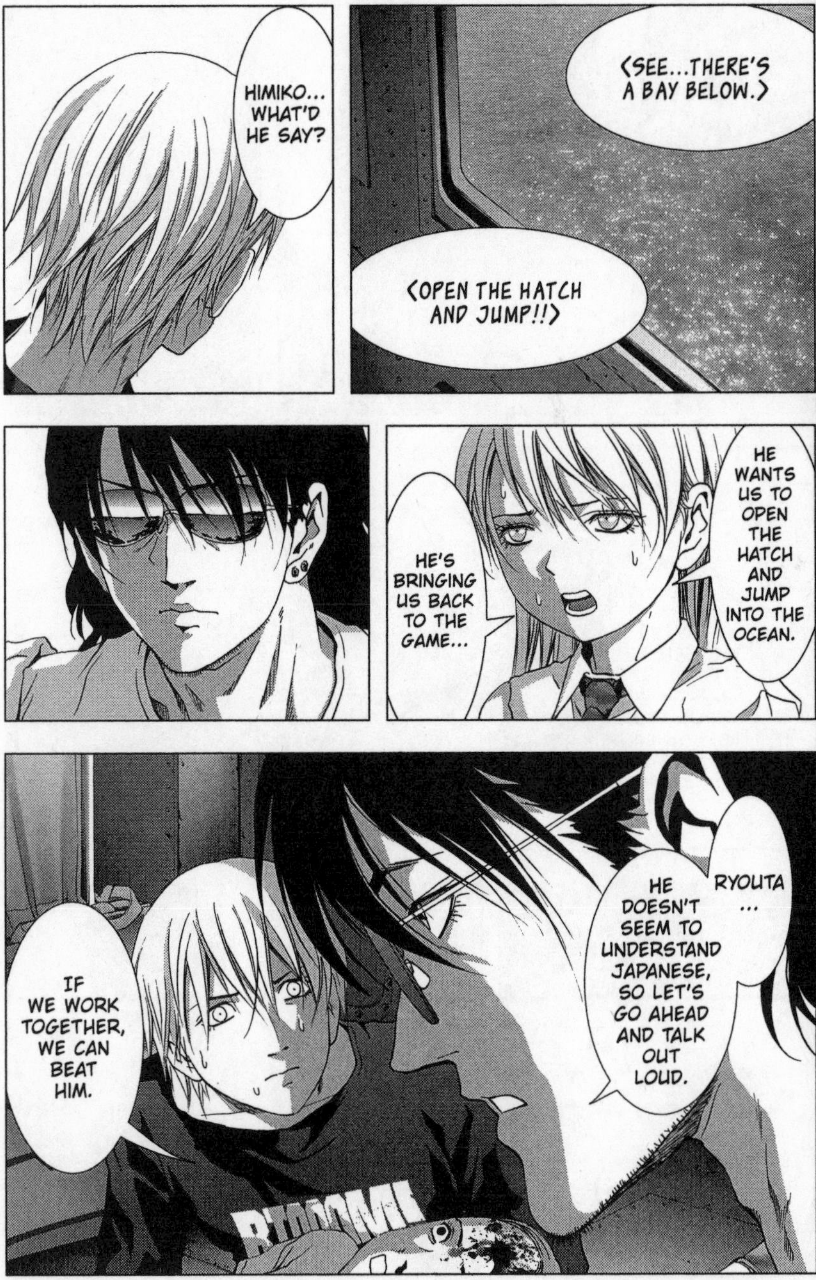

〈SEE...THERE'S A BAY BELOW.〉
〈OPEN THE HATCH AND JUMP!!〉
HIMIKO... WHAT'D HE SAY?
HE WANTS US TO OPEN THE HATCH AND JUMP INTO THE OCEAN.
HE'S BRINGING US BACK TO THE GAME...
RYOUTA...
HE DOESN'T SEEM TO UNDERSTAND JAPANESE, SO LET'S GO AHEAD AND TALK OUT LOUD.
IF WE WORK TOGETHER, WE CAN BEAT HIM.

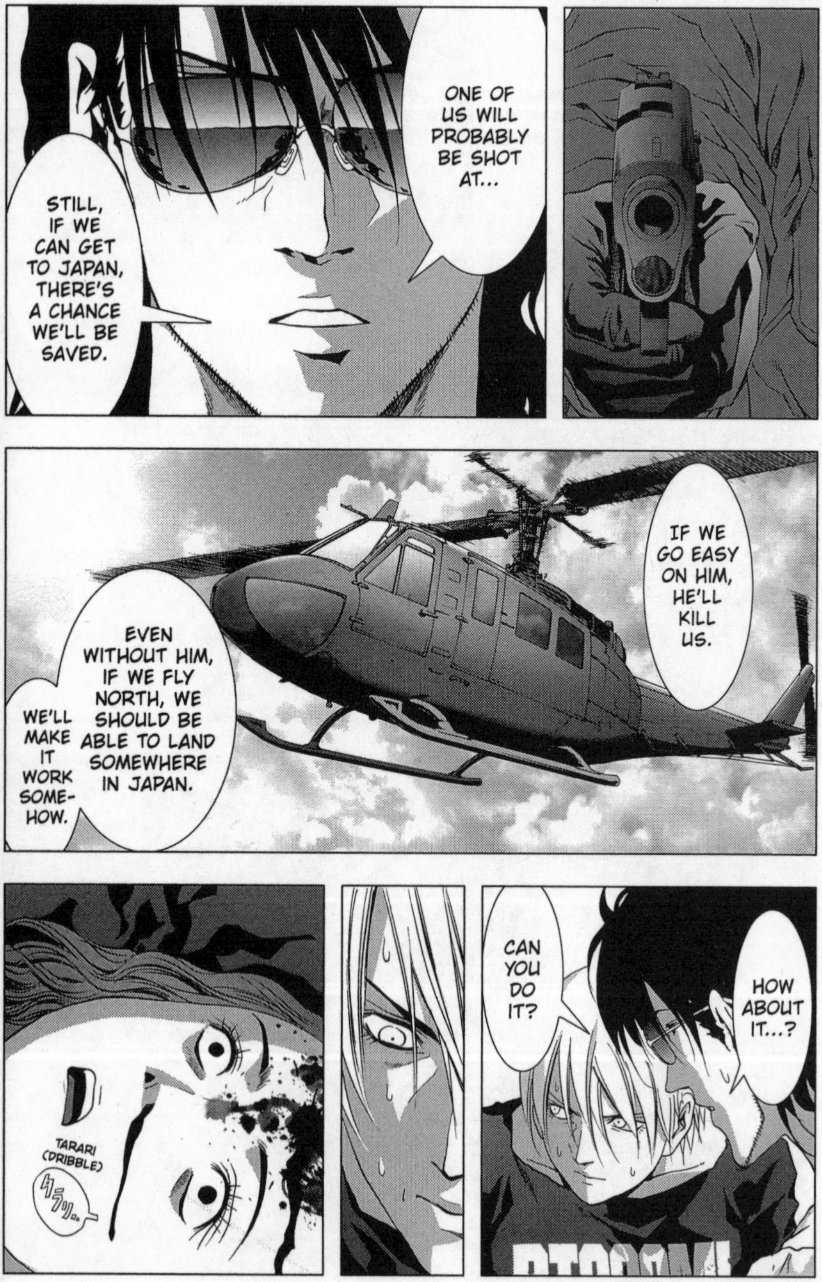
ONE OF US WILL PROBABLY BE SHOT AT...
STILL, IF WE CAN GET TO JAPAN, THERE'S A CHANCE WE'LL BE SAVED.
IF WE GO EASY ON HIM, HE'LL KILL US.
EVEN WITHOUT HIM, IF WE FLY NORTH, WE SHOULD BE ABLE TO LAND SOMEWHERE IN JAPAN.
WE'LL MAKE IT WORK SOME-HOW.
HOW ABOUT IT...?
CAN YOU DO IT?
TARARI (DRIBBLE)

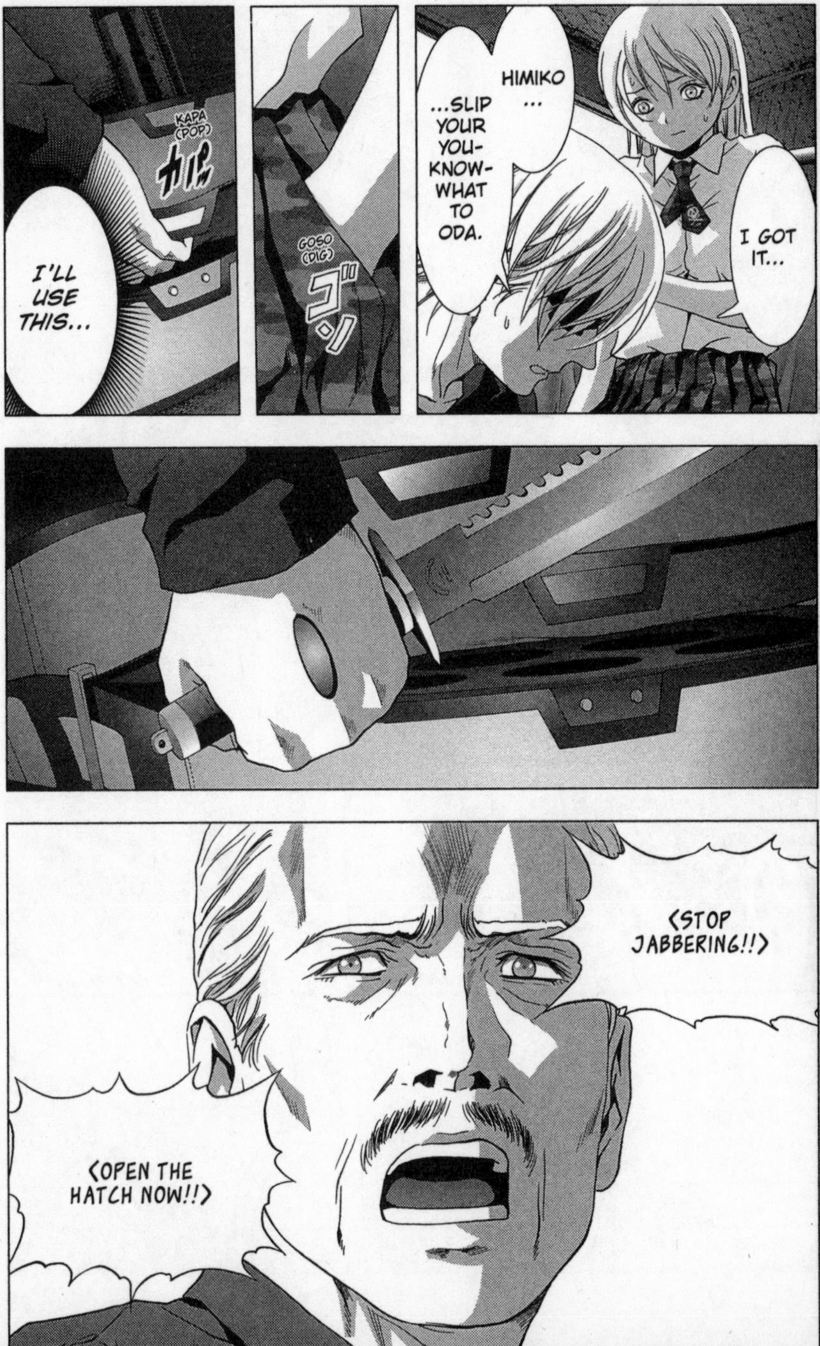
HIMIKO ...
...SLIP YOUR YOU-KNOW-WHAT TO ODA.
I GOT IT...
GOSO (DIG)
ゴソ
KAPA (POP)
カパ
I'LL USE THIS...
<STOP JABBERING!!>
<OPEN THE HATCH NOW!!>

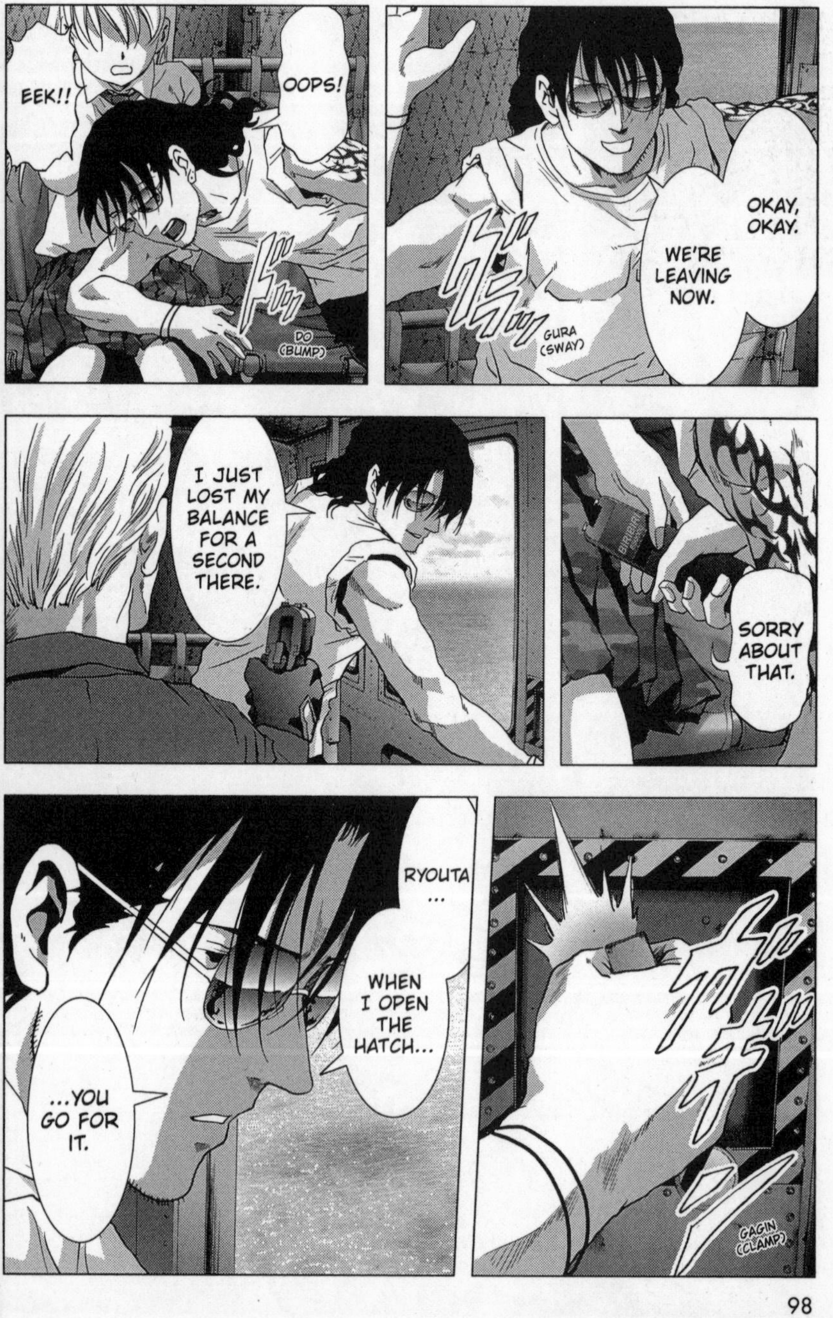
OKAY, OKAY.
WE'RE LEAVING NOW.
GURA (SWAY)
OOPS!
EEK!!
DO (BUMP)
SORRY ABOUT THAT.
I JUST LOST MY BALANCE FOR A SECOND THERE.
GAGIN (CLAMP)
RYOUTA...
WHEN I OPEN THE HATCH...
...YOU GO FOR IT.

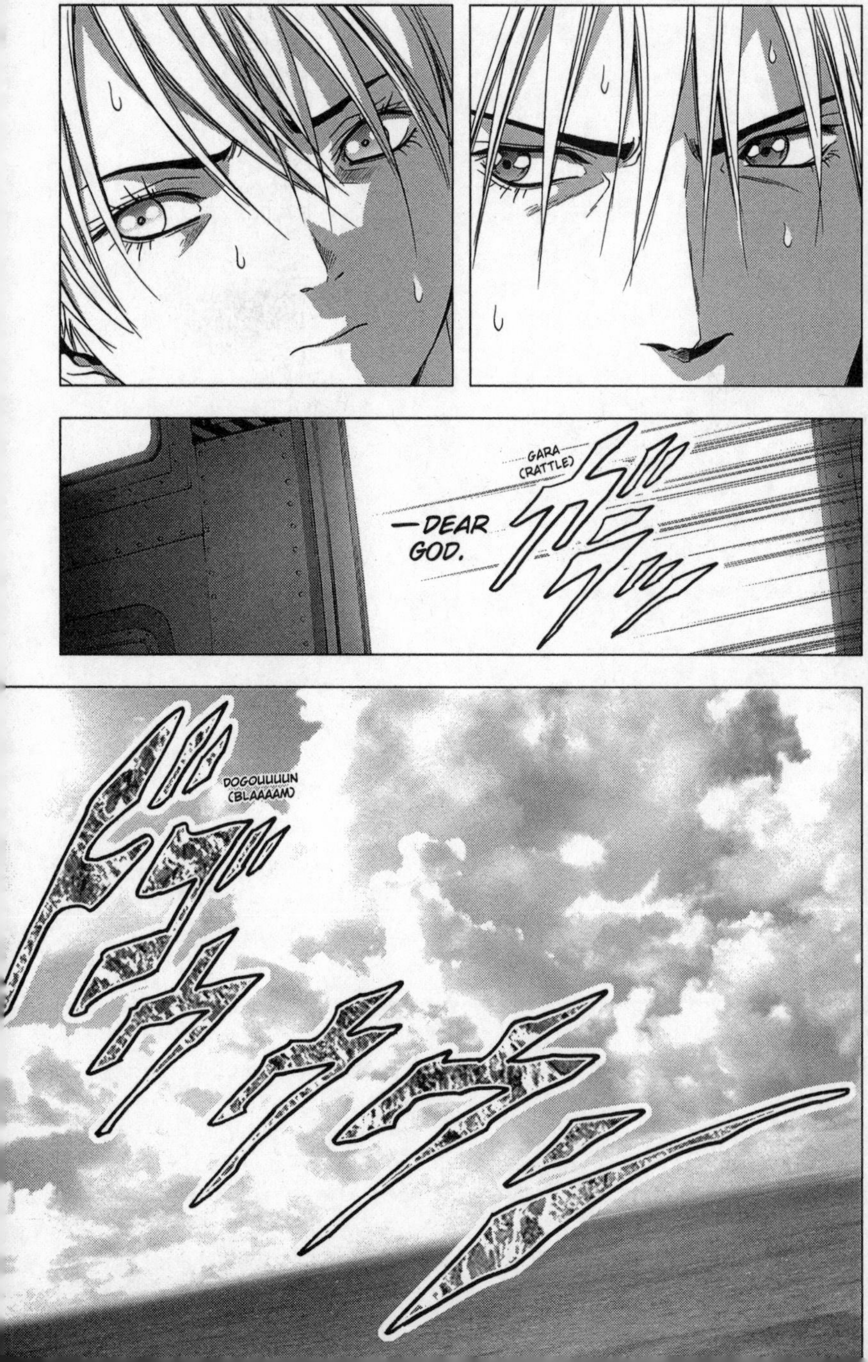
GARA (RATTLE)
—DEAR GOD.
DOGOUUUUN (BLAAAAM)

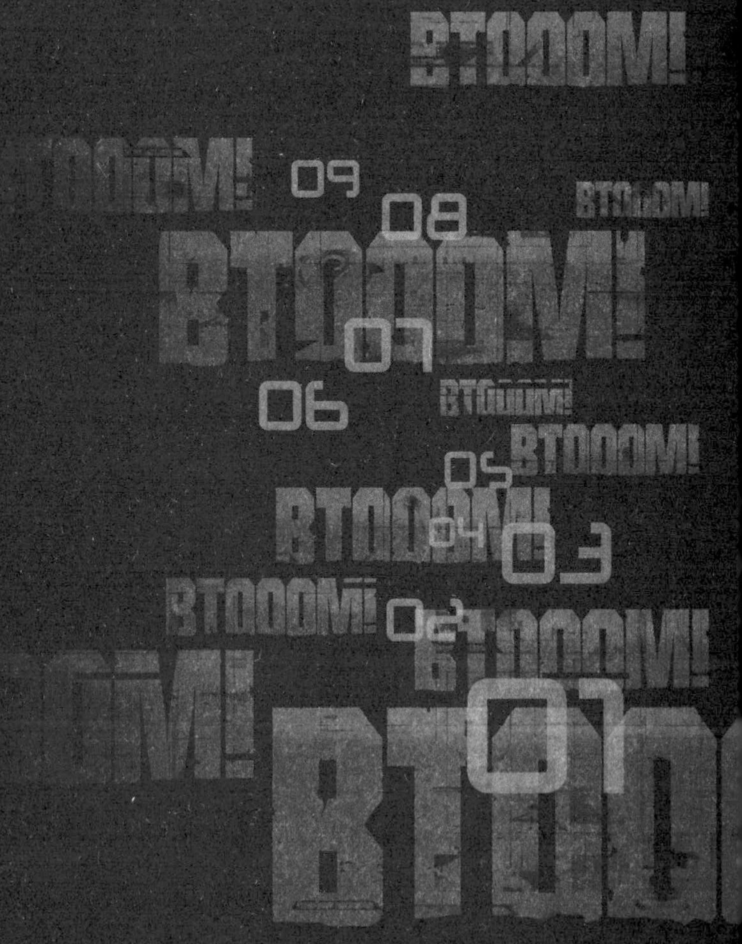
BTOOOM!
09
08
BTOOOM!
07
06
BTOOOM!
05
BTOOOM!
04
03
BTOOOM!
02
BTOOOM!
01

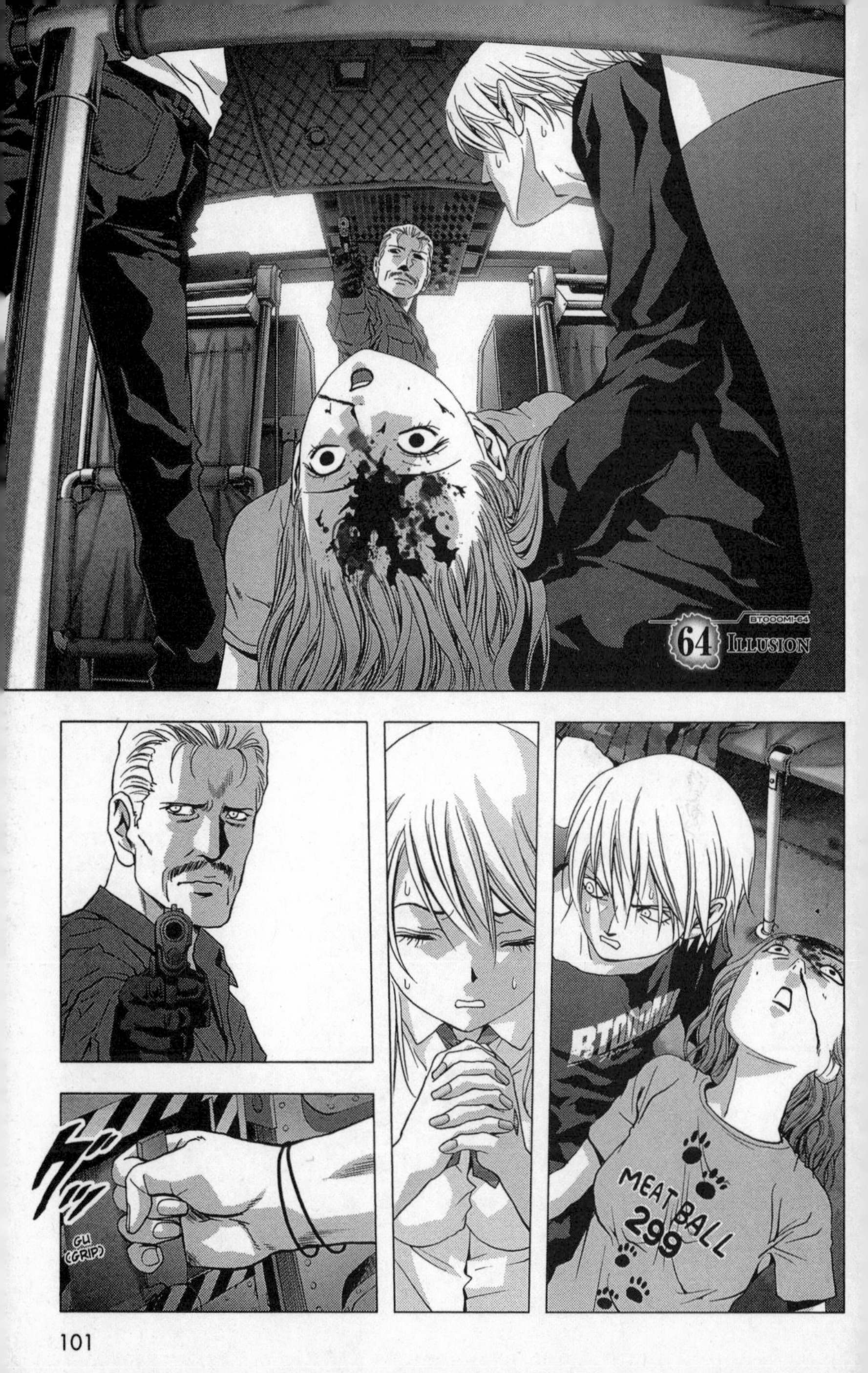
BTOOOM!-64
64 ILLUSION
MEAT BALL 299
GU (GRIP)

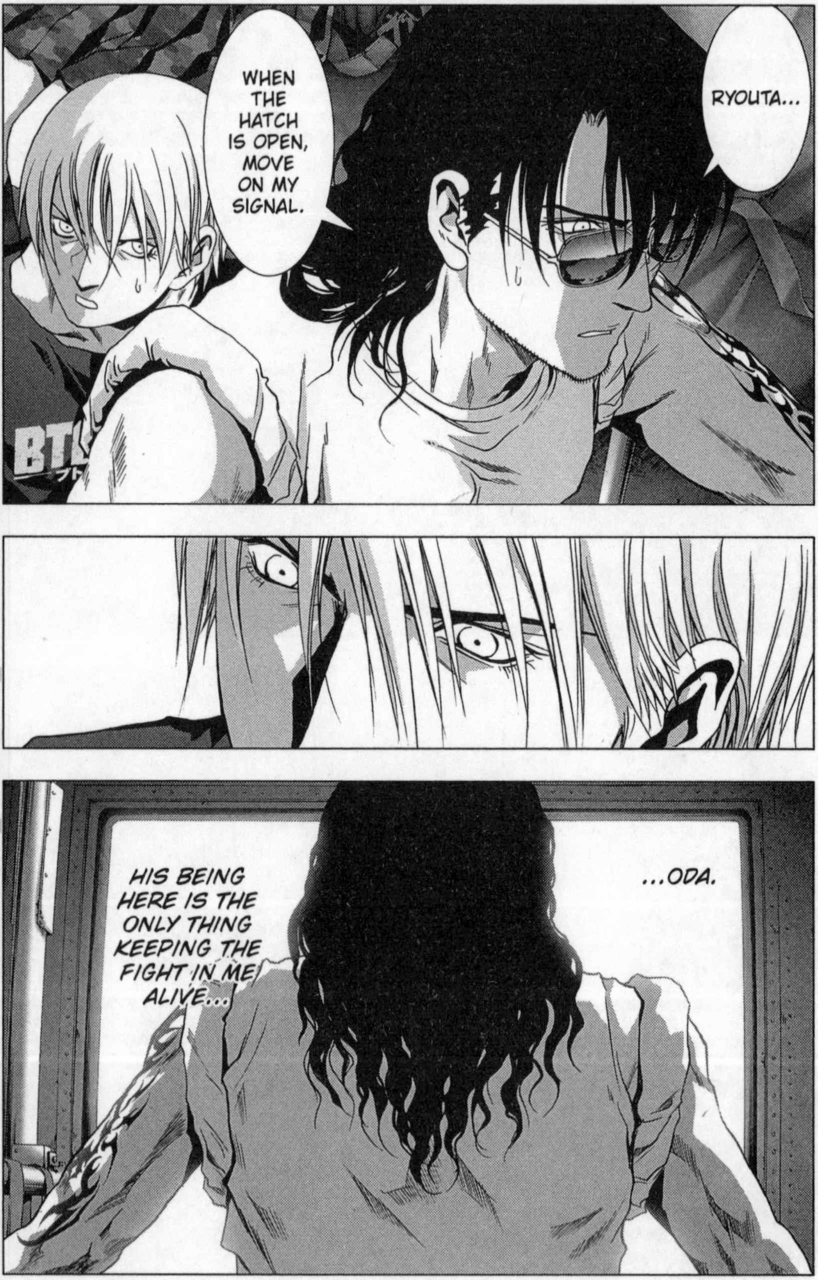
RYOUTA...
WHEN THE HATCH IS OPEN, MOVE ON MY SIGNAL.
...ODA.
HIS BEING HERE IS THE ONLY THING KEEPING THE FIGHT IN ME ALIVE...

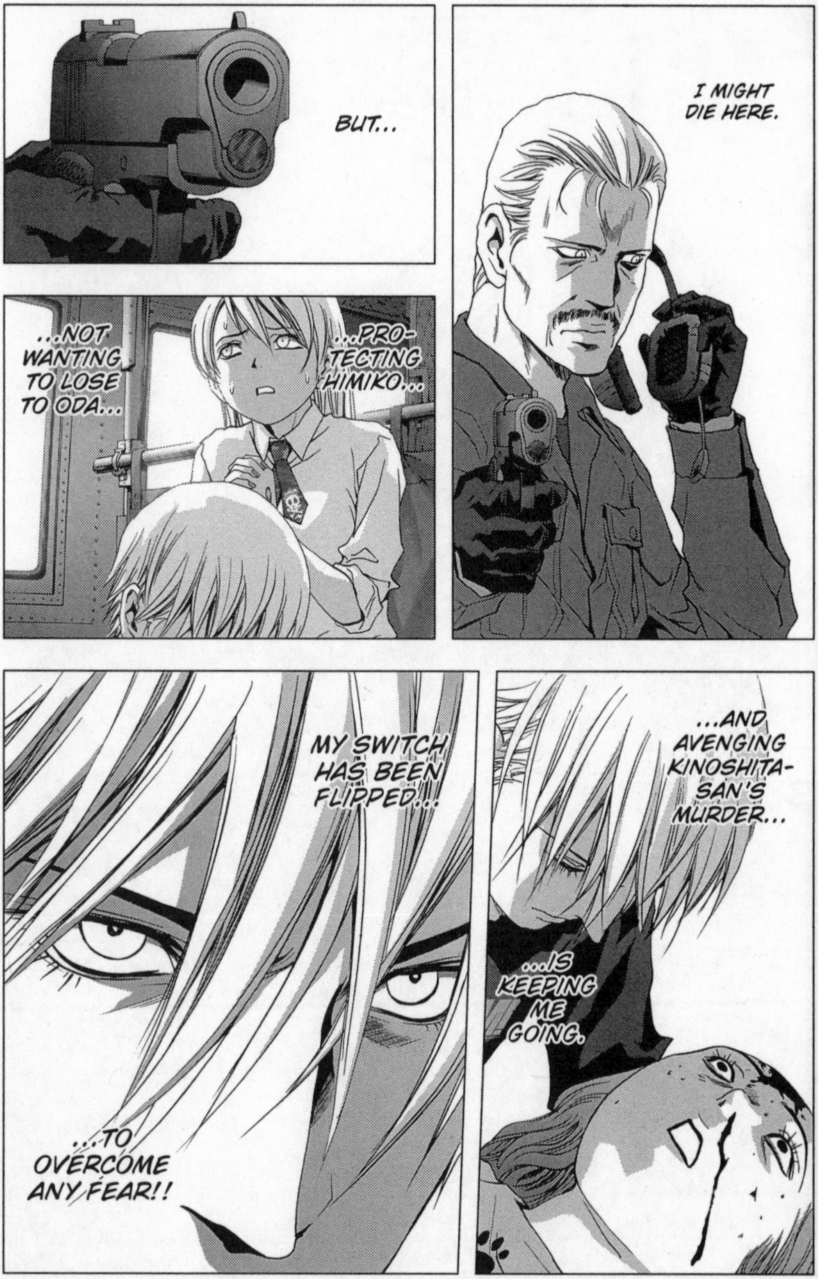
I MIGHT DIE HERE.
BUT...
...PRO-TECTING HIMIKO...
...NOT WANTING TO LOSE TO ODA...
...AND AVENGING KINOSHITA-SAN'S MURDER...
...IS KEEPING ME GOING.
MY SWITCH HAS BEEN FLIPPED...
...TO OVERCOME ANY FEAR!!

BTOOOM!-64

64 ILLUSION

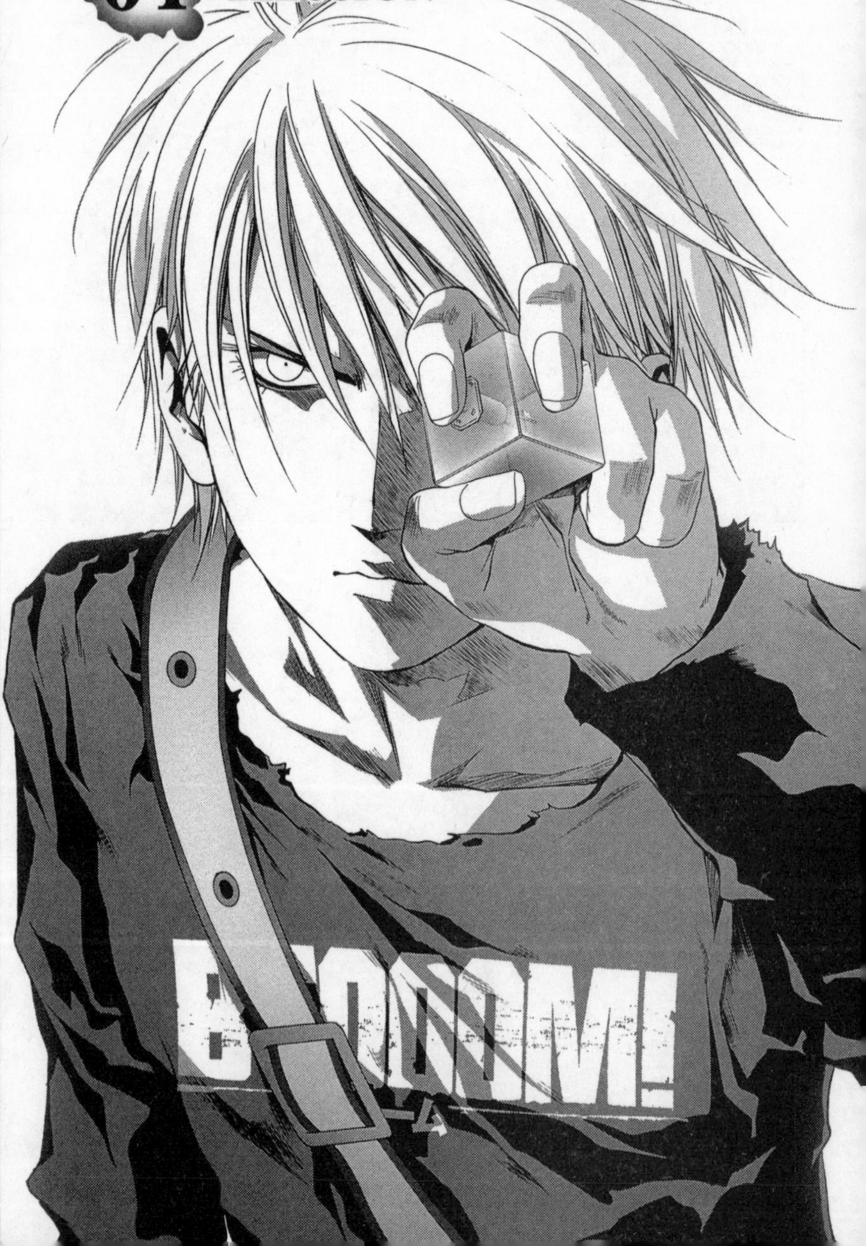

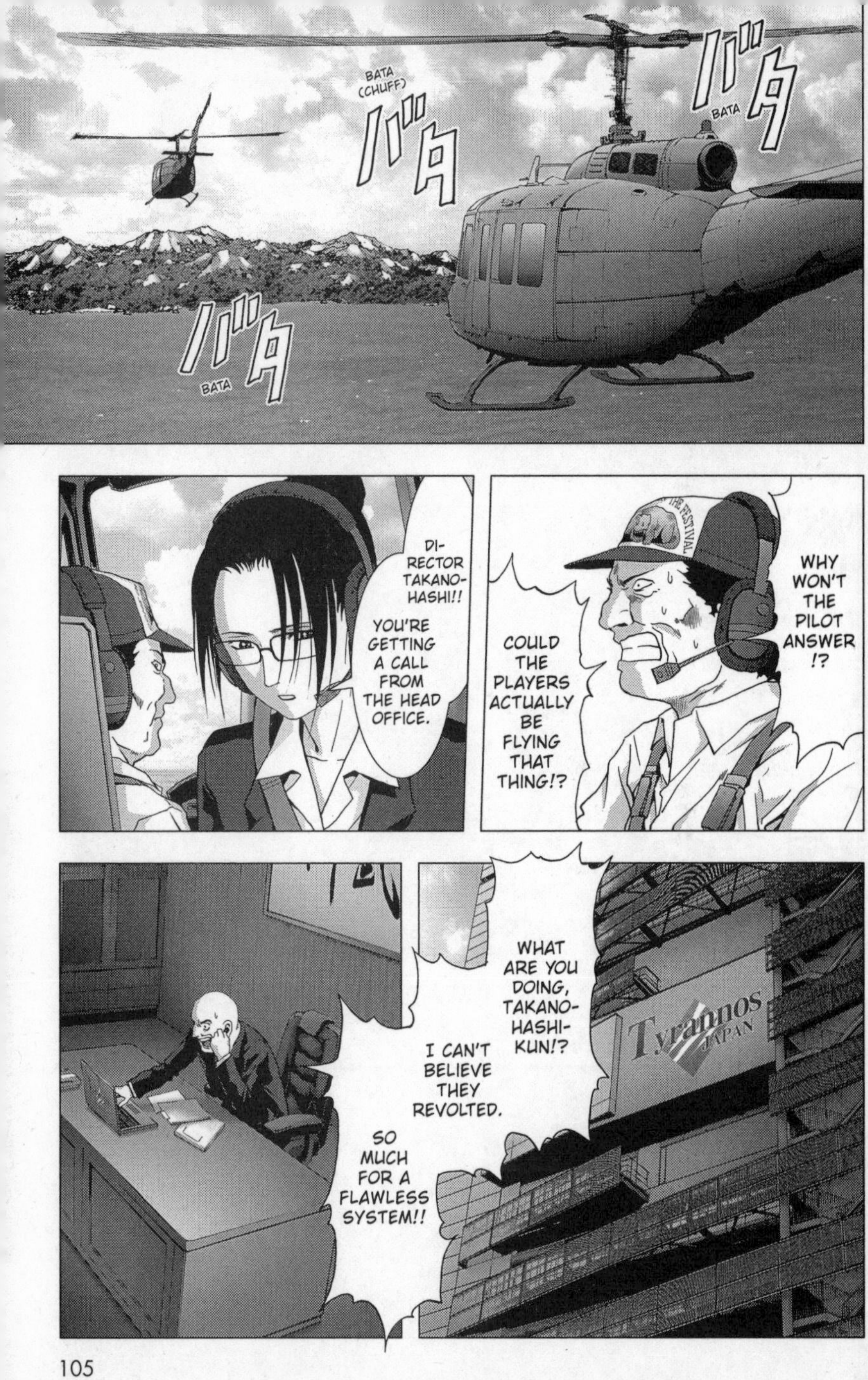
バタ
BATA
BATA (CHUFF)
バタ
バタ
BATA
WHY WON'T THE PILOT ANSWER!?
COULD THE PLAYERS ACTUALLY BE FLYING THAT THING!?
DI-RECTOR TAKANO-HASHI!!
YOU'RE GETTING A CALL FROM THE HEAD OFFICE.
Tyrannos JAPAN
WHAT ARE YOU DOING, TAKANO-HASHI-KUN!?
I CAN'T BELIEVE THEY REVOLTED.
SO MUCH FOR A FLAWLESS SYSTEM!!

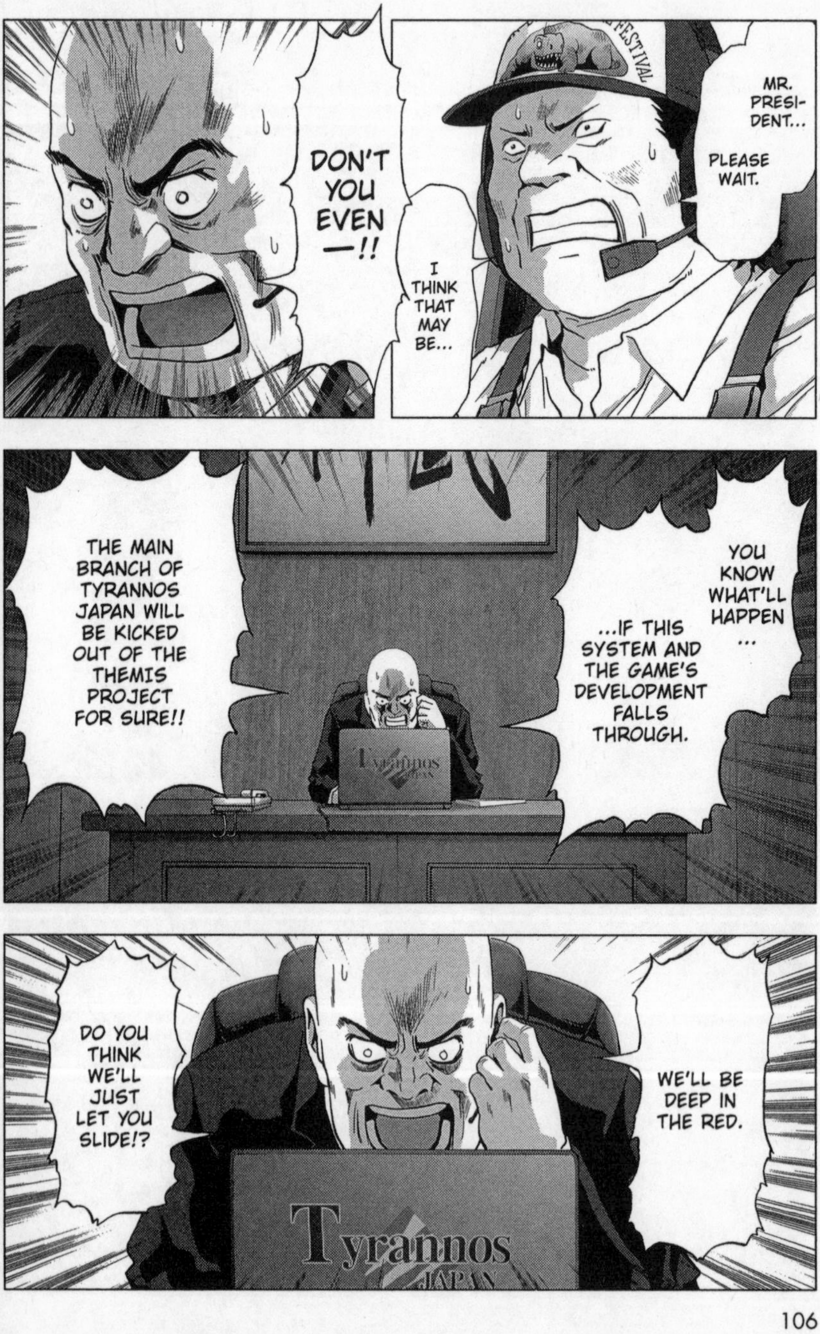
FESTIVAL
MR. PRESIDENT...
PLEASE WAIT.
I THINK THAT MAY BE...
DON'T YOU EVEN—!!
YOU KNOW WHAT'LL HAPPEN...
...IF THIS SYSTEM AND THE GAME'S DEVELOPMENT FALLS THROUGH.
THE MAIN BRANCH OF TYRANNOS JAPAN WILL BE KICKED OUT OF THE THEMIS PROJECT FOR SURE!!
WE'LL BE DEEP IN THE RED.
DO YOU THINK WE'LL JUST LET YOU SLIDE!?
Tyrannos
JAPAN

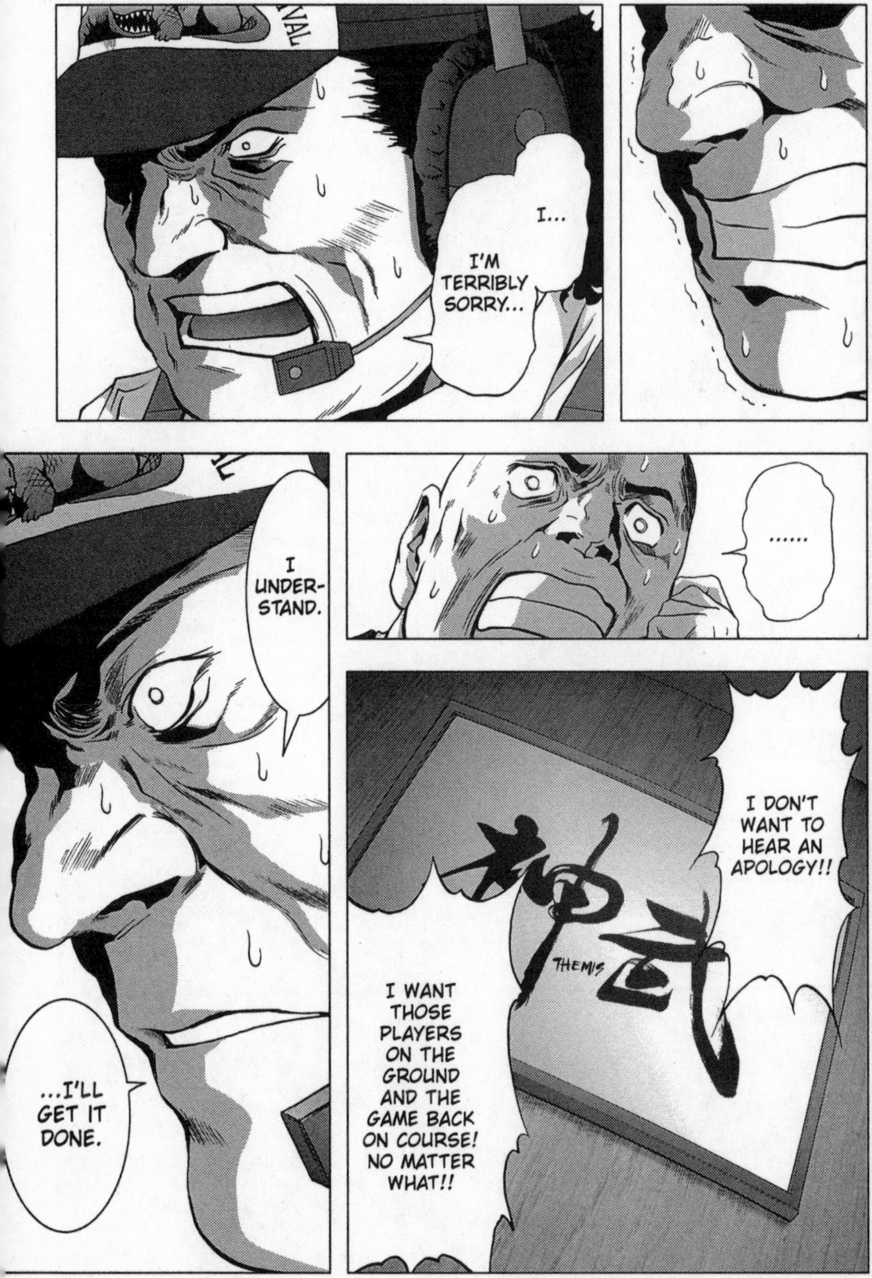
I...
I'M TERRIBLY SORRY...
......
I DON'T WANT TO HEAR AN APOLOGY!!
THEMIS
I WANT THOSE PLAYERS ON THE GROUND AND THE GAME BACK ON COURSE! NO MATTER WHAT!!
I UNDERSTAND.
...I'LL GET IT DONE.

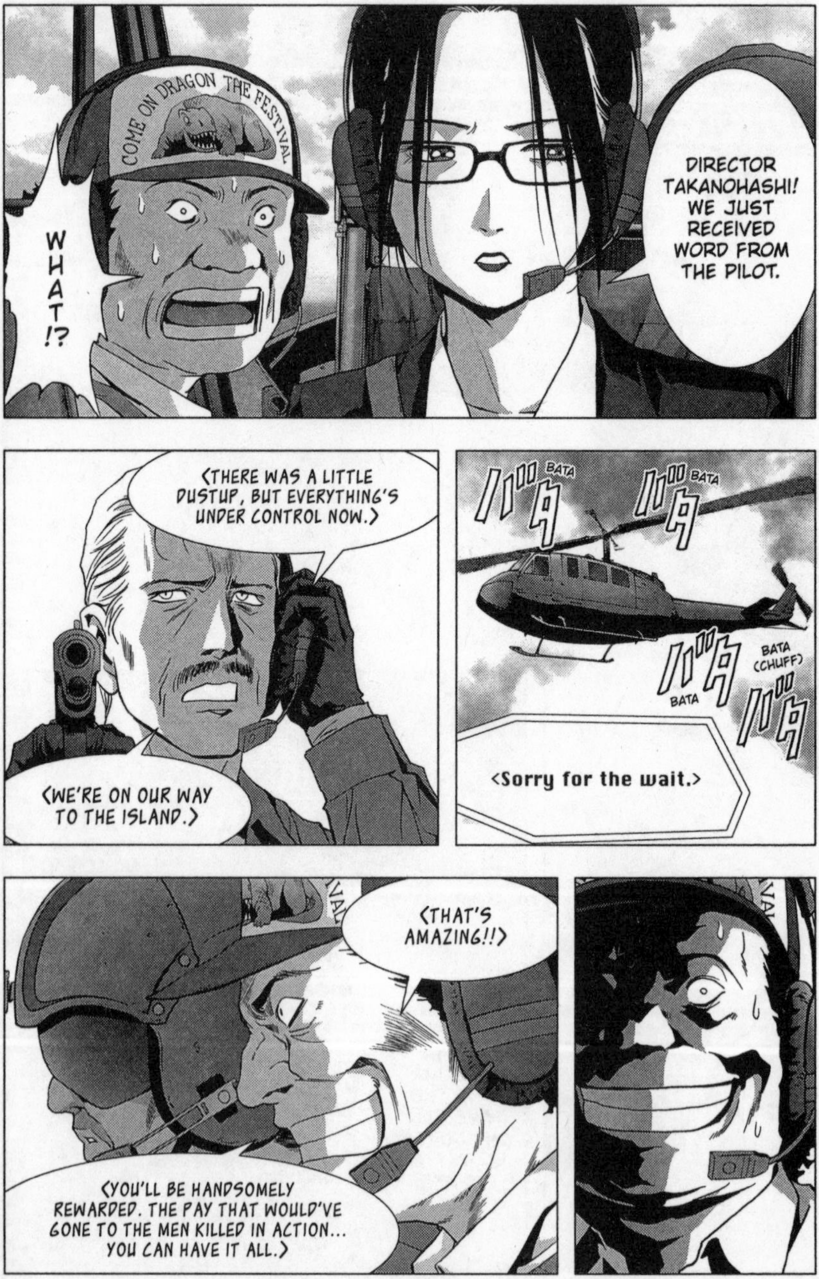
DIRECTOR TAKANOHASHI! WE JUST RECEIVED WORD FROM THE PILOT.
COME ON DRAGON THE FESTIVAL
WHAT!?
バタ BATA
バタ BATA
バタ BATA
バタ (CHUFF)
<Sorry for the wait.>
<THERE WAS A LITTLE DUSTUP, BUT EVERYTHING'S UNDER CONTROL NOW.>
<WE'RE ON OUR WAY TO THE ISLAND.>
<THAT'S AMAZING!!>
<YOU'LL BE HANDSOMELY REWARDED. THE PAY THAT WOULD'VE GONE TO THE MEN KILLED IN ACTION... YOU CAN HAVE IT ALL.>

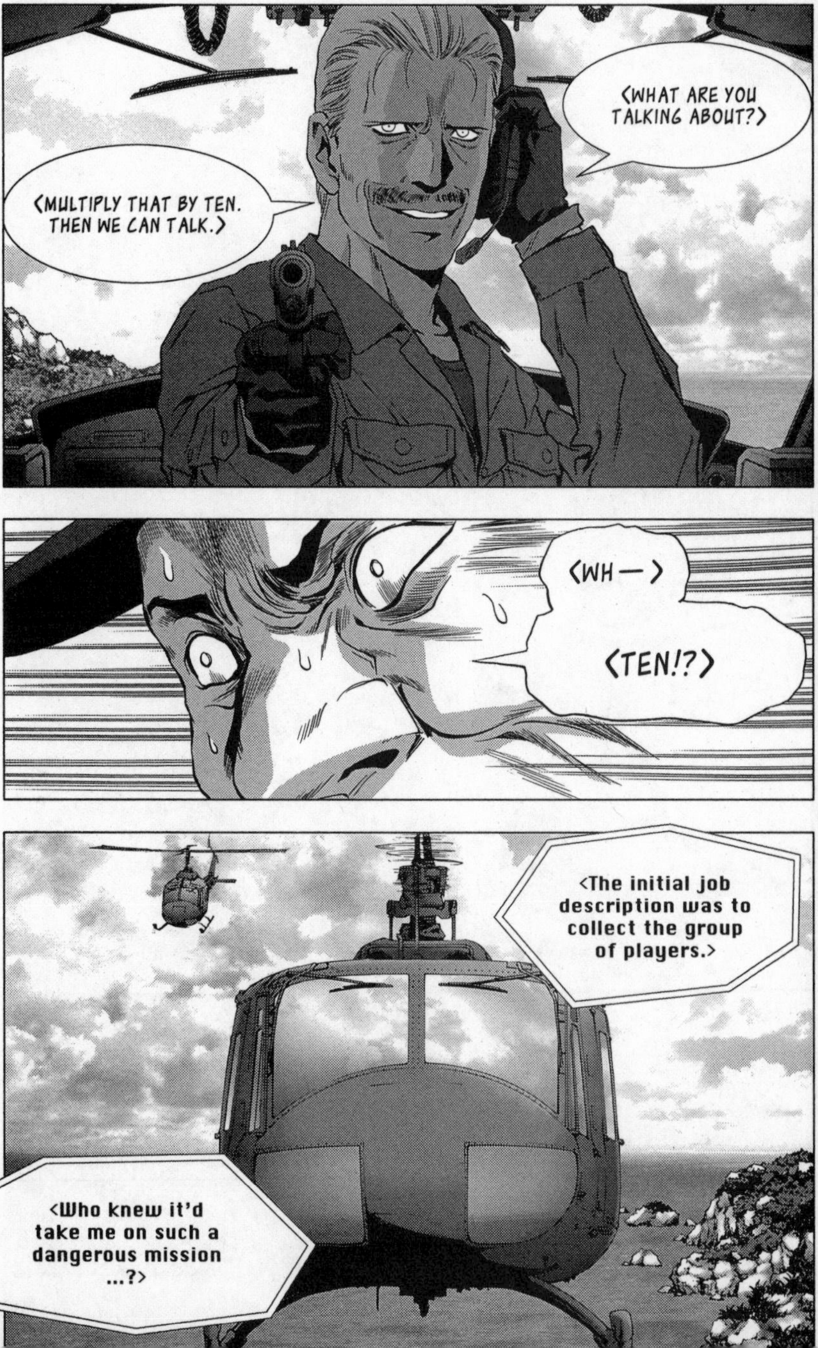
<WHAT ARE YOU TALKING ABOUT?>
<MULTIPLY THAT BY TEN. THEN WE CAN TALK.>
<WH—>
<TEN!?>
<The initial job description was to collect the group of players.>
<Who knew it'd take me on such a dangerous mission ...?>

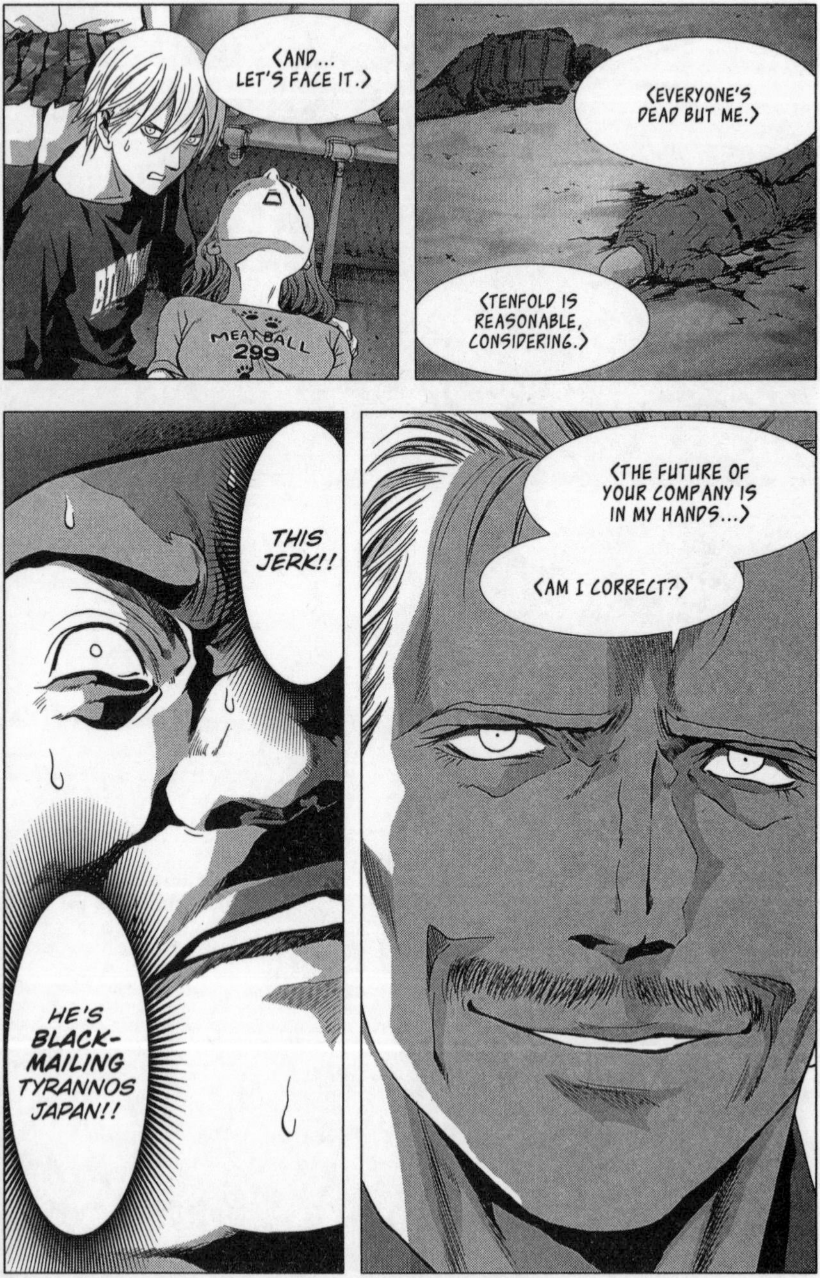
〈EVERYONE'S DEAD BUT ME.〉
〈TENFOLD IS REASONABLE, CONSIDERING.〉
〈AND... LET'S FACE IT.〉
MEATBALL 299
〈THE FUTURE OF YOUR COMPANY IS IN MY HANDS...〉
〈AM I CORRECT?〉
THIS JERK!!
HE'S BLACK-MAILING TYRANNOS JAPAN!!

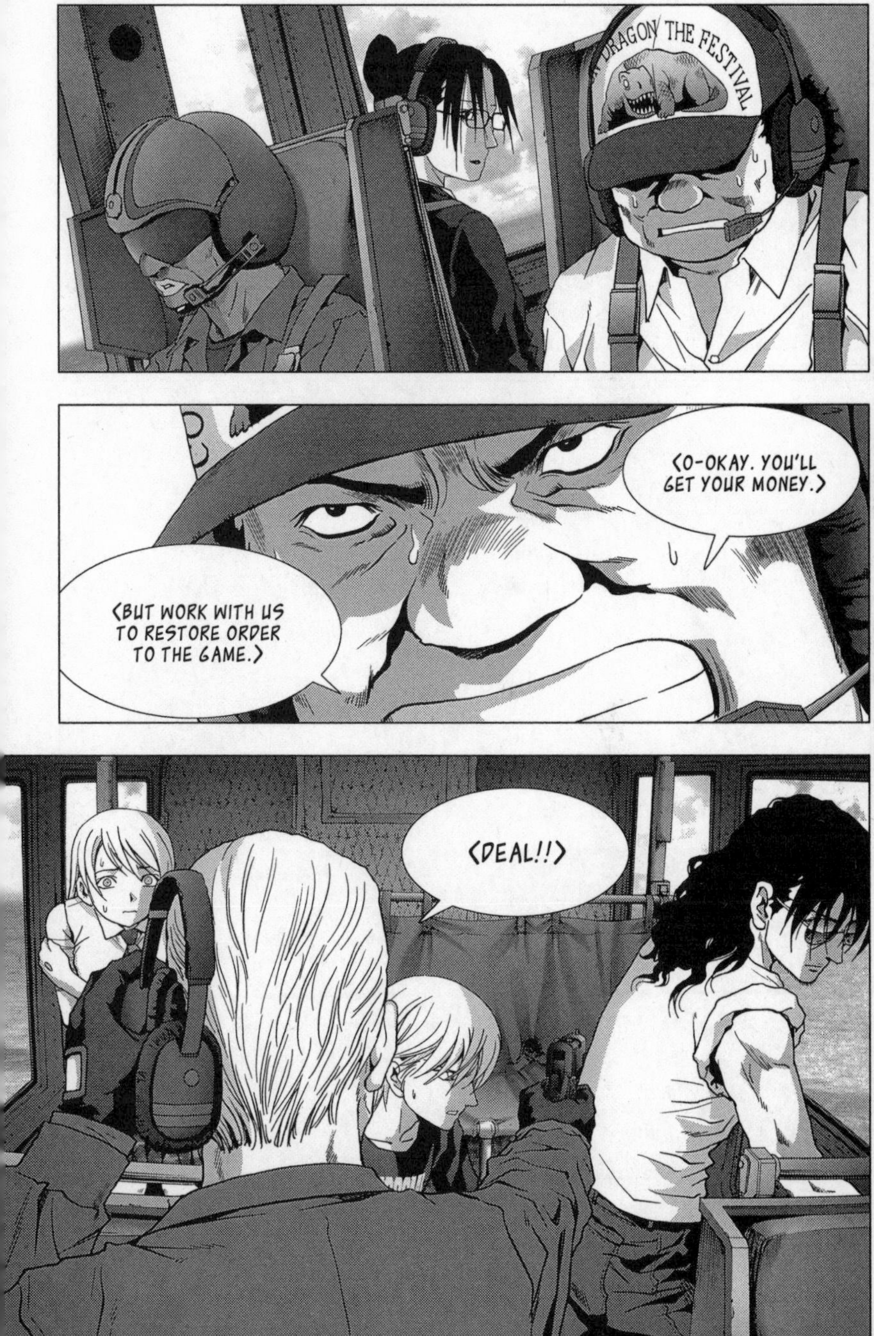
DRAGON THE FESTIVAL
<O-OKAY. YOU'LL GET YOUR MONEY.>
<BUT WORK WITH US TO RESTORE ORDER TO THE GAME.>
<DEAL!!>

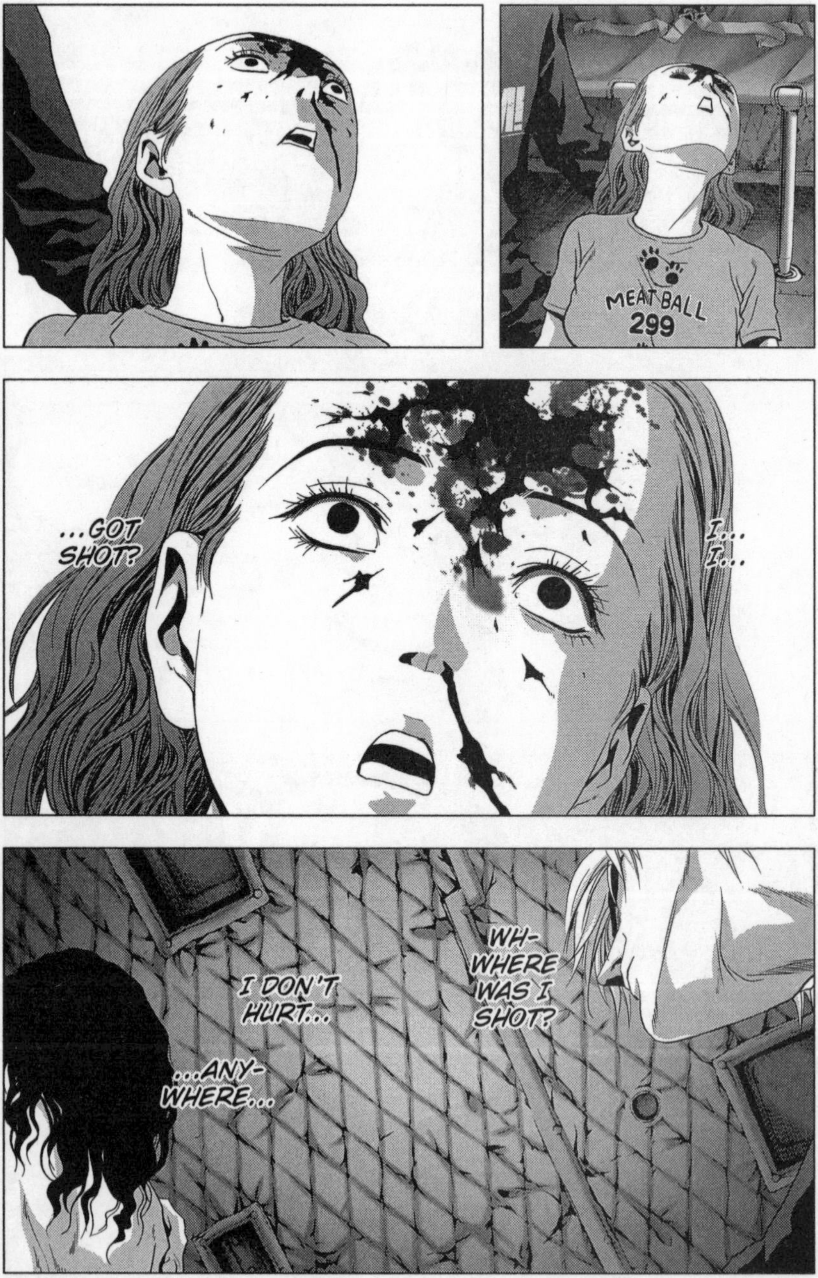
MEAT BALL
299
I...
I...
...GOT
SHOT?
WH-
WHERE
WAS I
SHOT?
I DON'T
HURT...
...ANY-
WHERE...

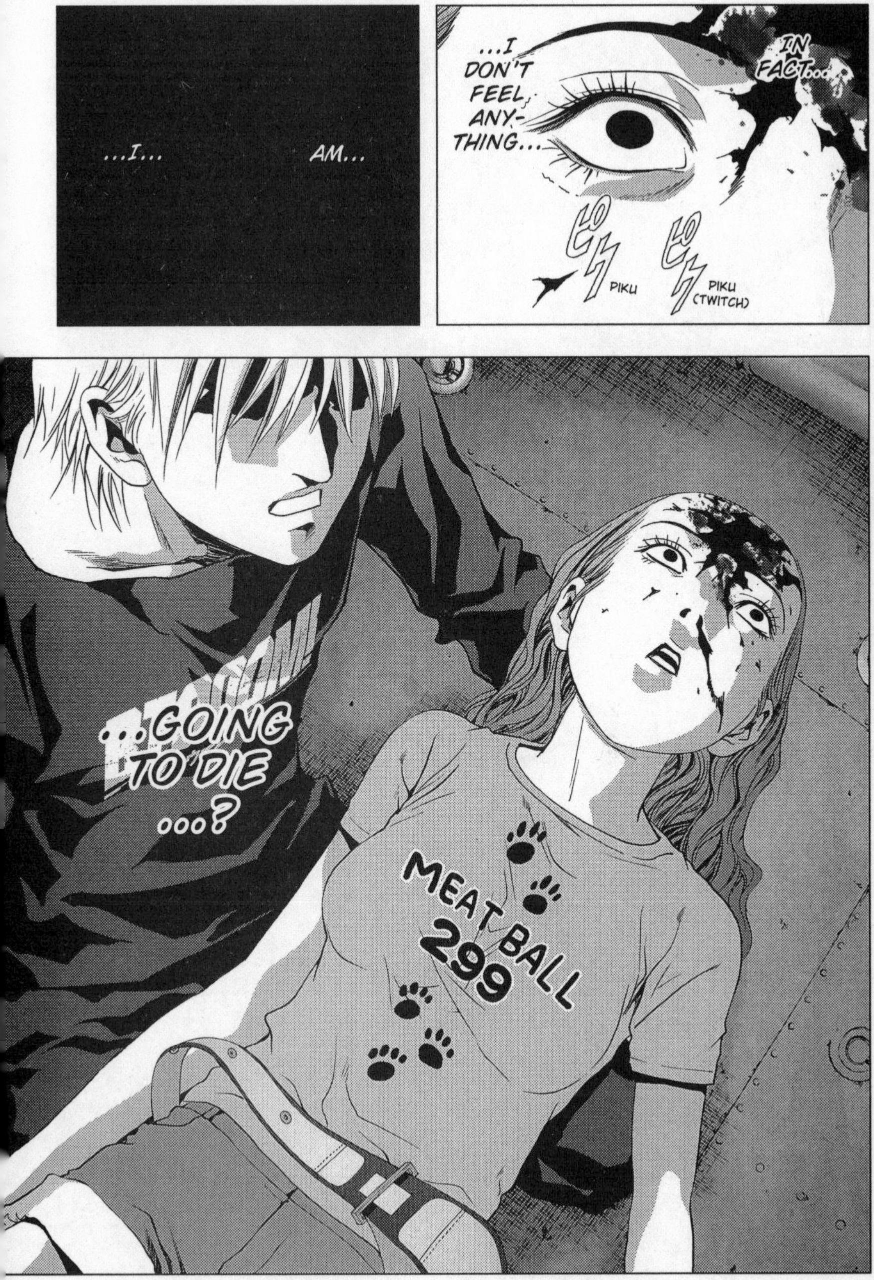
IN FACT...
...I DON'T FEEL ANY-THING...
PIKU
PIKU (TWITCH)
...I...
AM...
...GOING TO DIE...?
MEAT BALL 299

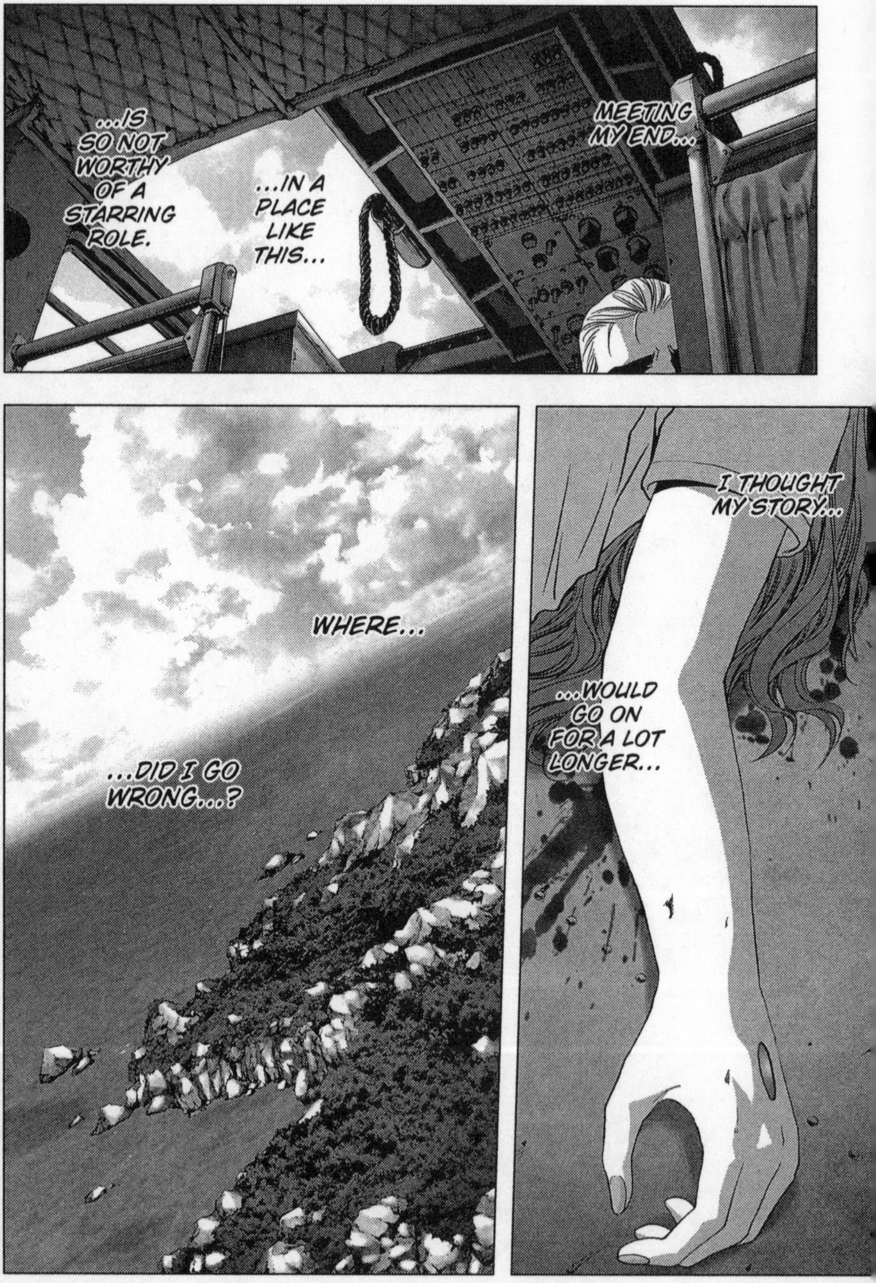
MEETING MY END...
...IN A PLACE LIKE THIS...
...IS SO NOT WORTHY OF A STARRING ROLE.
I THOUGHT MY STORY...
...WOULD GO ON FOR A LOT LONGER...
WHERE...
...DID I GO WRONG...?

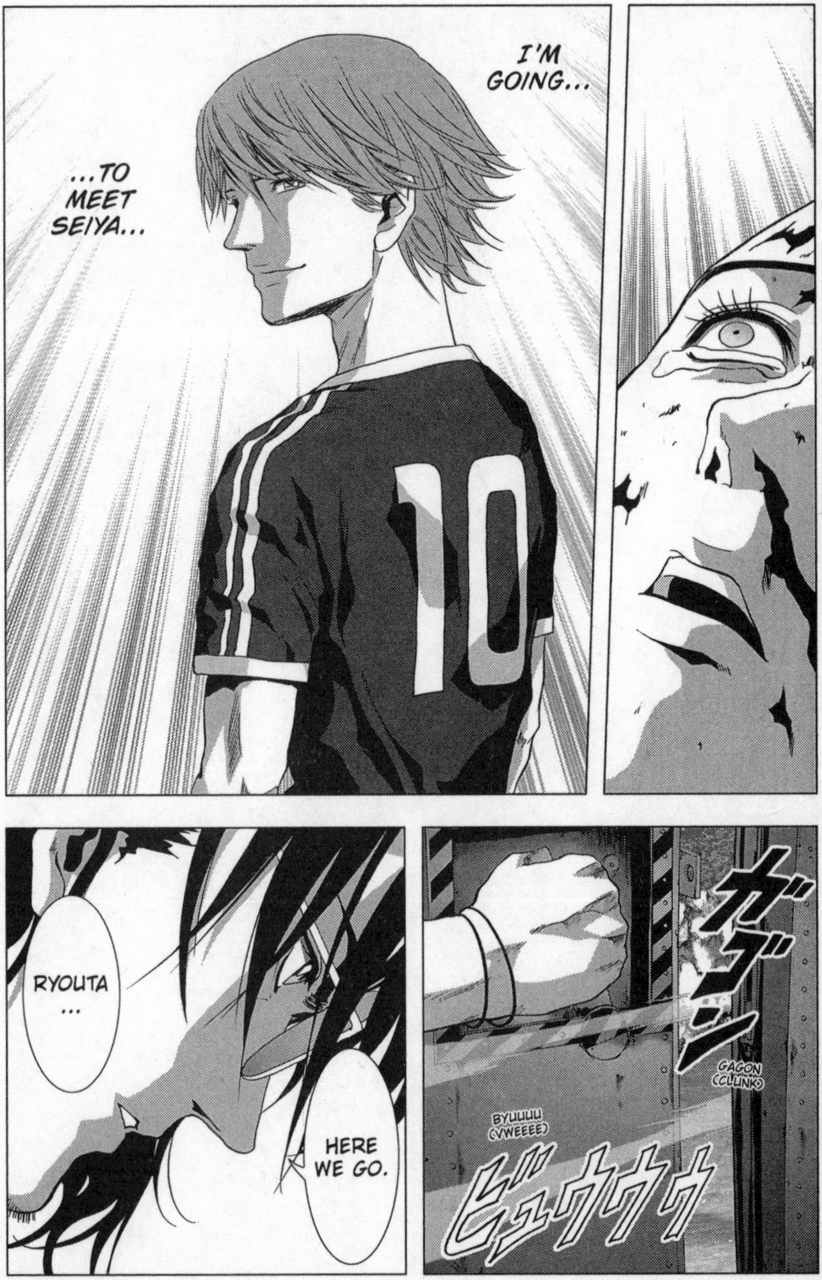
I'M GOING...
...TO MEET SEIYA...
ガゴン
GAGON (CLUNK)
BYUUUU (VWEEEE)
ビュウウウ
RYOUTA ...
HERE WE GO.

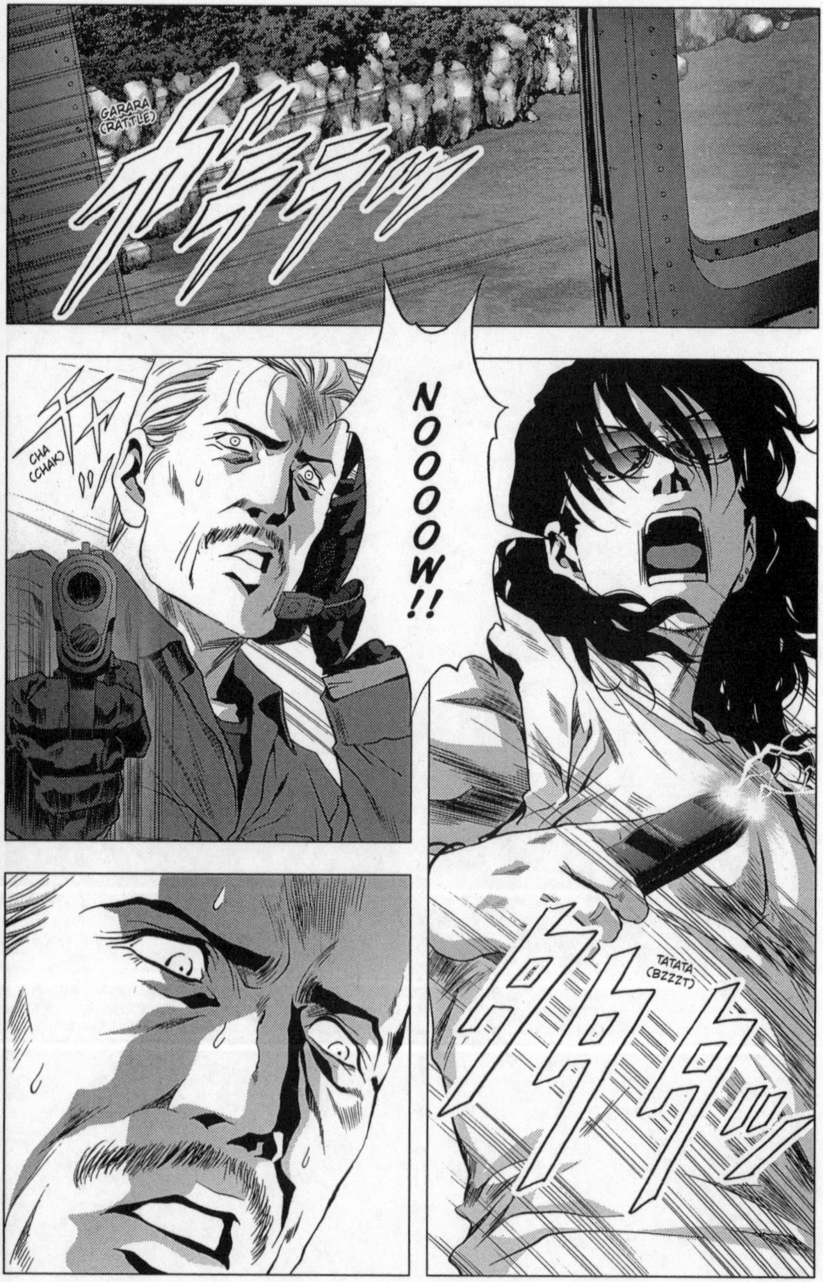
GARARA
(RATTLE)
NOOOOOW!!
CHA
(CHAK)
TATATA
(BZZZT)

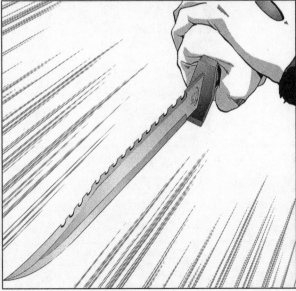

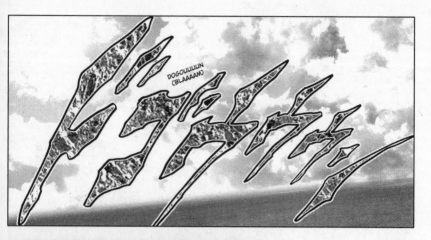

DOGOUUUUN
(BLAAAAM)

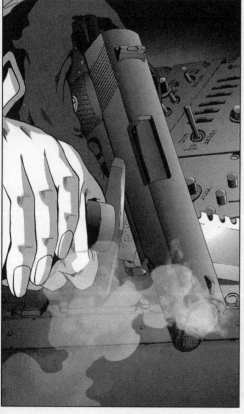

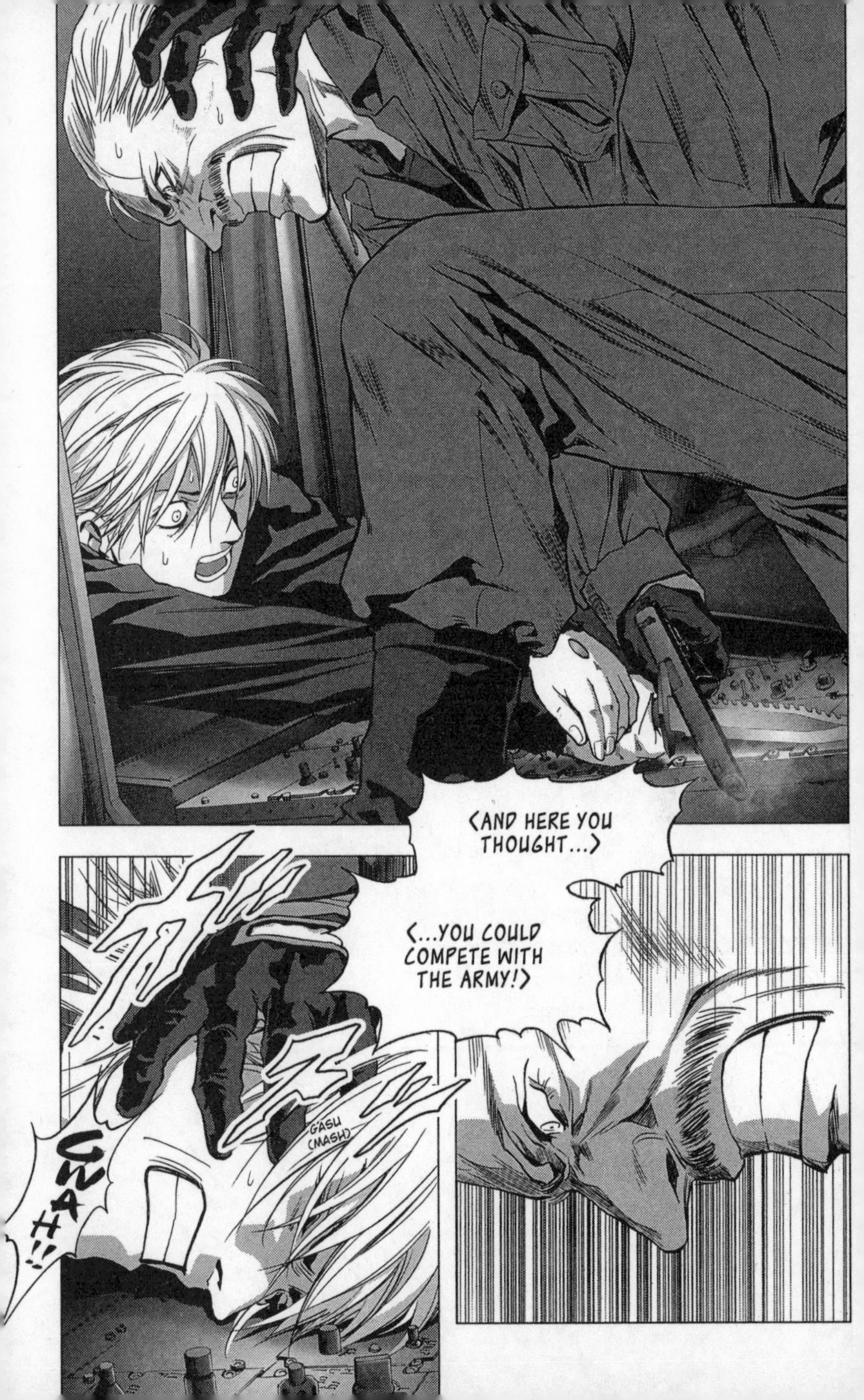

<AND HERE YOU THOUGHT...>
<...YOU COULD COMPETE WITH THE ARMY!>
GASU (MASH)
GWAH!!

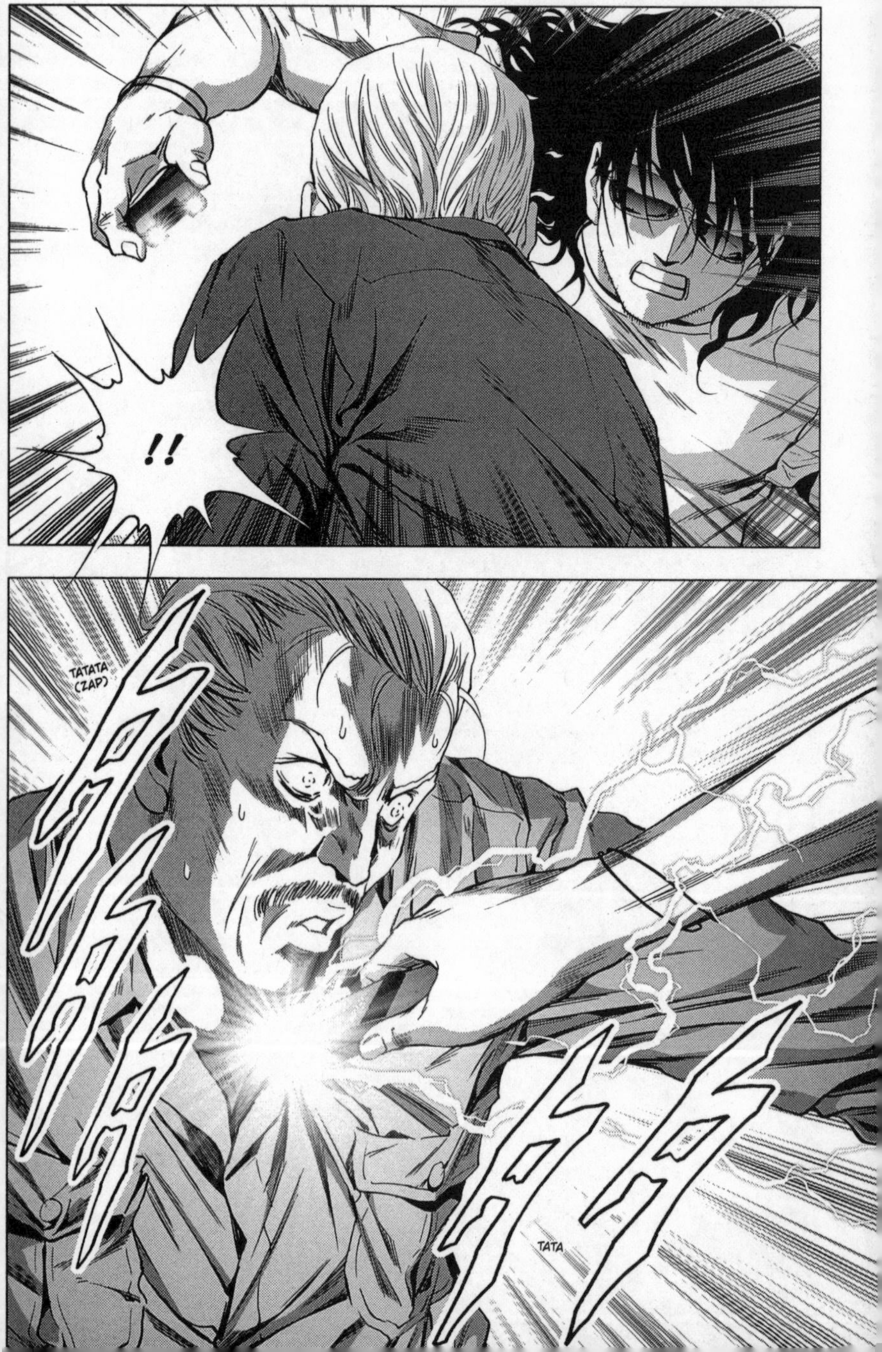
!!
TATATA
(ZAP)
TATA

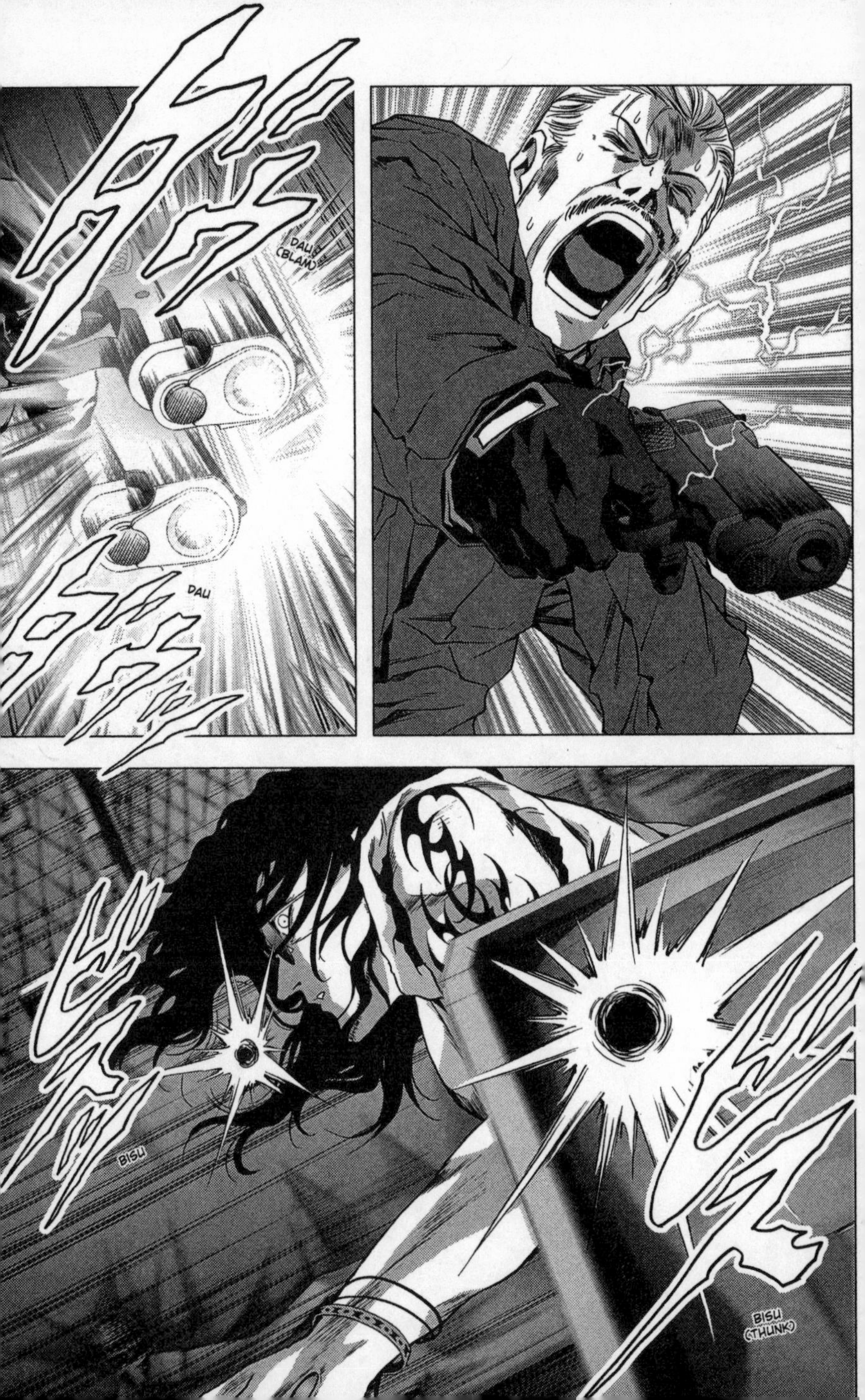
DAU (BLAM)
DAU
BISU (THUNK)
BISU

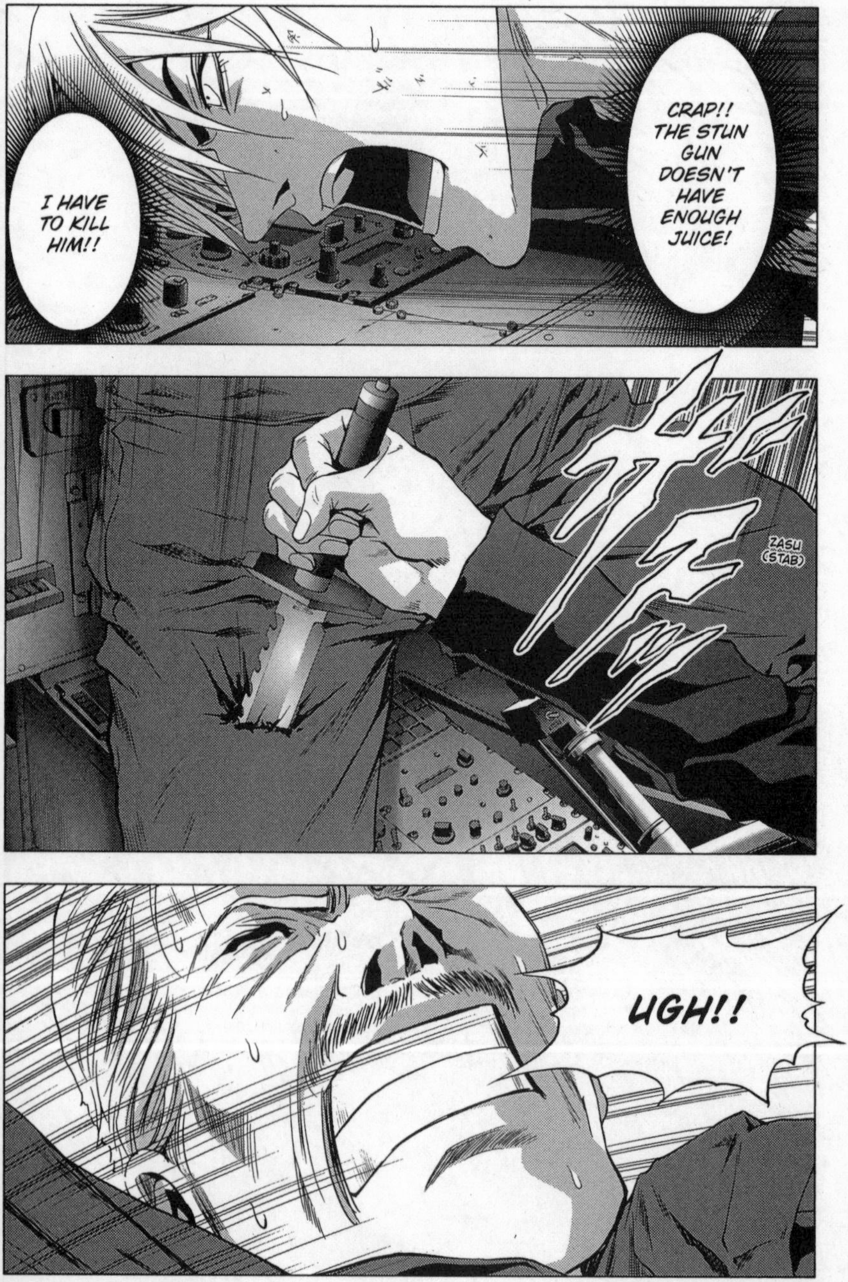
CRAP!! THE STUN GUN DOESN'T HAVE ENOUGH JUICE!
I HAVE TO KILL HIM!!
ZASU (STAB)
UGH!!

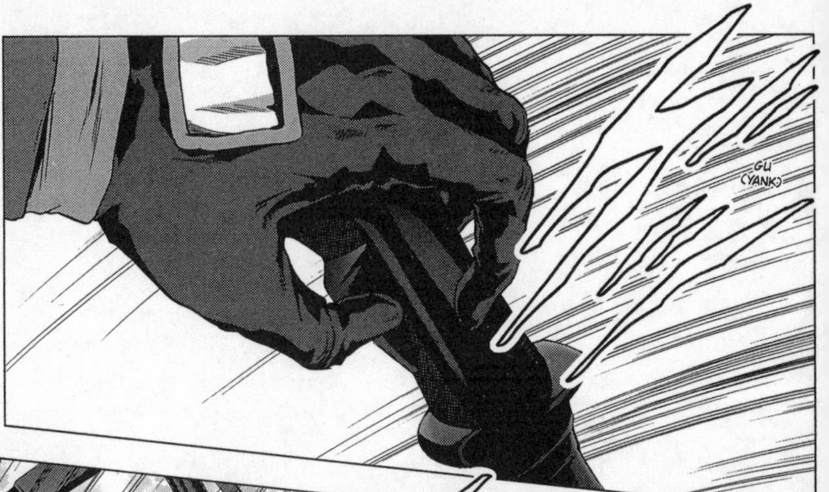
GU
(YANK)
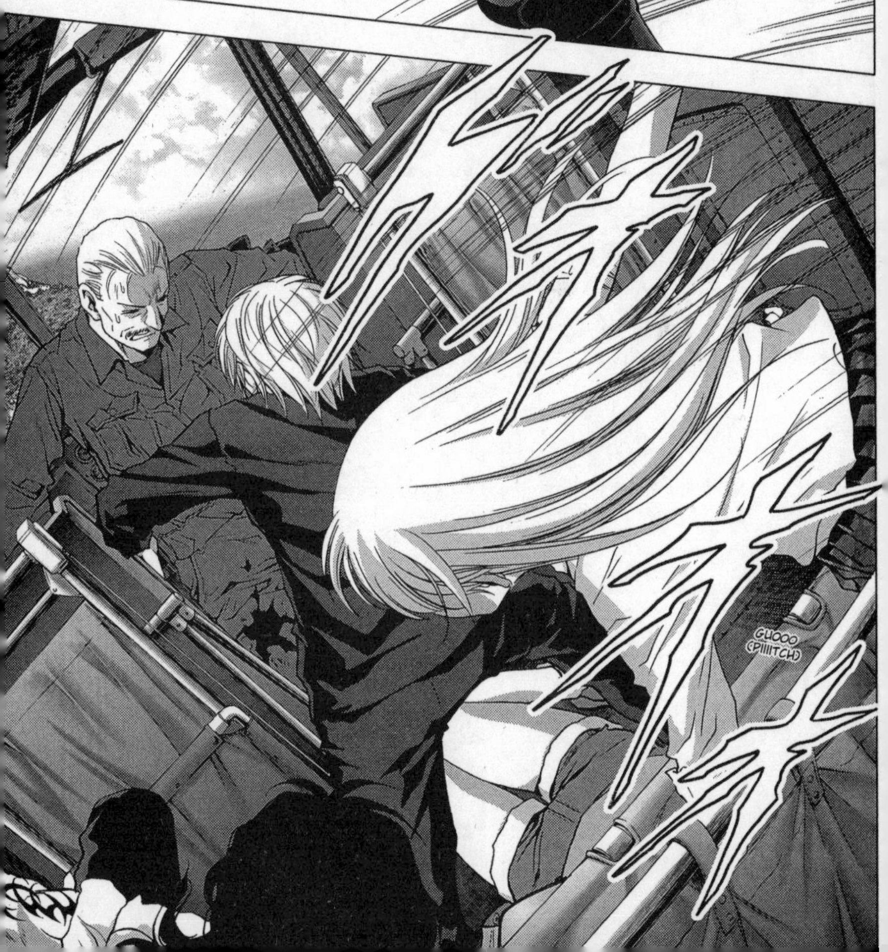
GUOOO
(PIIIITCH)

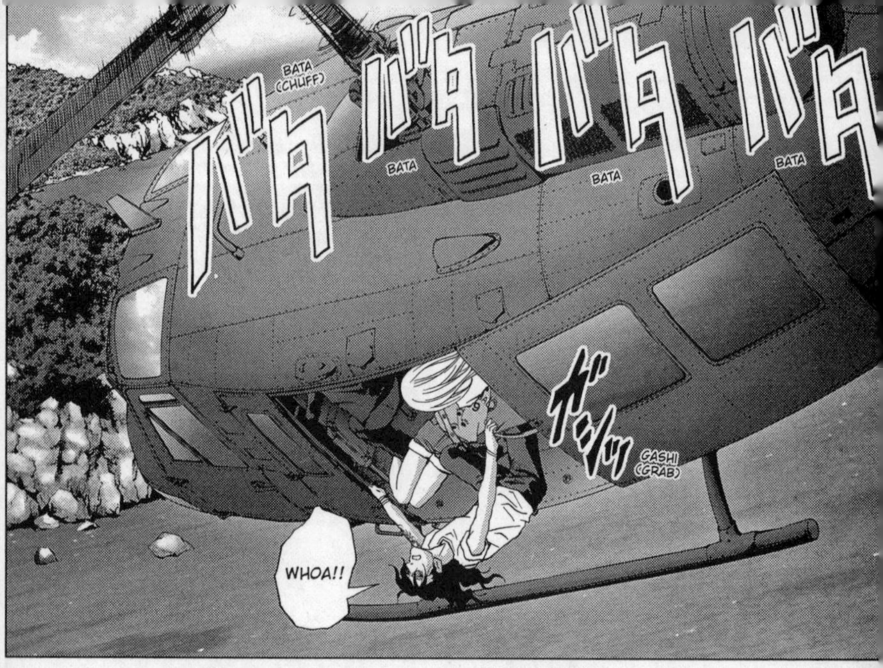
バタ
BATA
バタ
BATA
バタ
BATA
バタ
BATA (CHUFF)
ガシッ
GASHI (GRAB)
WHOA!!

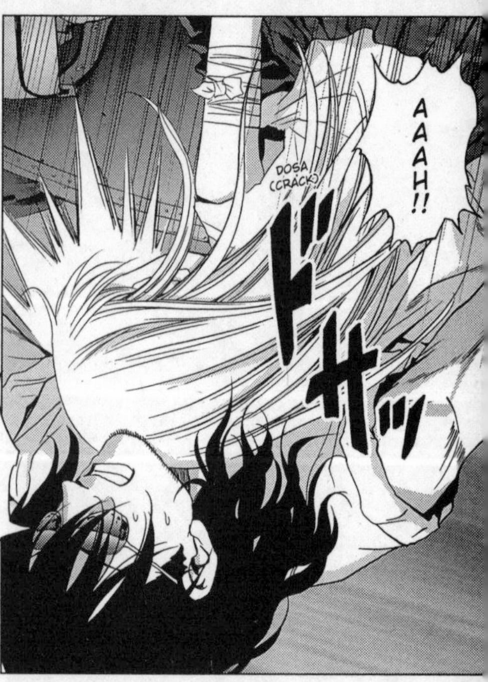
AAAAH!!
ドサッ
DOSA (CRACK)

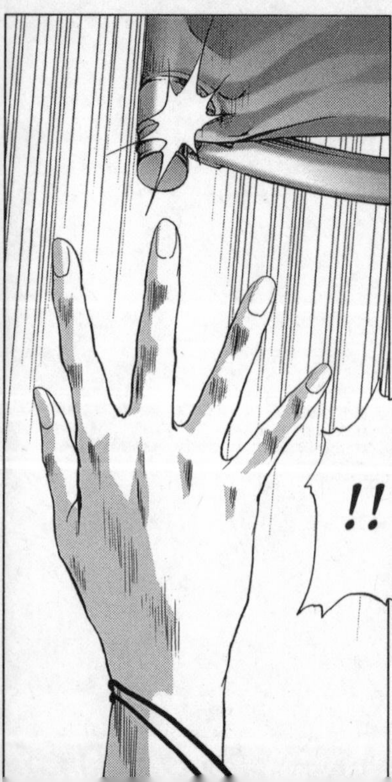
!!

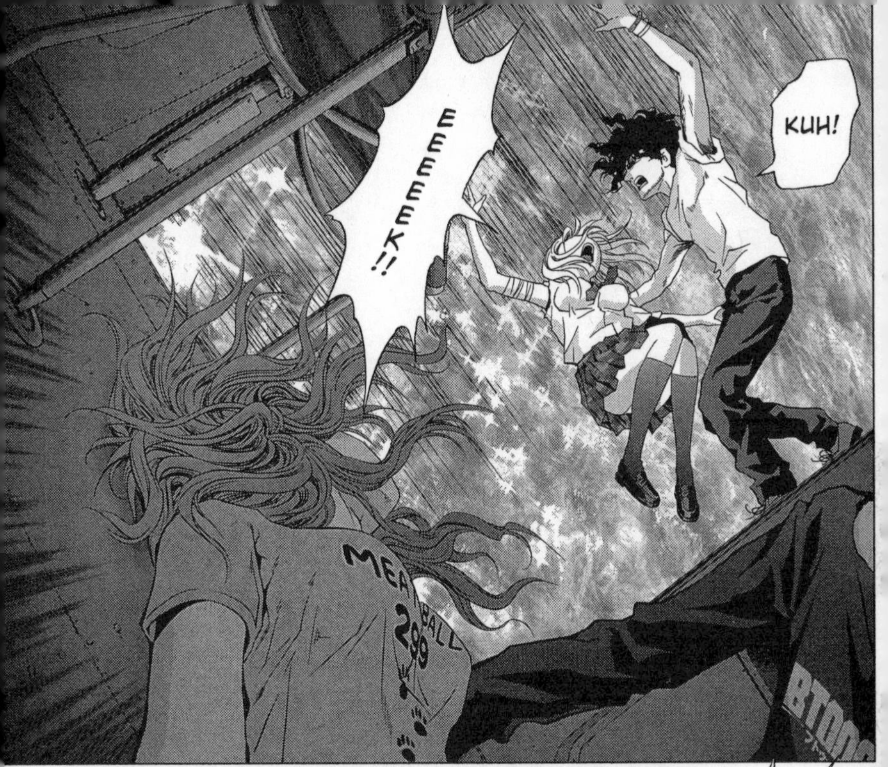
KUH!
EEEEEEK!!
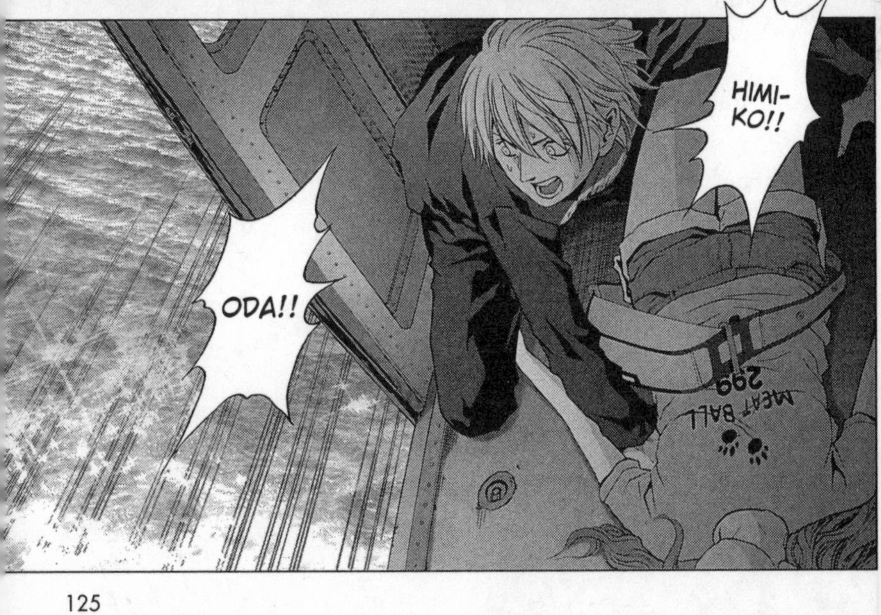
HIMI-KO!!
ODA!!

TWO FELL OUT.

WELL DONE!!

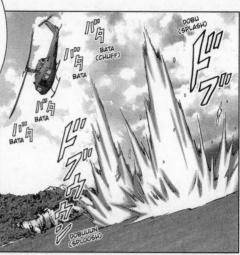

バタ
BATA

バタ
BATA

バタ
BATA

バタ
BATA

BATA
(CHUFF)

DOBU
(SPLASH)

ドブ

ドブウン

DOBUUUN
(SPLOOSH)

NOW HURRY UP AND DROP THE OTHER ONES!

バタ
BATA

バタ
BATA

バタ
BATA

バタ
BATA

グラン
GURAN
(LURCH)

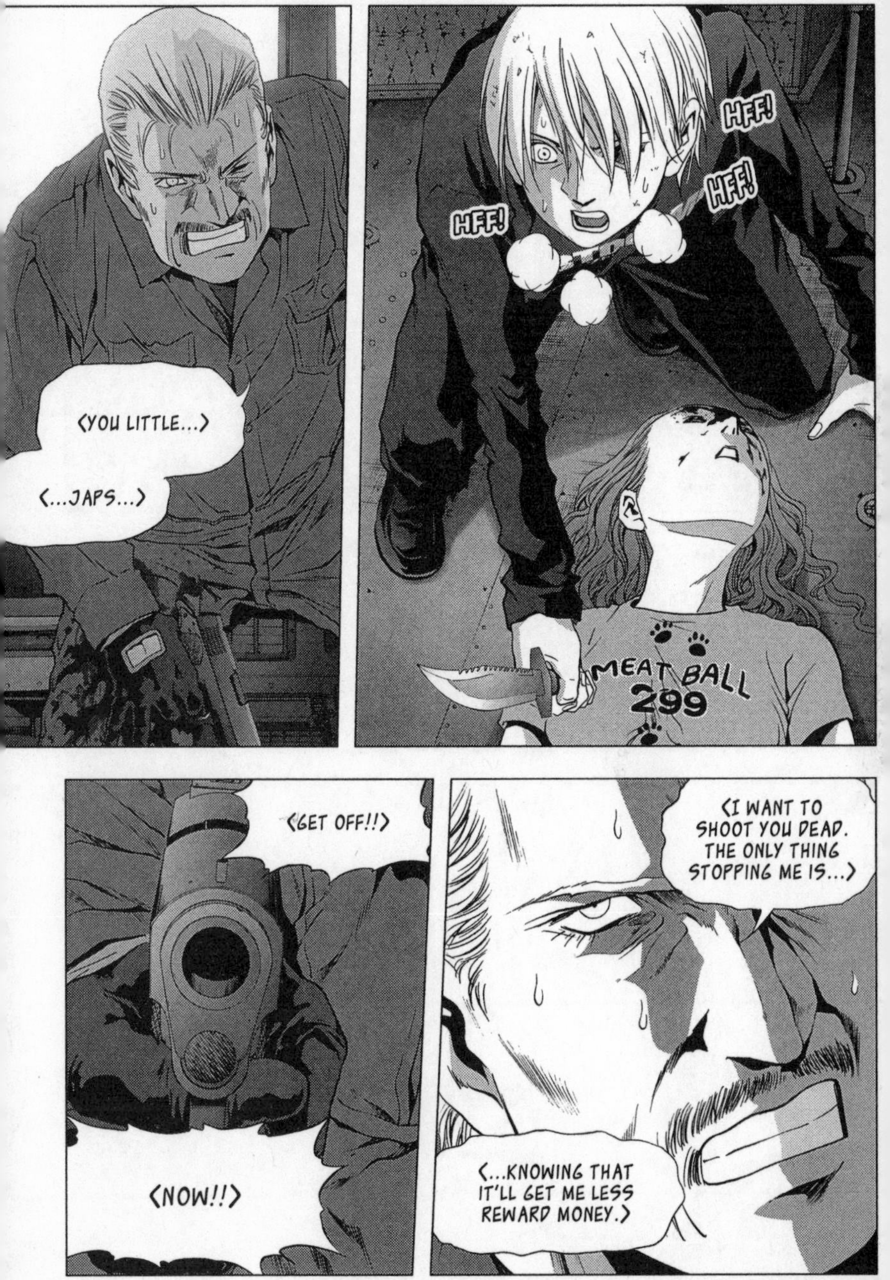
HFF!
HFF!
HFF!
MEAT BALL 299
〈YOU LITTLE...〉
〈...JAPS...〉
〈I WANT TO SHOOT YOU DEAD. THE ONLY THING STOPPING ME IS...〉
〈...KNOWING THAT IT'LL GET ME LESS REWARD MONEY.〉
〈GET OFF!!〉
〈NOW!!〉

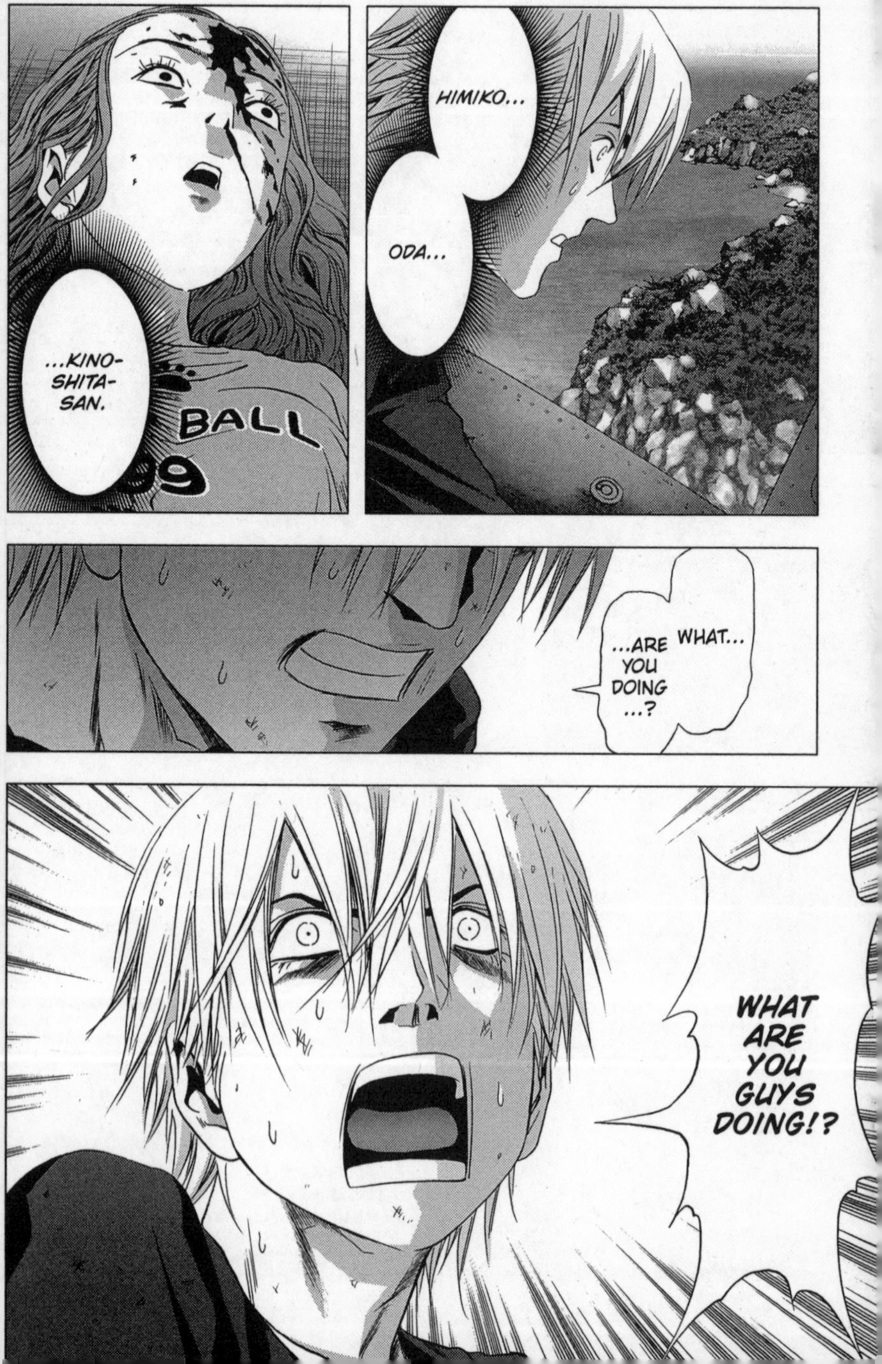

HIMIKO...
ODA...
...KINO-SHITA-SAN.
BALL
99
WHAT... ...ARE YOU DOING ...?
WHAT ARE YOU GUYS DOING!?

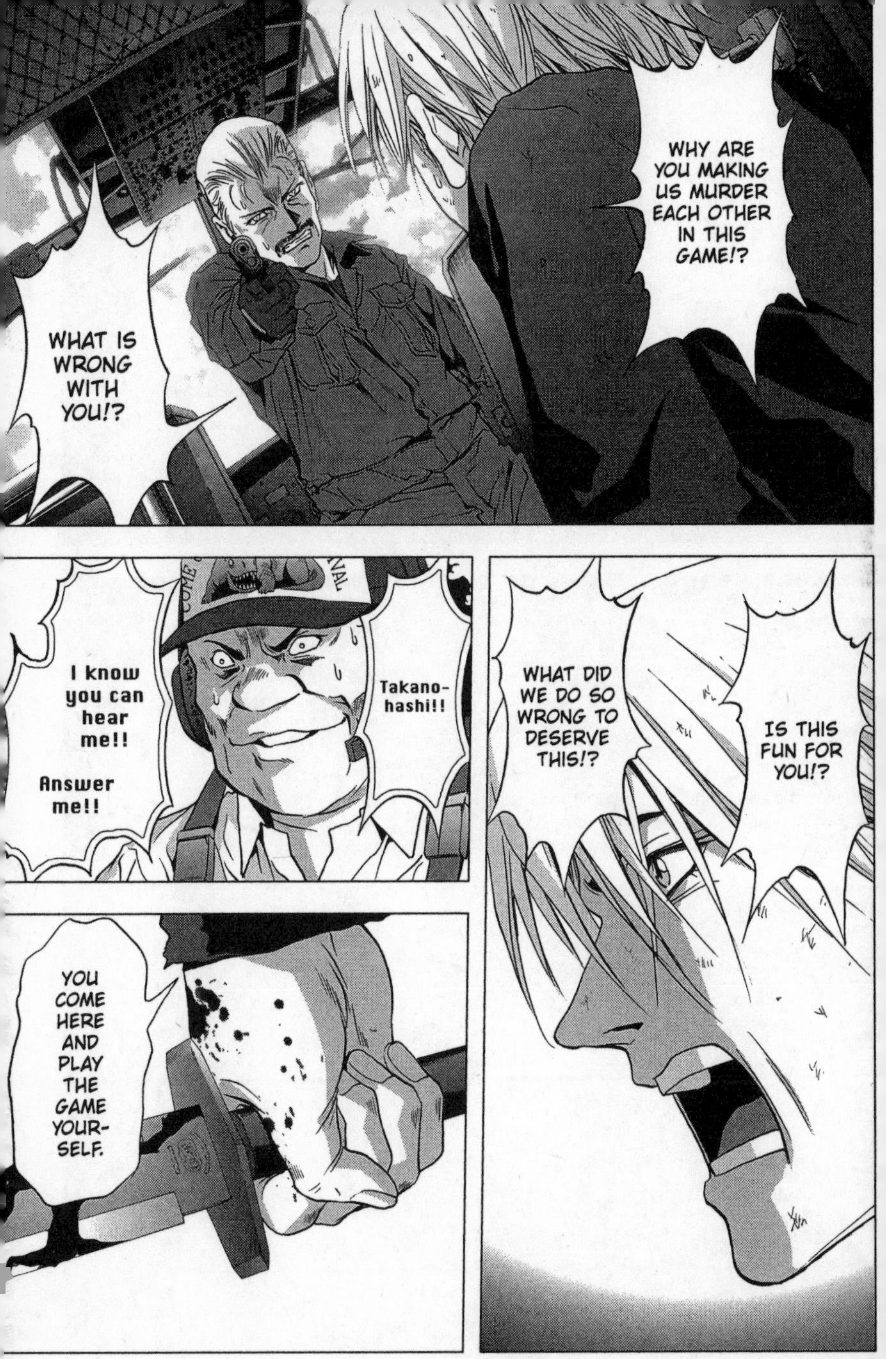
WHY ARE YOU MAKING US MURDER EACH OTHER IN THIS GAME!?
WHAT IS WRONG WITH YOU!?
IS THIS FUN FOR YOU!?
WHAT DID WE DO SO WRONG TO DESERVE THIS!?
Takano-hashi!!
I know you can hear me!!
Answer me!!
YOU COME HERE AND PLAY THE GAME YOUR-SELF.

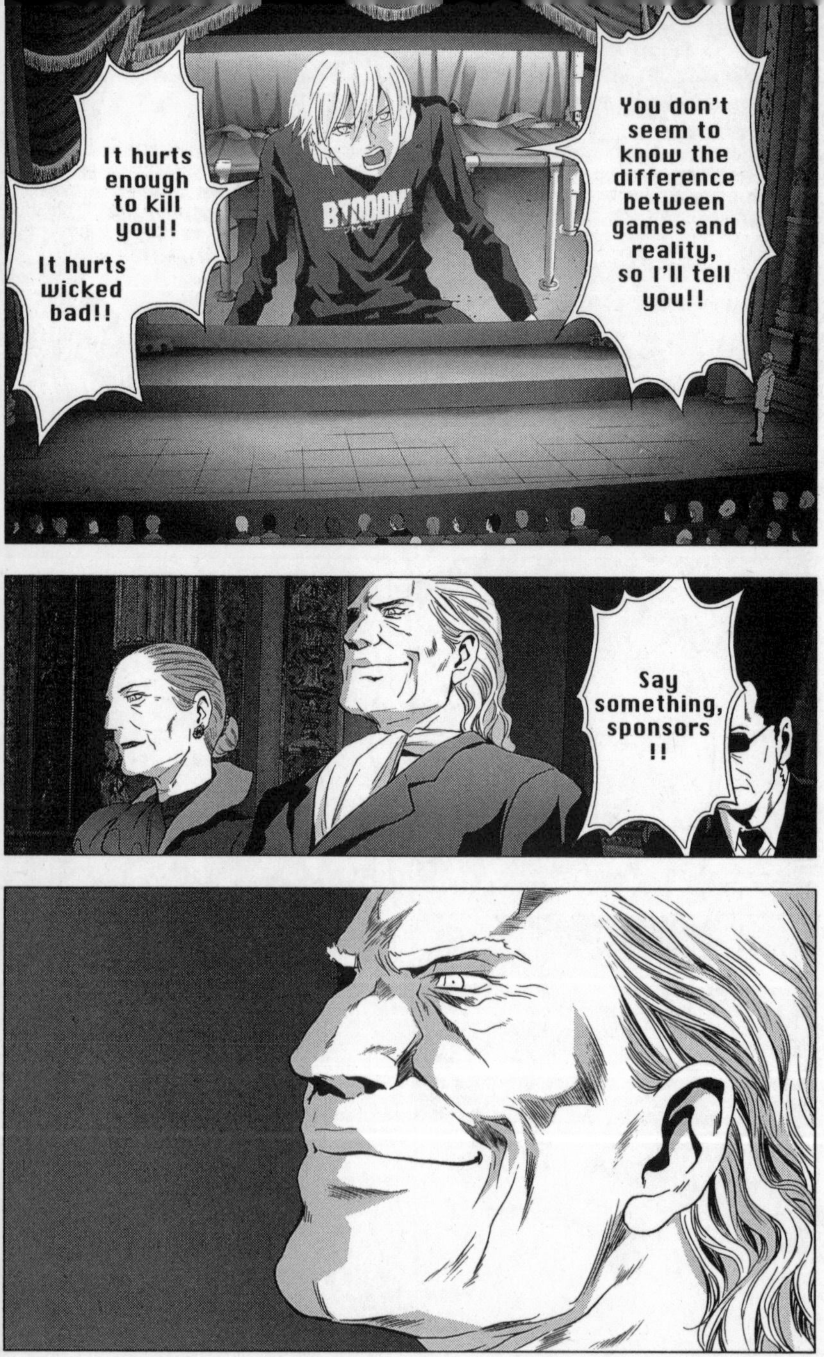
You don't seem to know the difference between games and reality, so I'll tell you!!
It hurts enough to kill you!!
It hurts wicked bad!!
Say something, sponsors !!

I'M SORRY...

I COULDN'T AVENGE YOU...

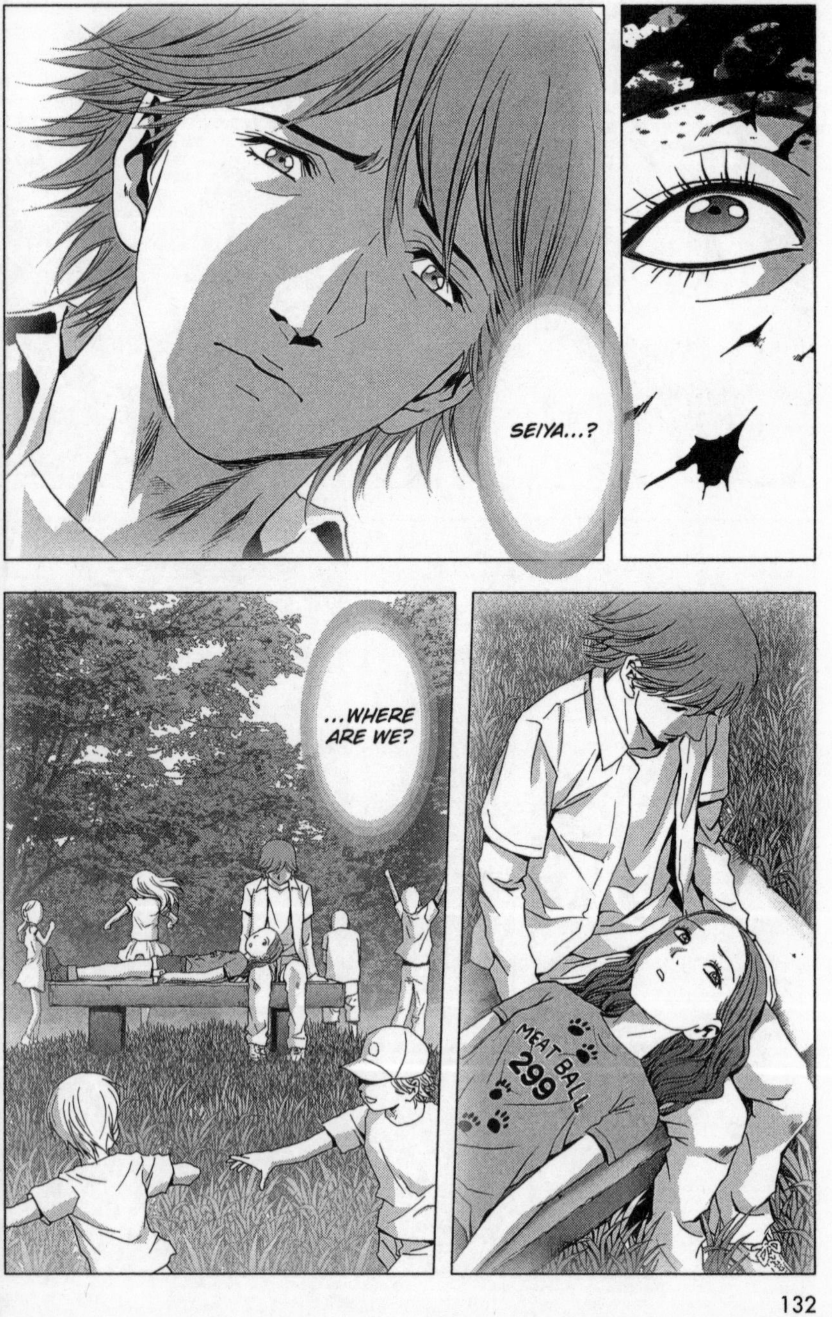
SEIYA...?
MEAT BALL
299
...WHERE ARE WE?

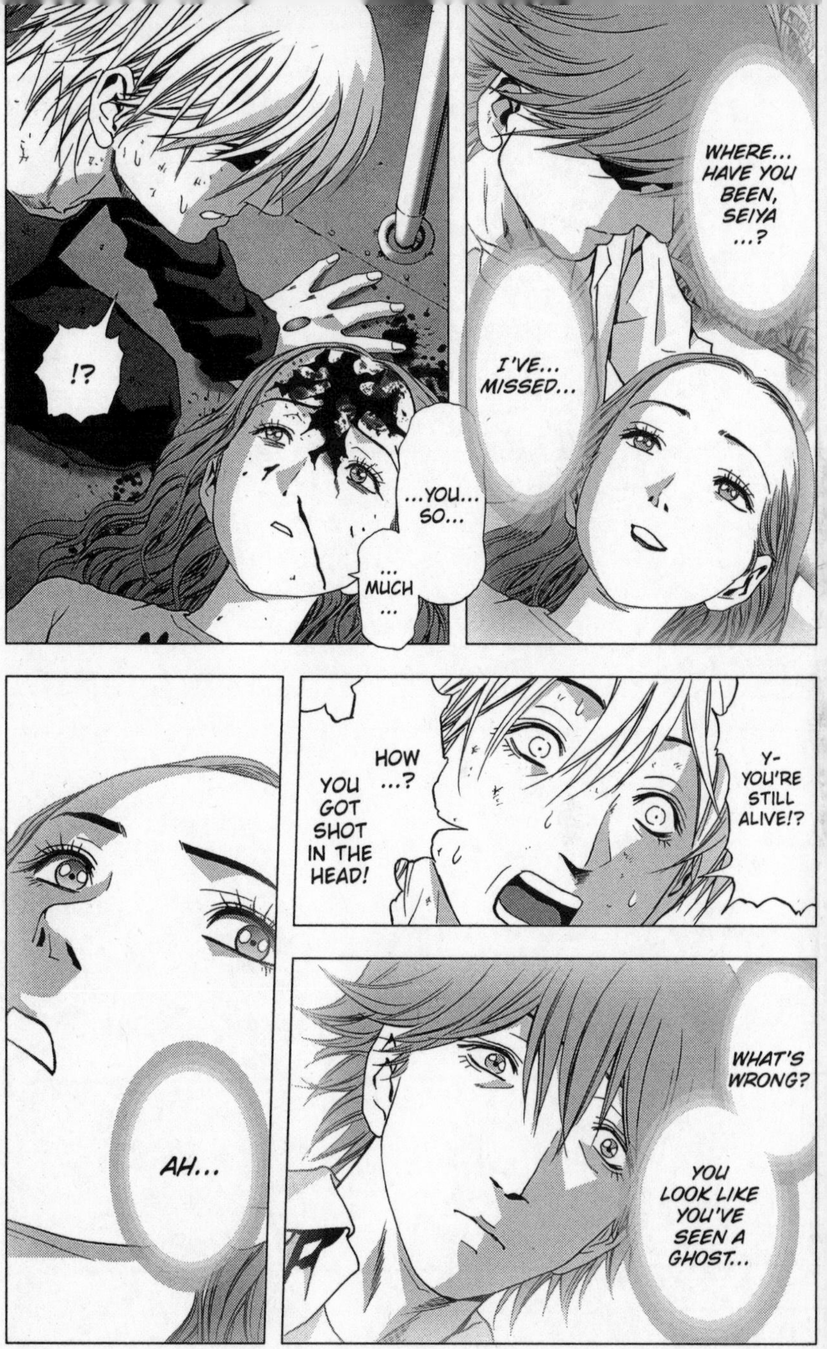
WHERE... HAVE YOU BEEN, SEIYA ...?
I'VE... MISSED...
...YOU... SO...
... MUCH ...
!?
Y- YOU'RE STILL ALIVE!?
HOW ...?
YOU GOT SHOT IN THE HEAD!
WHAT'S WRONG?
YOU LOOK LIKE YOU'VE SEEN A GHOST...
AH...

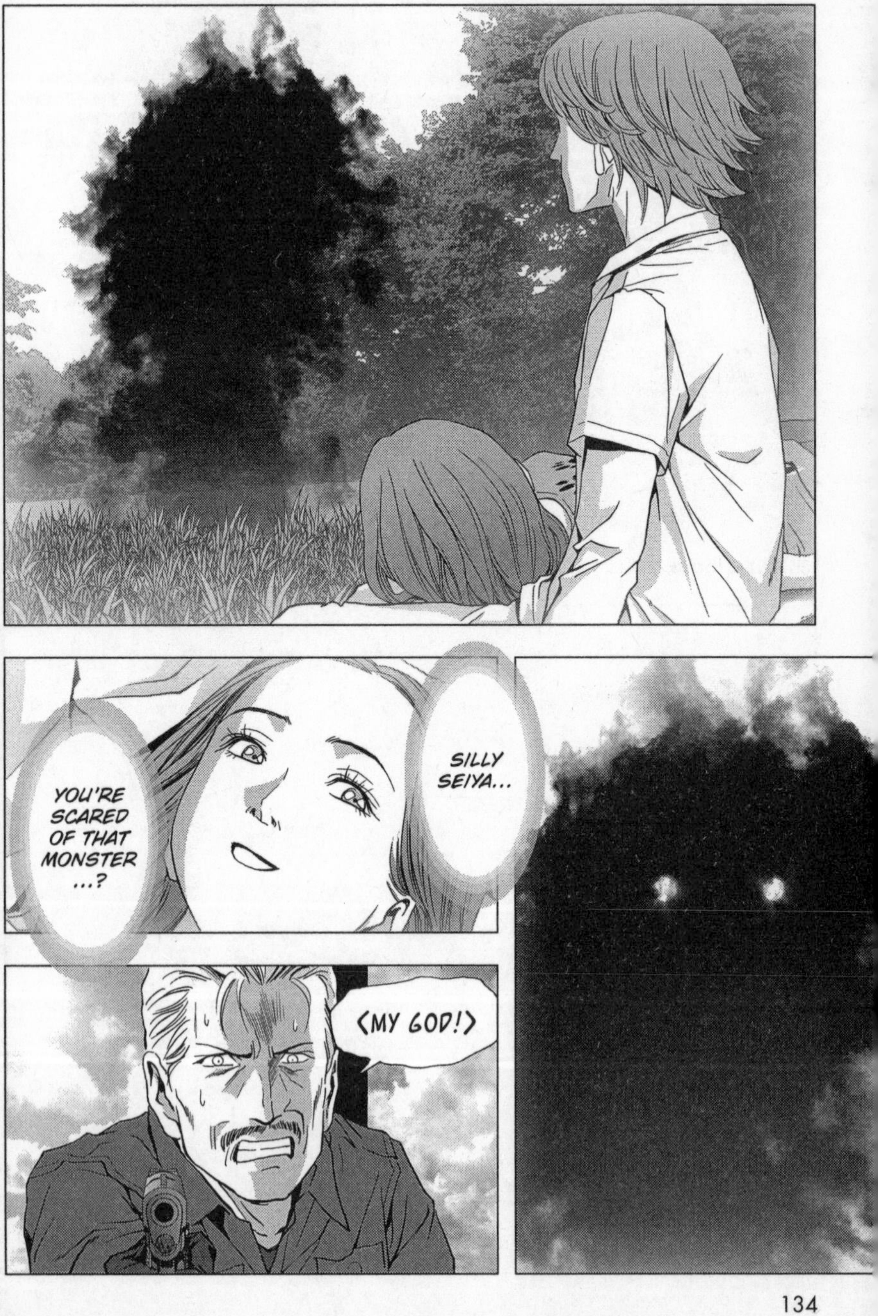
SILLY SEIYA...
YOU'RE SCARED OF THAT MONSTER ...?
〈MY GOD!〉

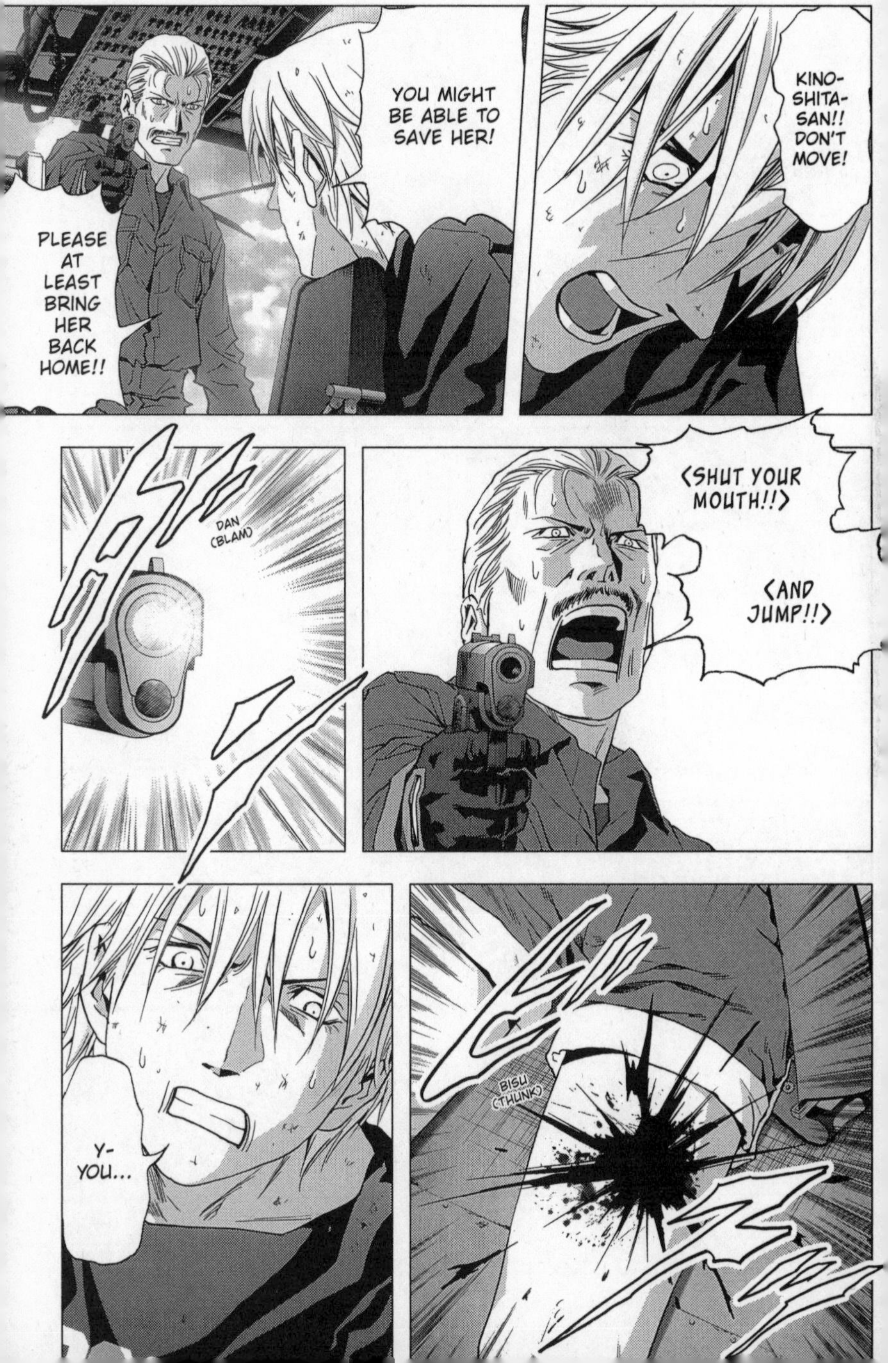
KINO-SHITA-SAN!! DON'T MOVE!
YOU MIGHT BE ABLE TO SAVE HER!
PLEASE AT LEAST BRING HER BACK HOME!!
<SHUT YOUR MOUTH!!>
<AND JUMP!!>
DAN (BLAM)
BISU (THUNK)
Y- YOU...

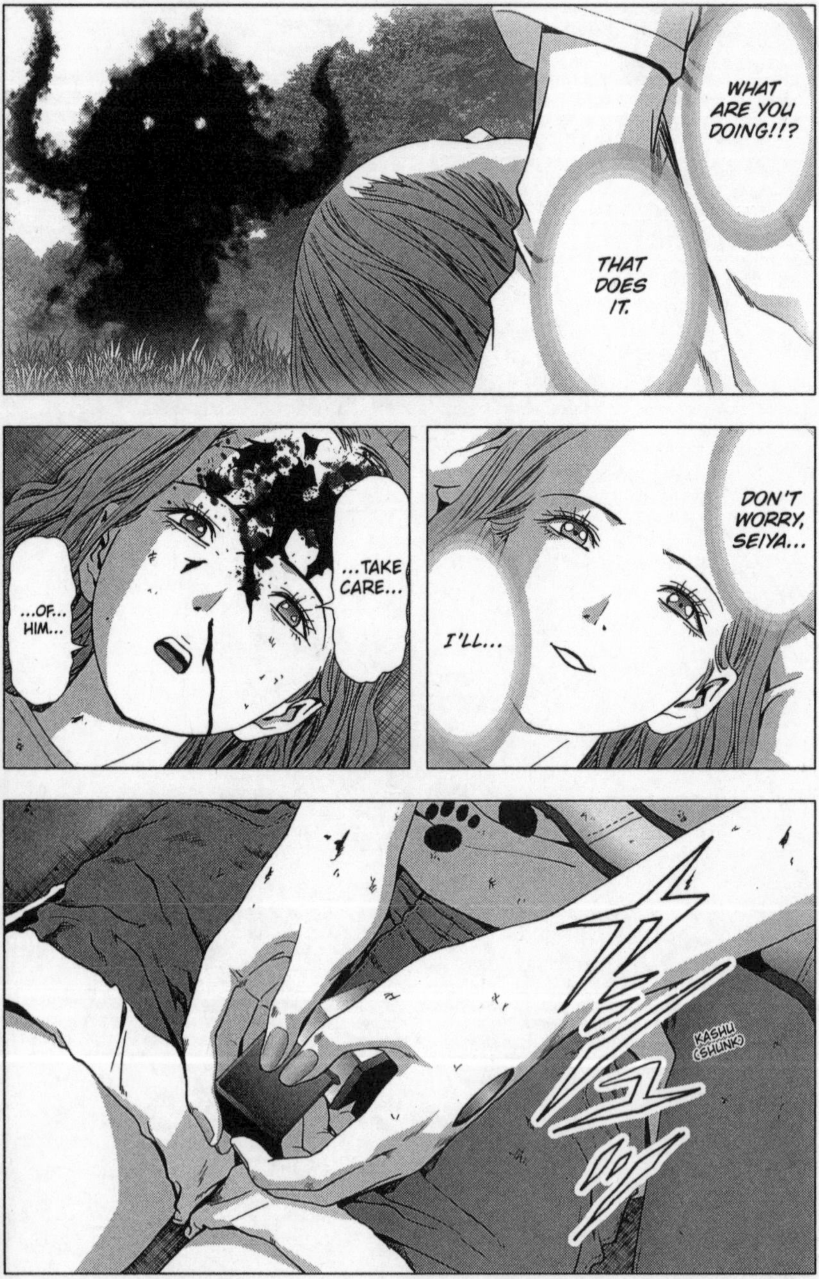
WHAT ARE YOU DOING!!?
THAT DOES IT.
DON'T WORRY, SEIYA...
I'LL...
...TAKE CARE...
...OF... HIM...
KASHU (SHUNK)

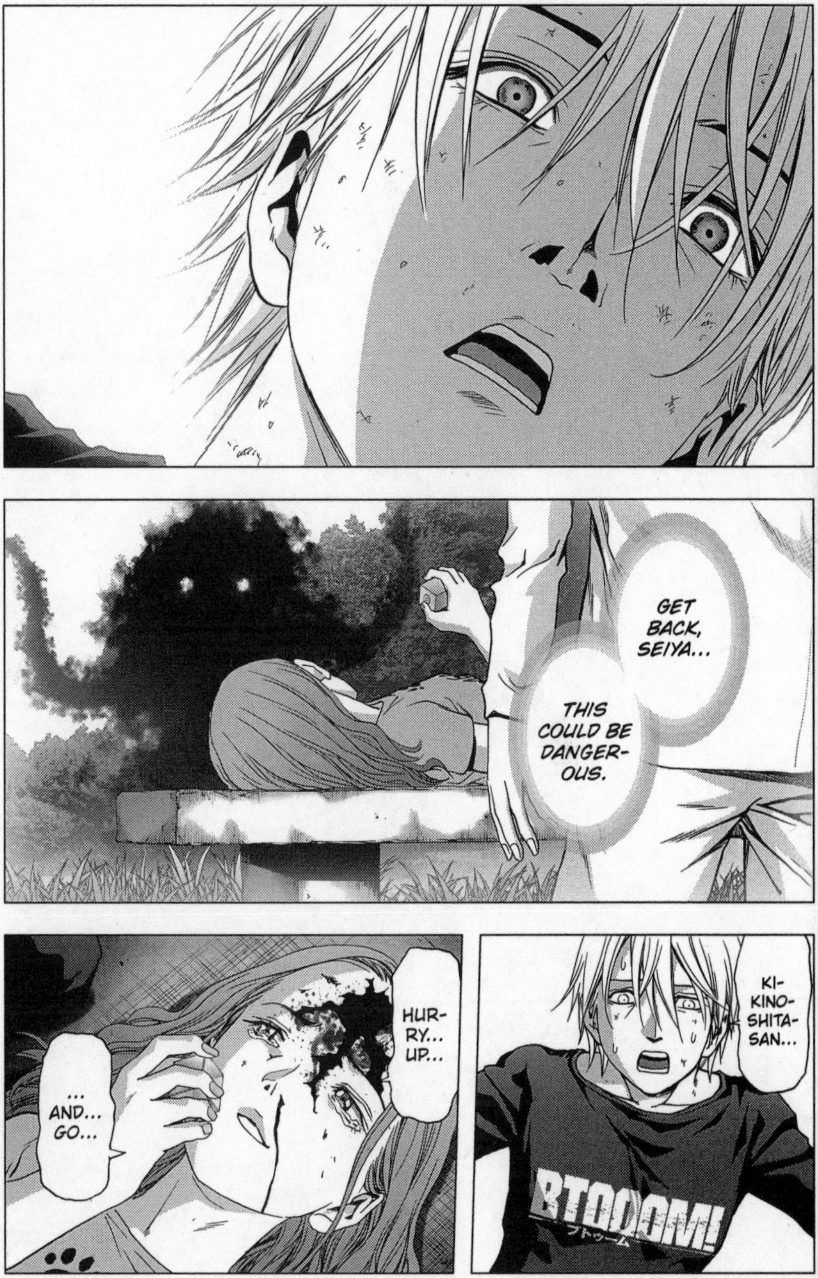
GET BACK, SEIYA...
THIS COULD BE DANGER-OUS.
KI-KINO-SHITA-SAN...
BTOOOM!
HUR-RY... UP...
... AND... GO...

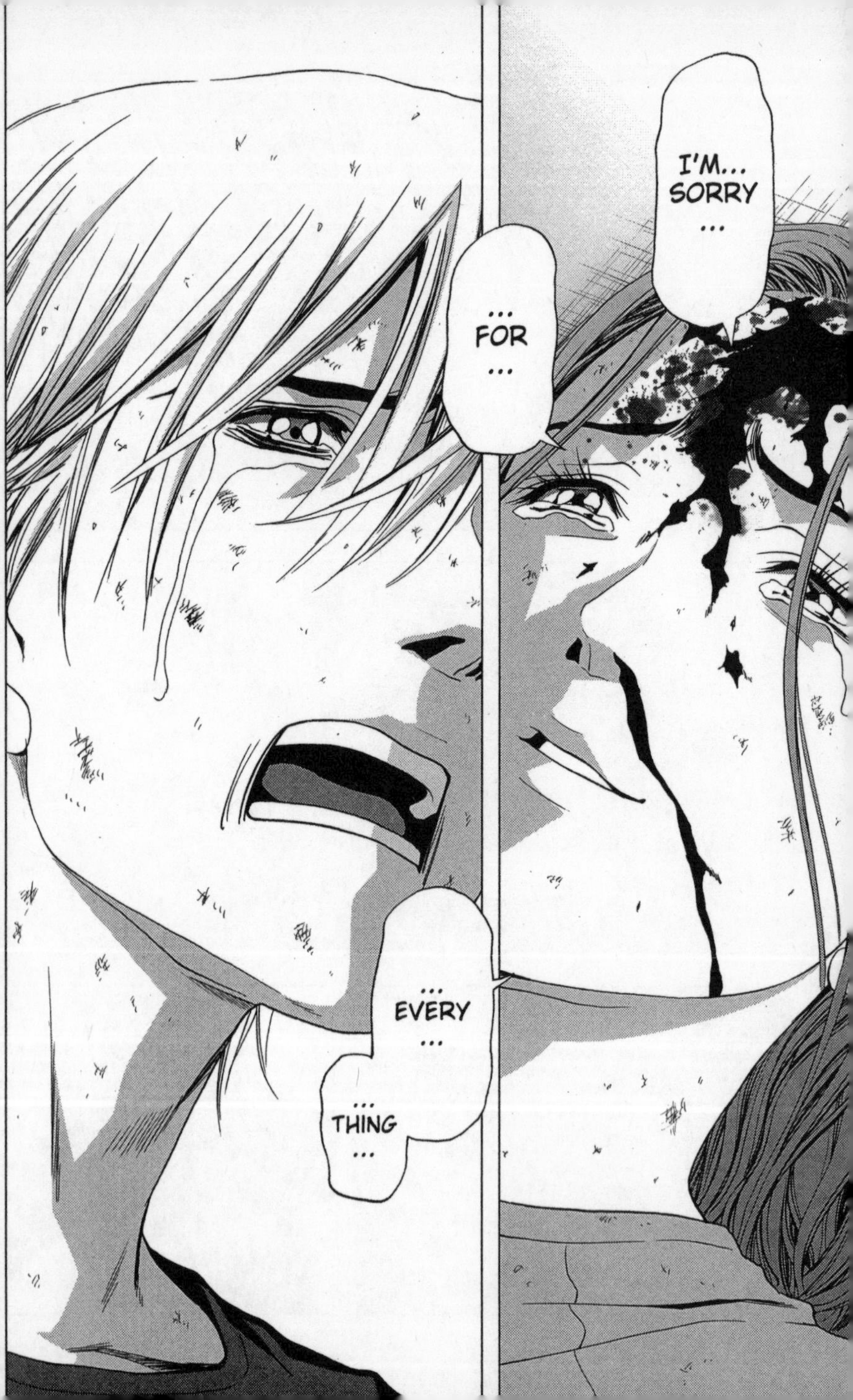
I'M... SORRY ...
... FOR ...
... EVERY ...
... THING ...

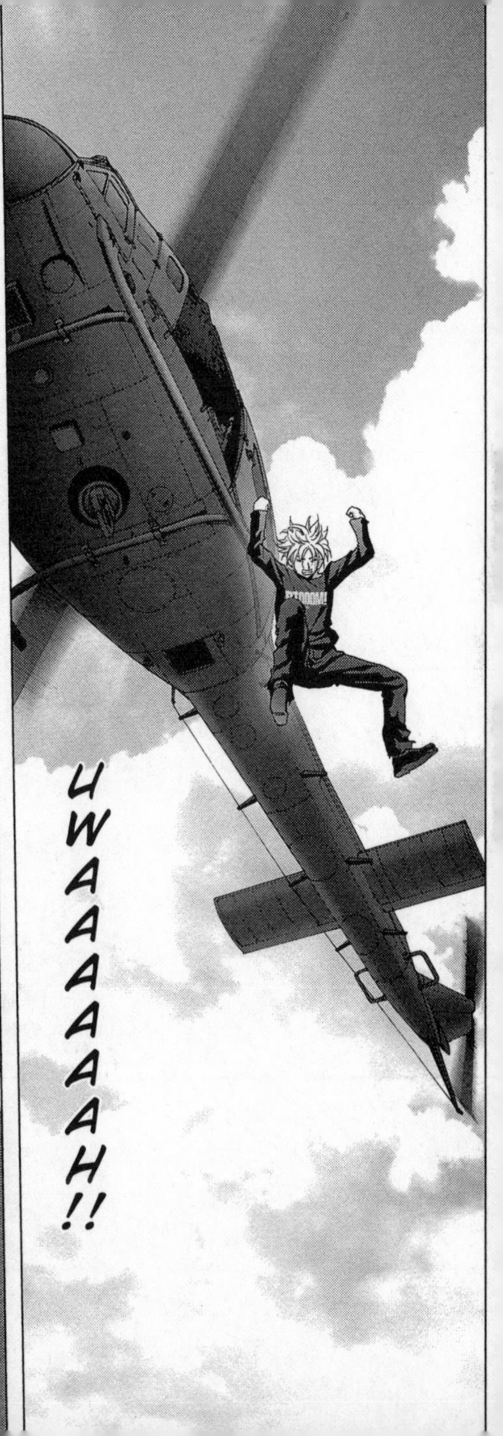
UWAAAAAAH!!
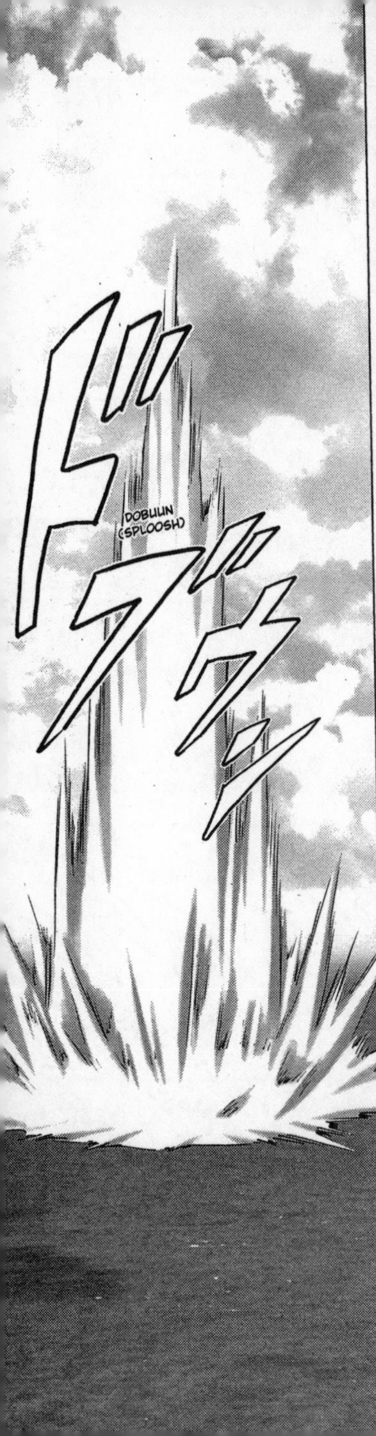
ドブゥン
DOBUUN
(SPLOOSH)

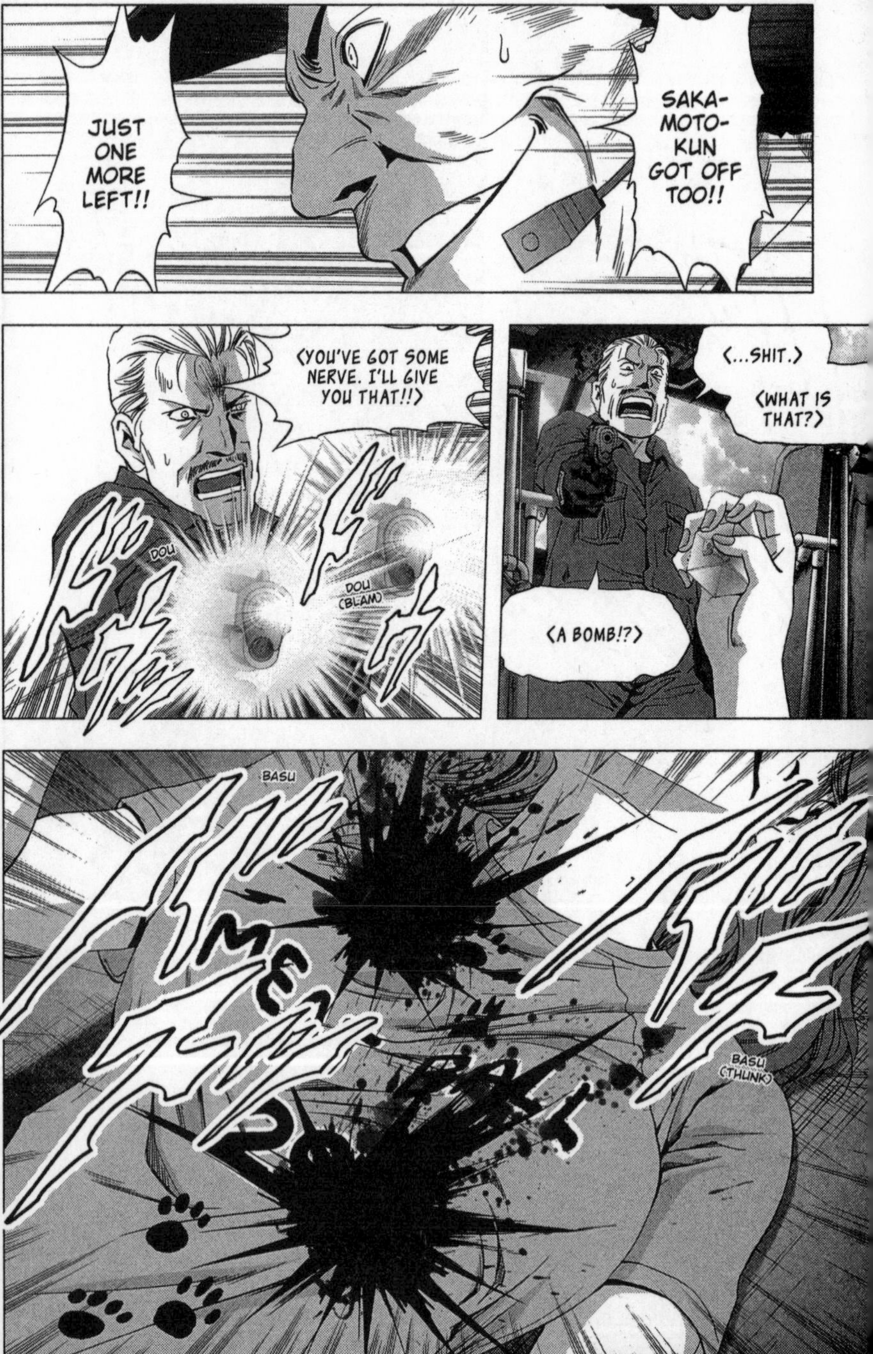
SAKA-MOTO-KUN GOT OFF TOO!!
JUST ONE MORE LEFT!!
〈...SHIT.〉
〈WHAT IS THAT?〉
〈A BOMB!?〉
〈YOU'VE GOT SOME NERVE. I'LL GIVE YOU THAT!!〉
DOU
DOU (BLAM)
BASU
BASU (THUNK)

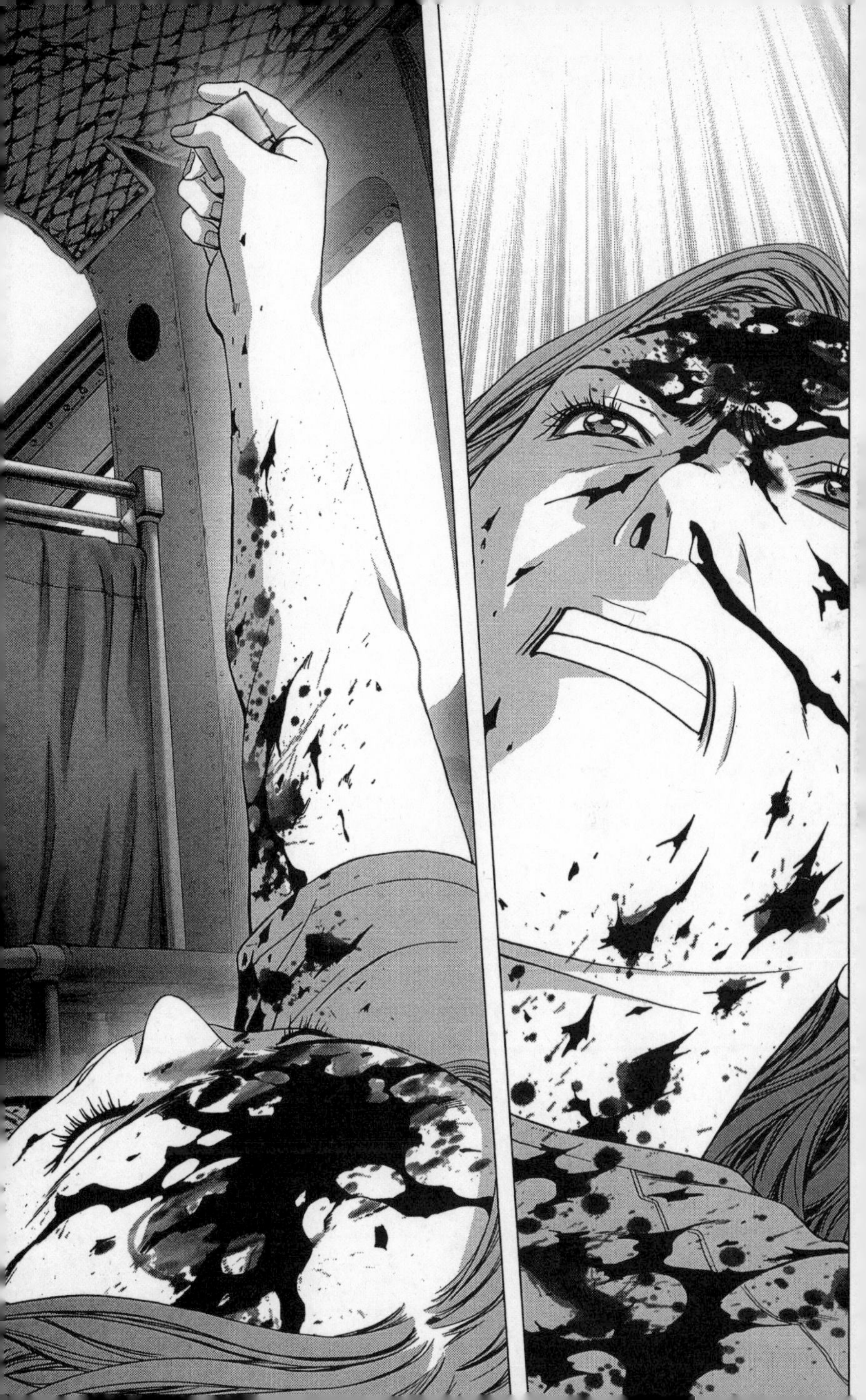

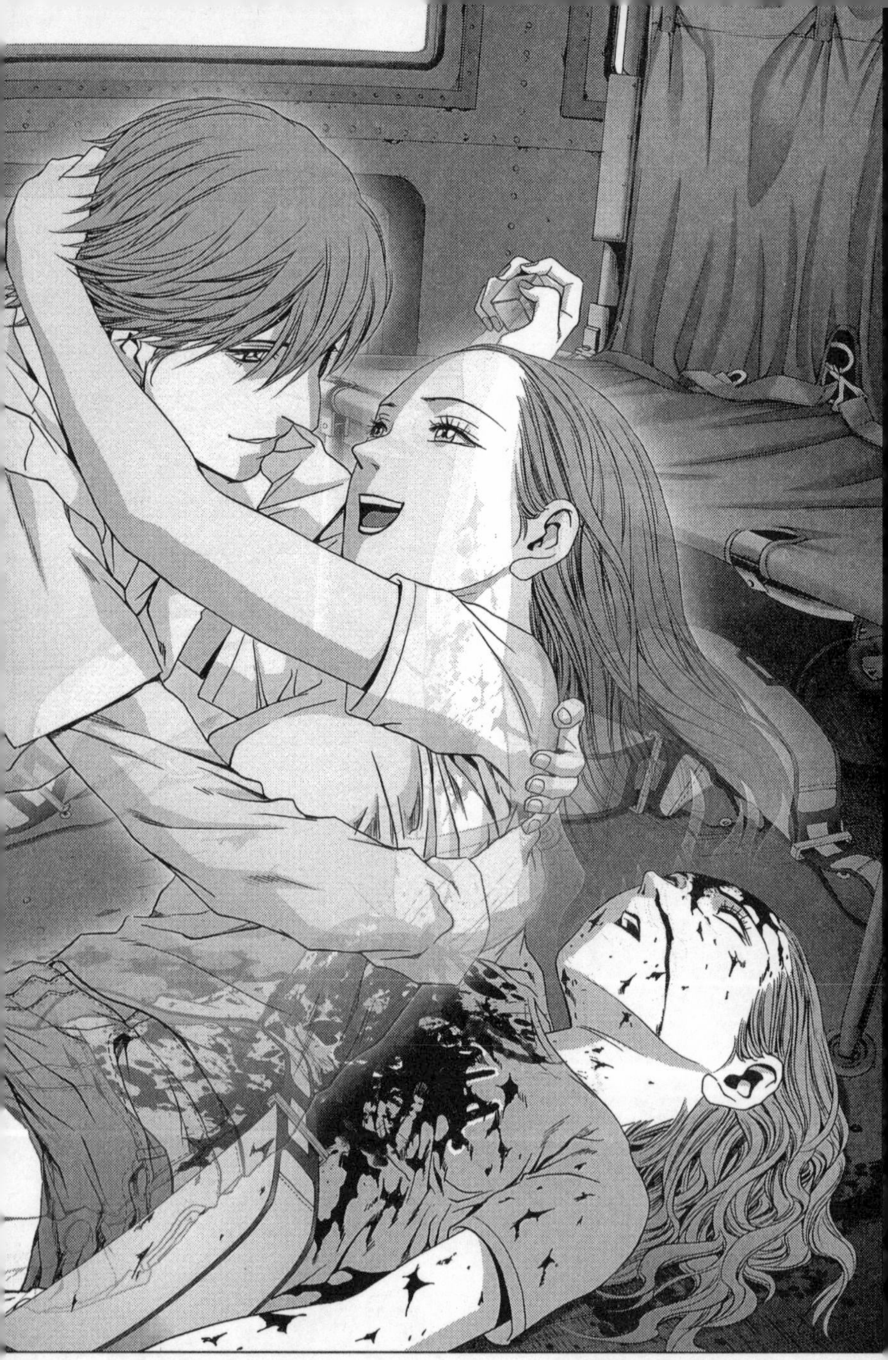

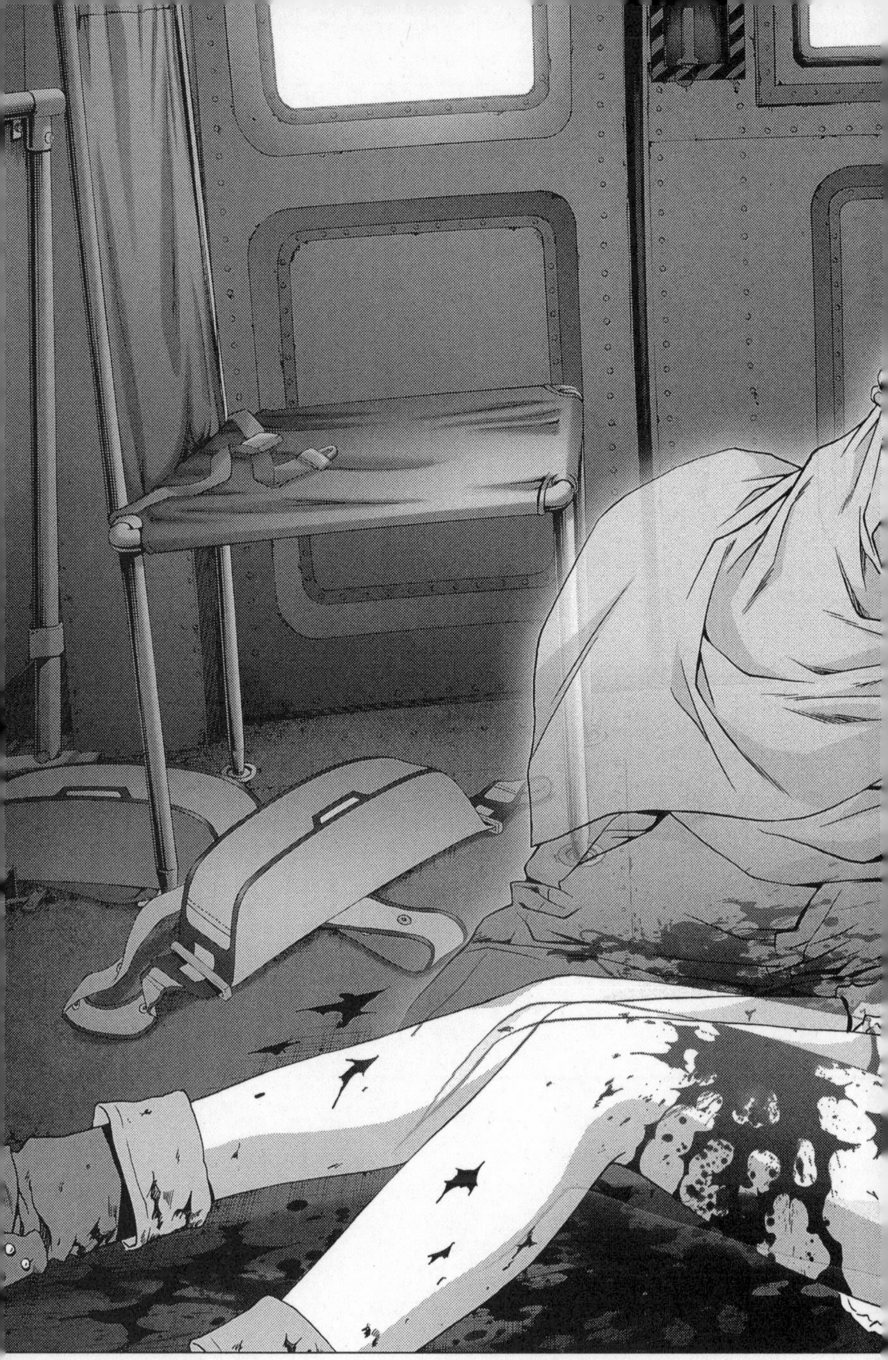

SEIYA...

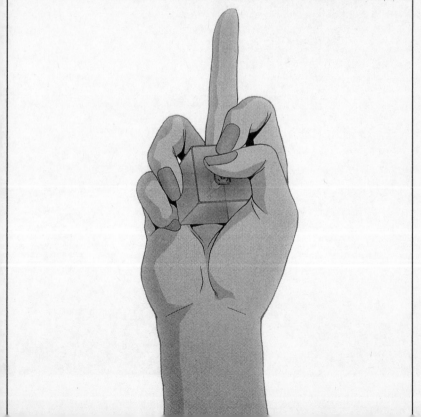

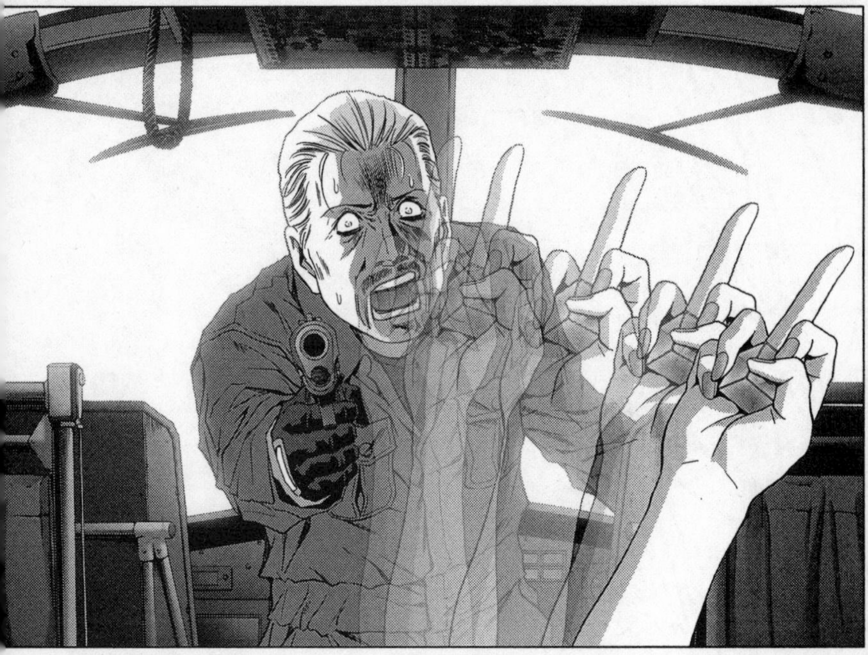
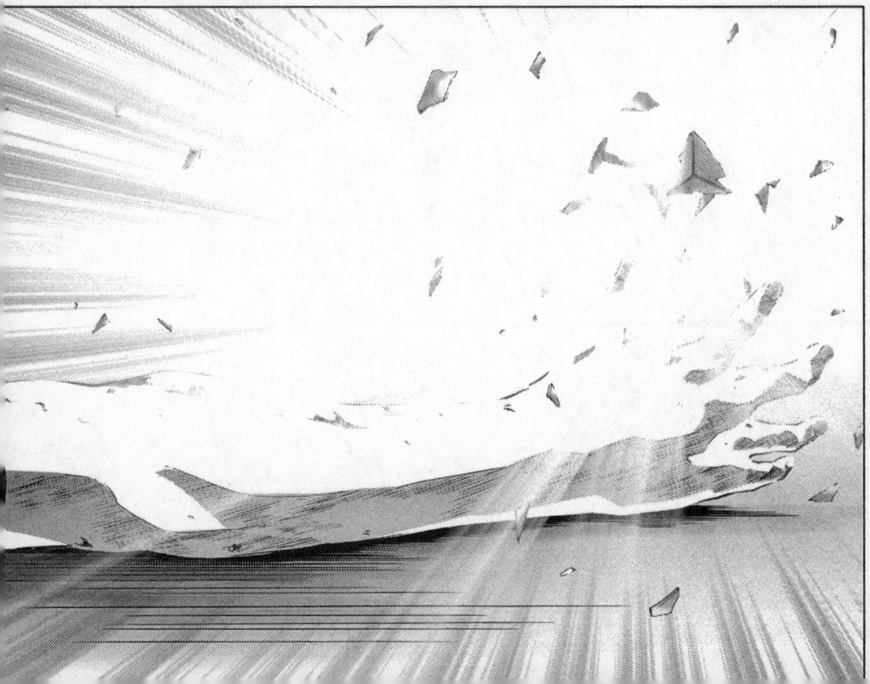

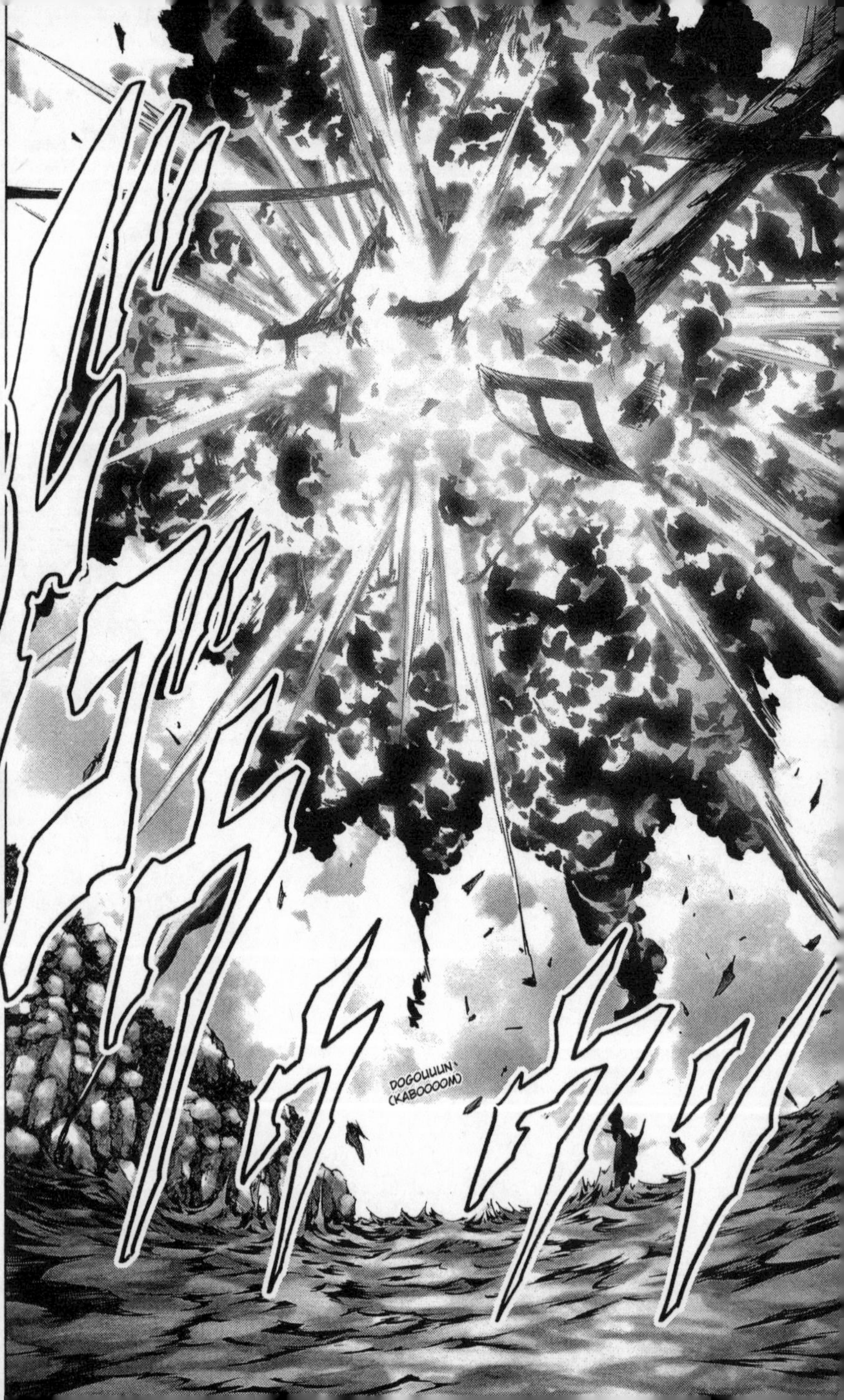
DOGOUUUN
(KABOOOOM)

65 The Secret Organization Takes Shape

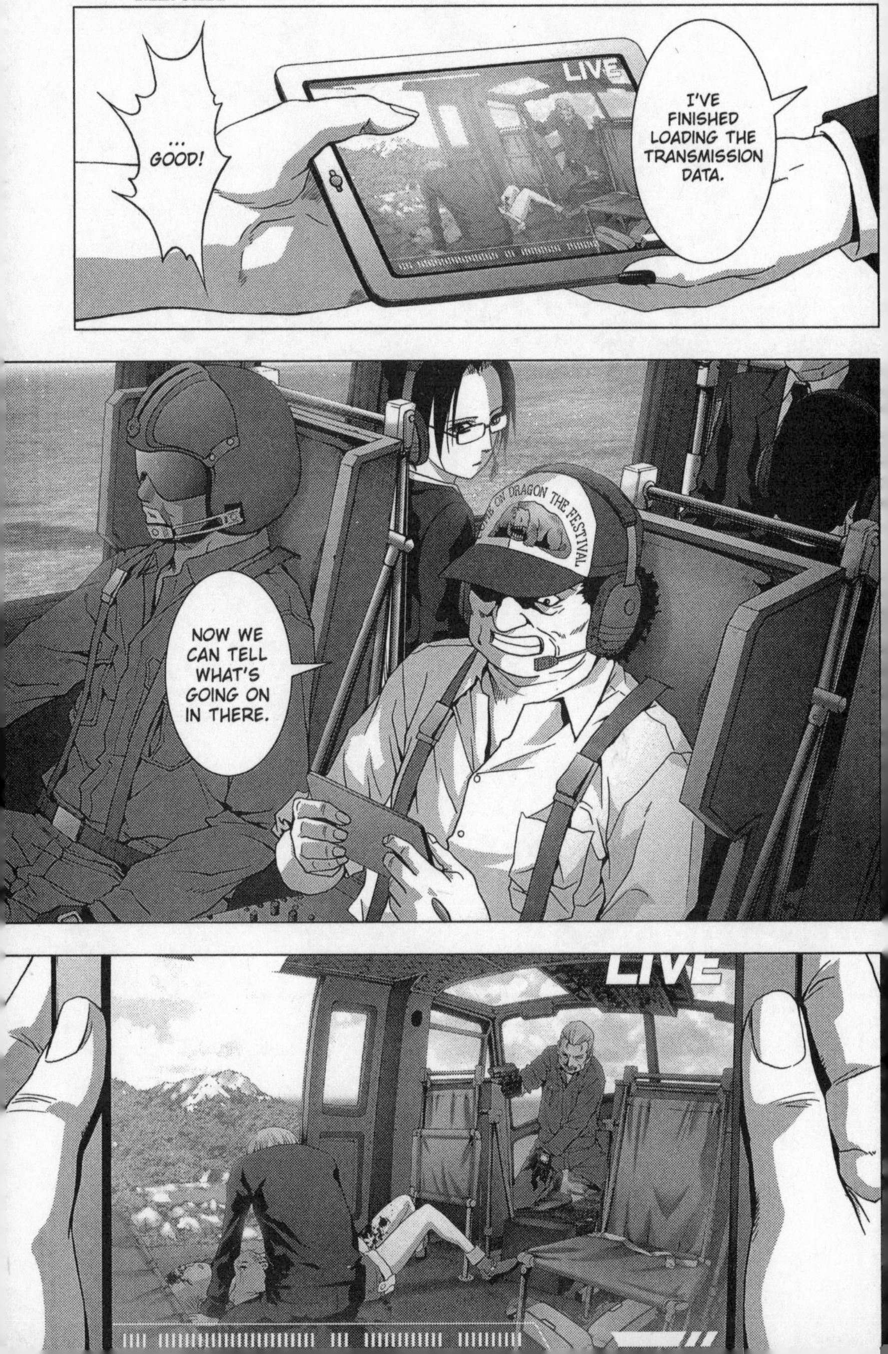
LIVE
I'VE FINISHED LOADING THE TRANSMISSION DATA.
... GOOD!
NOW WE CAN TELL WHAT'S GOING ON IN THERE.
LIVE

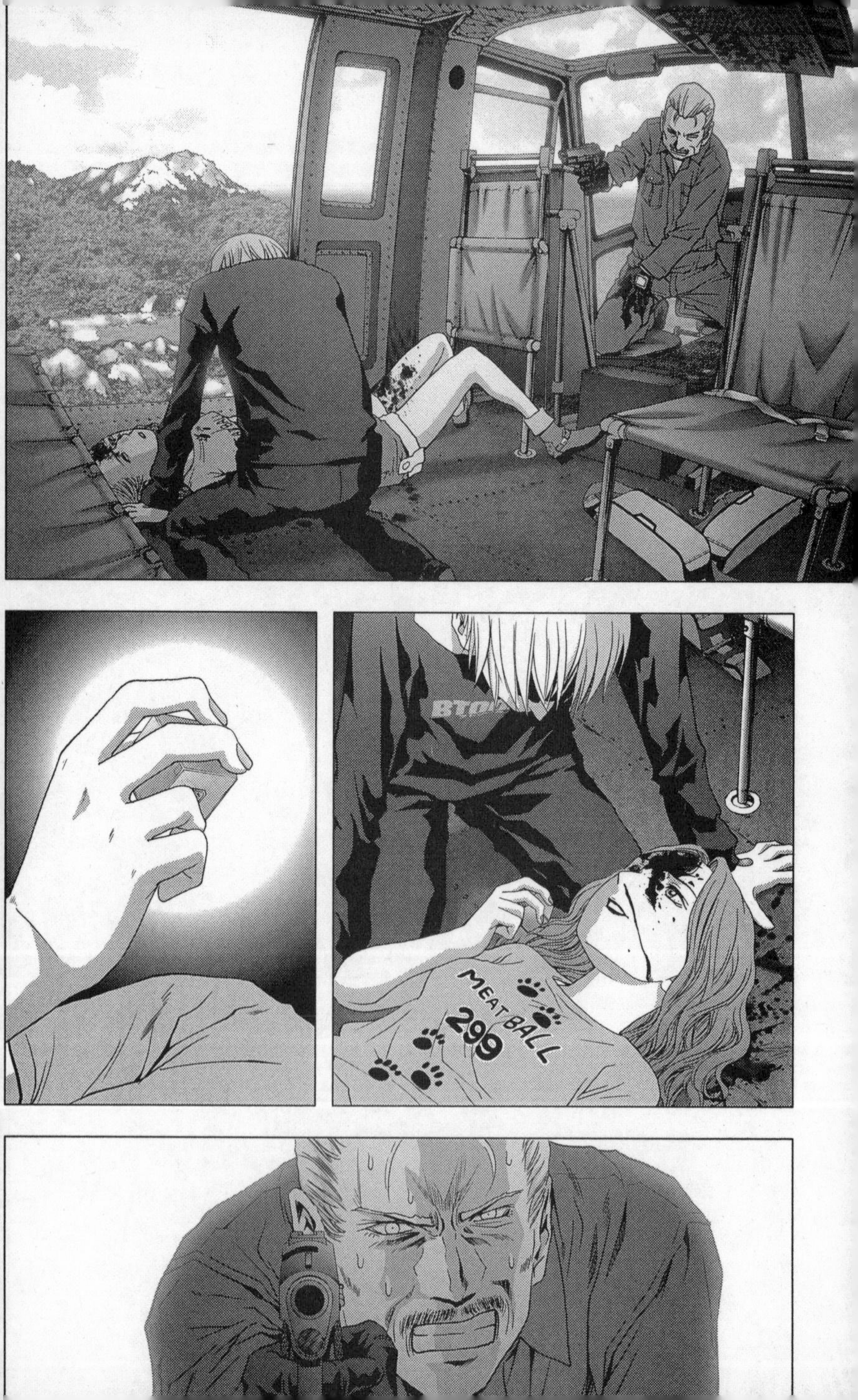
MEAT BALL
299

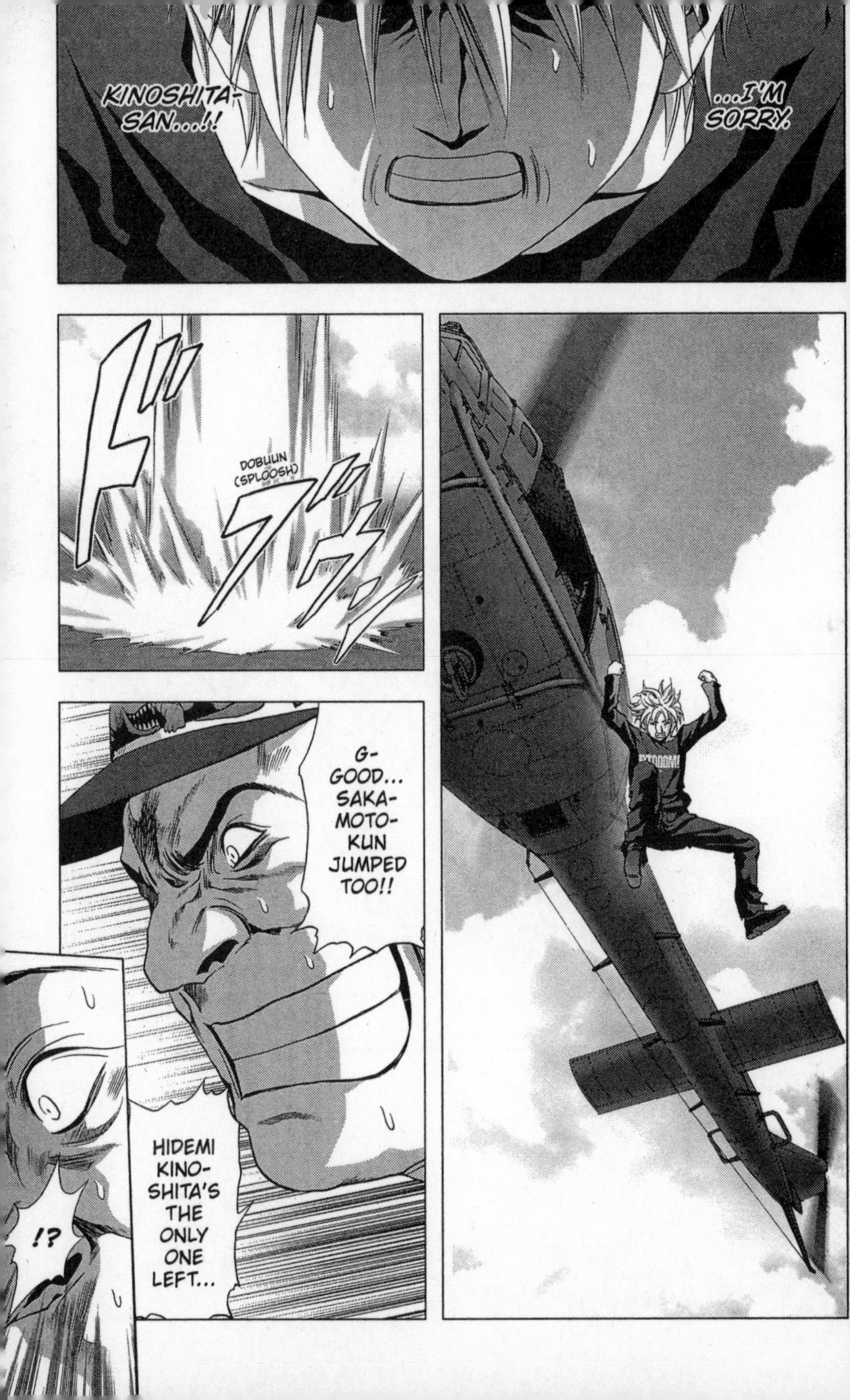
...I'M SORRY.
KINOSHITA-SAN...!!
DOBUUN (SPLOOSH)
G-GOOD... SAKAMOTO-KUN JUMPED TOO!!
HIDEMI KINOSHITA'S THE ONLY ONE LEFT...
!?

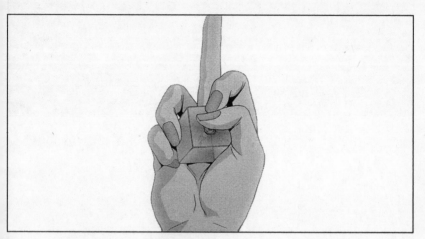

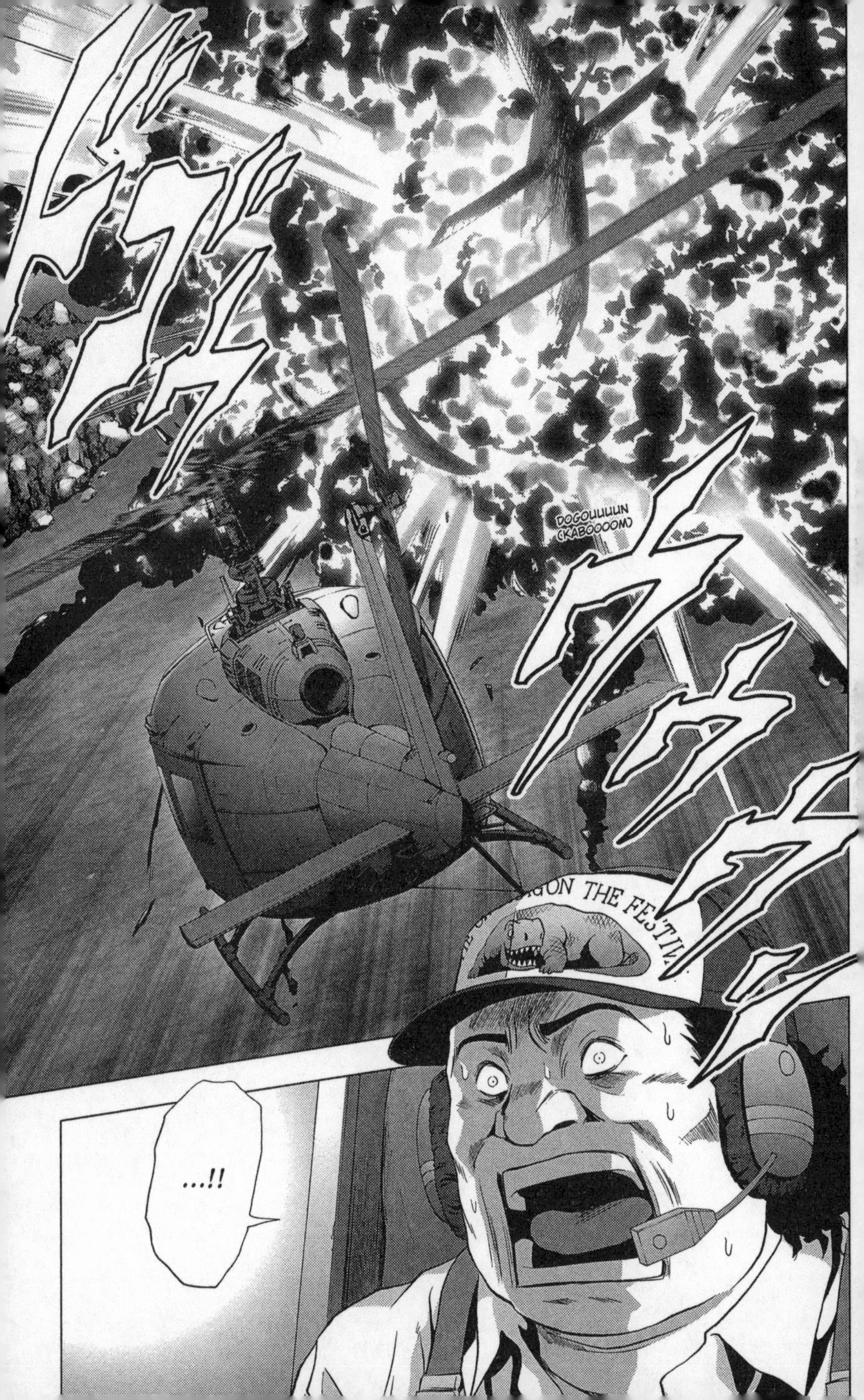
DOGOUUUUN (KABOOOOM)
GON THE FESTIV
...!!

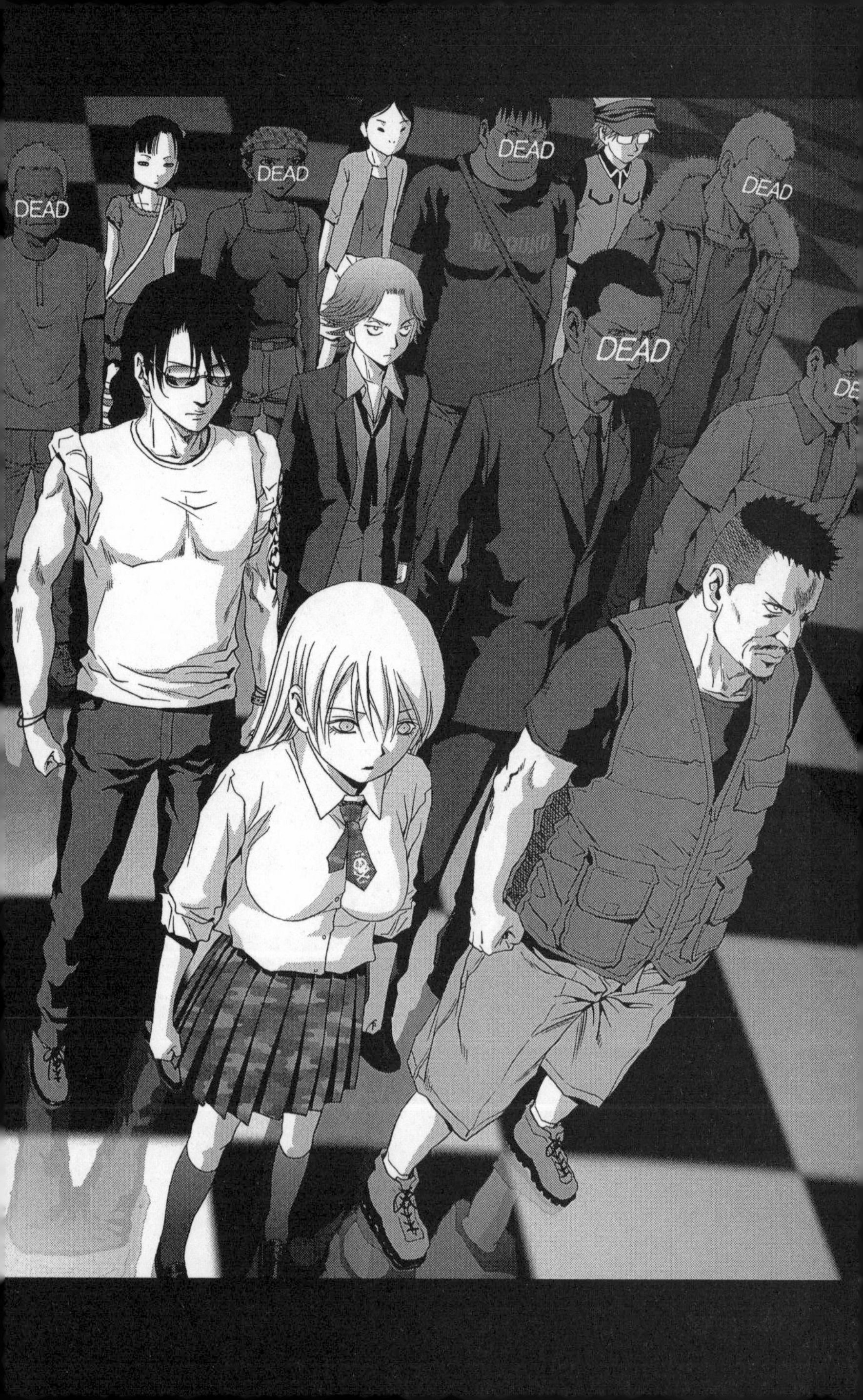
DEAD
DEAD
DEAD
DEAD
DE
DEAD

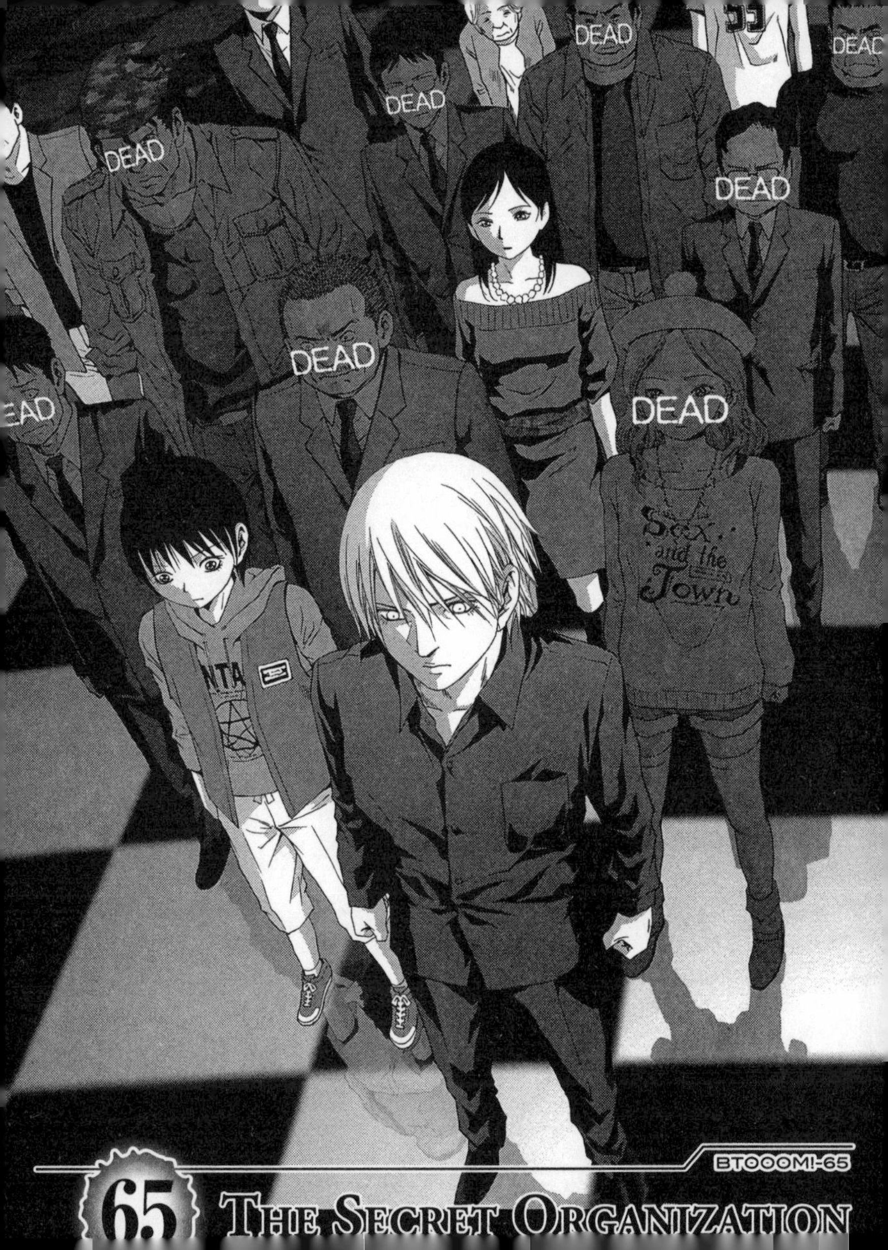
DEAD
DEAD
DEAD
DEAD
DEAD
DEAD
EAD
DEAD
Sex and the Town
BTOOOM!-65

65 The Secret Organization

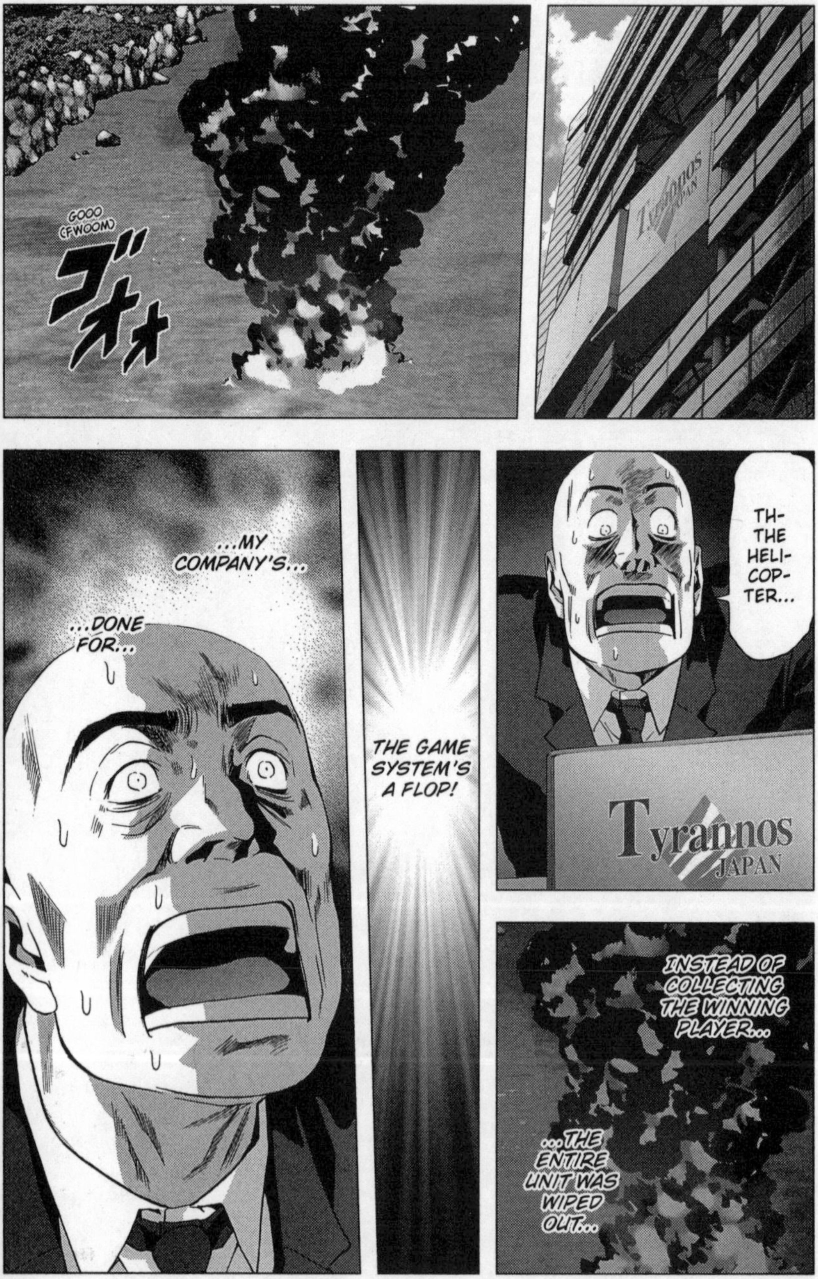
Tyrannos
GOOO (FWOOM)
ゴオォ
TH-THE HELICOPTER...
Tyrannos
JAPAN
INSTEAD OF COLLECTING THE WINNING PLAYER...
...THE ENTIRE UNIT WAS WIPED OUT...
THE GAME SYSTEM'S A FLOP!
...MY COMPANY'S...
...DONE FOR...

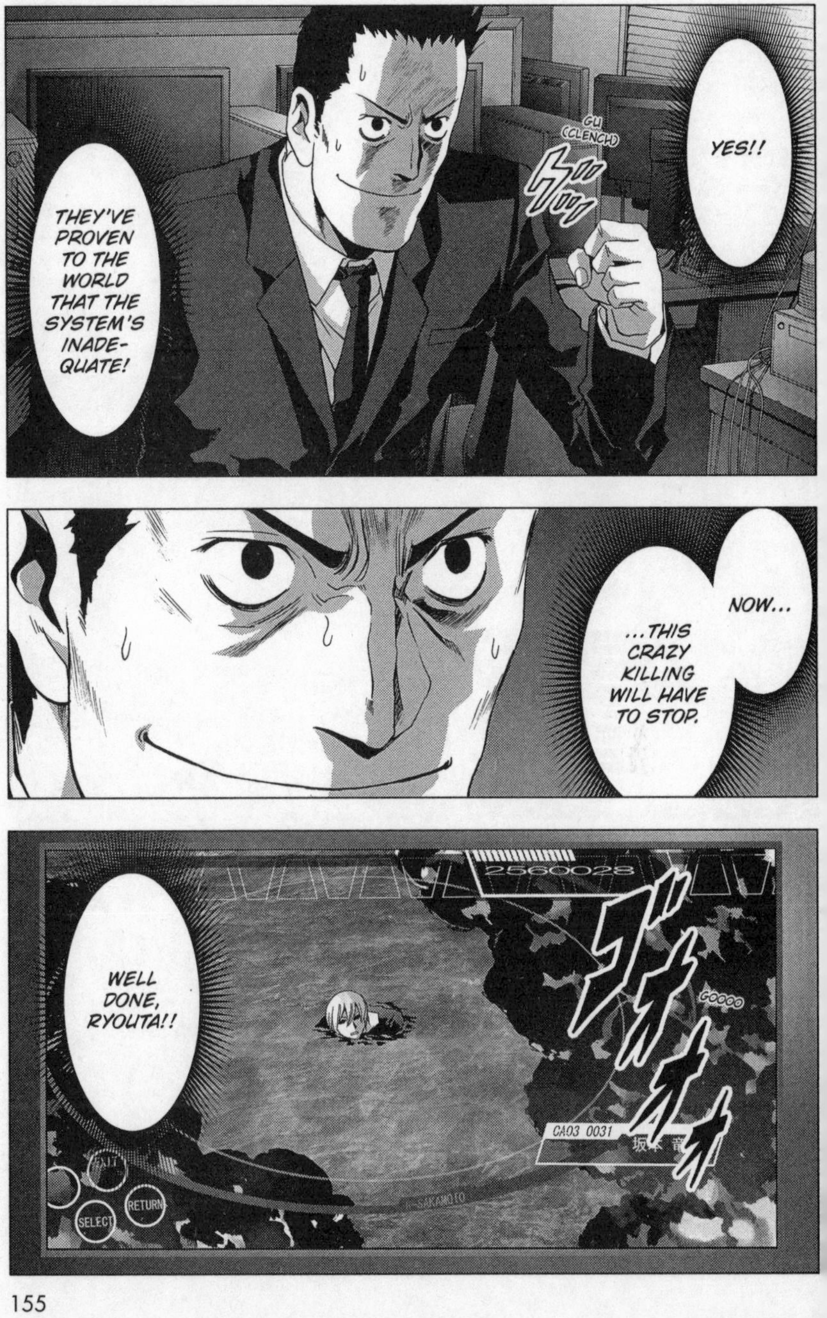
YES!!
GU (CLENCH)
THEY'VE PROVEN TO THE WORLD THAT THE SYSTEM'S INADE-QUATE!
NOW...
...THIS CRAZY KILLING WILL HAVE TO STOP.
2560028
GOOOO
WELL DONE, RYOUTA!!
CA03 0031
EXIT
RETURN
SELECT
SAKAMOTO

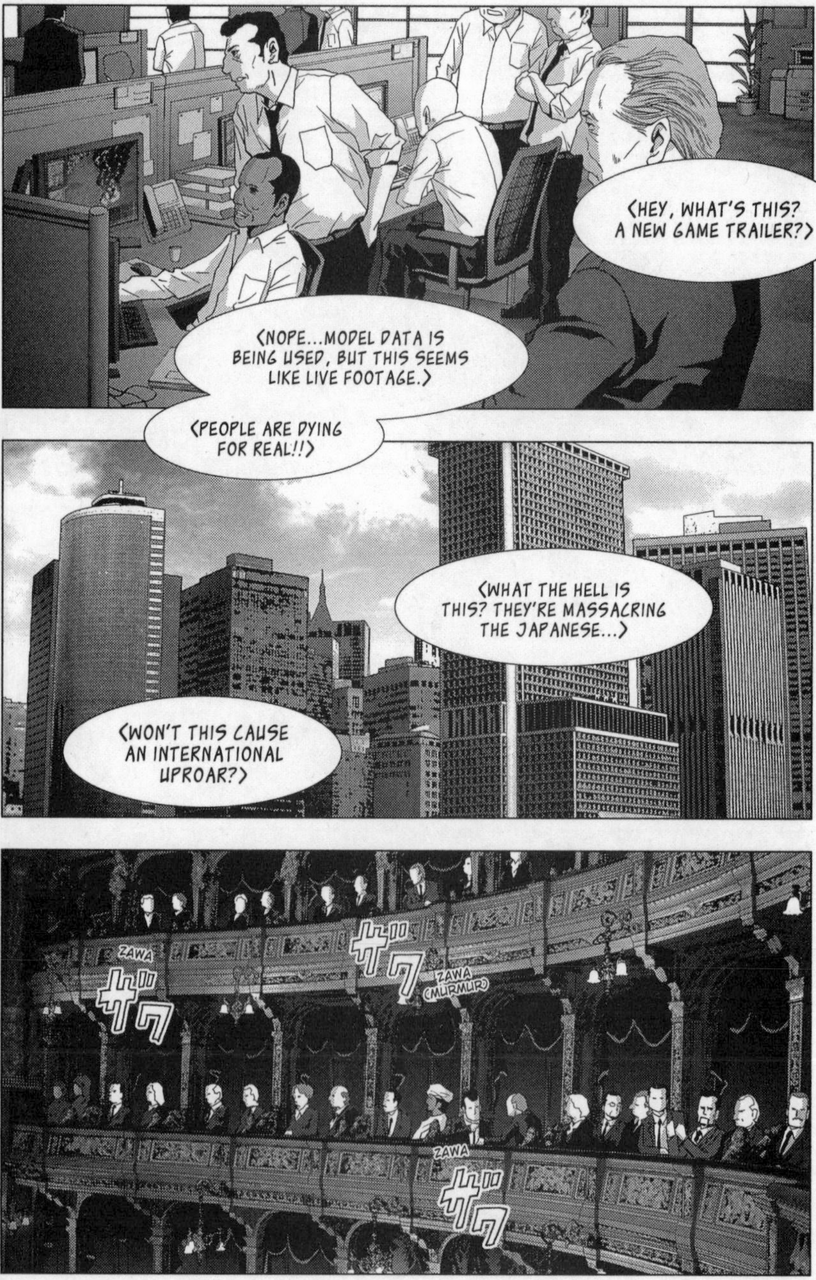
〈HEY, WHAT'S THIS? A NEW GAME TRAILER?〉
〈NOPE...MODEL DATA IS BEING USED, BUT THIS SEEMS LIKE LIVE FOOTAGE.〉
〈PEOPLE ARE DYING FOR REAL!!〉
〈WHAT THE HELL IS THIS? THEY'RE MASSACRING THE JAPANESE...〉
〈WON'T THIS CAUSE AN INTERNATIONAL UPROAR?〉
ザワ
ZAWA (MURMUR)
ZAWA
ザワ
ZAWA
ザワ

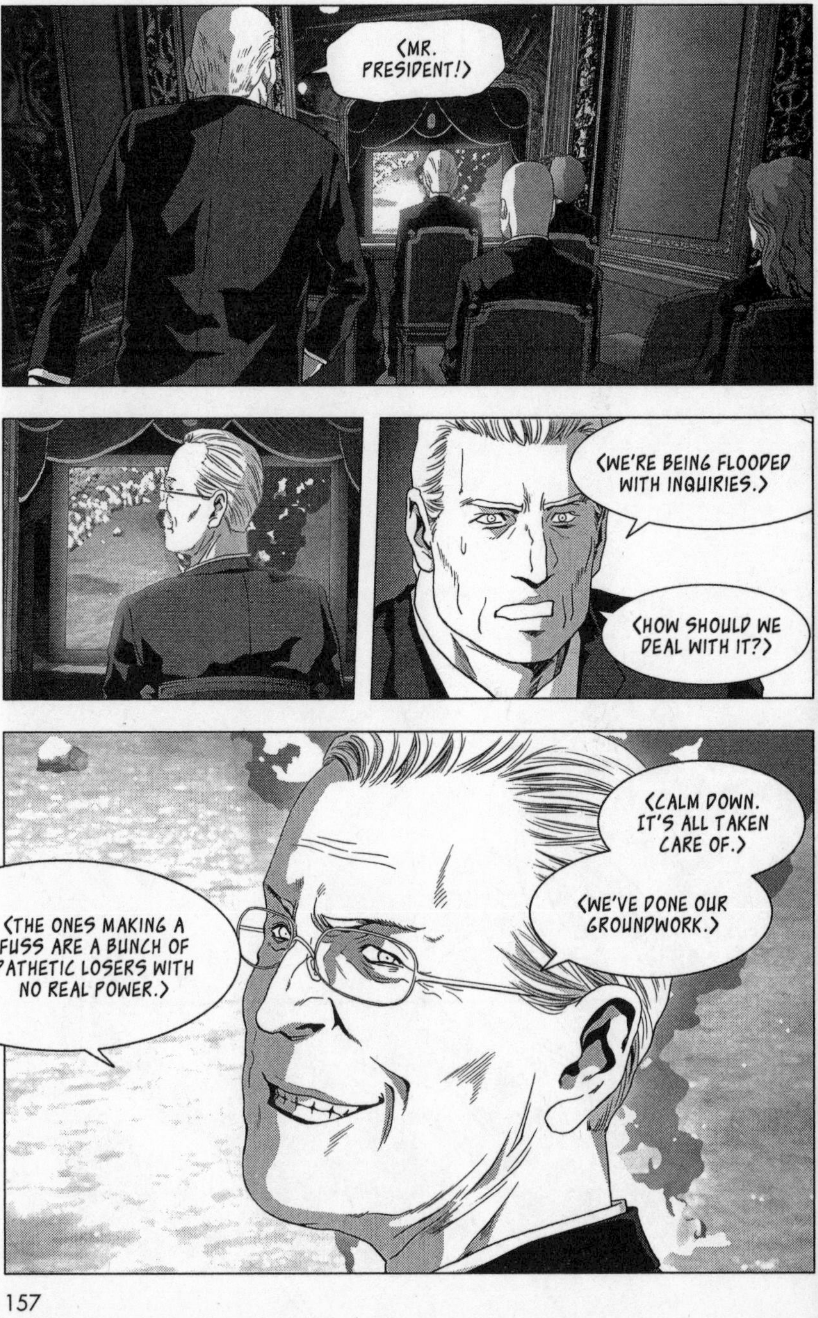
<MR. PRESIDENT!>
<WE'RE BEING FLOODED WITH INQUIRIES.>
<HOW SHOULD WE DEAL WITH IT?>
<CALM DOWN. IT'S ALL TAKEN CARE OF.>
<WE'VE DONE OUR GROUNDWORK.>
<THE ONES MAKING A FUSS ARE A BUNCH OF PATHETIC LOSERS WITH NO REAL POWER.>

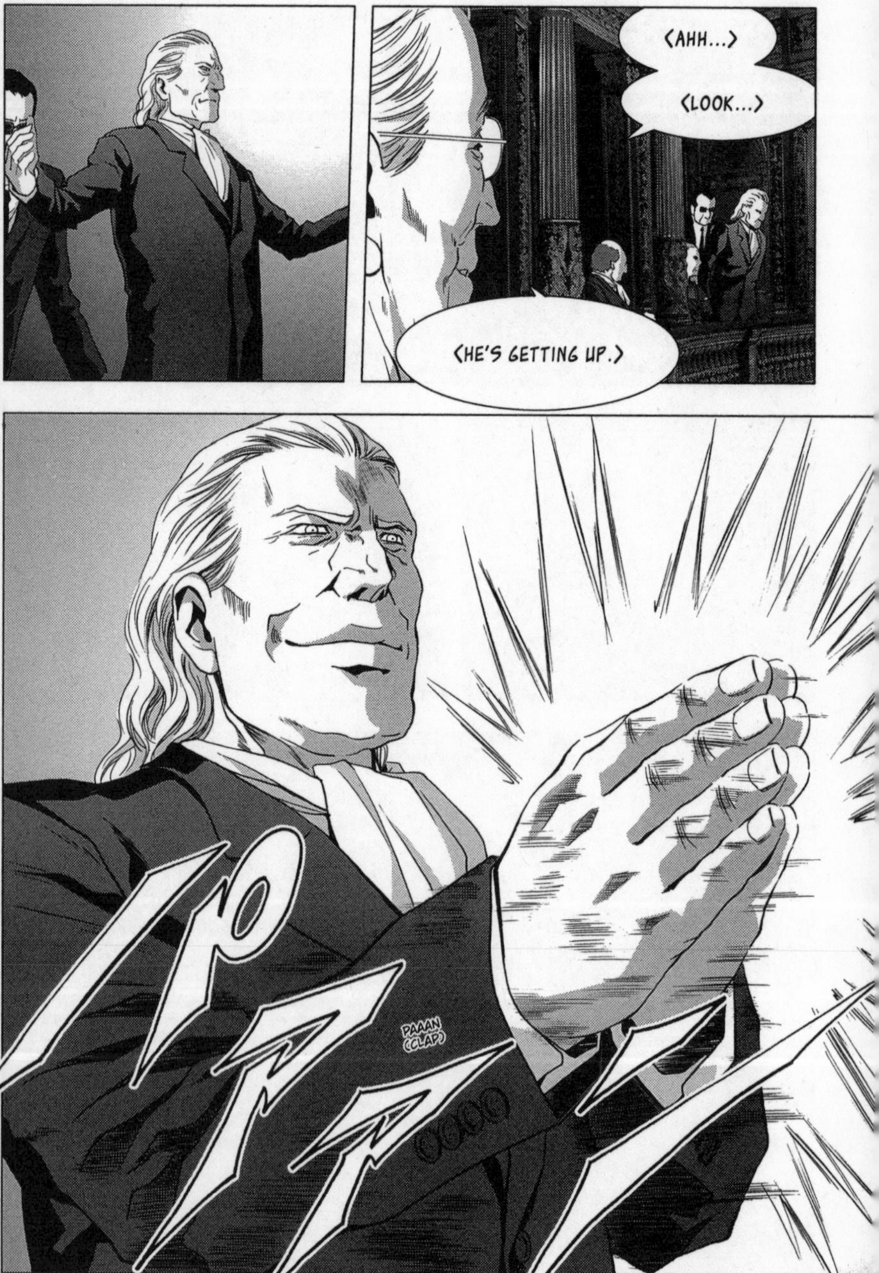
<AHH...>
<LOOK...>
<HE'S GETTING UP.>
PAAAN (CLAP)

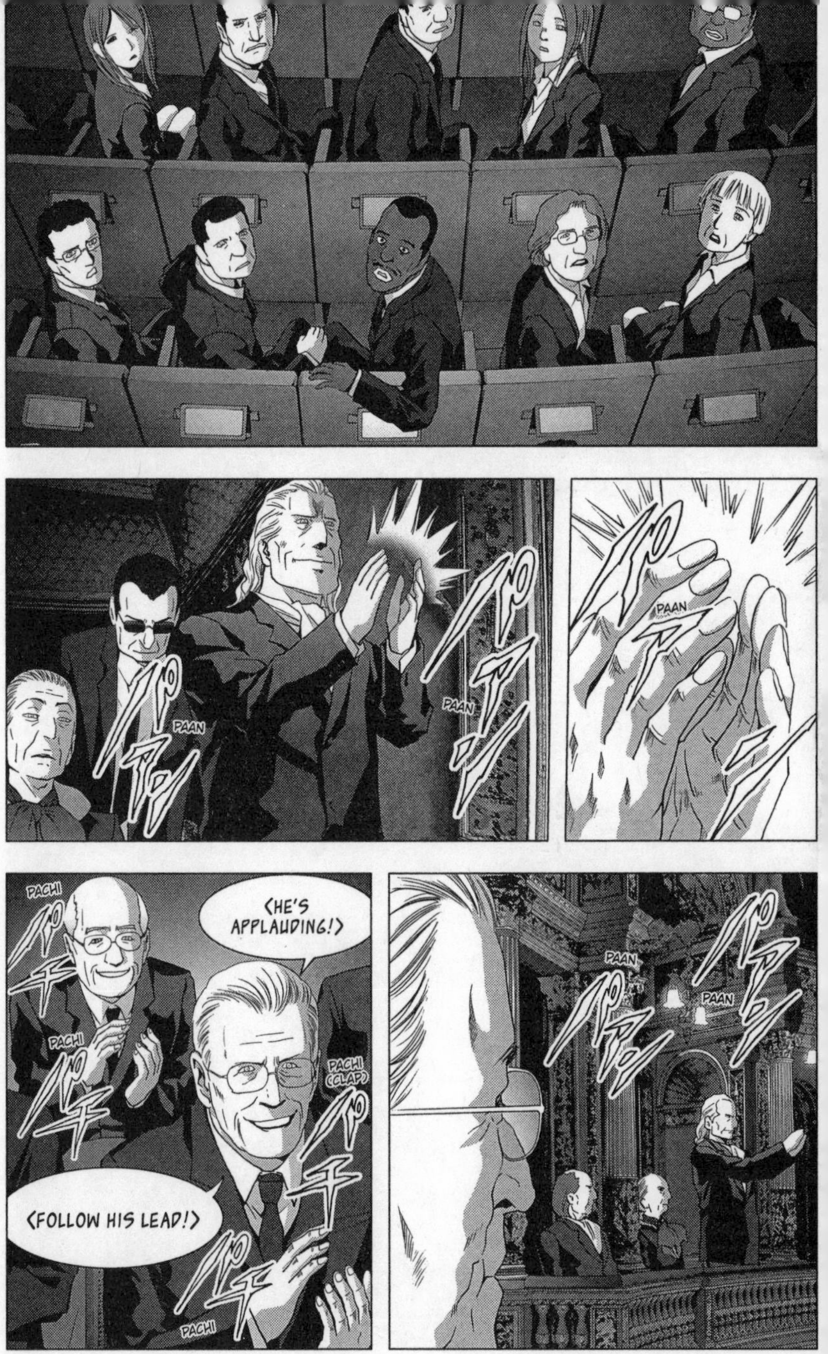
PAAN
PAAN
PAAN
PAAN
PAAN
PACHI
<HE'S APPLAUDING!>
PACHI
PACHI (CLAP)
<FOLLOW HIS LEAD!>
PACHI

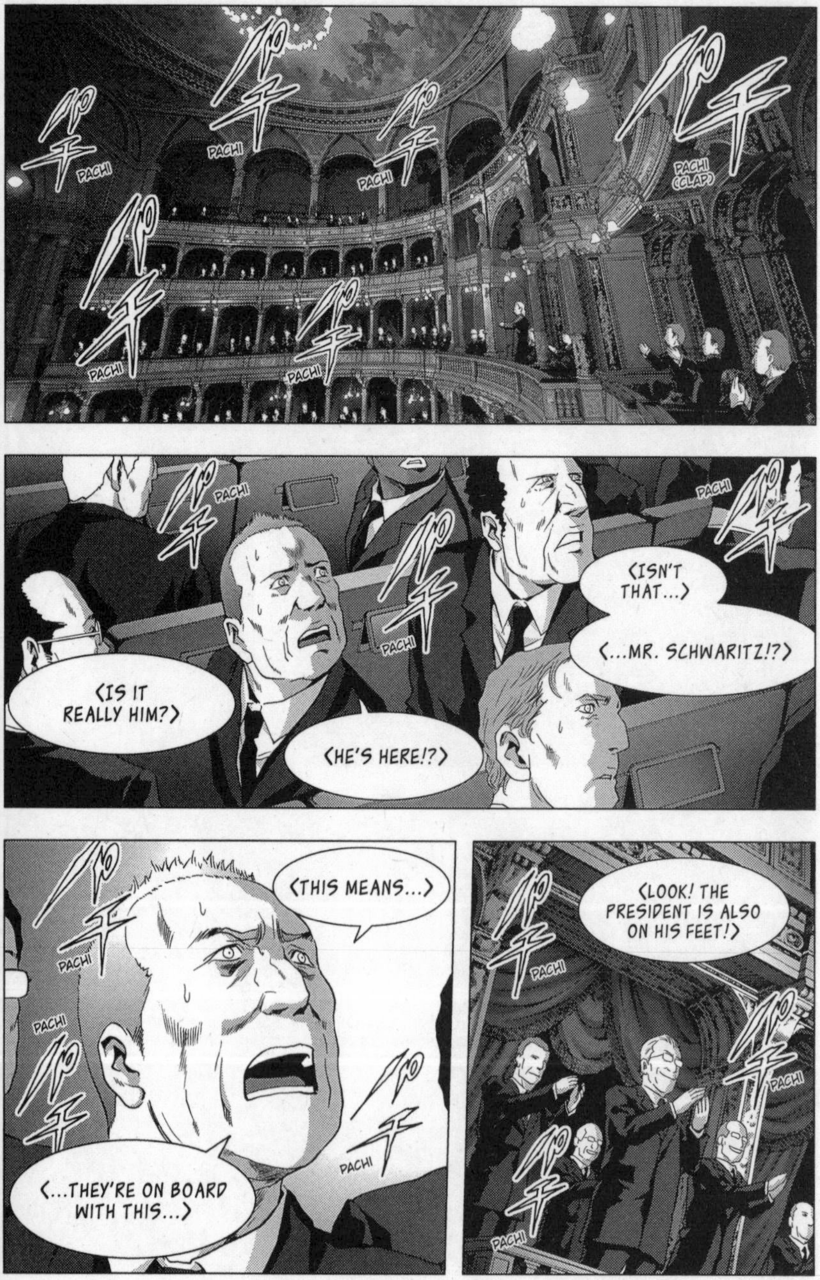
PACHI (CLAP)
PACHI
PACHI
PACHI
PACHI
PACHI
PACHI
<ISN'T THAT...>
<...MR. SCHWARITZ!?>
PACHI
PACHI
<HE'S HERE!?>
<IS IT REALLY HIM?>
<LOOK! THE PRESIDENT IS ALSO ON HIS FEET!>
PACHI
PACHI
PACHI
<THIS MEANS...>
PACHI
PACHI
PACHI
<...THEY'RE ON BOARD WITH THIS...>

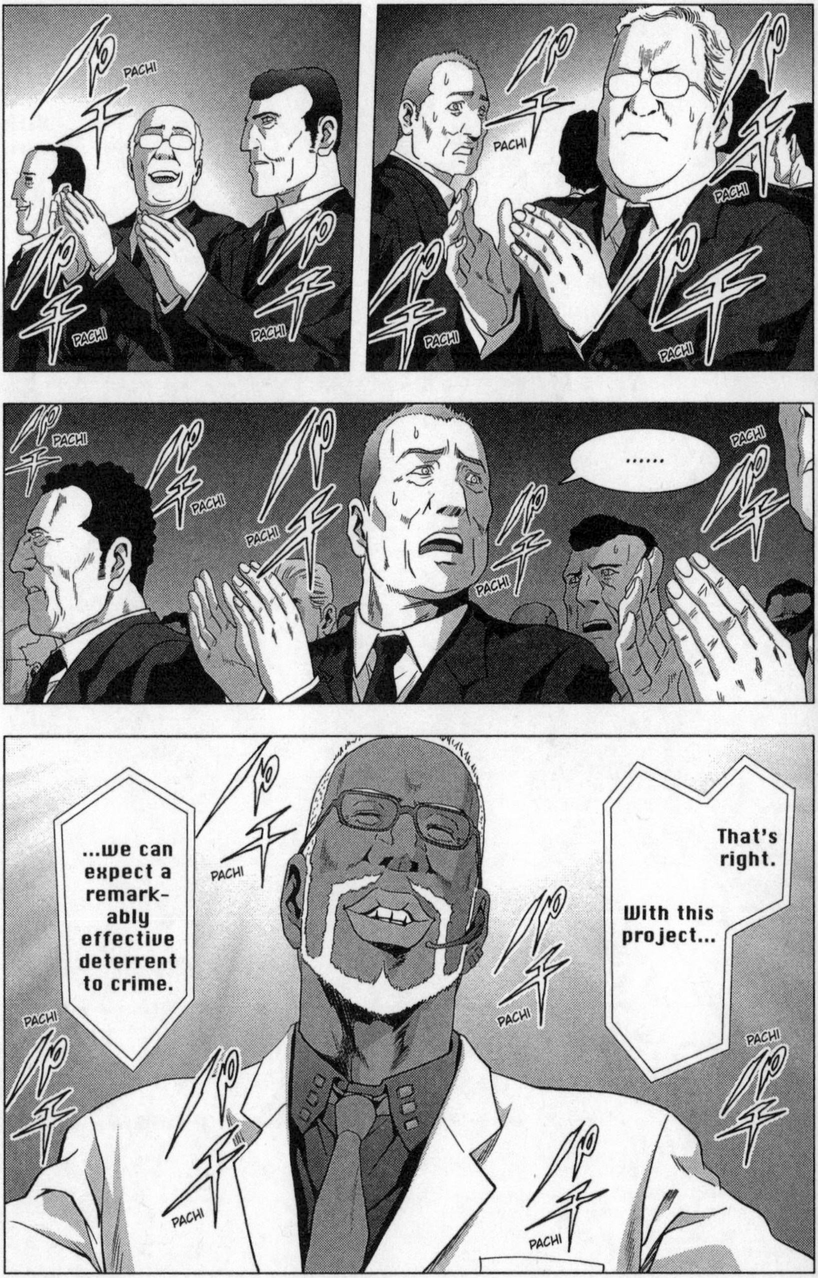
PACHI
PACHI
PACHI
PACHI
PACHI
PACHI
PACHI
PACHI
......
PACHI
PACHI
PACHI
PACHI
That's right.
With this project...
...we can expect a remarkably effective deterrent to crime.
PACHI
PACHI
PACHI
PACHI
PACHI
PACHI

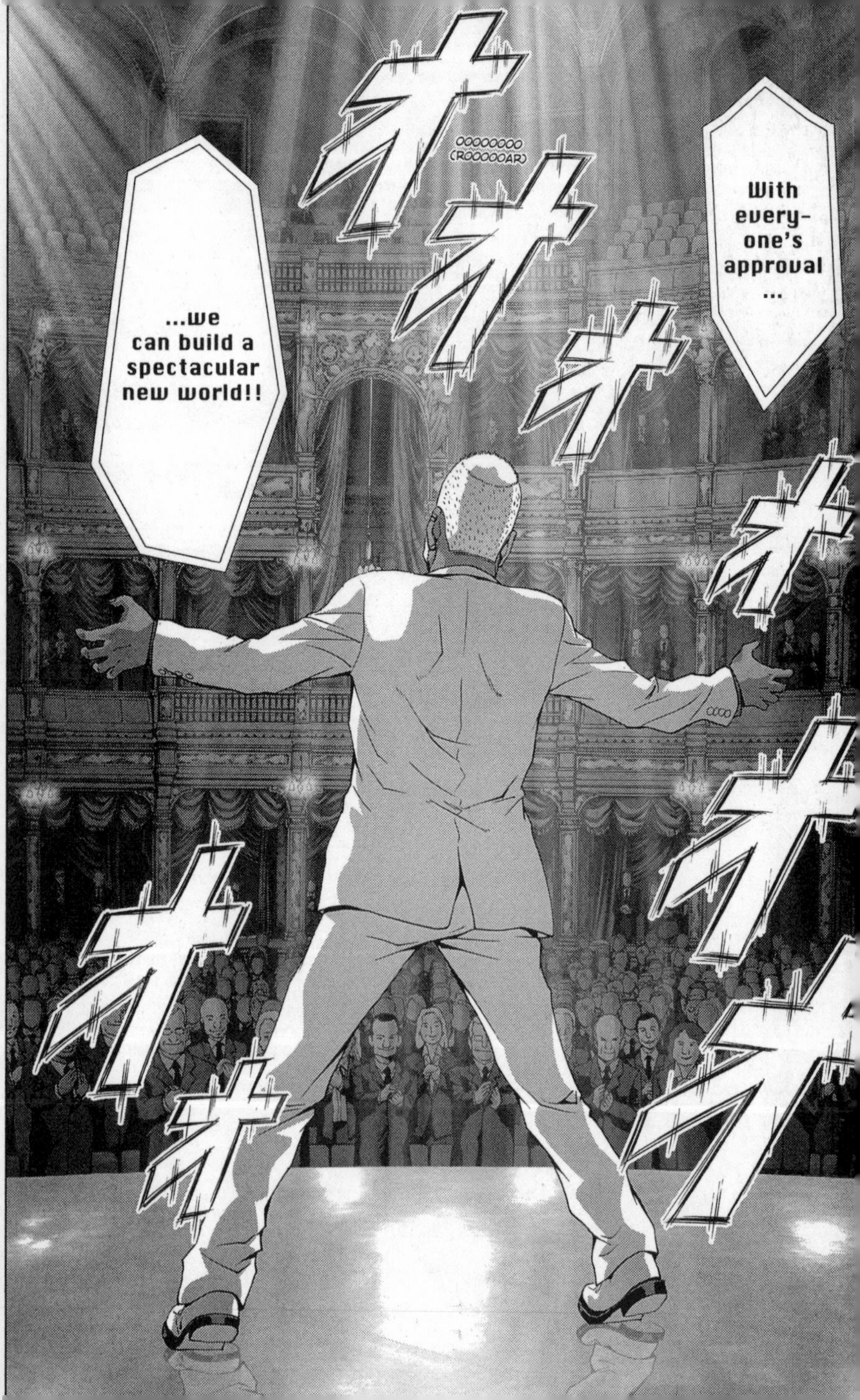
With every-one's approval ...
OOOOOOOOO (ROOOOOAR)
...we can build a spectacular new world!!

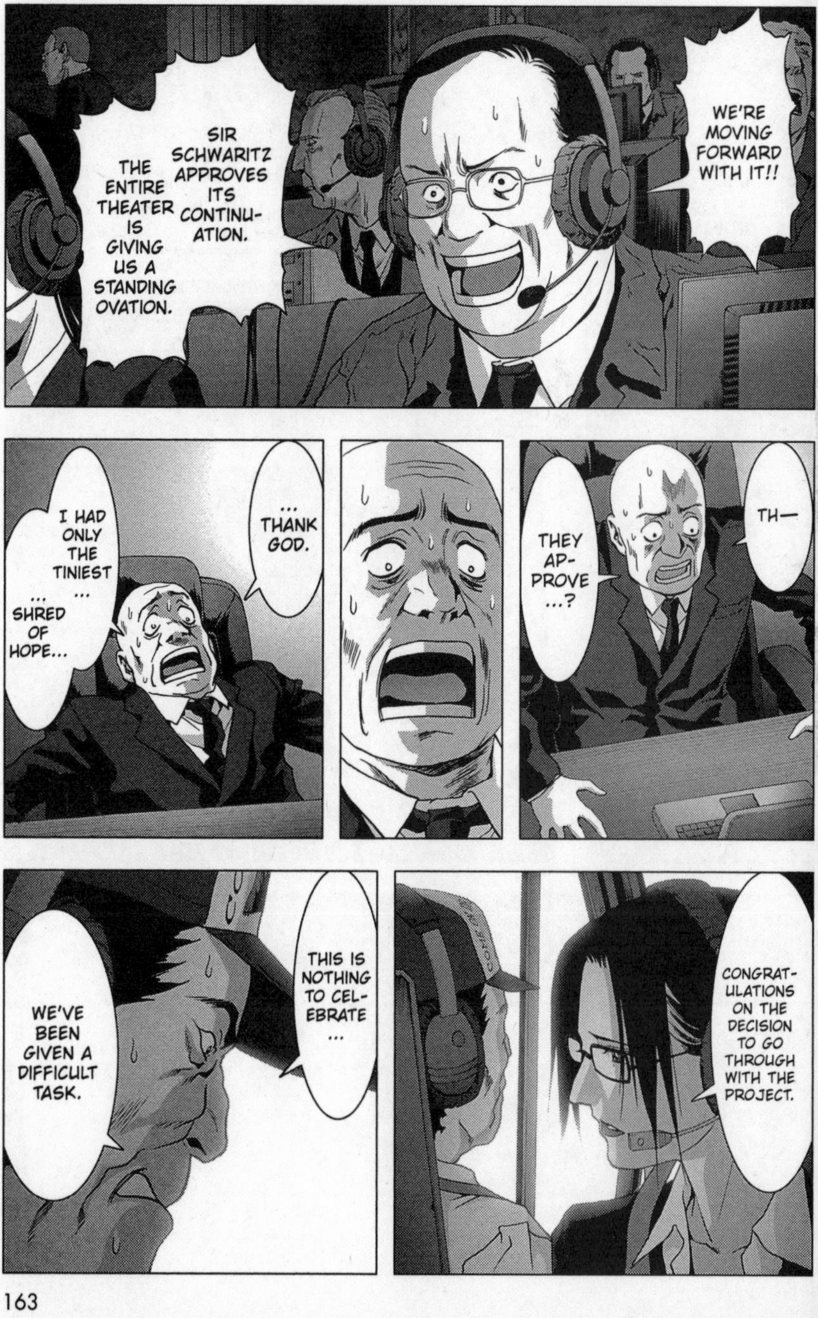
WE'RE MOVING FORWARD WITH IT!!
SIR SCHWARITZ APPROVES ITS CONTINUATION.
THE ENTIRE THEATER IS GIVING US A STANDING OVATION.
TH—
THEY APPROVE...?
... THANK GOD.
I HAD ONLY THE TINIEST ... SHRED OF HOPE...
CONGRATULATIONS ON THE DECISION TO GO THROUGH WITH THE PROJECT.
THIS IS NOTHING TO CELEBRATE ...
WE'VE BEEN GIVEN A DIFFICULT TASK.

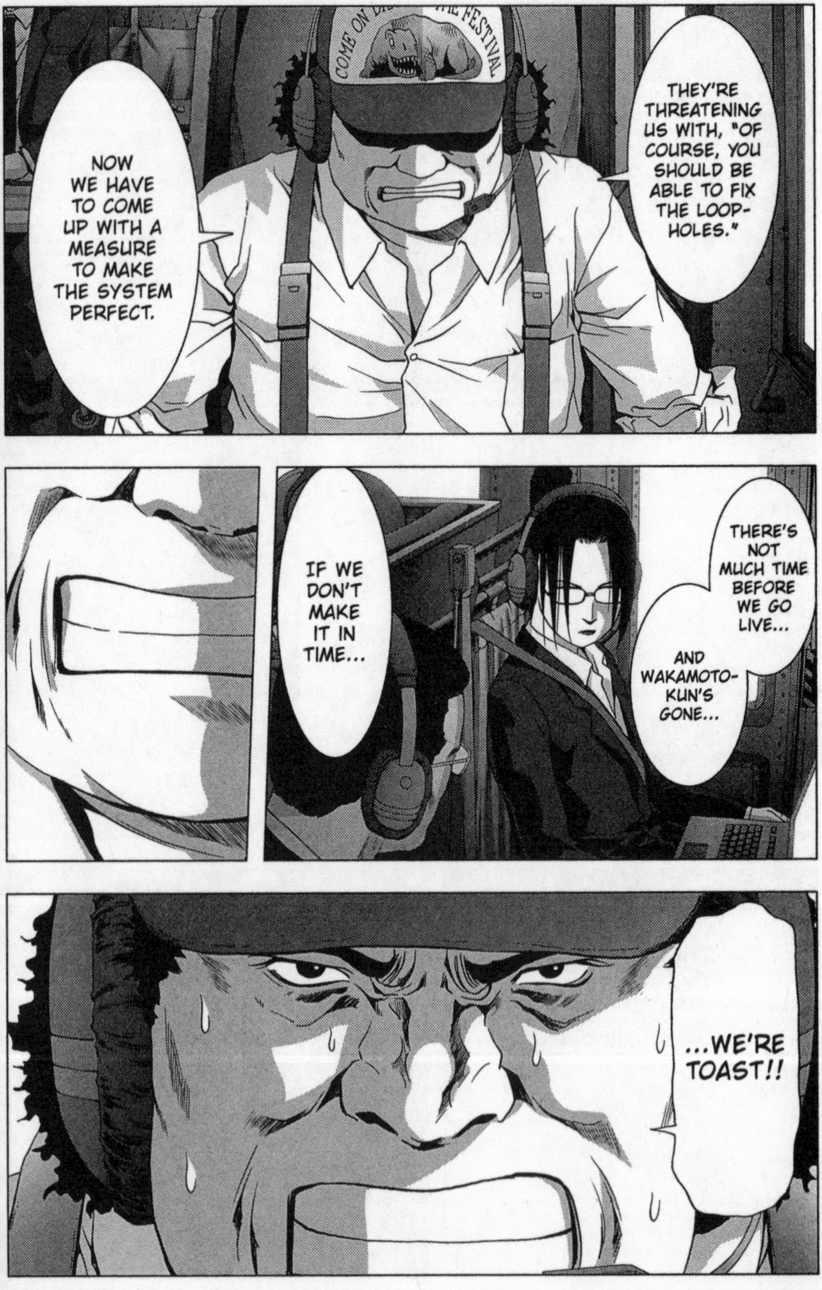
THEY'RE THREATENING US WITH, "OF COURSE, YOU SHOULD BE ABLE TO FIX THE LOOP-HOLES."
NOW WE HAVE TO COME UP WITH A MEASURE TO MAKE THE SYSTEM PERFECT.
THERE'S NOT MUCH TIME BEFORE WE GO LIVE...
AND WAKAMOTO-KUN'S GONE...
IF WE DON'T MAKE IT IN TIME...
...WE'RE TOAST!!

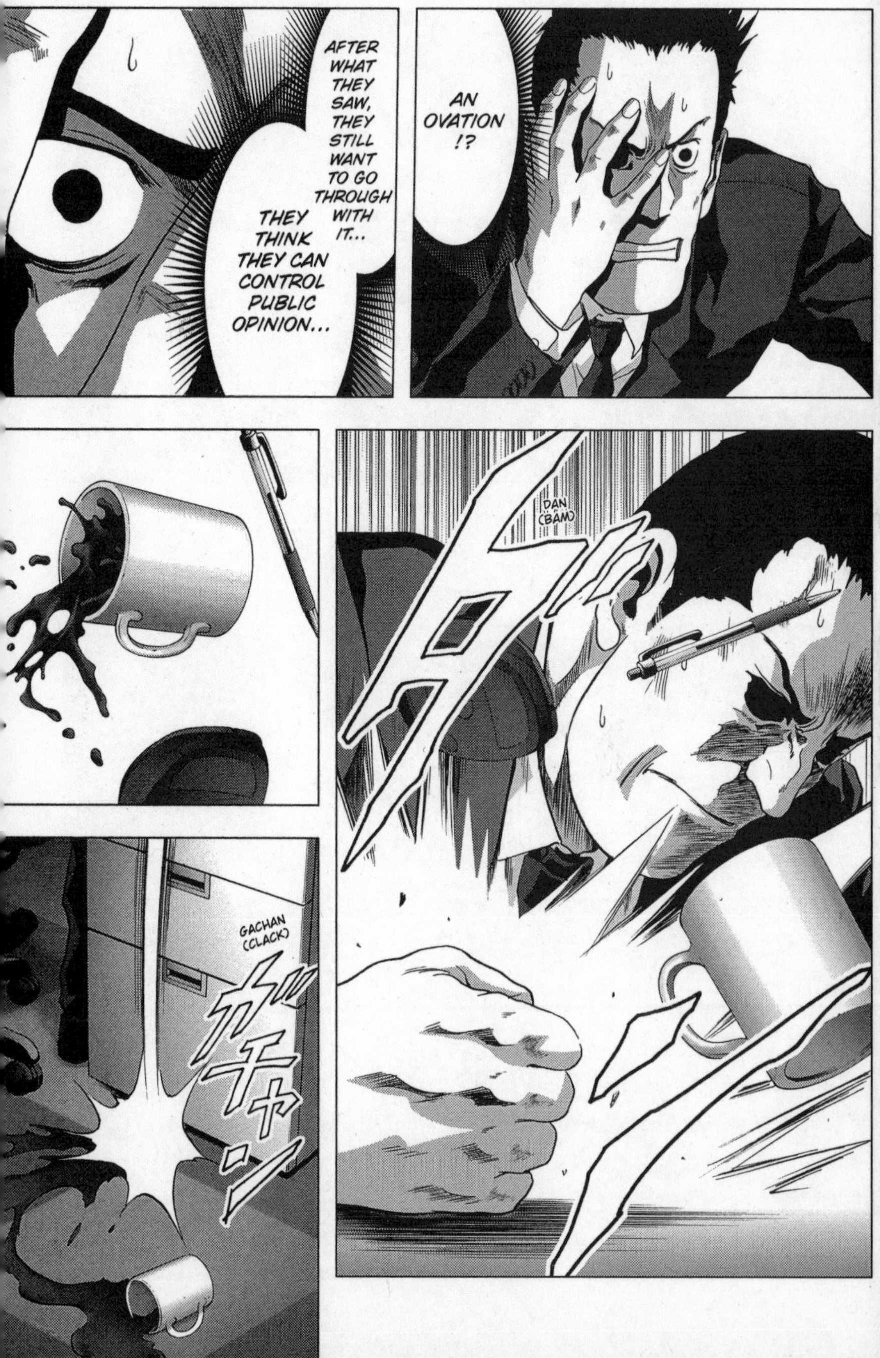
AN OVATION !?
AFTER WHAT THEY SAW, THEY STILL WANT TO GO THROUGH WITH IT...
THEY THINK THEY CAN CONTROL PUBLIC OPINION...
DAN (BAM)
GACHAN (CLACK)

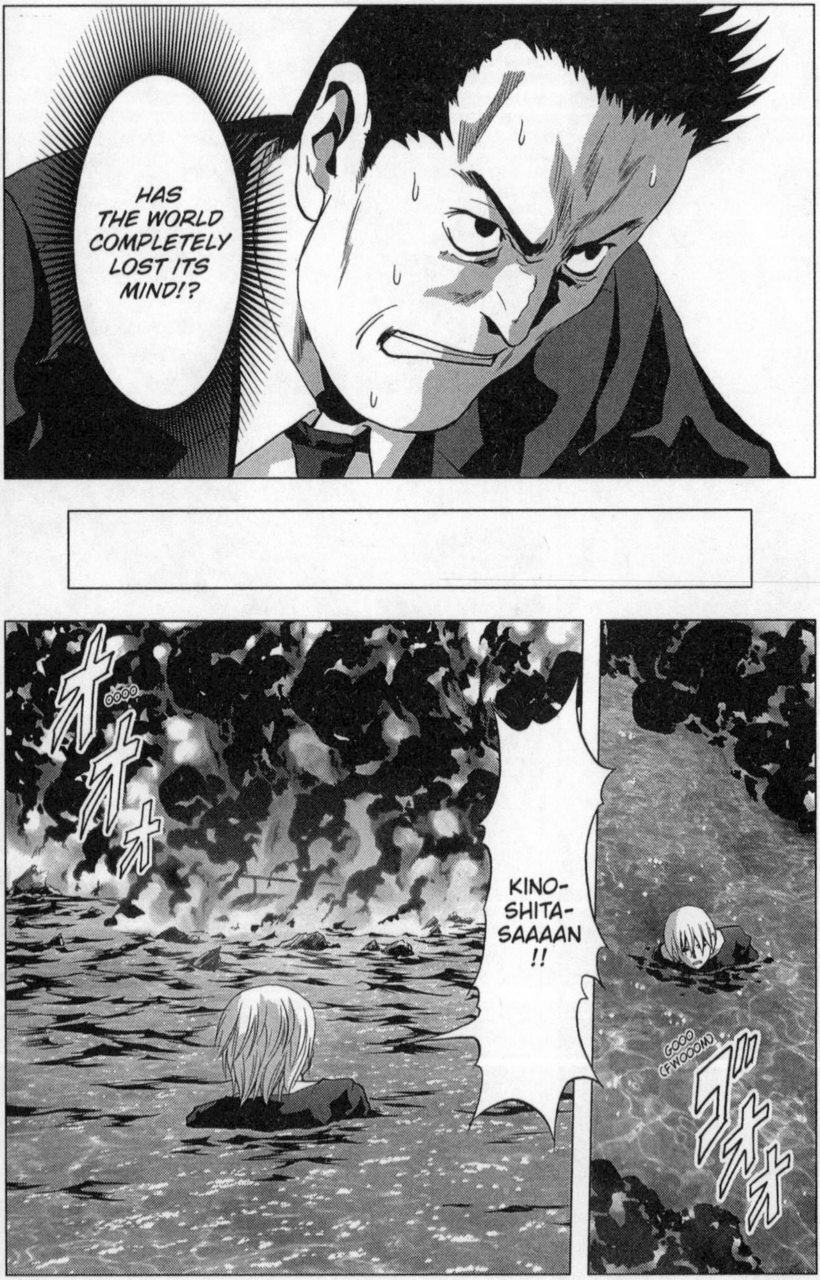
HAS THE WORLD COMPLETELY LOST ITS MIND!?
GOOO (FWOOOM)
KINO-SHITA-SAAAAN!!
OOOO

WE FAILED......

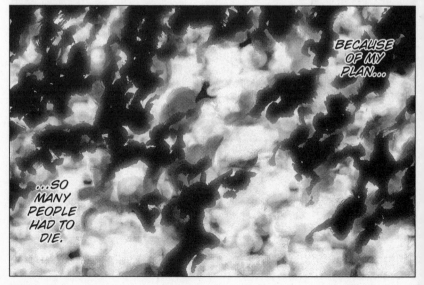

BECAUSE OF MY PLAN...

...SO MANY PEOPLE HAD TO DIE.

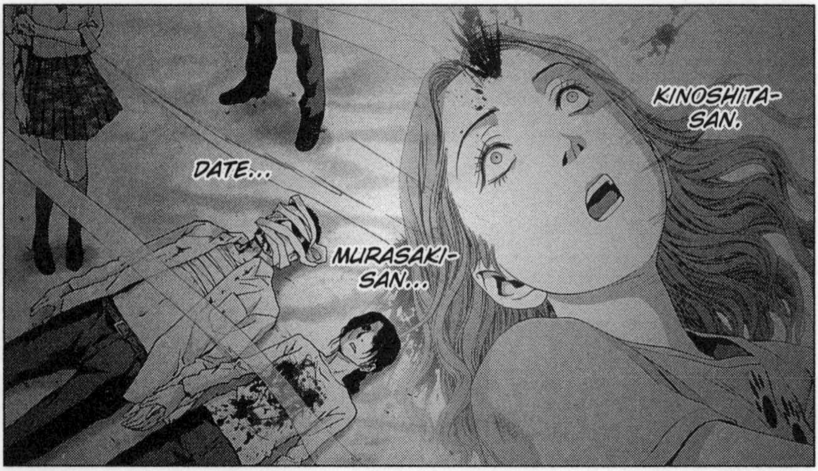
KINOSHITA-SAN.
DATE...
MURASAKI-SAN...

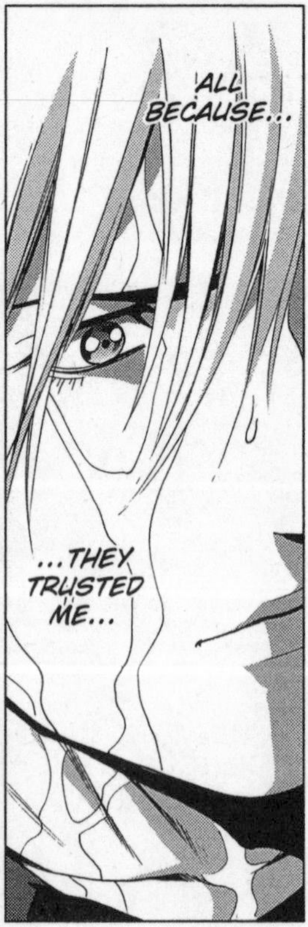
ALL BECAUSE...
...THEY TRUSTED ME...

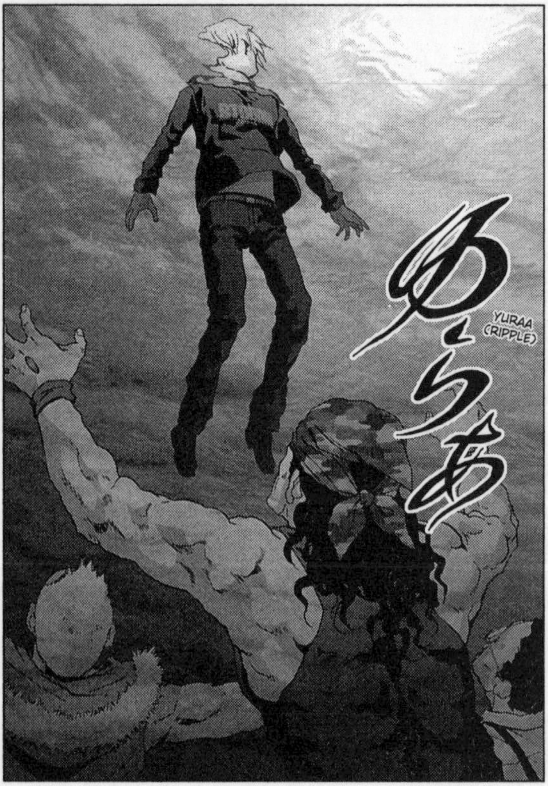
ゆらあ
YURAA (RIPPLE)

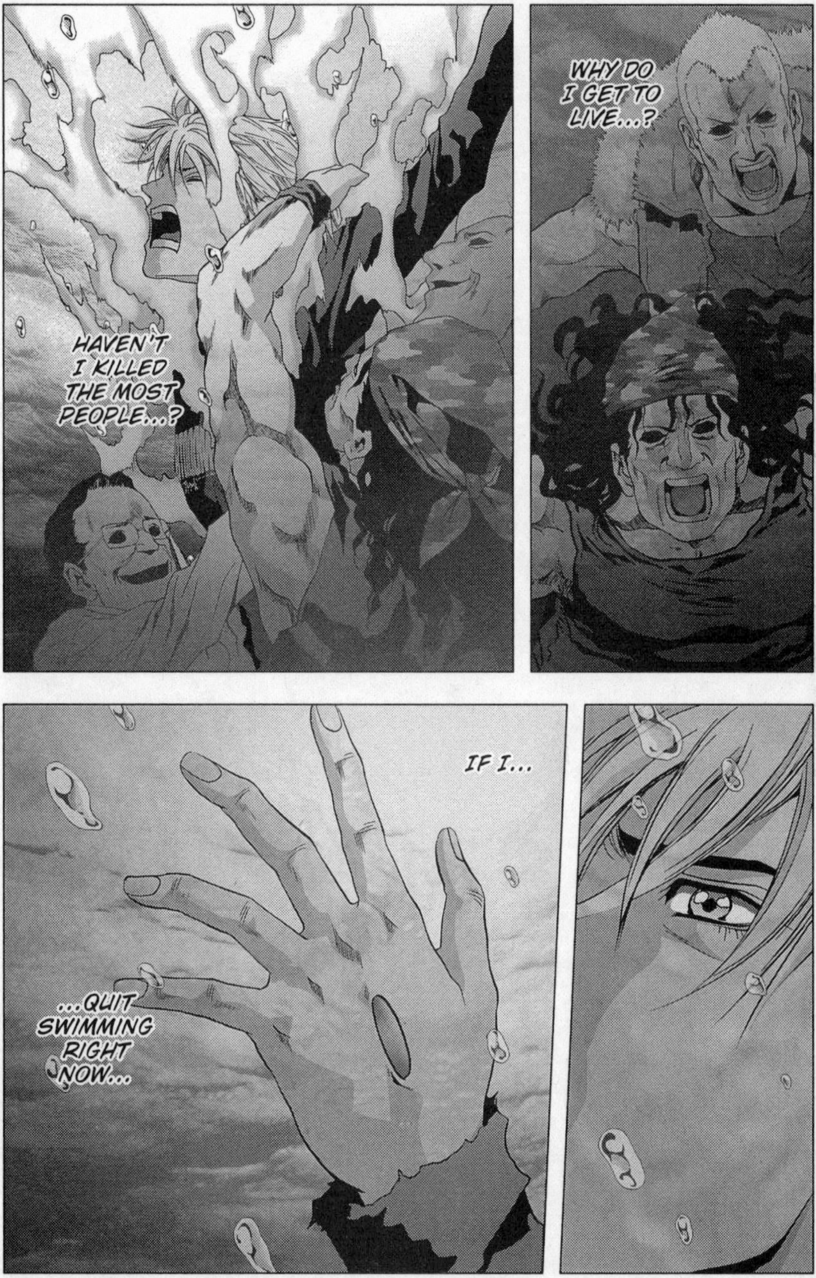
WHY DO I GET TO LIVE...?
HAVEN'T I KILLED THE MOST PEOPLE...?
IF I...
...QUIT SWIMMING RIGHT NOW...

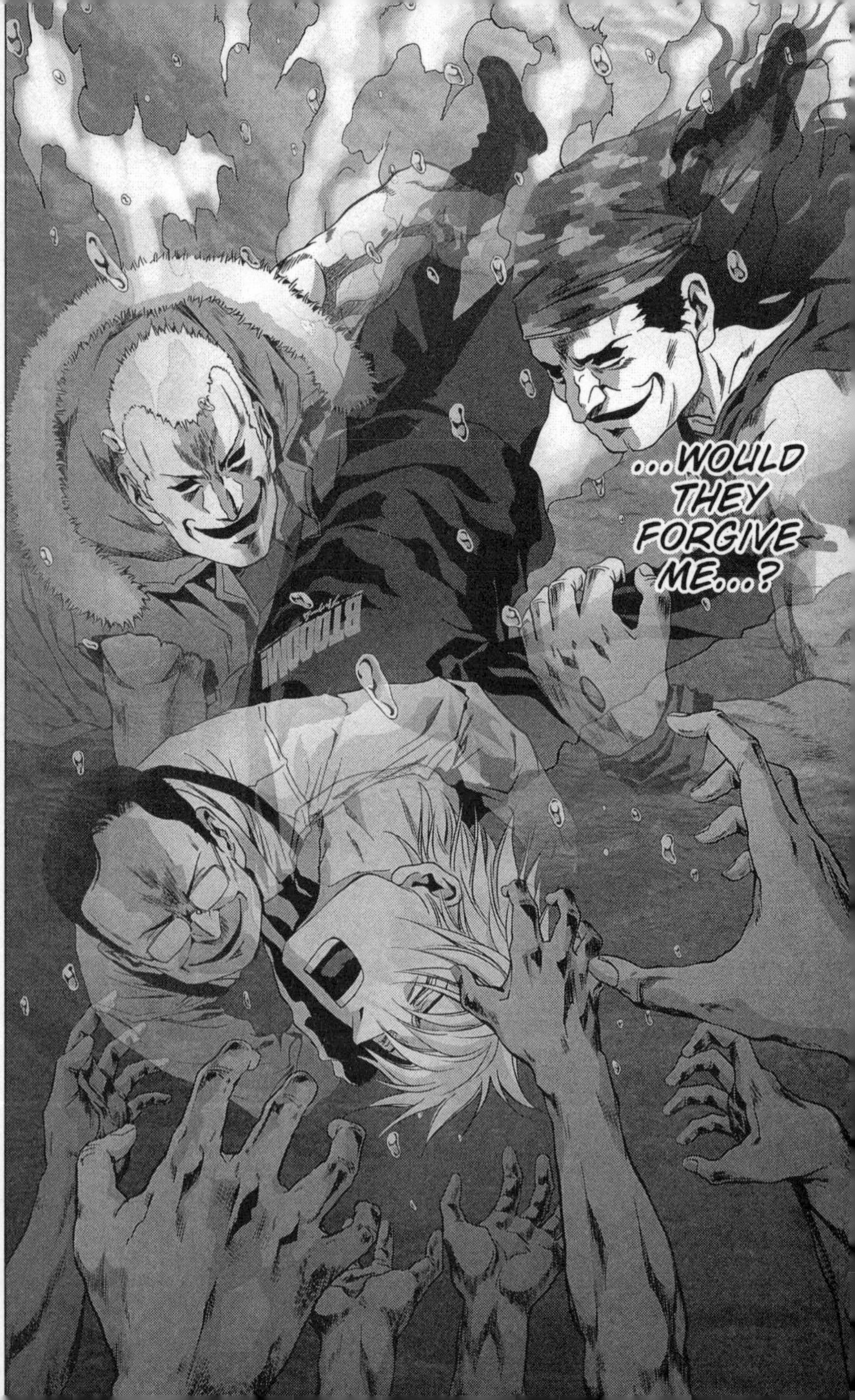
...WOULD THEY FORGIVE ME...?

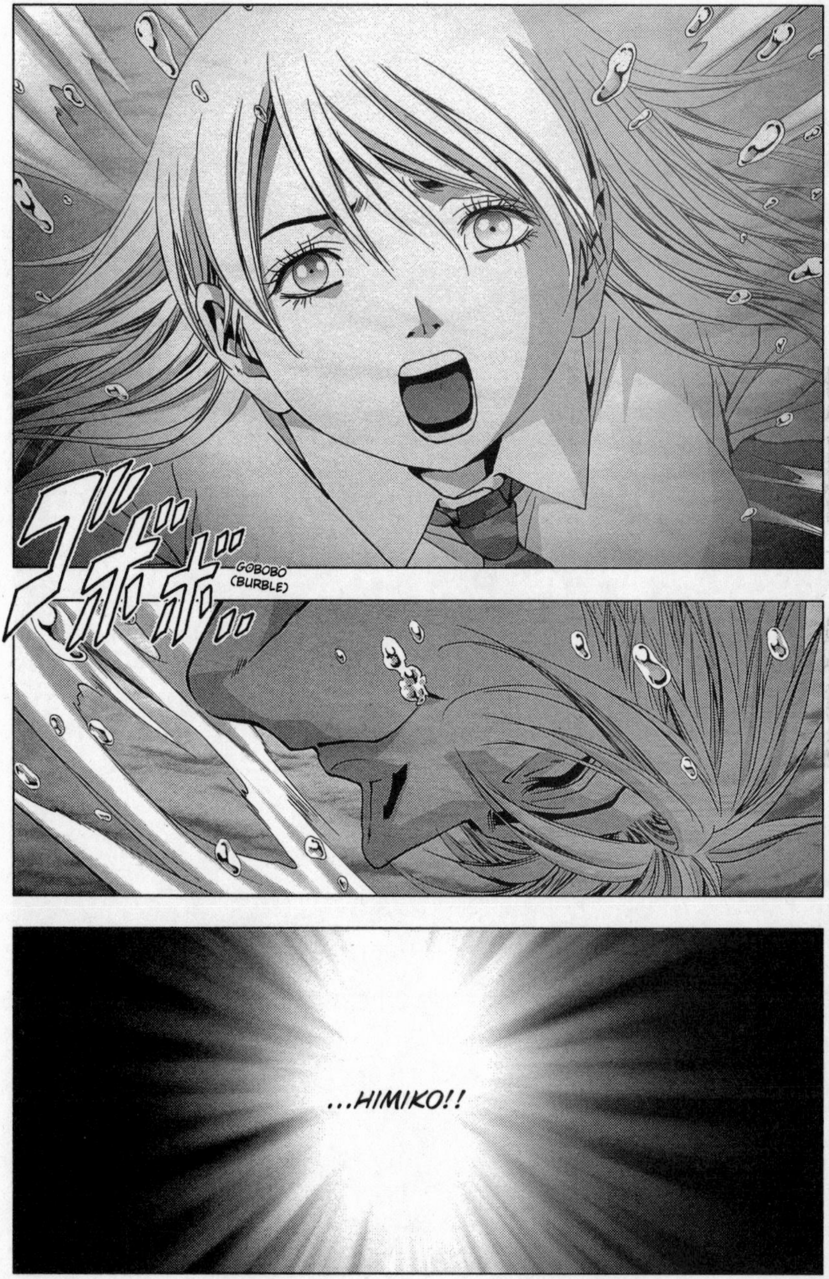
ゴボボ
GOBOBO
(BURBLE)
...HIMIKO!!

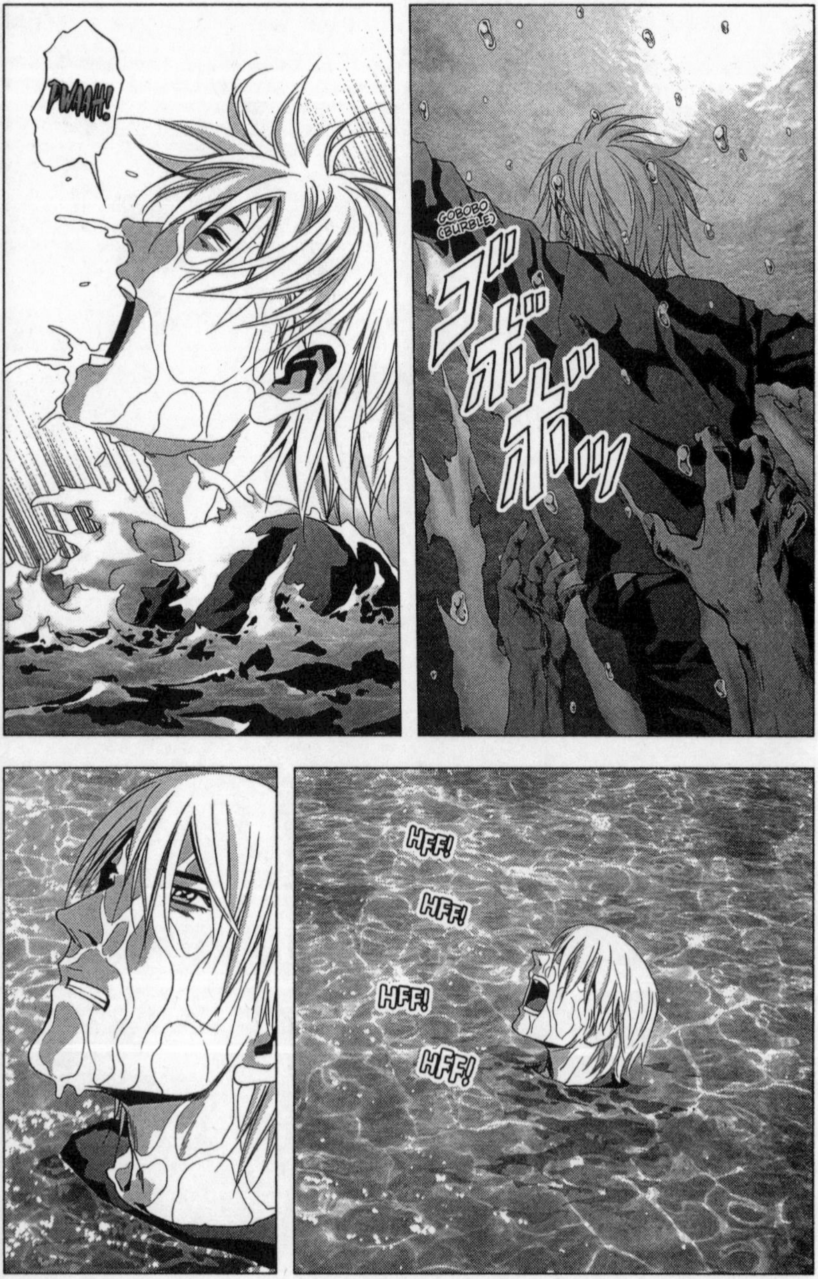
GOBOBO (BURBLE)
ゴボボッ
PWAAH!
HFF!
HFF!
HFF!
HFF!

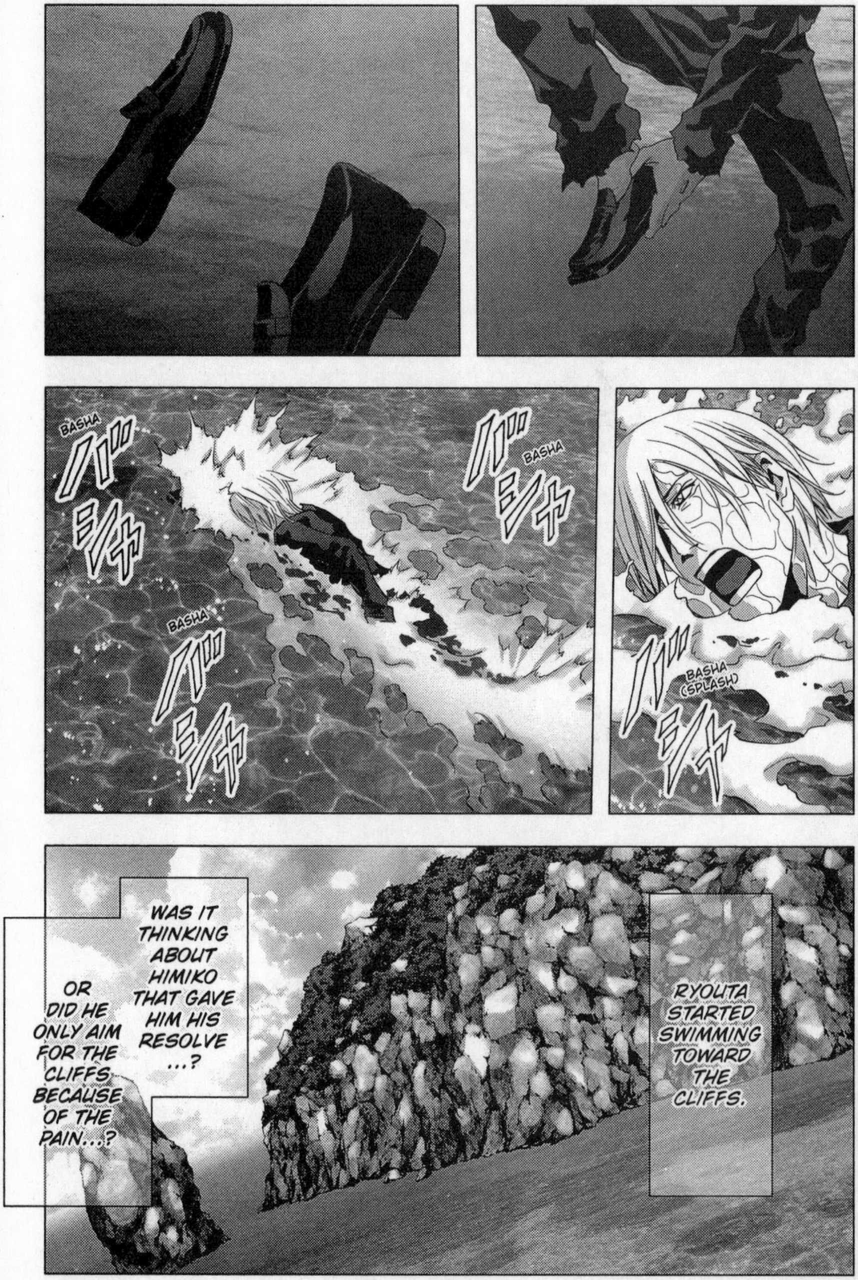
バシャ
BASHA
(SPLASH)
バシャ
BASHA
バシャ
BASHA
バシャ
BASHA
RYOUTA STARTED SWIMMING TOWARD THE CLIFFS.
WAS IT THINKING ABOUT HIMIKO THAT GAVE HIM HIS RESOLVE ...?
OR DID HE ONLY AIM FOR THE CLIFFS BECAUSE OF THE PAIN...?

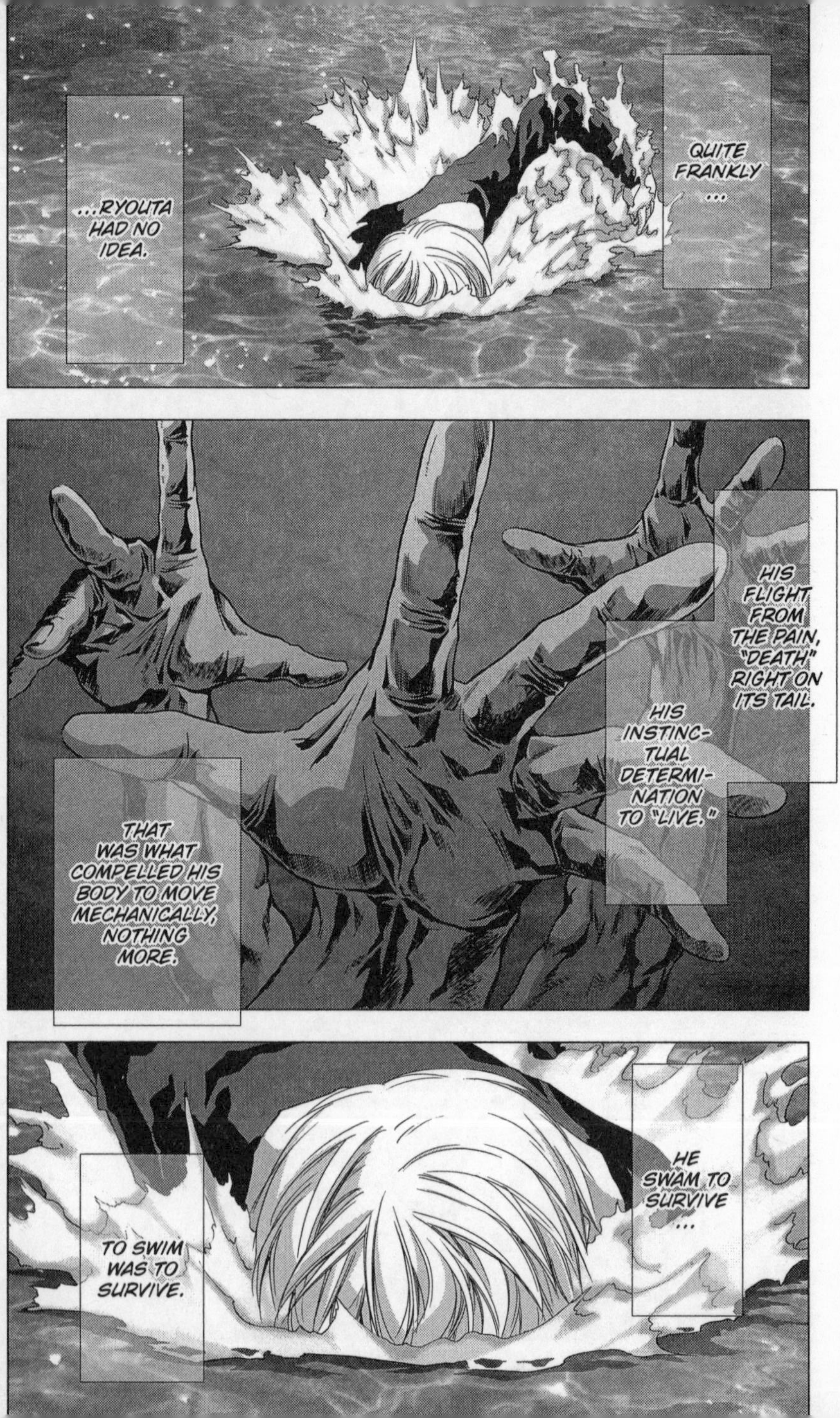
QUITE FRANKLY ...
...RYOUTA HAD NO IDEA.
HIS FLIGHT FROM THE PAIN, "DEATH" RIGHT ON ITS TAIL.
HIS INSTINCTUAL DETERMINATION TO "LIVE."
THAT WAS WHAT COMPELLED HIS BODY TO MOVE MECHANICALLY, NOTHING MORE.
HE SWAM TO SURVIVE ...
TO SWIM WAS TO SURVIVE.

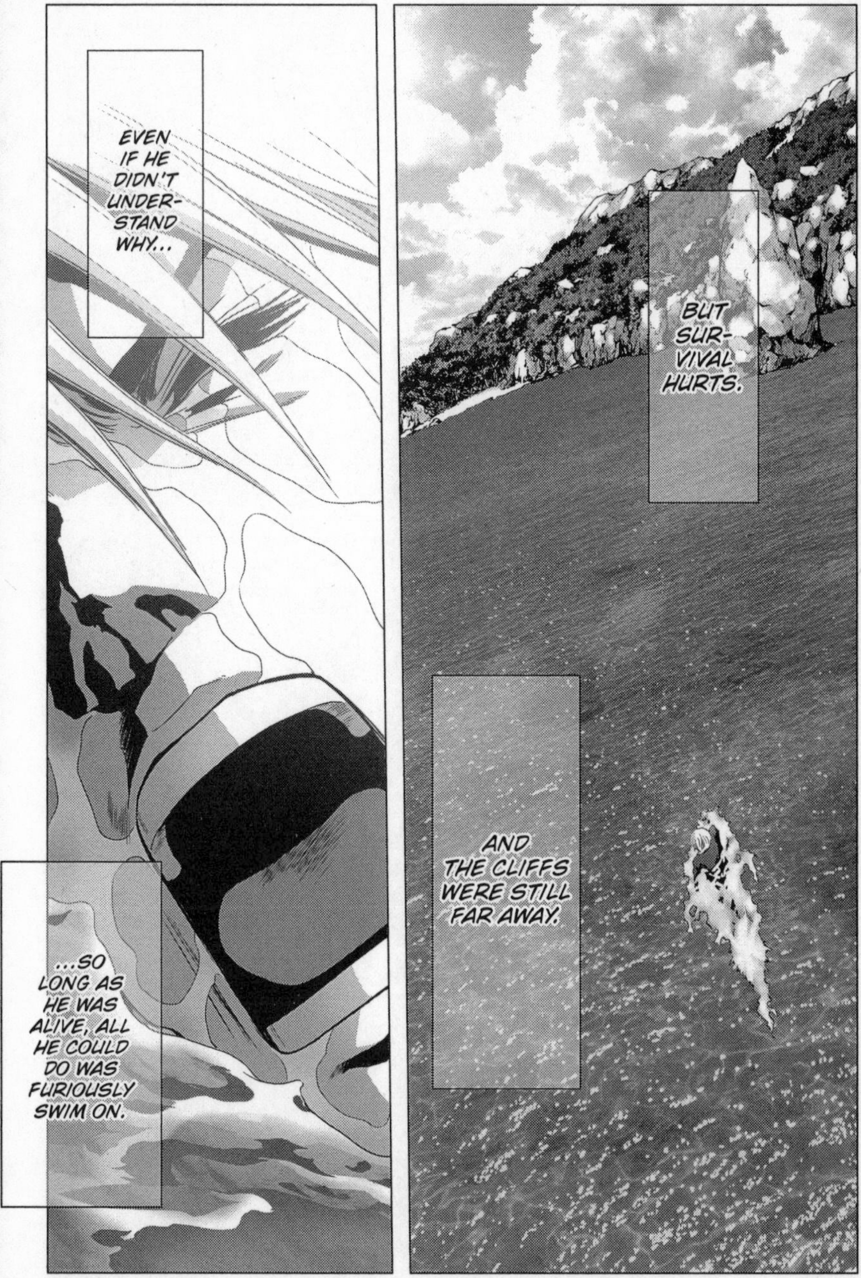
BUT SUR-VIVAL HURTS.
AND THE CLIFFS WERE STILL FAR AWAY.
EVEN IF HE DIDN'T UNDER-STAND WHY...
...SO LONG AS HE WAS ALIVE, ALL HE COULD DO WAS FURIOUSLY SWIM ON.

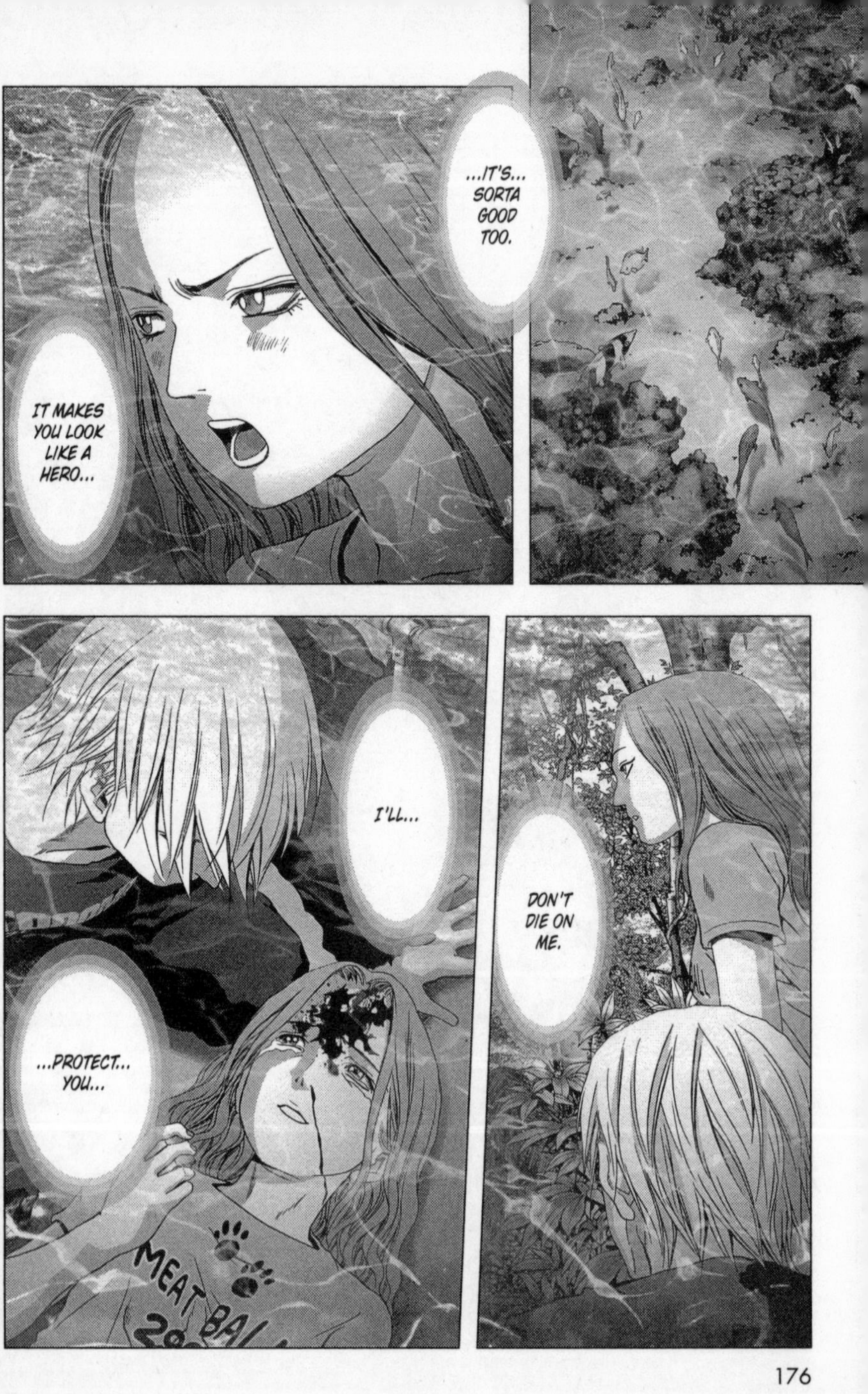
...IT'S... SORTA GOOD TOO.
IT MAKES YOU LOOK LIKE A HERO...
DON'T DIE ON ME.
I'LL...
...PROTECT... YOU...
MEAT BALL

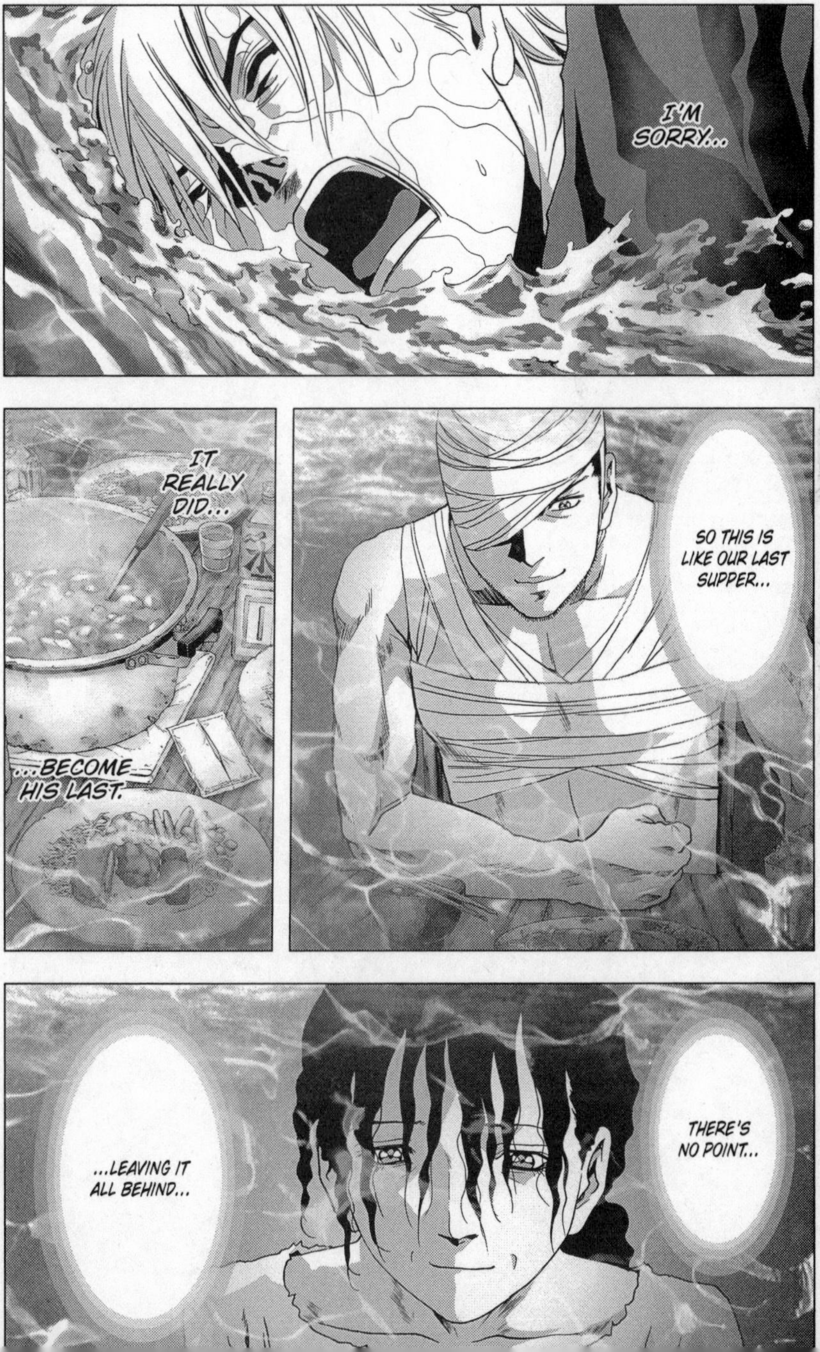
I'M SORRY...
SO THIS IS LIKE OUR LAST SUPPER...
IT REALLY DID...
...BECOME HIS LAST.
THERE'S NO POINT...
...LEAVING IT ALL BEHIND...

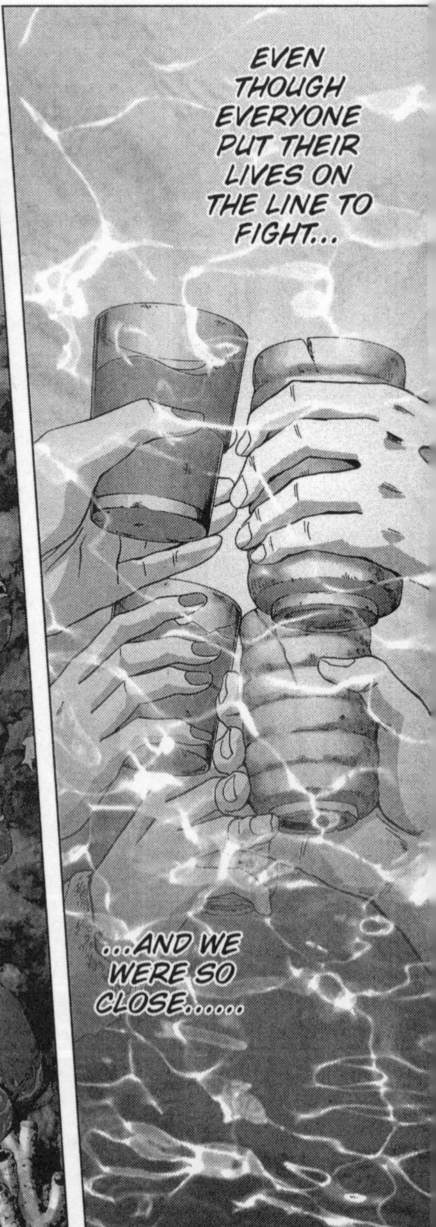
EVEN THOUGH EVERYONE PUT THEIR LIVES ON THE LINE TO FIGHT...
...AND WE WERE SO CLOSE......

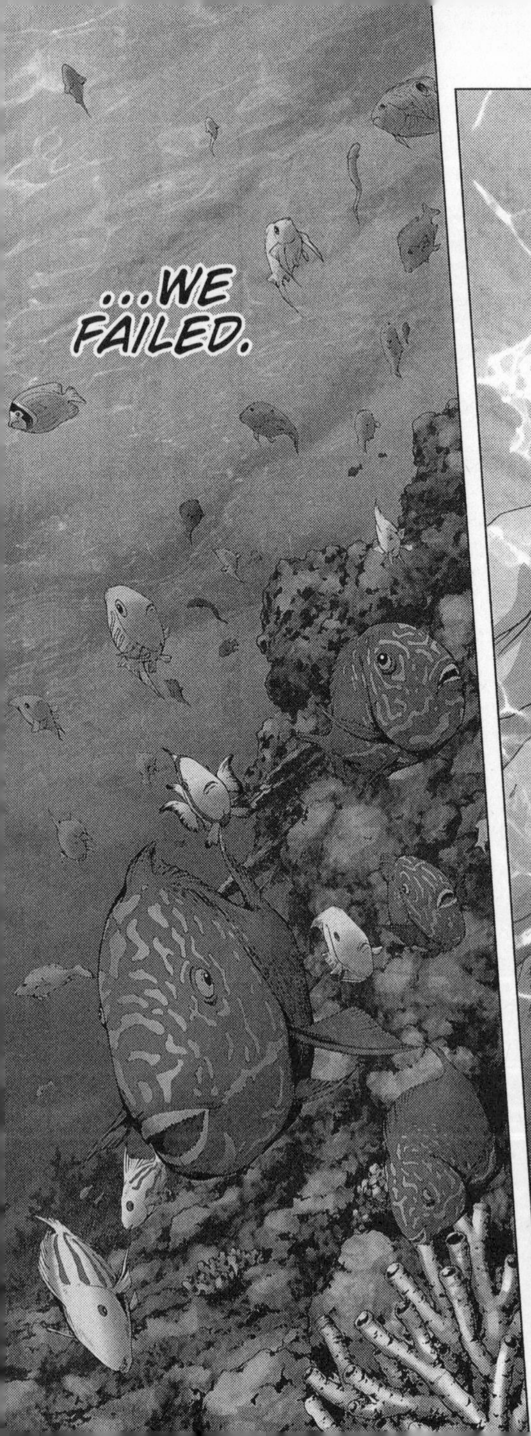
...WE FAILED.

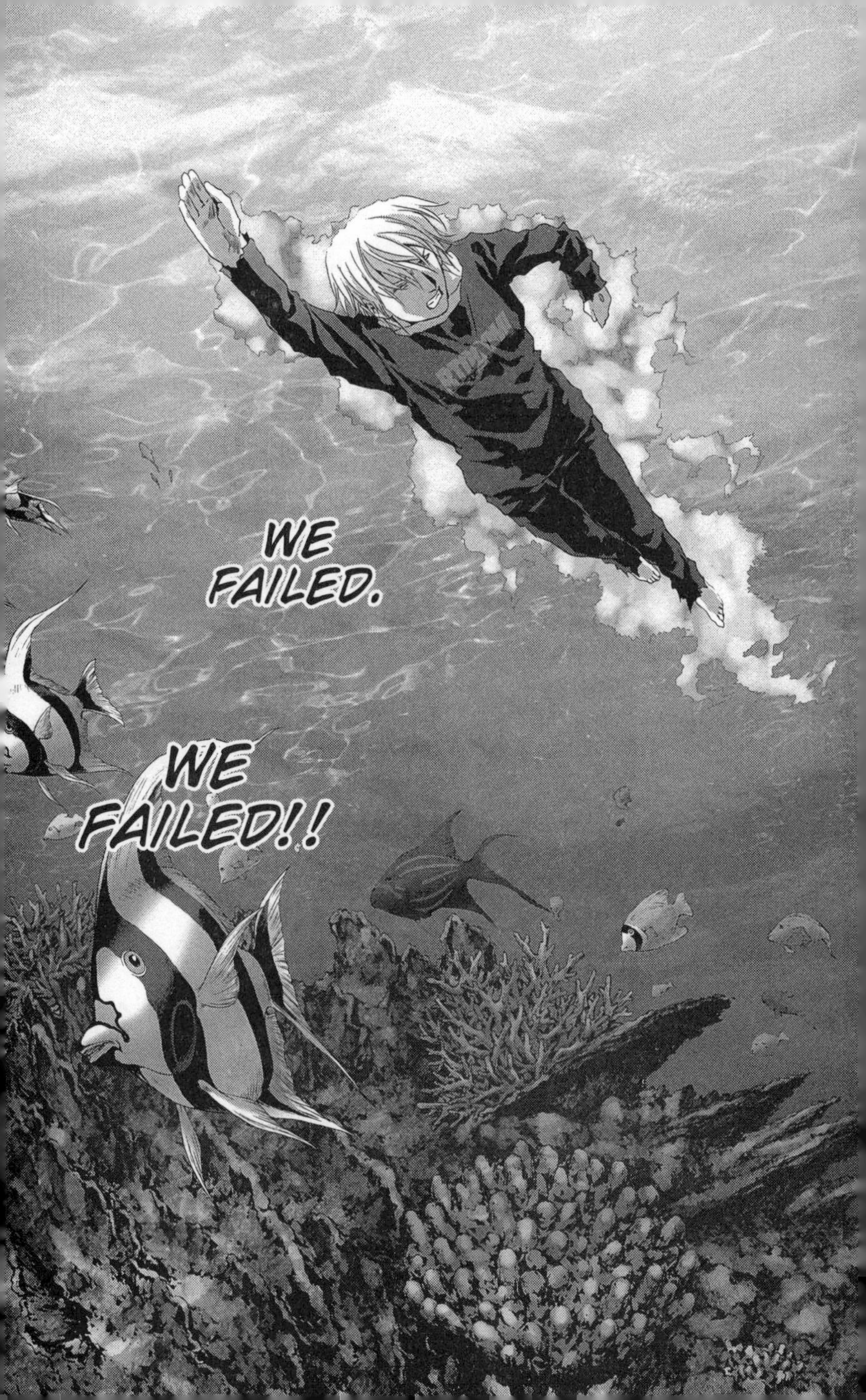
WE FAILED.
WE FAILED!!

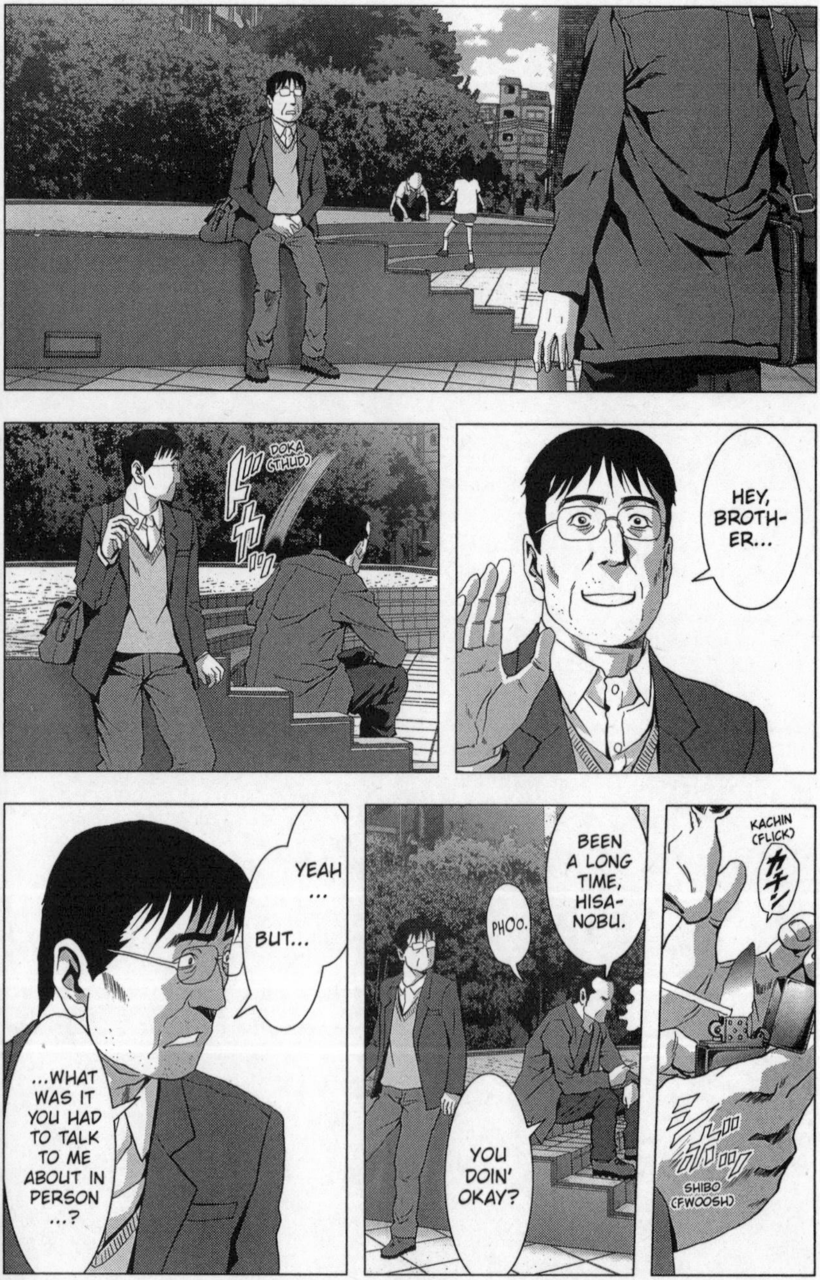
HEY, BROTHER-ER...
DOKA (THUD)
KACHIN (FLICK)
SHIBO (FWOOSH)
BEEN A LONG TIME, HISA-NOBU.
PHOO.
YOU DOIN' OKAY?
YEAH... BUT...
...WHAT WAS IT YOU HAD TO TALK TO ME ABOUT IN PERSON...?

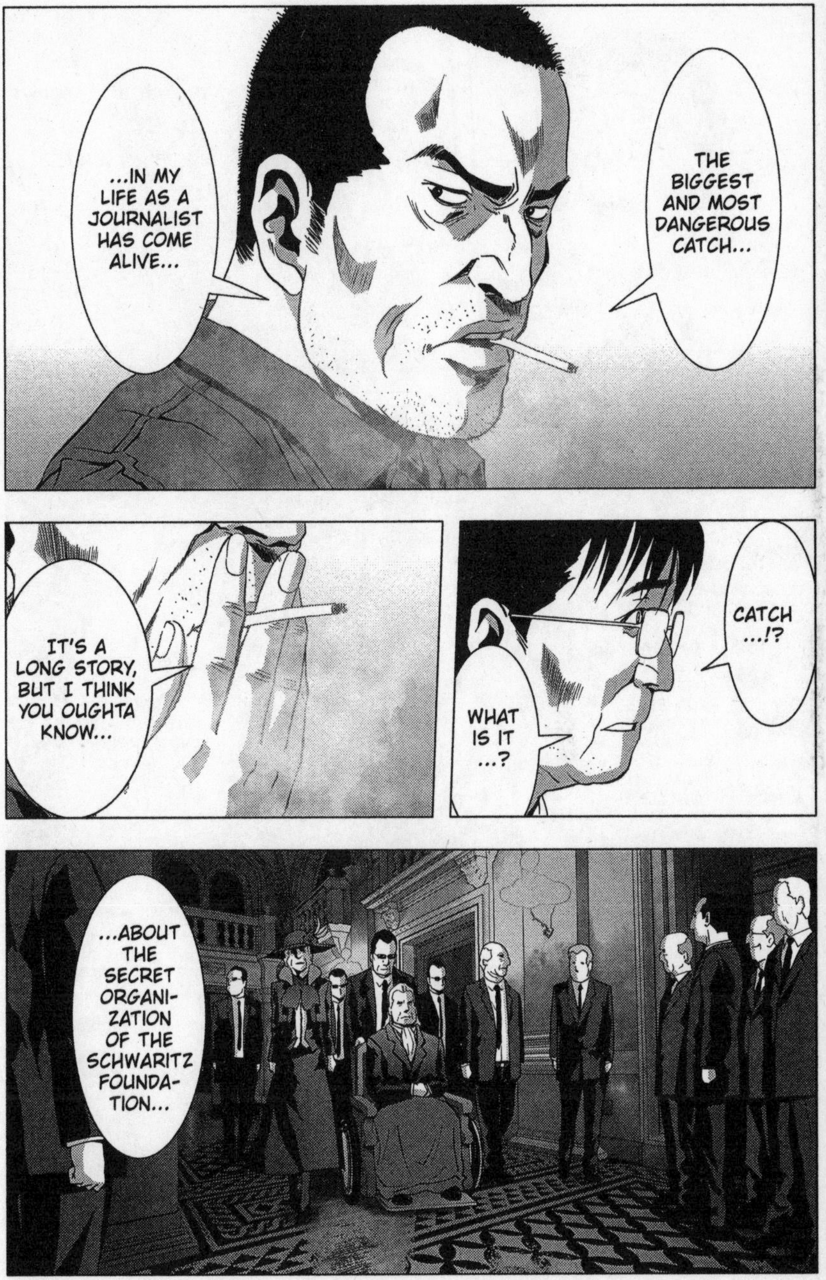
THE BIGGEST AND MOST DANGEROUS CATCH...
...IN MY LIFE AS A JOURNALIST HAS COME ALIVE...
CATCH ...!?
WHAT IS IT ...?
IT'S A LONG STORY, BUT I THINK YOU OUGHTA KNOW...
...ABOUT THE SECRET ORGANI-ZATION OF THE SCHWARITZ FOUNDA-TION...

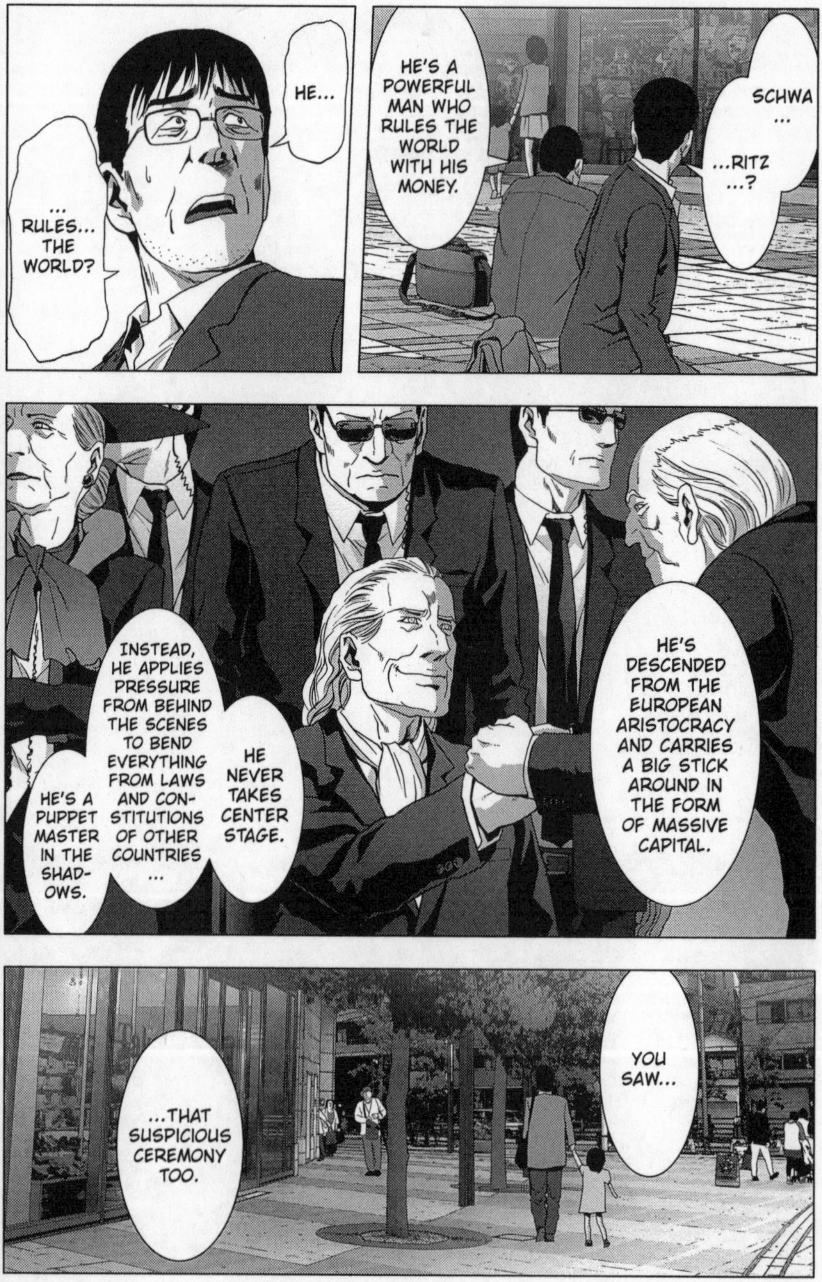
SCHWA ... ...RITZ ...?
HE'S A POWERFUL MAN WHO RULES THE WORLD WITH HIS MONEY.
HE...
... RULES... THE WORLD?
HE'S DESCENDED FROM THE EUROPEAN ARISTOCRACY AND CARRIES A BIG STICK AROUND IN THE FORM OF MASSIVE CAPITAL.
HE NEVER TAKES CENTER STAGE.
INSTEAD, HE APPLIES PRESSURE FROM BEHIND THE SCENES TO BEND EVERYTHING FROM LAWS AND CON-STITUTIONS OF OTHER COUNTRIES ...
HE'S A PUPPET MASTER IN THE SHAD-OWS.
YOU SAW...
...THAT SUSPICIOUS CEREMONY TOO.

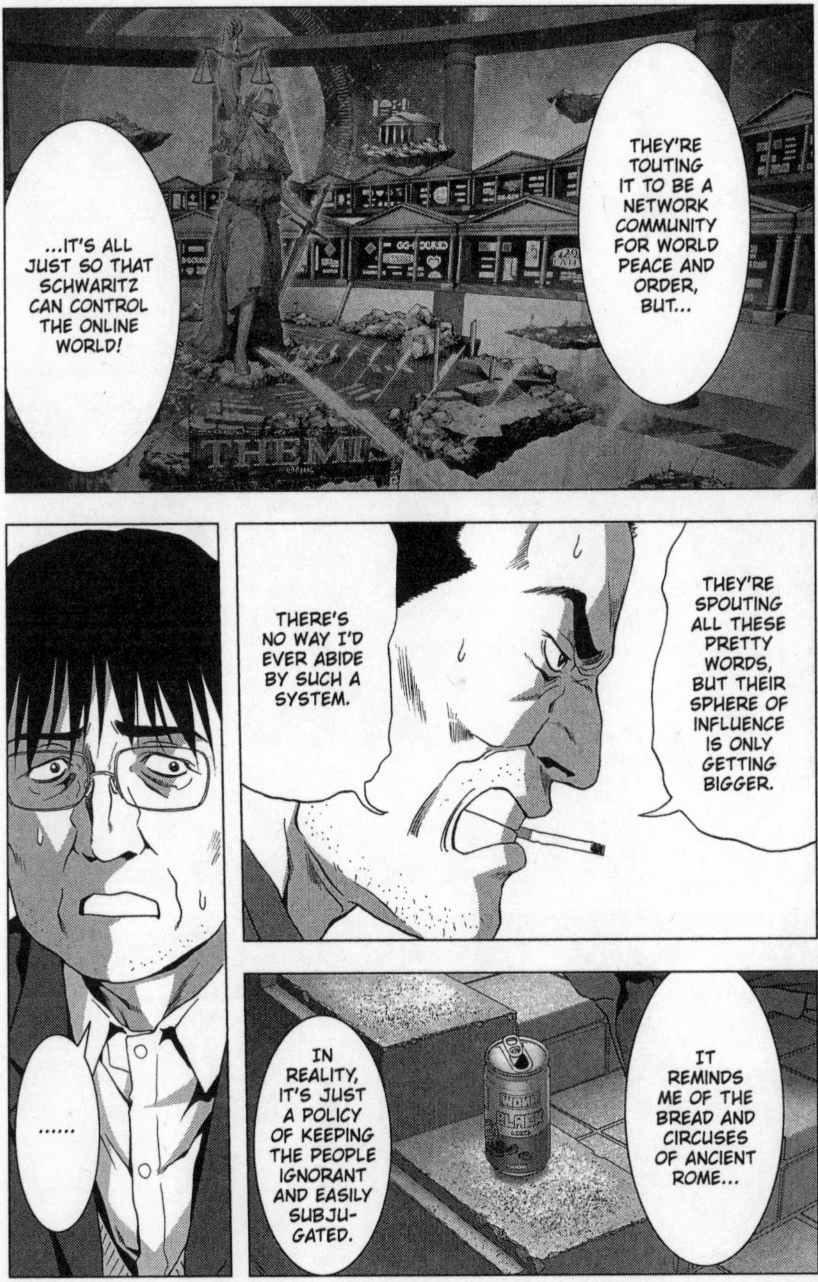
THEY'RE TOUTING IT TO BE A NETWORK COMMUNITY FOR WORLD PEACE AND ORDER, BUT...
...IT'S ALL JUST SO THAT SCHWARITZ CAN CONTROL THE ONLINE WORLD!
THEY'RE SPOUTING ALL THESE PRETTY WORDS, BUT THEIR SPHERE OF INFLUENCE IS ONLY GETTING BIGGER.
THERE'S NO WAY I'D EVER ABIDE BY SUCH A SYSTEM.
IT REMINDS ME OF THE BREAD AND CIRCUSES OF ANCIENT ROME...
IN REALITY, IT'S JUST A POLICY OF KEEPING THE PEOPLE IGNORANT AND EASILY SUBJU-GATED.
......

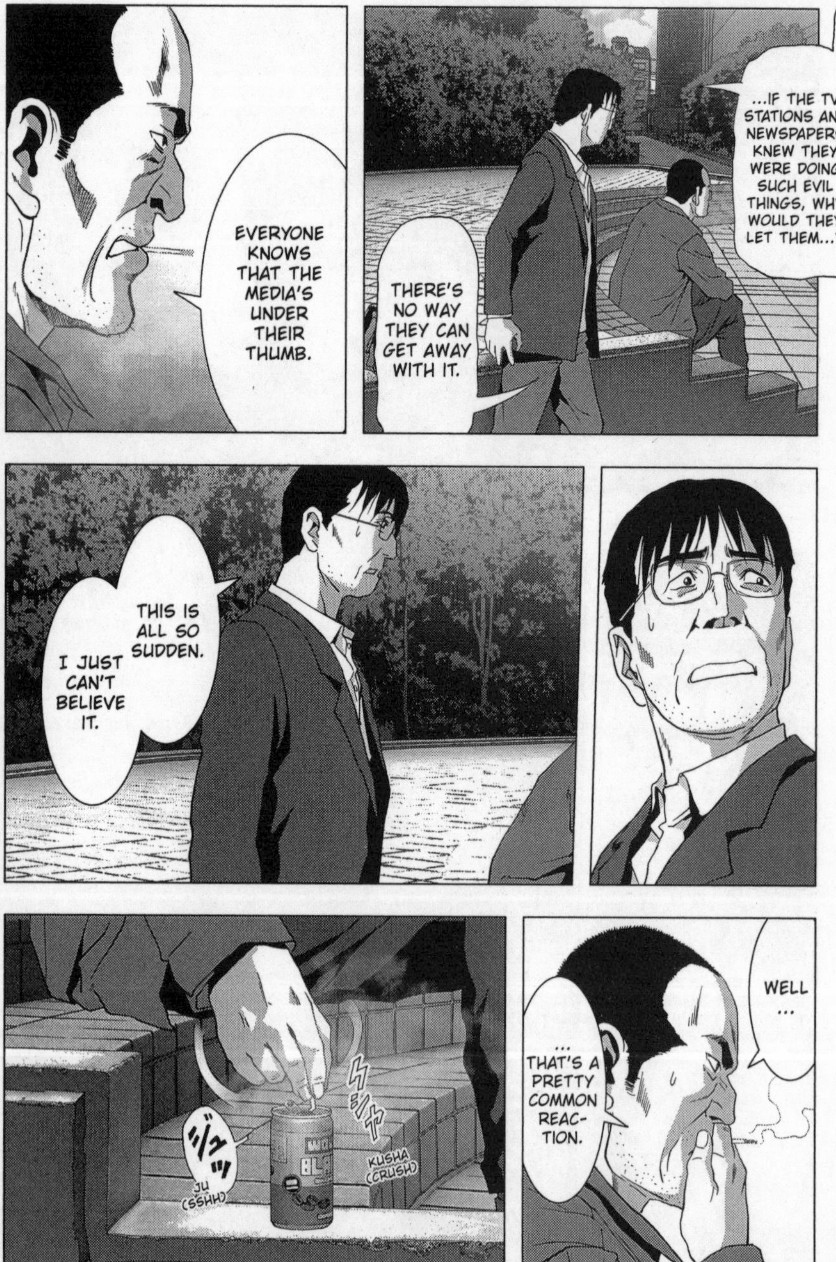
BUT...
...IF THE TV STATIONS AND NEWSPAPERS KNEW THEY WERE DOING SUCH EVIL THINGS, WHY WOULD THEY LET THEM...?
THERE'S NO WAY THEY CAN GET AWAY WITH IT.
EVERYONE KNOWS THAT THE MEDIA'S UNDER THEIR THUMB.
THIS IS ALL SO SUDDEN.
I JUST CAN'T BELIEVE IT.
WELL...
...THAT'S A PRETTY COMMON REACTION.
KUSHA (CRUSH)
JU (SSHH)

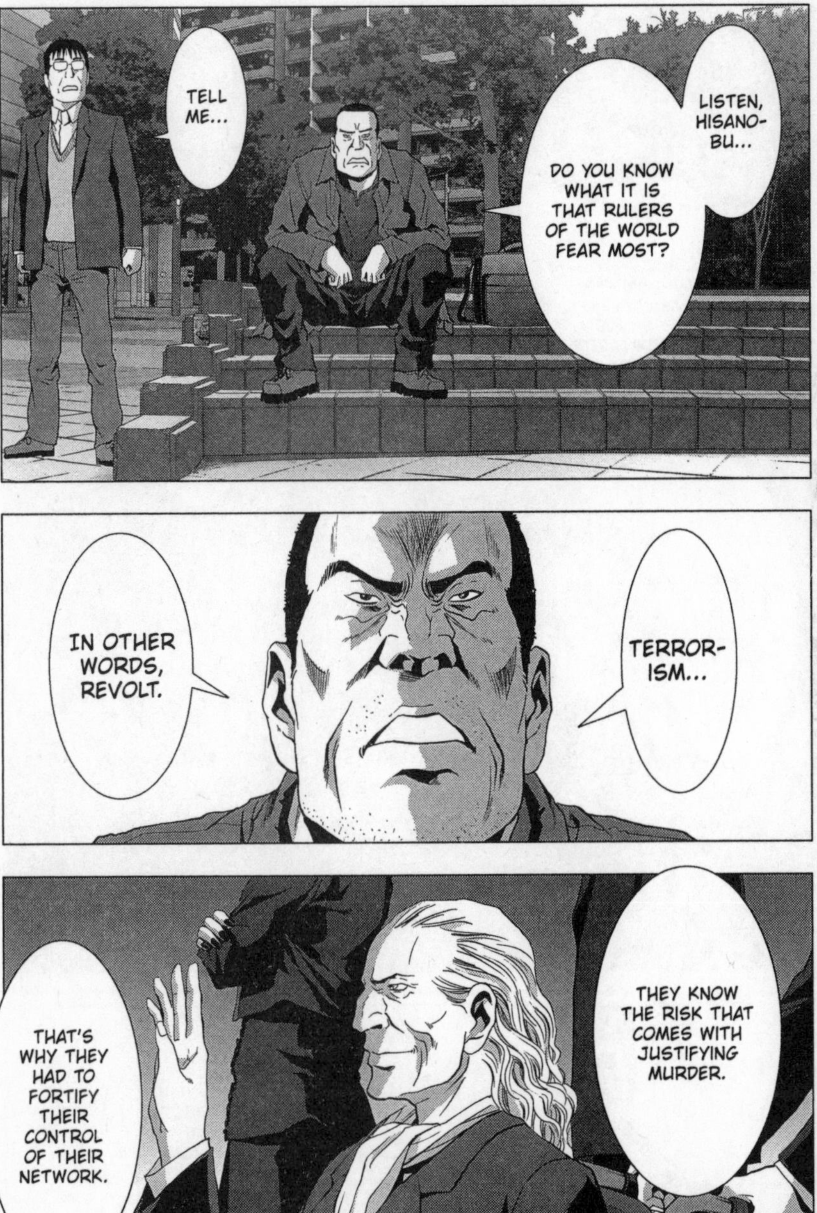
LISTEN, HISANO-BU...
DO YOU KNOW WHAT IT IS THAT RULERS OF THE WORLD FEAR MOST?
TELL ME...
TERROR-ISM...
IN OTHER WORDS, REVOLT.
THEY KNOW THE RISK THAT COMES WITH JUSTIFYING MURDER.
THAT'S WHY THEY HAD TO FORTIFY THEIR CONTROL OF THEIR NETWORK.

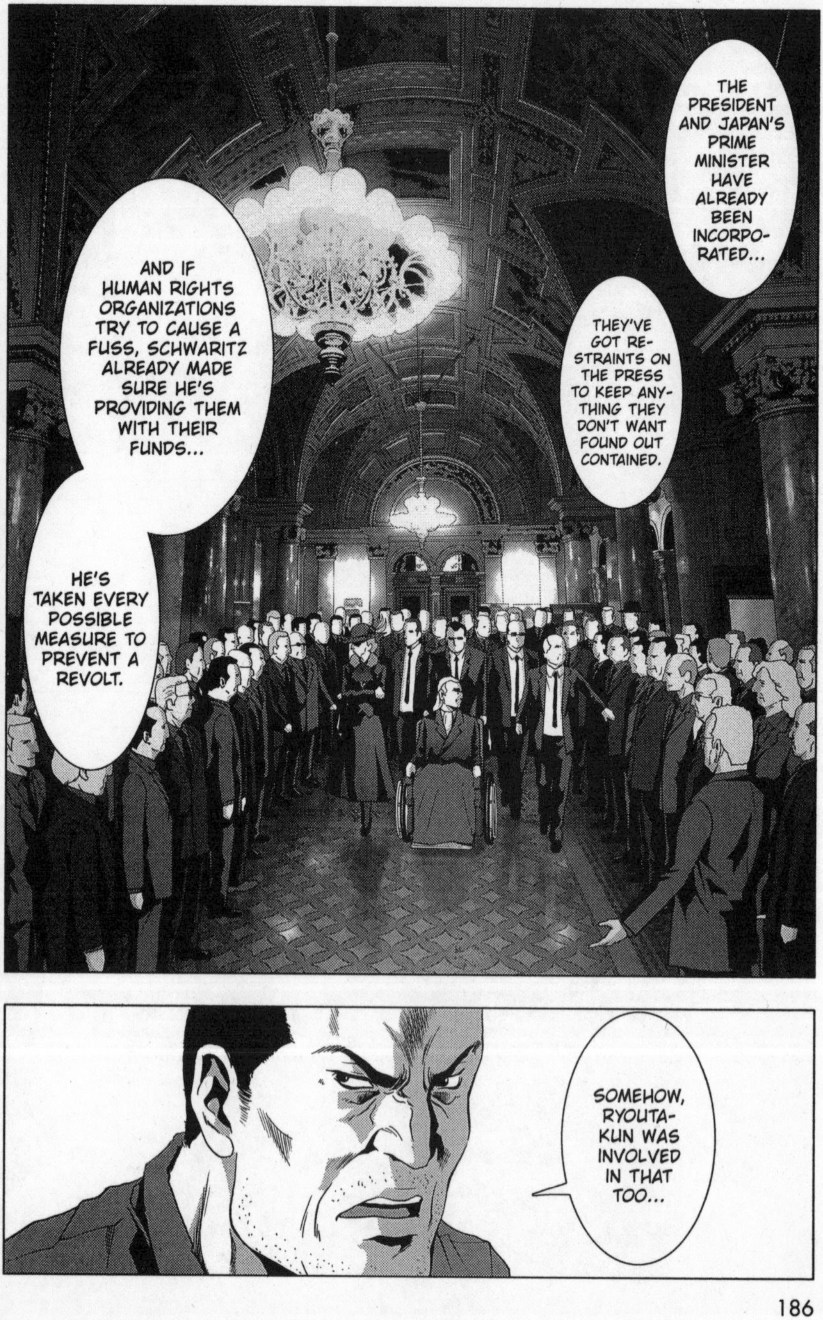
THE PRESIDENT AND JAPAN'S PRIME MINISTER HAVE ALREADY BEEN INCORPORATED...
THEY'VE GOT RESTRAINTS ON THE PRESS TO KEEP ANYTHING THEY DON'T WANT FOUND OUT CONTAINED.
AND IF HUMAN RIGHTS ORGANIZATIONS TRY TO CAUSE A FUSS, SCHWARITZ ALREADY MADE SURE HE'S PROVIDING THEM WITH THEIR FUNDS...
HE'S TAKEN EVERY POSSIBLE MEASURE TO PREVENT A REVOLT.
SOMEHOW, RYOUTA-KUN WAS INVOLVED IN THAT TOO...

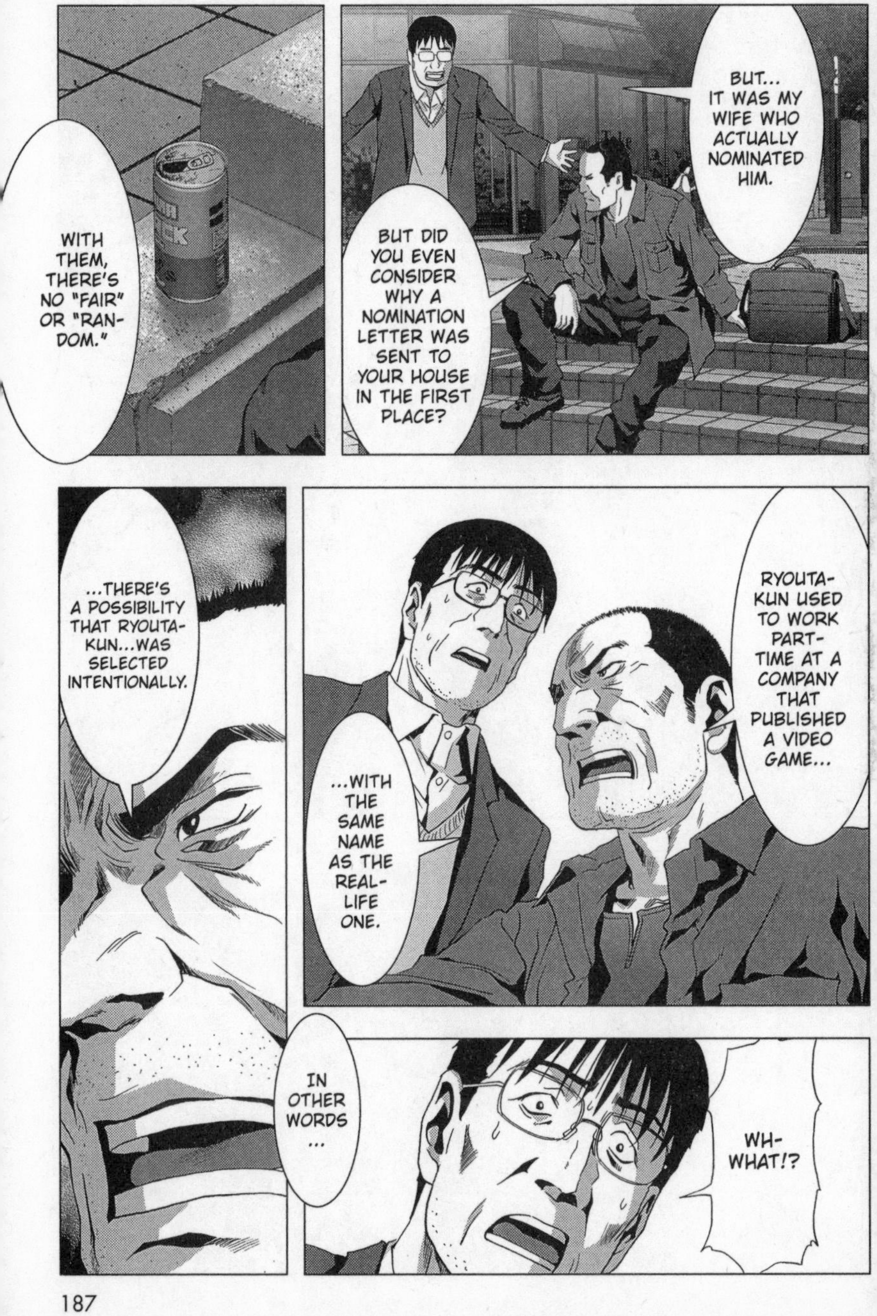
BUT... IT WAS MY WIFE WHO ACTUALLY NOMINATED HIM.
BUT DID YOU EVEN CONSIDER WHY A NOMINATION LETTER WAS SENT TO YOUR HOUSE IN THE FIRST PLACE?
WITH THEM, THERE'S NO "FAIR" OR "RAN-DOM."
RYOUTA-KUN USED TO WORK PART-TIME AT A COMPANY THAT PUBLISHED A VIDEO GAME...
...WITH THE SAME NAME AS THE REAL-LIFE ONE.
WH-WHAT!?
IN OTHER WORDS...
...THERE'S A POSSIBILITY THAT RYOUTA-KUN...WAS SELECTED INTENTIONALLY.

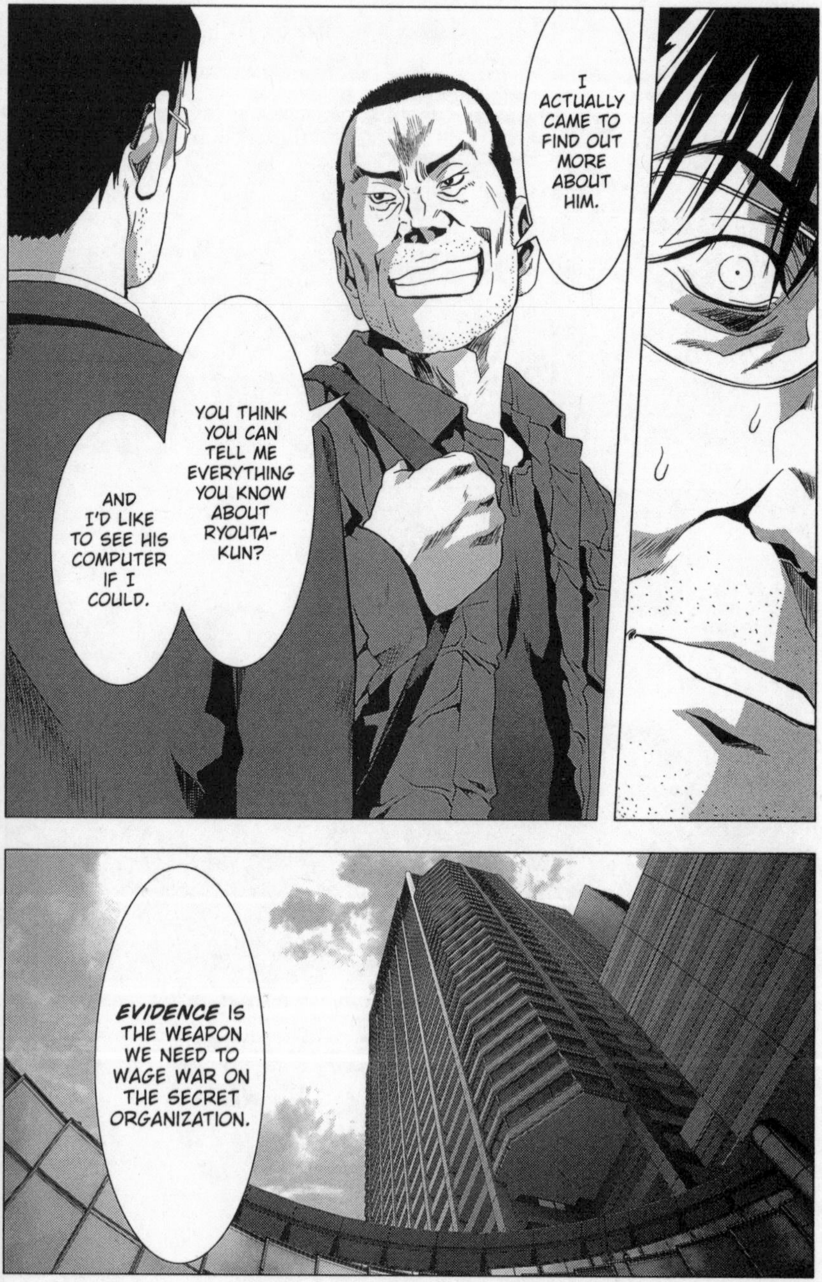
I ACTUALLY CAME TO FIND OUT MORE ABOUT HIM.
YOU THINK YOU CAN TELL ME EVERYTHING YOU KNOW ABOUT RYOUTA-KUN?
AND I'D LIKE TO SEE HIS COMPUTER IF I COULD.
EVIDENCE IS THE WEAPON WE NEED TO WAGE WAR ON THE SECRET ORGANIZATION.

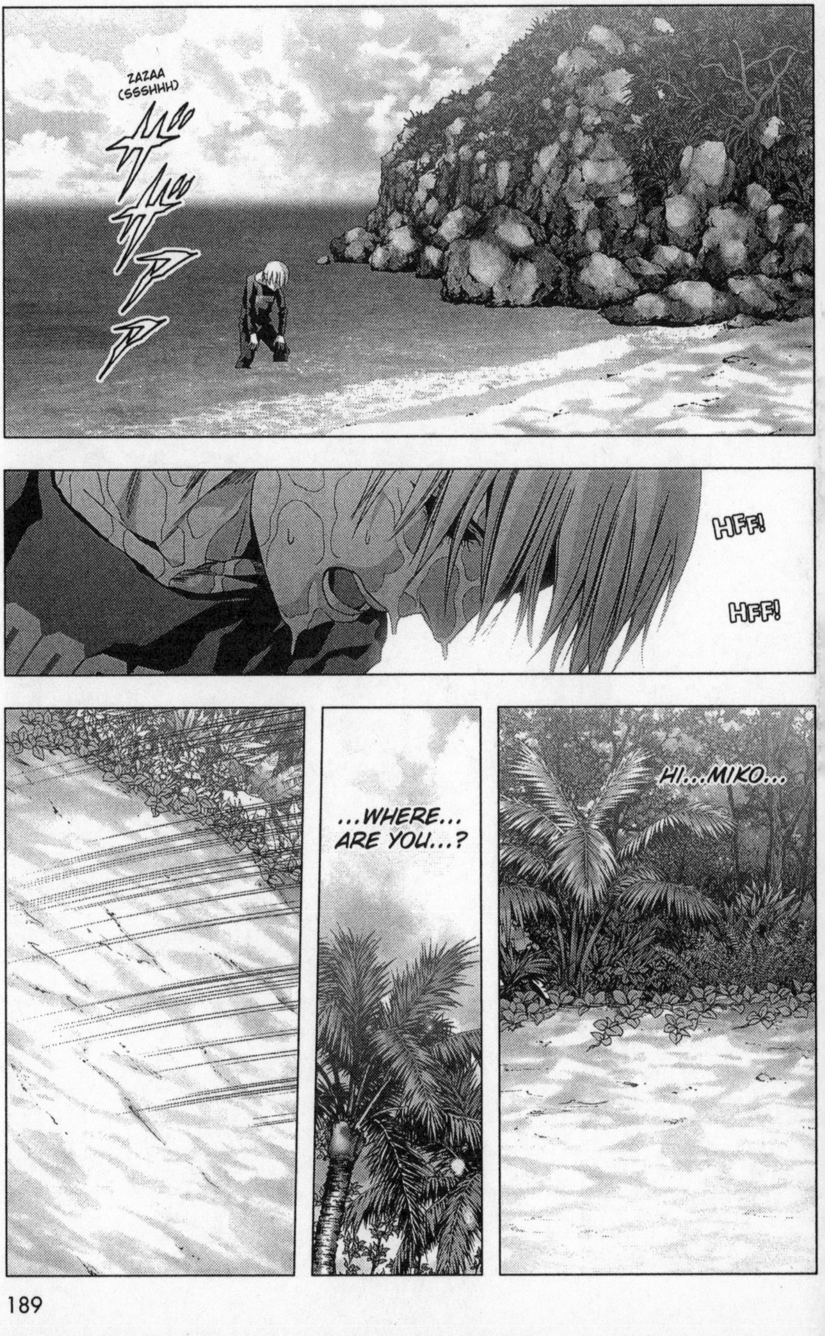
ZAZAA (SSSHHH)
HFF!
HFF!
HI...MIKO...
...WHERE... ARE YOU...?

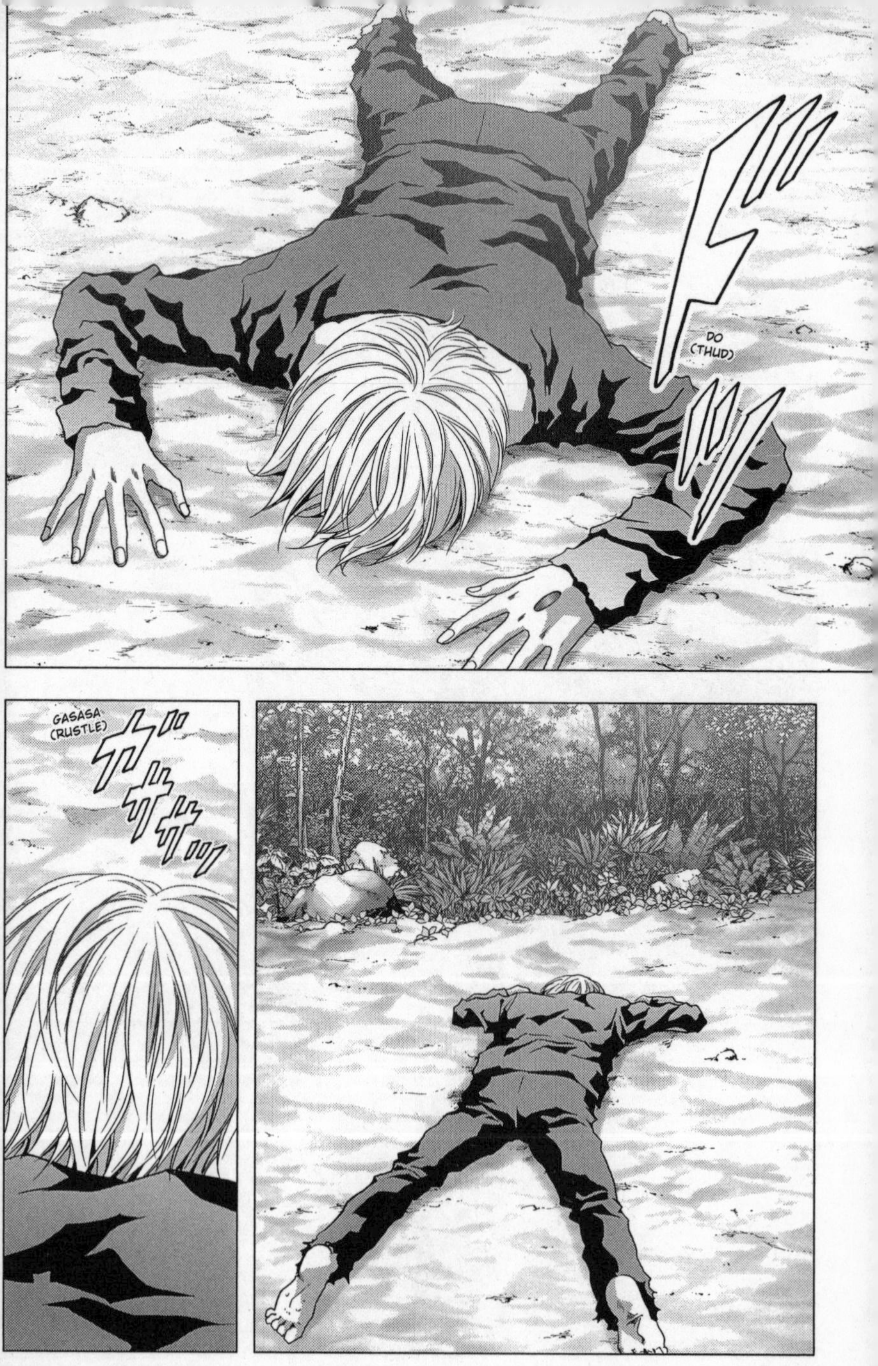
DO
(THUD)
GASASA
(RUSTLE)

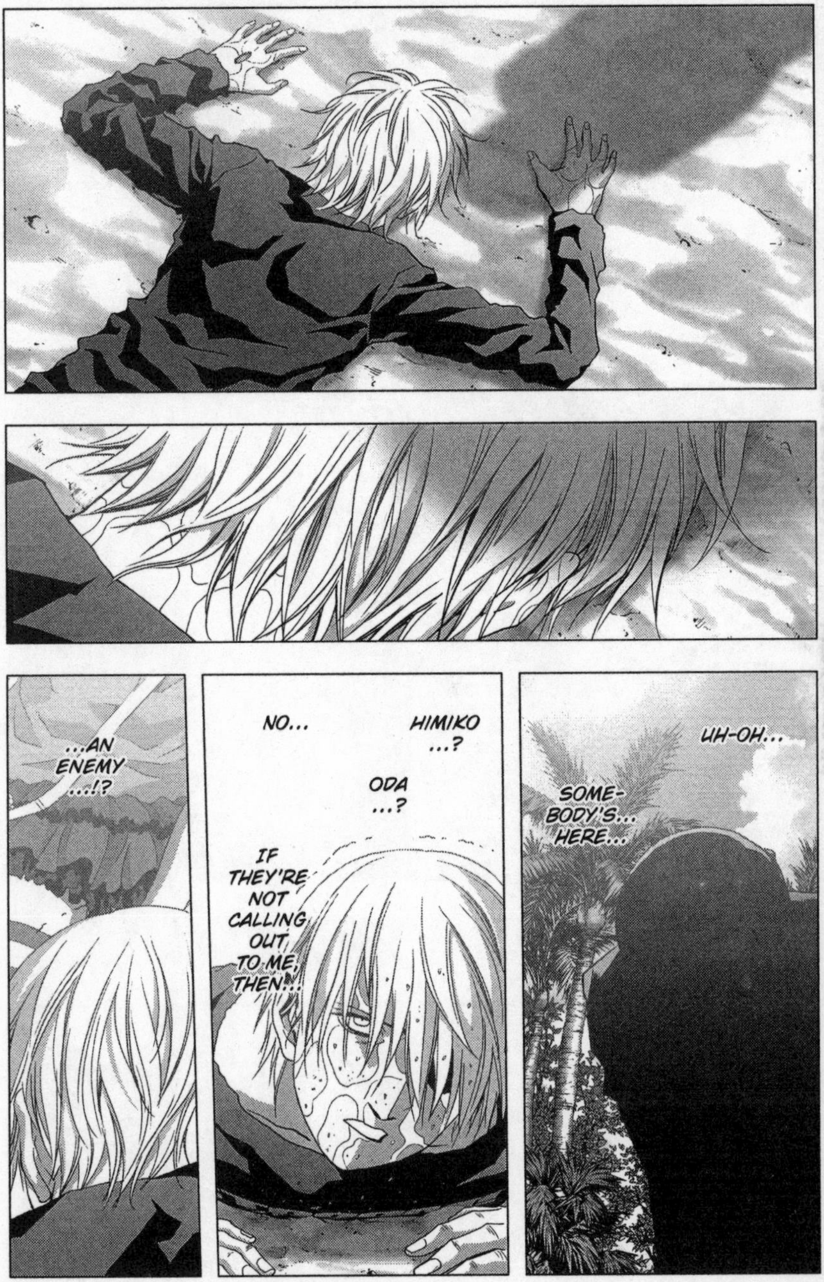
UH-OH...
SOME-BODY'S... HERE...
HIMIKO ...?
NO...
ODA ...?
IF THEY'RE NOT CALLING OUT TO ME, THEN...
...AN ENEMY ...!?

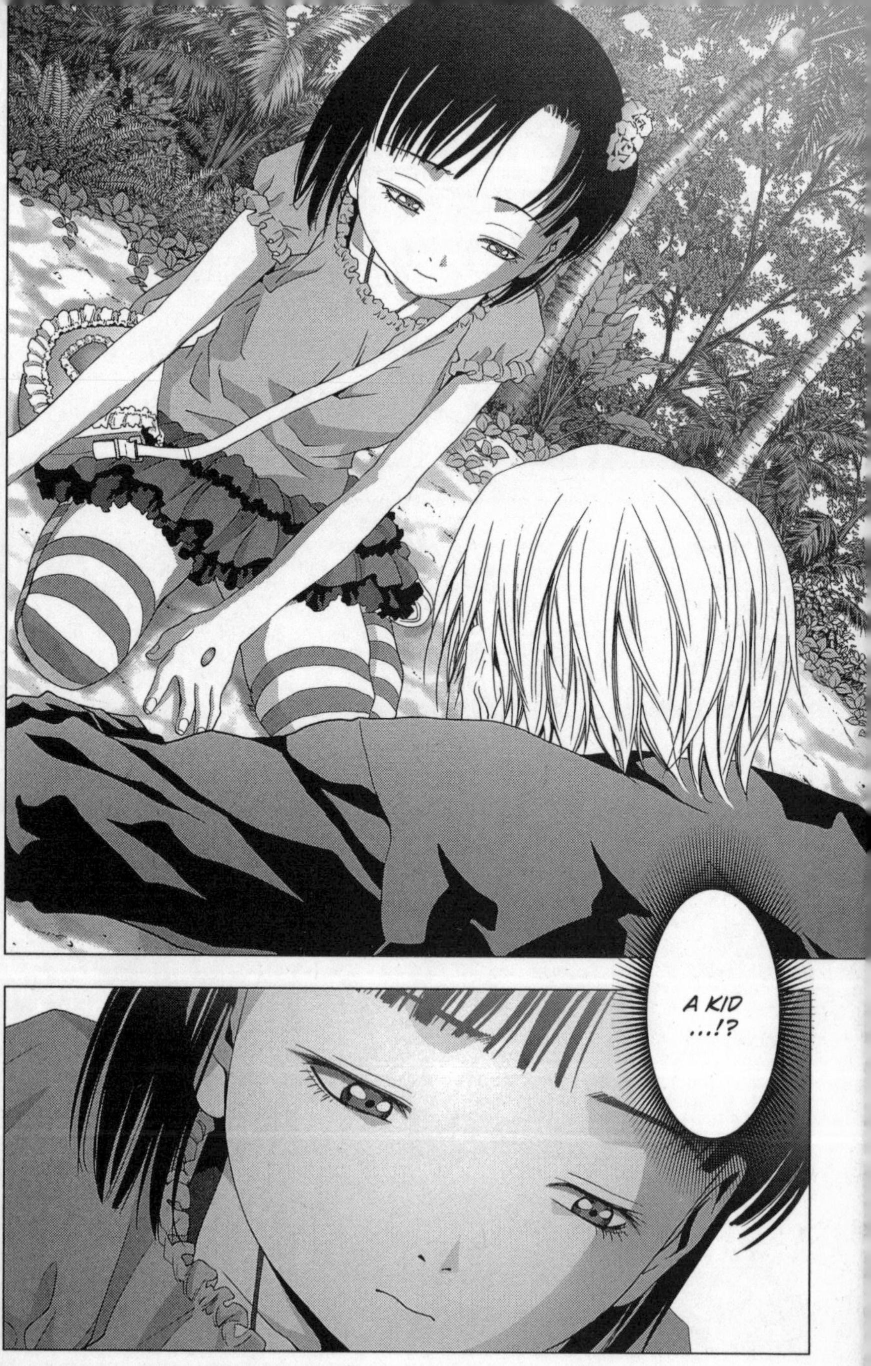
A KID ...!?

TO BE CONTINUED IN BTOOOM! ⑬

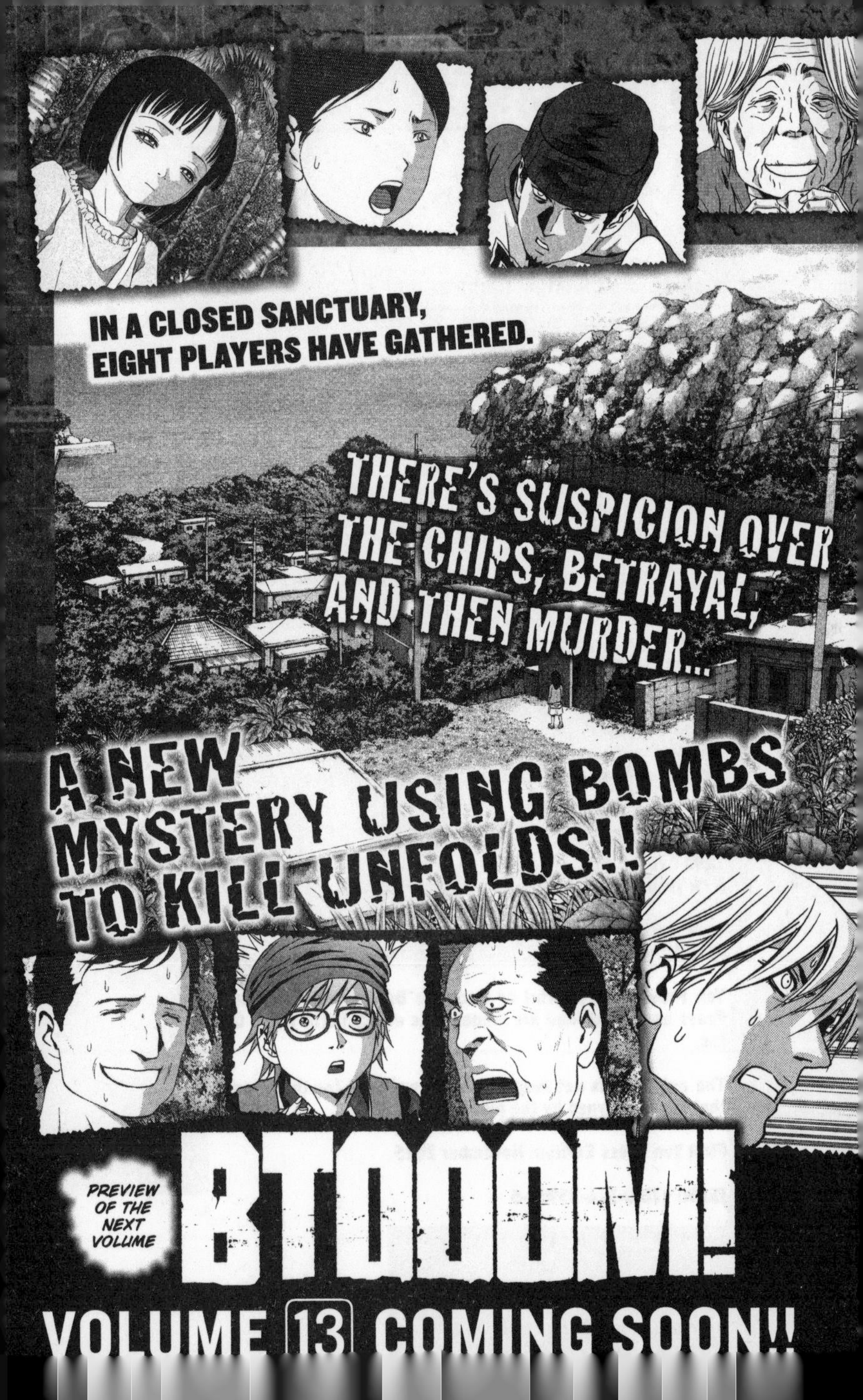

IN A CLOSED SANCTUARY,
EIGHT PLAYERS HAVE GATHERED.
THERE'S SUSPICION OVER THE CHIPS, BETRAYAL, AND THEN MURDER...
A NEW MYSTERY USING BOMBS TO KILL UNFOLDS!!
PREVIEW OF THE NEXT VOLUME
BTOOOM!
VOLUME 13 COMING SOON!!

BTOOOM! 12

JUNYA INOUE

Translation: Christine Dashiell

Lettering: Brndn Blakeslee

BTOOOM! © Junya INOUE 2009. All rights reserved. English translation rights arranged with SHINCHOSHA PUBLISHING CO. through Tuttle-Mori Agency, Inc., Tokyo.

English translation © 2015 by Hachette Book Group, Inc.

Yen Press
Hachette Book Group
1290 Avenue of the Americas
New York, NY 10104

www.HachetteBookGroup.com
www.YenPress.com

10 9 8 7 6 5 4 3 2 1

BVG

Printed in the United States of America